The Best Test Preparation for the

SAT Subject Test Spanish

5th EDITION

Gene M. Hammitt, Ph.D.
Professor of Modern Languages
Allegheny College, Meadville, Pennsylvania

Ricardo Gutiérrez Mouat, Ph.D.
Chairperson of Spanish Department
Emory University, Atlanta, Georgia

Mary Ellen Page, M.A.
Adjunct Professor of Spanish
St. Johns River Community College, St. Augustine, Florida

William Stivers, Ph.D.
Professor of Foreign Languages
Pepperdine University, Malibu, California

Patricia Valdez, M.A.
Professor of Spanish
Community College of Philadelphia, Philadelphia, Pennsylvania

REA
Research & Education Association
Visit our website at
www.rea.com

Research & Education Association
61 Ethel Road West
Piscataway, New Jersey 08854
E-mail: info@rea.com

The Best Test Preparation for the
SAT SUBJECT TEST IN SPANISH

Printed in the United States of America

Library of Congress Control Number 2005938160

International Standard Book Number 0-7386-0116-0

L05

ABOUT RESEARCH & EDUCATION ASSOCIATION

Founded in 1959, Research & Education Association is dedicated to publishing the finest and most effective educational materials—including software, study guides, and test preps—for students in middle school, high school, college, graduate school, and beyond.

REA's Test Preparation series includes books and software for all academic levels in almost all disciplines. Research & Education Association publishes test preps for students who have not yet entered high school, as well as high school students preparing to enter college. Students from countries around the world seeking to attend college in the United States will find the assistance they need in REA's publications. For college students seeking advanced degrees, REA publishes test preps for many major graduate school admission examinations in a wide variety of disciplines, including engineering, law, and medicine. Students at every level, in every field, with every ambition can find what they are looking for among REA's publications.

REA's practice tests are always based upon the most recently administered exams, and include every type of question that you can expect on the actual exams.

REA's publications and educational materials are highly regarded and continually receive an unprecedented amount of praise from professionals, instructors, librarians, parents, and students. Our authors are as diverse as the fields represented in the books we publish. They are well-known in their respective disciplines and serve on the faculties of prestigious high schools, colleges, and universities throughout the United States and Canada.

We invite you to visit us at *www.rea.com* to find out how "REA is making the world smarter."

ACKNOWLEDGMENTS

We would like to thank Larry B. Kling, Vice President, Editorial, for his overall direction; Pam Weston, Vice President, Publishing, for setting the quality standards for production integrity and managing the publication to completion; Diane Goldschmidt, Associate Editor, for coordinating the revision of this book; Patricia Van Arnum, Senior Editor, for preflight editorial contributions; and Network Typesetting, Inc. for typesetting the book.

We also extend special thanks to our REA production team, including Jeremy Rech, Graphic Designer, and Jeff LoBalbo, Senior Graphic Designer. Our cover was designed by Christine Saul, Senior Graphic Designer.

CONTENTS

THE SAT SUBJECT TEST IN

Spanish

Chapter 1

INTRODUCTION

Chapter 1

EXCELLING ON THE SAT SPANISH SUBJECT TEST

ABOUT THIS BOOK

This book provides you with an accurate and complete representation of the SAT Spanish Subject Test. Inside you will find a complete course review, as well as five REA practice tests based on the actual exam. Our practice tests contain every type of question that you can expect to encounter on the actual exam. Following each test you will find an answer key with detailed explanations designed to help you master the test material.

ABOUT THE TEST

Who takes the test and what is it used for?

Students planning to attend college take the SAT Spanish Subject Test for one of two reasons:

(1) Because it is an admission requirement of the college or university to which they are applying,

OR

(2) To demonstrate proficiency in Spanish.

The SAT Spanish exam is designed for students who have taken two to four years of Spanish.

Who administers the test?

The SAT Spanish Subject Test is developed by the College Board and administered by Educational Testing Service (ETS). The test development process involves the assistance of educators throughout the country, and is designed and implemented to ensure that the content and difficulty level of the test are appropriate.

When and where is the test given?

The SAT Spanish Subject Test is offered five times a year in October, December, January, May and June. (The SAT Subject Test in Spanish with Listening, which this book does not cover, is administered only in November.)

To receive information on upcoming administrations of the exam, consult the publication *Taking the SAT Spanish Subject Tests,* which can be obtained from your guidance counselor or by contacting:

College Board SAT Program
P.O. Box 6200
Princeton, NJ 08541-6200
Phone: (609) 771-7600
Website: *www.collegeboard.com*

Is there a registration fee?

You must pay a registration fee to take the SAT Spanish Subject Test. Consult the College Board website (*www.collegeboard.com*) for information on the fee structure. Financial assistance may be granted in certain situations. To find out if you qualify and to register for assistance, contact your academic advisor.

HOW TO USE THIS BOOK

What do I study first?

Remember that the SAT Spanish Subject Test is designed to test knowledge that you have acquired throughout your education. Therefore, the best way to prepare for the exam is to refresh yourself by thoroughly studying our review material and taking the sample tests provided in this book. Our practice tests will familiarize you with the types of questions, directions, and format of the SAT Spanish Subject Test.

To begin your studies, read over our course review and suggestions for test-taking. Then take the first practice test to determine your area(s) of weakness. When you're done, restudy the review material, focusing on your specific problem areas. The course review includes the information you need to know when taking the exam. Make sure to take the remaining practice tests to further test yourself and become familiar with the format of the SAT Spanish Subject Test. Further recommendations are detailed in our study schedule in the front of this book.

When should I start studying?

It is never too early to start studying for the SAT Spanish Subject Test. The earlier you begin, the more time you will have to sharpen your skills. Do not procrastinate! Cramming is *not* an effective way to study! The sooner you learn the format of the exam, the more comfortable you will be when you take it.

FORMAT OF THE SAT SPANISH SUBJECT TEST

The SAT Spanish Subject Test is a one-hour exam consisting of 85 multiple-choice questions that are designed to measure the gradual development of competence in the Spanish language acquired over a period of years.

About 33% of the test measures vocabulary and structure in context or grammar. Another third of the test measures reading comprehension. Paragraph completion accounts for the remaining 33%.

SCORING THE SAT SPANISH SUBJECT TEST

How do I score my practice tests?

The SAT Spanish Subject Test, like all other SAT Subject Tests, is scored on a 200–800 scale. Your exam is scored by crediting one point for each correct answer and deducting one-third of a point for each incorrect answer. There is no deduction for answers that are left blank. Use the worksheet below to calculate your raw score and to record your scores for the five practice tests. Use the Practice-Test Score Conversion Table that follows to convert your raw score to a scaled score.

SCORE CONVERSION TABLE

SAT: Subject Test in Spanish

Raw Score	Scaled Score	Raw Score	Scaled Score	Raw Score	Scaled Score
85	800	45	570	5	340
84	800	44	570	4	340
83	800	43	560	3	330
82	800	42	550	2	320
81	790	41	550	1	320
80	790	40	540	0	310
79	780	39	530	-1	310
78	780	38	530	-2	300
77	770	37	520	-3	290
76	770	36	520	-4	290
75	760	35	510	-5	280
74	760	34	500	-6	270
73	750	33	500	-7	260
72	750	32	490	-8	260
71	740	31	490	-9	250
70	730	30	480	-10	240
69	730	29	470	-11	230
68	720	28	470	-12	220
67	720	27	460	-13	220
66	710	26	460	-14	220
65	700	25	450	-15	210
64	700	24	450	-16	210
63	690	23	440	-17	210
62	680	22	430	-18	200
61	680	21	430	-19	200
60	670	20	420	-20	200
59	670	19	420	-21	200
58	660	18	410	-22	200
57	650	17	410	-23	200
56	650	16	400	-24	200
55	640	15	400	-25	200
54	630	14	390	-26	200
53	630	13	390	-27	200
52	620	12	380	-28	200
51	620	11	380		
50	610	10	370		
49	600	9	360		
48	590	8	360		
47	590	7	350		
46	580	6	350		

This chart has been designed to help you find your scaled score on the SAT Subject Test in Spanish. Locate your raw score in the left hand column; the corresponding score in the right column approximates the actual scaled score used for the SAT Subject Test in Spanish.

PRACTICE-TEST SCORING WORKSHEET

________	– (________ x 1/3)	= ________
Number correct	Number incorrect (do not include unanswered questions)	Raw Score (round to nearest whole point)

	Raw Score	Scaled Score
Test 1	58-9 -	49
Test 2		
Test 3		
Test 4		
Test 5		

When will I receive my score report and what will it look like?

You can expect to receive your score report within about five weeks after you take the test. This report will include your scores, percentile ranks, and interpretive information.

STUDYING FOR THE SAT SPANISH SUBJECT TEST

It is critical to choose the time and place for studying that works best for you. Some students may set aside a certain number of hours every morning to study, while others may choose to study at night before going to sleep. Only you can determine when and where your study time will be most effective. Be consistent and use your time wisely. Work out a study routine and stick to it!

When you take the practice tests, try to make your testing conditions as much like the actual test as possible. Turn your television and radio off, and sit down at a quiet desk or table free from distraction. Make sure to clock yourself with a timer.

As you complete each practice test, score it and thoroughly review the explanations to the questions you answered incorrectly; however, do not review too much at any one time. Concentrate on one problem area at a time by reviewing the questions and explanations, and by studying our review until you are confident you completely understand the material.

Keep track of your scores. By doing so, you will be able to gauge your progress and discover general weaknesses in particular sections. You should carefully study the reviews that cover your areas of difficulty, as this will build your skills in those areas.

TEST-TAKING TIPS

Although you may be unfamiliar with standardized tests such as the SAT Spanish Subject Test, there are many ways to acquaint yourself with this type of examination and help alleviate your test-taking anxieties. Here are six specific ways you can give yourself a leg up:

Become comfortable with the format of the exam. When you are practicing, simulate the conditions under which you will be taking the actual test. Stay calm and pace yourself. This will allow you to sit down for the actual exam with much more confidence.

Read all of the possible answers. Just because you think you have found the correct response, do not automatically assume that it is the best answer. Read through each choice to be sure that you are not making a mistake by jumping to conclusions.

Use the process of elimination. Go through each answer to a question and eliminate as many of the answer choices as possible. By eliminating just two answer choices, you give yourself a better chance of getting the item correct, since there will only be two choices left from which to make your guess.

Work quickly and steadily. You will have only 1 hour, so avoid focusing on any one question too long. Taking the practice tests in this book will help you learn to budget your time.

Learn the directions and format for each section of the test. Familiarizing yourself with the directions and format of the exam will save you valuable time on the day of the actual test.

Be sure that the answer oval you are marking corresponds to the number of the question in the test booklet. Since the exam is graded by machine, marking one wrong answer can throw off your answer key and your score. Be extremely careful when filling in your answer sheet.

Before the Test

Make sure you know where your test center is well in advance of your test day so you do not get lost on the day of the test. On the night before the test, gather together the materials you will need the next day:

- Your admission ticket
- Two forms of identification (e.g., driver's license, student identification card, or current alien registration card)
- Two No. 2 pencils with erasers
- Directions to the test center
- A wristwatch (if you wish) but not one that makes noise, as it may disturb other test-takers

On the day of the test, you should wake up early (it is hoped after a decent night's rest) and have a good breakfast. Dress comfortably so that you are not distracted by being too hot or too cold while taking the test. Also, plan to arrive at the test center early. This will allow you to collect your thoughts and relax before the test, and will also spare you the stress of being late. If you arrive after the test begins, you will not be admitted and you will not receive a refund.

During the Test

When you arrive at the test center, try to find a seat where you feel you will be comfortable. Follow all the rules and instructions given by the test supervisor. If you do not, you risk being dismissed from the test and having your scores canceled.

Once all the test materials are passed out, the test instructor will give you directions for filling out your answer sheet. Fill this sheet out carefully since the information you supply will appear on your score report.

After the Test

When you have completed the SAT Spanish Subject Test, you may hand in your test materials and leave. Then, go home and relax!

INDEPENDENT STUDY SCHEDULE
SAT SPANISH SUBJECT TEST

This study schedule is set up to thoroughly prepare you for the SAT Spanish Subject Test. Although it is designed to allow you to pace yourself comfortably over an eight-week preparation period, it can be condensed into a four-week course by collapsing each two-week period into one. Be sure to set aside enough time—at least two hours each day—to study. No matter which study schedule works best for you, however, the more time you spend acquainting yourself with the subject matter and the test, the more prepared and relaxed you will feel on Test Day.

Week	*Activity*
1	Read the introduction to this book, which details critical aspects of the SAT Spanish Subject Test for you. Then take Practice Test 1 to determine your strengths and weaknesses. Score each section by using the worksheet on page 7. You'll now have a baseline for your study needs.
2	Carefully read and study the Review included in this book. Cover all the material, but highlight those areas that gave you trouble in Practice Test 1. Go through each of the items you answered incorrectly and make sure you understand how to arrive at the correct answer. Recognizing where you went wrong will boost your confidence and, as a practical matter, help you avoid making the same mistakes come Test Day.
3 and **4**	Take Practice Test 2 and Practice Test 3. After scoring each exam, flag your incorrect answers. For any types of questions or particular subjects that continue to pose difficulty for you, check our detailed explanations and consult our Review.

Week	*Activity*
5 and **6**	Take Practice Test 4. After scoring each exam, flag your incorrect answers. For any types of questions or particular subjects that continue to pose difficulty for you, check our detailed explanations and consult our Review.
7	Take Practice Test 5. After scoring your exam, carefully review the explanations for all your incorrect answers. By this point, you should be nearing mastery of the subject matter. Again, consult our Review as often as possible to ensure that you're sufficiently at ease with our model tests.
8	This is the week you'll consolidate your gains and eliminate any continuing subject-matter weaknesses. Retake one or more of the practice tests (as you deem necessary), paying particular attention to the questions with which you had difficulty the first time around. Going through the practice tests once again will put you on completely familiar terms with the subject matter and the SAT Subject Test itself.

Good Luck on the SAT Subject Test in Spanish!

THE SAT SUBJECT TEST IN

Spanish

Chapter 2
Review

Chapter 2

SAT SPANISH REVIEW

THE ALPHABET

Spanish uses the same Latin alphabet as English except for the addition of one letter: ***ñ***. Spanish letters use the following pronunciation guidelines:

ch is pronounced like "ch" in "chief."

ll is pronounced like the "y" in "beyond."

ñ is pronounced like "ni" in "opinion."

c sounds like "s" before "e" and "i," and like "k" in all other cases.

g sounds like the "h" in "humid" before "e" and "i," and like the "g" in "go" or "get" in front of "a," "o," and "u." In order to obtain the hard sound before "e" and "i," Spanish interpolates the vowel "u": *guerra, guión.* In these cases the "u" is silent; a dieresis indicates that it must be pronounced: *vergüenza, güero.*

h is always silent: *ahora, húmedo, horrible.*

v is pronounced like "b" in all cases.

y sounds like "ll" at the beginning of a word or syllable. When it stands alone or comes at the end of a word, it is equivalent to the vowel "i."

z is pronounced like "s."

(This pronunciation guide follows Latin American usage. In Castilian Spanish the soft "*c*" and the "*z*" are pronounced like "th" in "thin." Either pronunciation is acceptable in the event you take the SAT Spanish Subject Test with Listening.)

Letter		Spanish Example	English Example
b	[b]	*bomba*	boy
c	[k]	*calco*	keep
	[s]	*cero*	same
ch	[ch]	*mucho*	chocolate
d	[d]	*andar*	dog
f	[f]	*fama*	fake
g	[h]	*general*	humid
	[g]	*rango*	get
h	always silent	*hombre*	honor
j	[h]	*justo*	humid
k	[k]	*kilogramo*	kite
l	[l]	*letra*	light
ll	[y]	*ella*	beyond
m	[m]	*mano*	mad
n	[n]	*pan*	no
ñ	[ni]	*uña*	onion
p	[p]	*padre*	poke
q	[k]	*que*	kite
r	[r]	*rápido*	(this is a trilled or "rolling" sound with no English equivalent)
s	[s]	*casa*	some
	[z]	*mismo*	rose
t	[t]	*patata*	tame
v	[b]	*vamos*	boy
x	[ks]	*máximo*	fox
y	[j]	*yo*	yes
z	[s]	*zapato*	same

The sounds of the Spanish vowels are invariable.

a sounds approximately like "a" in "ah."
e sounds approximately like "e" in "men."
i sounds approximately like "ee" in "eel."
o sounds approximately like "o" in "or."
u sounds approximately like "oo" in "moon."

Letter		Spanish Example	English Example
a	[a]	*pata*	father
e	[e]	*pelo*	men
i	[i]	*filo*	eel
o	[o]	*poco*	or
u	[u]	*luna*	moon

A combination of one strong (a, e, o) and one weak vowel (i, u) or of two weak ones is a diphthong and counts as one syllable:

ai, ay	*aire, hay*	pronounce like "eye"
ei, ey	*reino, ley*	pronounce like "may"
oi, oy	*oigo, hoy*	pronounce like "toy"
iu	*triunfo*	pronounce like "you"
ui, uy	*cuidar, muy*	pronounce like "Louie"
ue	*hueso, muerte*	pronounce like "west"

RULES FOR STRESS IN SPANISH

There are two rules that indicate stress in Spanish. If either of these two rules is broken, a written accent mark will appear on the word.

1. If a word ends in a vowel, *–n,* or *–s,* the **normal** stress is on the penultimate (next to last) syllable.

   mano (over the *–a*) *tribu* (over the *–i*)
   esposa (over the *–o*) *hablan* (over first *–a*)
   clase (over the *–a*) *tomaban* (over first *–a*)

2. If the word ends in any other letter (than those mentioned above), the **normal** stress will fall on the last syllable.

   hablar (over the *–a*) *papel* (over the *–e*)
   comer (over the *–e*) *ejemplar* (over the *–a*)
   vivir (over the *–i*) *nivel* (over the *–e*)

3. Spanish words will have an accent for the following specific reasons:

   a. There is another identical word and the accent distinguishes the one from the other.

   de (of, from) vs. *dé* (give—formal command)
   se (reflexive pronoun) vs. *sé* (I know, verb)

mas (but, conjunction)	vs.	*más* (more, adverb)
si (if)	vs.	*sí* (yes)

b. A pronoun has been added to a verb form.

diciéndolo	saying it
diciéndomelo	saying it to me
explíquelo	explain it
explíquemelo	explain it to me
decírselo	to say it to him

Note: Infinitives require two pronouns before an accent is necessary.

c. The accent is the result of a stem-change.

reunir (ú) – The *ú* will appear in the first, second, and third person singular and third person plural of the present indicative/subjunctive.

Other examples:

continuar (*ú*), *enviar* (*í*)
graduarse (*ú*)

d. There may be a diphthong (two weak vowels or a weak with a strong) where the weak vowel (*u* or *i*) needs to be stressed.

Examples:

divertíos	Enjoy yourselves!
creíste	you believed

SYLLABIC DIVISION

A consonant between two vowels joins the second vowel to form a syllable: *li-te-ra-tu-ra, e-ne-mi-go, a-ho-ra.*

- Two consonants together must be separated: *cuer-no, pac-to.*
- "*ch,*" "*ll,*" and "*rr*" are considered one letter and are not separated.
- "*l*" or "*r*" preceded by "*b,*" "*c,*" "*d,*" "*f,*" "*g,*" "*p,*" and "*t*" are not separated: *ha-blar, a-brup-to, te-cla, pul-cri-tud, me-lo-dra-ma, in-flu-jo, a-gra-de-cer.*
- "*ns*" and "*bs*" are not separated in groups of three or four consonants: *ins-cri-bir, obs-tá-cu-lo.*
- In words formed with prefixes, the prefix stands alone as one syllable: *sub-ra-yar, in-ú-til, des-a-gra-dar.*

ARTICLES

The forms of the definite article are:

	Masculine	Feminine
Singular	*el*	*la*
Plural	*los*	*las*

El is used instead of *la* before feminine nouns beginning with stressed "a" or "ha": ***el** agua, **el** hacha, **el** alma, **el** hambre.*

El contracts to *al* when the article follows the preposition *a* (*a* + *el*) and to *del* when the article follows the preposition *de* (*de* + *el*).

Uses of the Definite Article

The definite article is used in Spanish (but not in English):

- when the noun represents an abstraction: **life** is short; **time** is money; **freedom** is worth fighting for; **politics** is a practical art. (***la** vida, **el** tiempo, **la** libertad, **la** política)*
- when the noun includes the totality of a category: **books** are good; **man** is mortal; the Incas were acquainted with **gold**; **bread** is a staple. (***los** libros, **el** hombre, **el** oro, **el** pan)*
- with the days of the week (except after a form of the verb *ser*) and the seasons of the year: ***el** lunes* (but *hoy es lunes*), ***la** primavera, **el** otoño*
- with the hours of the day: *son **las** tres de la tarde; a **las** doce **del** día* (or ***al** mediodía*)
- with personal or professional forms of address in the third person: ***el** señor Jiménez, **la** señorita Méndez, **el** doctor Márquez, **el** licenciado Vidriera.* (It is omitted when the individual is directly addressed and in front of titles such as *Don, Doña, San,* or *Santo[a]: venga, señor Jiménez; no se preocupe, señorita Méndez.*)
- with the parts of the body or articles of clothing instead of the possessive adjective: I brushed **my** teeth. *Me cepillé **los** dientes.* I put on **my** shirt. *Me puse **la** camisa.*
- with the names of languages except after the prepositions *en* and *de* and the verb *hablar: **el** francés es difícil* (but *no hablo francés; ese texto está en francés*)
- with weights and measures: *un dólar **la** libra,* one dollar per pound; *diez pesos **la** docena,* ten pesos per dozen

- with infinitives used as nouns (gerunds): Lying is a vice. ***El** mentir es un vicio*. (This use is optional, especially in proverbs.) Seeing is believing. *Ver es creer*.
- with names of "generic" places: jail, ***la** cárcel*; class, ***la** clase*; church, ***la** iglesia*; market, ***el** mercado*
- with family names: The Garcías, ***los** Garcías*
- with adjectives to make them nouns: the pretty one, ***la** bonita*; the poor, ***los** pobres*; the old man, ***el** viejo*
- with nouns in apposition with a pronoun: We Americans . . . *Nosotros **los** americanos . . .*

Omission of the Definite Article in Spanish

The definite article in Spanish is omitted in the following cases:

1. With fields of knowledge, in general, one needs an article unless one . . .

a. gives a **definition**	*¿Qué es astronomía?* *Astronomía es una ciencia.*
b. uses ***estudiar*** or ***examinar***	*Estudiamos química.*

2. With the expressions ***de . . . a***

   En casa comemos ***de seis a ocho***.
   At home we eat from 6:00 to 8:00.

3. With expressions such as

por primera vez	for the first time
por segunda vez	for the second time
en primer lugar	in the first place

4. With ***con*** and ***sin*** before an unmodified abstract noun.

   *No puedo vivir **sin libertad.***
   I cannot live without liberty.

   ***Con amor** la vida tiene sentido.*
   With love life has meaning.

5. With a numeral that denotes the order of a monarch.

Carlos Quinto	Charles the Fifth

The Neuter Article *Lo*

This article is used exclusively in the singular as follows:

1. *Lo* + adjective = **part/thing**

Examples:	*lo importante*	the important thing/part
	lo mejor	the best thing/part

2. *Lo* + adj/adv + *que* = **how**

   Examples: *Tú no sabes lo importante que es.*
   You don't know **how** important it is.

   Él no entiende lo despacio que va.
   He doesn't know **how** slowly it goes.

3. *Lo de* = All that or everything that (happened)

   Example: *Vamos a cubrir lo de ayer.*
   We'll cover everything we did yesterday.

4. *Lo* is used in sentences with the pronoun ***todo*** as the direct object.

   Example: *Lo entiendo todo.*
   I understand everything.

5. *Todo lo que* = All that

   Example: *Todo lo que oí no es verdad.*
   All that I heard isn't true.

6. *Lo* is used as a complement to replace adjectives, pronouns, or nouns with ***ser***, ***estar,*** and ***parecer***.

   Examples: *Pareces enojada.* [adj-*enojada*]
   You seem angry.

   —Quizás ***lo*** *parezca, pero no* ***lo*** *estoy.*
   Perhaps I seem it, but I'm not.

   ¿Estas llaves son tuyas? [noun-*llaves*]
   Are these keys yours?

   —No, no ***lo*** *son.*
   No, they're not.

Forms of the Indefinite Article

The indefinite article must agree in gender and number with the noun it modifies. Its forms are the following:

	Masculine	Feminine
Singular	*un*	*una*
Plural	*unos*	*unas*

Examples: *un perro* – a dog
unos perros – some dogs

Note: Feminine nouns beginning with a stressed "*a*" or "*ha*" take *un* instead of *una: **un** alma, **un** hacha, **un** hada madrina.* This rule only applies if the noun is singular.

Uses of the Indefinite Article

Spanish *omits* the indefinite article (but not English) as follows:

- after the verb *ser* with nouns denoting profession, religion, or nationality: *soy profesor, son católicos, es española.* (This rule does not apply when the noun is followed by an adjective or some other modifier: *soy **un** profesor exigente* (I'm a demanding teacher).)
- with words such as *otro* (other), *medio* (half), *cien* (one hundred or a hundred), *mil* (one thousand or a thousand), *tal* (such a), *cierto* (a certain), and *qué* (what a): *cierta mujer* (a certain woman), *¡qué día!* (What a day!), *cien libros* (a hundred books), *mide un metro y medio* (it measures one and one-half meters), *otra respuesta* (another answer), *tal hombre* (such a man).
- after ***sin:***

Salío sin abrigo.	He left without a coat.

- after ***haber*** used impersonally, ***buscar,*** and ***tener*** (otherwise it means **one**)*:*

No hay respuesta.	There isn't **an** answer.
Estoy buscando trabajo.	I'm looking for **a** job.
No tiene coche.	He doesn't have **a** car.

GENDER

In Spanish, nouns are either masculine or feminine. Most nouns ending in ***-o*** or ***-or*** are masculine and most of those ending in ***-a** ,**-d**, **-ión**, **-umbre**, **-ie**, **-sis**, **-itis*** are feminine.

Masculine	Feminine
el dinero – money	*la muchedumbre* – crowd
el otoño – autumn	*la serie* – series
el amor – love	*la crisis* – crisis
	la presencia – presence
	la bronquitis – bronchitis
	la acción – action

Note: Drop the accent on *–ión* words when made plural: *nación, naciones*

Many masculine nouns become feminine by changing the *-o* ending to *-a* or by adding an *-a* if the word ends in a consonant:

Masculine	Feminine
el escritor – the writer	*la escritor**a*** – the writer
el doctor – the doctor	*la doctor**a*** – the doctor
el hijo – the son	*la hij**a*** – the daughter
el muchacho – the young man	*la muchach**a*** – the young woman

Exceptions

A few common words ending in *-o* are feminine:

la mano – the hand
la foto (la fotografía) – the photo, picture
la moto (la motocicleta) – the motorcycle

There is a large number of words ending in ***-ma***, ***-pa***, and ***-ta*** that are masculine. For the most part, if these are easily identifiable in English, they are probably masculine.

el clima – climate	*el problema* – problem
el diploma – diploma	*el sistema* – system
el drama – drama	*el mapa* – map
el poema – poem	*el profeta* – prophet
el tema – theme	*el aroma* – aroma

There are also other ways of forming the feminine than by adding an *-a* ending:

Masculine	Feminine
el rey – the king	*la reina* – the queen
el actor – the actor	*la actriz* – the actress
el poeta – the poet	*la poetisa* – the poet
el gallo – the rooster	*la gallina* – the hen

Sometimes the masculine and feminine words corresponding to a matched pair of concepts are different:

Masculine	Feminine
el yerno – the son-in-law	*la nuera* – the daughter-in-law
el varón – the male	*la hembra* – the female
el toro – the bull	*la vaca* – the cow

Masculine words that appear to be feminine:

el día – day	*el césped* – turf
el sofá – sofa	*el colega* – colleague
el ataúd – coffin	*el tranvía* – trolley

Nouns of Invariable Gender

Some nouns can be either masculine or feminine depending on their content or reference, without undergoing any formal alterations:

Masculine	Feminine
el artista – the artist	*la artista* – the artist
el estudiante – the student	*la estudiante* – the student
el joven – the young man	*la joven* – the young woman

Gender and Meaning Change

There are nouns that have different meanings depending on whether they are used as masculine or feminine:

el policía – the policeman	*la policía* – the police (force)
el papa – the Pope	*la papa* – the potato
el cometa – the comet	*la cometa* – the kite
el orden – order (as in a command)	*la orden* – the order (to do something)
el cura – the priest	*la cura* – the cure
el guía – the guide (person)	*la guía* – the guide (book, as in *guía de teléfonos*)
el frente – the front	*la frente* – the forehead

Use of *El* Before a Feminine Noun

If the feminine noun begins with a stressed ***a*** or ***ha***, the singular forms of the article used are ***el*** or ***un***. If anything intercedes between these two items, use the normal ***la*** or ***una***.

el *águila* (eagle)	*las águilas*	*la gran águila*
un *hacha* (hatchet)	*unas hachas*	*una gran hacha*

Other examples: *el alma* – soul, *el aula* – classroom, *el agua* – water, *el ala* – wing, *el alba* – dawn, *el hada* – fairy, *el hambre* – hunger.

el *agua tibi**a***	the warm water
el *alba bonit**a***	the pretty dawn
el *águila maravillos**a***	the marvelous eagle

Other Feminine Words

la pirámide – pyramid	*la vez* – time
la torre – tower	*la razón* – reason
la leche – milk	*la imagen* – image
la carne – meat	*la luz* – light
la gente – people	*la catedral* – cathedral
la frase – sentence	*la suerte* – luck

NUMBER

In Spanish, as in English, nouns can be singular or plural. The most common way to form the plural is by adding the *-s* ending to the singular form of the word. (Note that the following examples are of words ending in an unstressed vowel.)

Singular	**Plural**
hombre – man	*hombres* – men
niño – boy	*niños* – boys
perro – dog	*perros* – dogs

Formation of the Plural by Addition of *-es*

In other cases (words ending in a consonant or in a stressed vowel other than *-é*), the plural is formed by adding an *-es* ending to the singular form of the word:

Singular	Plural
mujer – woman	*mujeres* – women
razón – reason	*razones* – reasons
jabalí – boar	*jabalíes* – boars

Exceptions: *mamá* (mother), pl. *mamás; ley* (law), pl. *leyes.*

Nouns of Invariable Number

Nouns ending in *-s* are the same in the singular and the plural if the final syllable is unstressed:

el (los) rascacielos – the skyscraper(s)
el (los) paraguas – the umbrella(s)
el (los) lunes – Monday(s)

Diminutives

The Spanish endings *-ito, -cito*, and their feminine forms are used to indicate affection or to emphasize smallness of size:

Tú eres mi ***amor.***
You are my **love.**

Tú eres mi ***amorcito.***
You are my **sweetheart.**

Quiero chocolate. Dame un ***poco.***
I want chocolate. Give me **some.**

Quiero chocolate. Dame un ***poquito.***
I want chocolate. Give me **a little.**

Ese ***hombre*** *tiene buen aspecto.*
That **man** is good looking.

Ese ***hombrecito*** *debe ser muy desgraciado.*
That **poor man** must be very unfortunate.

Augmentatives

The endings *-ote, -ón,* and *-ona* are added to express increased size:

hombre – man	*hombrón* – big man
mujer – woman	*mujerona* – big woman
casa – house	*casona* – big house

ADJECTIVES

Adjectives agree in gender and number with the noun they modify.

a) Adjectives ending in *-o* change their ending to *-a* when they modify a feminine noun:

bueno, buena – good; *malo, mala* – bad; *bello, bella* – beautiful

b) Adjectives ending in *-or* (or *-on* or *-an*) add an *-a* to become feminine:

hablador, habladora – talkative; *alemán, alemana* – German

Exceptions:

mejor – better
superior – upper, superior
exterior – outer, external
anterior – earlier, anterior
peor – worse
inferior – lower, inferior
interior – inner, internal
posterior – later, posterior

c) Most other adjectives have the same ending for both genders:

verde – green
azul – blue
cortés – courteous
grande – big, great
frágil – fragile
soez – mean, vile

d) Adjectives of nationality have four forms. If they end in *-o,* they follow the normal pattern of change. All others may be changed by adding *-a* to make them feminine and *-as* to make them feminine plural:

inglés, inglesa, ingleses, inglesas
alemán, alemana, alemanes, alemanas
español, española, españoles, españolas

Number

a) Adjectives ending in a vowel add an *-s* to form the plural:

bello, bellos – beautiful; *grande, grandes* – big, great

b) Adjectives ending in a consonant add *-es* to form the plural:

azul, azules – blue; *débil, débiles* – weak; *vulgar, vulgares* – vulgar

c) If an adjective modifies more than one noun and one of those nouns is masculine, the adjective must be **masculine** and **plural:**

Mis tíos y tías eran ***ricos.*** My uncles and aunts were **rich.**
Los hombres y las mujeres ***viejos****...* **Old** men and women...

Shortening of Adjectives

Some adjectives that directly precede the noun lose their final vowel or syllable:

ciento → cien
*bueno → buen***
*Santo → San***
*tercero → tercer***
*ninguno→ ningún***
*grande → gran**
*malo → mal***
*primero → primer***
*alguno→ algún***
*cualquiera→ cualquier**

* The shortening of this adjective only happens in front of singular nouns, either masculine or feminine. Compare:

El acontecimiento fue ***grande.***
The event was **big.**

el ***gran*** *acontecimiento* – the **big** event

** These adjectives only shorten in front of masculine singular nouns. Compare:

El hombre es ***bueno****.*
The man is **good.**

el ***buen*** *hombre* – the **good** man

Qualifying Adjectives

Qualifying adjectives usually follow the noun:

un día ***frío*** – a **cold** day
unas sábanas ***limpias*** – some **clean** sheets

Change of Meaning with Location

Some common adjectives change their meaning with their location:

el hombre ***pobre*** – the poor man (having no money)
el ***pobre*** *hombre* – the poor man (pitiable)

un cuadro ***grande*** – a large painting
un ***gran*** *cuadro* – a great painting

el policía ***mismo*** – the policeman himself
el ***mismo*** *policía* – the same policeman

***ciertas** palabras* – certain words (specific words from among many)
*palabras **ciertas*** – certain (sure)

***nueva** casa* – new house (different)
*casa **nueva*** – new house (brand new)

*un **simple** empleado* – a mere employee
*un empleado **simple*** – a simple-minded employee

COMPARISON OF ADJECTIVES AND ADVERBS

Adverbs modify verbs, adjectives, and other adverbs and are invariable.

The following is a list of frequently used adverbs:

bien – well	*mal* – badly
más – more	*menos* – less
siempre – always	*nunca* – never
cerca – near	*lejos* – far
antes – before	*después* – afterwards
bastante – enough	*demasiado* – too much
temprano – early	*tarde* – late
así – thus, so	*casi* – almost
entonces – then	*luego* – later, afterward
todavía – still	

Aún is a common adverb whose meaning depends on whether the sentence is affirmative or negative:

***Aún** quiere trabajar.*
He **still** wants to work.

***Aún** no está despierta.*
She's not **yet** awake.

Aun (no accent) normally has the meaning **even** and commonly precedes the word it modifies.

¿Aun no ha llegado Juan?
Juan hasn't even arrived?

Adverbs Ending in *-mente*

Many adverbs are derived from the **feminine** form of the adjective (when such a form is available) by the addition of *-mente:*

claro/claramente – clearly
rápido/rápidamente – quickly

feliz/felizmente – happily
hábil/hábilmente – skillfully
dulce/dulcemente – sweetly

When two or more adverbs are used in a sequence, only the last adverb ends in *–mente*. All others are written as feminine adjectives (if they have a feminine form).

*Habla lent**a** y elocuente**mente**.*
He speaks slowly and eloquently.

*Juan corre rápid**a** y hábil**mente**.*
Juan runs rapidly and skillfully.

Con, Sin + Noun

At times an adverb can be formed by using the preposition *con* (with) or *sin* (without) + a noun.

con cuidado – carefully
sin cuidado – carelessly
con rápidez – rapidly

Recientemente vs. *Recién*

Recientemente becomes *recién* before a past participle.

los recién llegados – the recent arrivals
los recién casados – the newlyweds

Adverbs Replaced by Adjectives

Adverbs may be replaced by adjectives with verbs of motion.

Ellos van y vienen silenciosos.
They come and go silently.

Comparison of Equality

This is constructed in the following ways:

Tanto, a, os, as + (noun) + *como*
Tan + (adverb or adjective) + *como*

*Tuve **tantas** deudas **como** el mes pasado.* I had **as many** debts **as** last month.

*Su música es **tan** clara **como** el agua.*
Her music is **as** clear **as** water.

*Llegué **tan** tarde **como** ayer.*
I arrived **as** late **as** yesterday.

Tanto como (without intervening expressions) means "as much as."

*Tu amigo estudia **tanto como** yo.*
Your friend studies **as much as** I [do].

Comparison of Inequality

The formula for describing levels of superiority is:

más + (noun, adjective, or adverb) + ***que***

*Tengo **más** dinero **que** tú.*
I have **more** money **than** you.

*Su auto es **más** caro **que** el mío.*
His car is **more** expensive **than** mine.

*Me levanto **más** temprano **que** ella.*
I get up **earlier than** she does.

The above formula changes to ***más de*** if a numerical expression is involved and the sentence is in the affirmative:

*Vimos **más de** mil estrellas en el cielo.*
We saw **more than** a thousand stars in the sky.

But:

*No tengo **más que** cinco dólares en el bolsillo.*
I don't have **more than** five dollars in my pocket.

The formula for describing levels of inferiority is:

menos + (noun, adjective, or adverb) + ***que***

*Nos dieron **menos** tiempo **que** a ustedes para completar el examen.*
They gave us **less** time **than** they gave you to finish the exam.

*Eres **menos** pobre **que** ella.*
You are **less** poor **than** she is.

*Tiene **menos** problemas **que** su madre.*
She has **fewer** problems **than** her mother.

The same change applies to the comparison of inferiority **except** that even in negative sentences ***de*** is used instead of ***que:***

No eran **menos de** *cinco los asaltantes.*
The assailants were no **fewer than** five.

If the second part of the comparison has a different verb from the first, **than** is expressed in one of five ways: *del que, de la que, de los que, de las que* (which all have gender and refer to nouns that are objects of both verbs), and *de lo que* (which is used when adjectives or adverbs are being compared).

Ella gasta más dinero **del que** *gana su esposo.* [*dinero*]
She spends more money **than** her husband earns.

Tengo más coches **de los que** *puedo contar.* [*coches*]
I have more cars **than** I can count.

Es más fácil **de lo que** *crees.* [*fácil*]
It is easier **than** you believe.

Anda más despacio **de lo que** *corre.* [*despacio*]
He walks more slowly **than** he runs.

Special Comparatives

Adjective (Adverb)	Comparative
bueno (bien) – good, well	*mejor* – better
malo (mal) – bad, badly	*peor* – worse
grande – big	*mayor** – older
pequeño – small	*menor** – younger

* *Mayor* and *menor* only refer to age; otherwise, *más (menos) grande (pequeño) que* is used.

Mi padre es **mayor** *que yo; mi hijo es* **menor.**
My father is **older** than I; my son is **younger.**

Esta ciudad es **más grande que** *la capital.*
This city is **bigger than** the capital.

Superlatives

In English the true or relative superlative is rendered by **the most (least) of** a category:

El, la, los, las + *más (menos)* + (adjective) + *de*
Lo + *más (menos)* + adverb + *de*

*Estos anillos son **los más** caros **de** la tienda.*
These rings are **the most** expensive **in** the store.

*Tienes **los** ojos **más** lindos **del** mundo.*
You have **the prettiest** eyes **in** the world.

*Corre **lo más** rápidamente **de** todos.*
He runs **the most** quickly **of** all.

Previously, the special comparatives noted have a superlative form:

El, la, los, las + (special comparatives) + *de*
*Mi hijo es **el mayor de** la clase.* My son is **the oldest in** the class.

Absolute Superlative

Superlatives can also be formed by adding the *-ísimo* ending to adjectives and adverbs. (Some spelling adjustments may be necessary.)

The absolute superlative is usually rendered in English as "very pretty," "very ugly," etc.

lindo/lindísimo (a) – very pretty
feo/feísimo (a) – very ugly
tarde/tardísimo (a) – very late
cerca/cerquísimo (a) – very near
rico/riquísimo (a) – very rich
fácil/facilísimo (a) – very easy

The adjective *malo* has the special superlative *pésimo* in addition to the more informal *malísimo.*

☞ Drill 1

1. Ramiro es más guapo . . . Felipe.

(A) que
(B) como
(C) de
(D) tan

2. . . . arma de fuego es peligrosa.

(A) El
(B) La
(C) Los
(D) Las

3. Mercedes lavó los platos . . .

(A) rápidamente y cuidadosamente.
(B) rápida y cuidadosa.
(C) rápida y cuidadosamente.
(D) rápidamente y cuidadosa.

4. Los explicaron . . . nosotros.

(A) menor que
(B) tanto
(C) mayor que
(D) mejor que

5. Elena tiene más amigas . . . puede contar.

(A) de los que
(B) que
(C) de las que
(D) de lo que

6. Pablo trabaja mejor . . . usted cree.

(A) que
(B) de lo que
(C) del que
(D) de la que

7. Anita es menos alta . . . Elena.

(A) tan
(B) de
(C) como
(D) que

8. Estas películas son . . . interesantes como ésas.

(A) tan
(B) tantos
(C) tantas
(D) como

9. Roberto y Ana son . . . inteligentes de la clase.

(A) las más
(B) los más
(C) más
(D) menos

10. Ellos corren . . . y hábilmente.

(A) rápida
(B) rápido
(C) rápidamente
(D) rápidos

11. Las chicas hablan . . . lentamente de todos.

(A) el más
(B) las más
(C) lo más
(D) más

12. Hay . . . torres como palacios en aquel país.

(A) tan
(B) tantos
(C) tan muchos
(D) tantas

13. . . . persona puede estudiar este curso.

(A) Algún
(B) Cualquier
(C) Ningún
(D) Cualquiera

14. Wilhelm y Kerstin son . . .

(A) alemanas.
(B) de alemanes.
(C) alemanes.
(D) alemanos.

15. La Reina Isabela I . . .

(A) una gran mujer.
(B) una grande mujer.
(C) una mujer gran.
(D) mujer grande.

16. Mis notas son . . . las de Juan.

(A) mayor que
(B) mayores de
(C) mejores que
(D) mejores de

17. Tú no sabes . . . importantes . . . son las tareas.

(A) los . . . que
(B) las . . . que
(C) lo . . . que
(D) lo . . . de

18. ¿Estas llaves son tuyas? –No, no . . . son.

(A) las
(B) lo
(C) ellas
(D) nothing needed

19. Juan lo hizo . . . ayer.

(A) para primera vez
(B) por primer vez
(C) por primera vez
(D) por la primera vez

20. Todo . . . oí ayer no es verdad.

(A) que
(B) lo que
(C) la que
(D) de

Drill 1—Detailed Explanations of Answers

1. **(A)** The most common pattern to express a **comparison** of superiority (i.e., to show that one thing or person is superior to another in some respect) is "más . . . que" (more than); for example, "Yo soy más delgado que tú" (I am thinn**er than** you); "Hablas español más fácilmente que yo" (You speak Spanish more easily than I); "Tengo más años que ella" (I am older than she). Notice from these three examples that we may use either adjectives, adverbs, or nouns between the words "más" and "que." The only time we use "de," as in (C) after "más," is when there is a number immediately afterwards: "Tenemos más de tres pesos" (We have more than three pesos).

2. **(A)** "Arma de fuego" means "firearm." Of the possible choices, we can immediately eliminate (C) and (D) because they are plural definite articles and cannot be placed before a singular noun such as "arma." This reduces our choices to "El" or "La." We know that most nouns that end in -a are feminine. By looking at the sentence carefully, we also see that the adjective "peligrosa" (dangerous) is feminine and most certainly modifies "arma." Therefore, you might have been tempted to choose (B), "La." This is not correct, however. Feminine singular nouns which end in -a but begin with "a" or "ha" and have their **stress** on the **first syllable**, as in "arma," require that we use the masculine singular definite article in front of them. This does not change the gender of the noun, however. It still stays feminine. We can see this in our sentence because we used the feminine adjective "peligrosa" to describe "arma." Remember that this rule applies only to feminine **singular** nouns. In the plural, we use the feminine plural definite article: "Las armas de fuego son peligrosas."

3. **(C)** When two or more adverbs are used together to refer to the same verb, the last one is the only one with the **–mente** ending.

4. **(D)** The verb "explicaron" in our sentence means "they explained." Comparisons of superiority, i.e., comparisons which show that in some respect someone or something is superior to someone or something else, are usually formed according to the following pattern: "más" + adjective or adverb or noun + "que." Example: "Enrique es **más rico que** yo." (Enrique is richer than I.) There are some adjectives and adverbs which have irregular comparatives. For example, "menor," which appears in (A), is the comparative form of "pequeño." "Mayor," in (C), is the comparative for "grande." Neither of these could be used in the blank because we are

not talking about size. On the other hand, "mejor que" would mean "better than" and makes sense in our sentence. The word "tanto," in (B), means "as much" or sometimes "so much." It is usually followed by "como" to form comparisons of equality, i.e., to show that two persons or things are equal in some respect: "Tengo **tanto dinero como** tú" (I have as much money as you). In (B), however, we have omitted the word "como," which is obligatory in comparisons of equality.

5. **(C)** When the verbs in each half of the comparison are both referring to the same noun ("amigas"), the longer form of **than** is required. Because "amigas" is a feminine noun, "de las que" is used. For this reason (A) would be incorrect because it is masculine plural, and (D) is also incorrect because it is neuter. Answer (B) would be used in a simple comparison where the verb is not repeated in the second half.

6. **(B)** Because an adjective is the point of comparison for each verb ("trabaja" and "cree"), the neuter form of **than** is used. Therefore, (C), the masculine form, and (D), the feminine form, are not correct. Answer (A) would be used in a simple comparison where the verb is not repeated in the second half.

7. **(D)** This is a simple comparison where the verb in the second half of the comparison is not stated but understood to be from the same infinitive (**ser** in this case). Choice (A) is used in the first half of an equal comparison and means **as**. Choice (C) is used in the second half of an equal comparison to mean **as**. Choice (B) is used in an unequal comparison when followed by a number.

8. **(A)** When there is an equal comparison that involves using an adjective or adverb, the word preceding this adjective or adverb is **tan** meaning **as**. The second half of this comparison requires using **como**, which is already in the sample. Therefore, choice (D) cannot be used to precede the adjective. Choices (B) and (C) each have gender and would precede nouns.

9. **(B)** Superlative statements require the use of the definite article and are followed by **de**. In this sample, because Roberto is masculine and Ana is feminine, the masculine plural "los" is required. Therefore, choice (A), the feminine plural, is incorrect. In order to use either choice (C) or (D), the sentence would need to be in the comparative form (not the superlative) and **que** would then need to follow the adjective.

10. **(A)** Whenever there are two or more adverbs modifying a verb, only the last adverb ends in **-mente**. The other must be written in the feminine form of the adjective (if there is one). This would eliminate choice (B), which is a masculine adjective, and (D), which is a masculine plural adjective. Choice (C) is incorrect because it ends in **-mente**.

11. **(C)** When dealing with the superlative forms of adverbs instead of using the definite article, which has gender, **lo** is used with **más** or **menos**. Therefore, (A), which is masculine, and (B), which is feminine plural, are incorrect. Choice (D) is incomplete because **lo** is needed.

12. **(D)** Because "torres" is a feminine plural noun, the feminine plural form of **tanto** is required. Choice (A) means **as** and does not translate correctly with a noun after it. Choice (C) is a completely incorrect form since forms of **tanto** mean **as much** or **as many**.

13. **(B)** Before any singular noun, "cualquiera" apocopates (drops the -a). Therefore, (D) is incorrect. Choices (A) and (C), although apocopated, are used with masculine singular nouns. To be correct, each would need to end in -a.

14. **(C)** Adjectives of nationality have four forms. The masculine plural form is required here because the adjective is modifying both a masculine and feminine subject. Because the masculine singular form is **alemán**, the plural adds -**es** to that form. (Note that the accent is dropped on the plural form.) This would eliminate (A), which is feminine plural, and (D), which is nonexistent. Choice (B) is incorrect because adjectives of this sort are not preceded by **de**.

15. **(A)** There are two grammatical points here: "grande" becomes "gran" before any singular noun and means **great**; the indefinite article ("una") is required before predicate nouns of occupation that are modified (have adjectives). Choice (B) is incorrect because "grande" is not apocopated, and (C) is incorrect because the apocopated form precedes, not follows, the noun. Choice (D) requires an indefinite article.

16. **(C)** This answer requires knowing the meaning of "mejor" (better) and "mayor" (older). Also, a comparison is followed by **que** not **de**. "Mejor" must be plural in this sample to match "notas." Although choices (B) and (D) are plural, they are followed by **de**. Choices (A) and (B) also mean "older," which doesn't make sense in this context. Although (D) is plural, it is also followed by **de** and is, therefore, incorrect.

17. **(C)** To express **how** followed by an adjective or adverb, use **lo** before that adjective/adverb and follow it with **que**. This would eliminate (A), (B), and (D) as correct choices.

18. **(B)** **Lo** is used as a complement to replace adjectives, pronouns, or nouns used with **ser**, **estar**, and **parecer**. In this sample, the noun "llaves" (keys) is being replaced in the answer with **lo**. **Lo** used in this sense is invariable and will not, therefore, have the same gender and number as the noun it replaces.

19. **(C)** The definite article is omitted with expressions such as this one (por primera vez, en primer lugar, etc.) Also, "vez" is feminine.

20. **(B)** "Todo lo que" is an expression meaning "all that."

PRESENT INDICATIVE

	amar **to love**	***comer*** **to eat**	***vivir*** **to live**
yo	*amo*	*como*	*vivo*
tú	*amas*	*comes*	*vives*
él/ella/Ud.	*ama*	*come*	*vive*
nosotros, –as	*amamos*	*comemos*	*vivimos*
*vosotros, –as**	*amáis*	*coméis*	*vivís*
ellos/ellas/Uds.	*aman*	*comen*	*viven*

* This pronoun and corresponding forms of the verb are used in Spain only.

Verbs irregular in ***yo*** form only:

caber	to fit	*quepo*	*saber*	to know	*sé*
caer	to fall	*caigo*	*salir*	to leave	*salgo*
dar	to give	*doy*	*traer*	to bring	*traigo*
hacer	to make/do	*hago*	*valer*	to be worth	*valgo*
poner	to put	*pongo*	*ver*	to see	*veo*

Verbs irregular in more than one form:

decir **to tell or say**	***estar*** **to be**	***haber*** **to have (auxiliary)**	***ir*** **to go**
digo	*estoy*	*he*	*voy*
dices	*estás*	*has*	*vas*
dice	*está*	*ha*	*va*
decimos	*estamos*	*hemos*	*vamos*
decís	*estáis*	*habéis*	*vais*
dicen	*están*	*han*	*van*

oír **to hear**	***ser*** **to be**	***tener*** **to have**	***venir*** **to come**
oigo	*soy*	*tengo*	*vengo*
oyes	*eres*	*tienes*	*vienes*
oye	*es*	*tiene*	*viene*
oímos	*somos*	*tenemos*	*venimos*
oís	*sois*	*tenéis*	*venís*
oyen	*son*	*tienen*	*vienen*

Verbs Ending in *-cer, -cir*

The ***yo*** form ends in ***–zco*** if preceded by a vowel. If the ending is preceded by a consonant, the form ends in ***–zo***.

conocer	to know	*conozco*
traducir	to translate	*traduzco*
vencer	to conquer	*venzo*

Others:

merecer – to deserve
carecer – to lack
aparecer – to appear
parecer – to seem
crecer – to grow
convencer – to convince
nacer – to be born

Verbs that Have Stem-changes

There are five types of stem-changes that may occur in the present tense: (*ie*), (*ue*), (*i*), (*ú*), (*í*). This will occur in all forms except nosotros/vosotros and appears in the stressed syllable.

ie ***pensar*** **to think**	**ue** ***dormir*** **to sleep**	**i** ***pedir*** **to ask for**	**ú** ***actuar*** **to act**	**í** ***enviar*** **to send**
pienso	*duermo*	*pido*	*actúo*	*envío*
piensas	*duermes*	*pides*	*actúas*	*envías*
piensa	*duerme*	*pide*	*actúa*	*envía*
pensamos	*dormimos*	*pedimos*	*actuamos*	*enviamos*
pensáis	*dormís*	*pedís*	*actuáis*	*enviáis*
piensan	*duermen*	*piden*	*actúan*	*envían*

Other examples:

ie: *comenzar/empezar* – to begin, *nevar* – to snow, *cerrar* – to close, *apretar* – to tighten, *perder* – to lose, *querer* – to want, *mentir* – to lie, *sentir* – to feel, *herir* – to wound

ue: *morir* – to die, *dormir* – to sleep, *volar* – to fly, *poder* – to be able, *volver* – to return, *rogar* – to beg, *jugar* – to play

i: *elegir* – to elect, *repetir* – to repeat, *servir* – to serve, *corregir* – to correct

ú: *graduarse* – to graduate, *continuar* – to continue

í: *confiar* – to confide, *guiar* – to guide, *variar* – to vary

Verbs Ending in *-ger, -gir*

In the ***yo*** form there will be a spelling change because the ***-go*** combination will produce a ***g*** sound and the infinitive has an ***h*** sound.

coger	to catch	***cojo***
elegir (i)	to elect	***elijo***

Others:

escoger	to choose	***escojo***
corregir	to correct	***correjo***
recoger	to gather	***recojo***

Verbs Ending in *-uir*

All forms except *nosotros/vosotros* have a ***y***.

huir **to flee**	***construir*** **to build**
huyo	*construyo*
huyes	*construyes*
huye	*construye*
huimos	*construimos*
huís	*construís*
huyen	*construyen*

Verbs Ending in *-guir*

The ***yo*** form drops the ***u***.

seguir (i) – to follow	***sigo***
perseguir (i) – to pursue	***persigo***

Uses of the Present Indicative

There are three possible translations for the present tense as expressed below with the verb to eat (*comer*).

I eat./I do eat./I am eating. = *Como.*

Immediate Future

The present tense is commonly used to express the immediate future.

Mañana voy a casa.
Tomorrow I will go home.

The "*Hace*" Sentence

When an action began in the past and is still continuing in the present, the Spanish sentence is rendered with the following formula:

hace + time + *que* + Present/Present Progressive

Hace dos horas que comemos/estamos comiendo.
We have been eating for two hours.

¿Cuánto tiempo hace que ella canta/está cantando?
How long has she been singing?

PRETERITE AND IMPERFECT

Preterite Indicative–Regular: *-ar, -er, -ir*

	amar **to love**	***comer*** **to eat**	***vivir*** **to live**
yo	*amé*	*comí*	*viví*
tú	*amaste*	*comiste*	*viviste*
él/ella/Ud.	*amó*	*comió*	*vivió*
nosotros, –as	*amamos*	*comimos*	*vivimos*
vosotros, –as	*amasteis*	*comisteis*	*vivisteis*
ellos/ellas/Uds.	*amaron*	*comieron*	*vivieron*

Preterite Indicative–Irregular

The following group of preterites shares the same set of irregular endings: *–e, –iste, –o, –imos, –isteis, –ieron.*

andar **to walk**	***caber*** **to fit**	***estar*** **to be**	***haber*** **to have**	***hacer*** **to make/do**
anduve	*cupe*	*estuve*	*hube*	*hice*
anduviste	*cupiste*	*estuviste*	*hubiste*	*hiciste*
anduvo	*cupo*	*estuvo*	*hubo*	*hizo*
anduvimos	*cupimos*	*estuvimos*	*hubimos*	*hicimos*
anduvisteis	*cupisteis*	*estuvisteis*	*hubisteis*	*hicisteis*
anduvieron	*cupieron*	*estuvieron*	*hubieron*	*hicieron*

poder* **to be able**	***poner*** **to put**	***querer**** **to want**
pude	*puse*	*quise*
pudiste	*pusiste*	*quisiste*
pudo	*puso*	*quiso*
pudimos	*pusimos*	*quisimos*
pudisteis	*pusisteis*	*quisisteis*
pudieron	*pusieron*	*quisieron*

saber* **to know**	***tener**** **to have**	***venir*** **to come**
supe	*tuve*	*vine*
supiste	*tuviste*	*viniste*
supo	*tuvo*	*vino*
supimos	*tuvimos*	*vinimos*
supisteis	*tuvisteis*	*vinisteis*
supieron	*tuvieron*	*vinieron*

* These verbs have an altered translation in the preterite and will be discussed later in this chapter.

Irregular Preterites with a *–J*

decir **to say/tell**	***traer*** **to bring**	***–ducir*** **types** ***conducir*** **to drive**
dije	*traje*	*conduje*
dijiste	*trajiste*	*condujiste*
dijo	*trajo*	*condujo*
dijimos	*trajimos*	*condujimos*
dijisteis	*trajisteis*	*condujisteis*
dijeron	*trajeron*	*condujeron*

Note: The third plural does not have an *i* after the *j*.

Irregulars of *Dar, Ir, Ser*

Dar is irregular in that it takes the endings of the *-er*/*-ir* verbs (without accents). *Ser* and *ir* are identical in this tense.

dar **to give**	***ir/ser*** **to go/to be**
di	*fui*
diste	*fuiste*
dio	*fue*
dimos	*fuimos*
disteis	*fuisteis*
dieron	*fueron*

Stem-Changing Verbs

Stem-changes commonly occur in the preterite for *–ir* verbs that have a stem-change in the present. These changes have a pattern (*ue/u*), (*ie/i*), and (*i/i*). The second vowel in parenthesis will surface in the preterite third person singular and plural.

dormir **(ue, u)** **to sleep**	***sentir*** **(ie, i)** **to regret or feel**	***pedir*** **(i, i)** **to ask for**
dormí	*sentí*	*pedí*
dormiste	*sentiste*	*pediste*
durmió	*sintió*	*pidió*
dormimos	*sentimos*	*pedimos*
dormisteis	*sentisteis*	*pedisteis*
durmieron	*sintieron*	*pidieron*

Others:

morir — to die	*divertirse* — to enjoy oneself	*servir* — to serve
	herir — to wound	*repetir* — to repeat
	mentir — to lie	*seguir* — to follow

Verbs ending in *–car, –gar, –zar*

Verbs ending in *–car*, *–gar*, and *–zar* are affected in the ***yo*** form of the preterite by the final *–é*. This vowel will cause the consonants before it (*c, g, z*) to change in sound. To maintain the original sound of the infinitive, these verbs will require a spelling change in that form as follows.

–car = qué *–gar = gué* *–zar = cé*

Examples:	*atacar = ataqué*	I attacked.
	entregar = entregué	I delivered.
	rezar = recé	I prayed.

Verbs that Change *I* to *Y*

All *–er* and *–ir* verbs with double vowels in the infinitive (with the exception of *traer/atraer*) will require this change in the third person singular and plural.

oír **to hear**	***creer*** **to believe**	***leer*** **to read**
oí	*creí*	*leí*
oíste	*creíste*	*leíste*
oyó	*creyó*	*leyó*
oímos	*creímos*	*leímos*
oísteis	*creísteis*	*leísteis*
oyeron	*creyeron*	*leyeron*

An added requirement for these verbs is the accent mark over the *i* in the *tú, nosotros*, and *vosotros* forms to split the diphthong.

Verbs Ending in *–ller, –llir, –ñir, –ñer*

Although these verbs are used with less frequency, they can surface on an AP exam. Because of the double *l* and the tilde over the *ñ,* these verbs in the third person singular and plural do not need the *i* of those endings.

bruñir **to polish**	***bullir*** **to boil**
bruñí	*bullí*
bruñiste	*bulliste*
*bruñ**ó***	*bull**ó***
bruñimos	*bullimos*
bruñisteis	*bullisteis*
*bruñ**eron***	*bull**eron***

Verbs Ending in *–uir*

Just like the present tense of these verbs, the preterite also needs a *y*. It will occur in the third person singular and plural only.

huir **to flee**	***construir*** **to build**
huí	*construí*
huiste	*construiste*
huyó	*construyó*
huimos	*construimos*
huisteis	*construisteis*
huyeron	*construyeron*

Verbs Ending in *–guar*

In this particular combination of letters, the ***u*** is heard as a separate letter, not treated as a diphthong with the ***a*** that follows. This sound will be altered in the ***yo*** form because of the final ***–é***. To maintain the sound of the ***u***, a dieresis mark is placed over it.

averiguar (to verify) = *averi**güé***

Note: This also occurs in other Spanish words:

la vergüenza (shame), *el agüero* (omen)

Imperfect Indicative–Regular: *–ar, –er, –ir*

This tense may be translated as "used to + verb," "was or were verb + ing," or the normal past tense ending "–ed."

	amar **to love**	***comer*** **to eat**	***vivir*** **to live**
yo	*amaba*	*comía*	*vivía*
tú	*amabas*	*comías*	*vivías*
él/ella/Ud.	*amaba*	*comía*	*vivía*
nosotros, –as	*amábamos*	*comíamos*	*vivíamos*
vosotros, –as	*amabais*	*comíais*	*vivíais*
ellos/ellas/Uds.	*amaban*	*comían*	*vivían*

Imperfect Indicative–Irregulars

There are only three irregular verbs in this tense.

ser **to be**	***ir*** **to go**	***ver*** **to see**
era	*iba*	*veía*
eras	*ibas*	*veías*
era	*iba*	*veía*
éramos	*íbamos*	*veíamos*
erais	*ibais*	*veíais*
eran	*iban*	*veían*

Continuation vs. Completion of an Action

The imperfect is used for an action **continuing** in the past; the preterite designates a **finished** action or an action whose beginning, duration, or end is emphasized by the speaker.

Estaba nublado. (Imperfect)
It was cloudy. (No indication of when it got that way.)

Estuvo nublado. (Preterite)
It was cloudy. (But now it has changed.)

Ella quería a su marido. (Imperfect)
She loved her husband. (Indefinitely in the past.)

Ella quiso a su marido. (Preterite)
She loved her husband. (While he was alive, while she was married to him, etc.)

Description vs. Narration

The imperfect is used to **describe** a quality or a state in the past; the preterite is used to **narrate** an action.

Los soldados ***marcharon*** (pret.) *toda una mañana y* ***llegaron*** (pret.) *al fuerte enemigo al mediodía cuando* ***hacía*** (imp.) *mucho calor. Se* ***sentían*** (imp.) *cansados y* ***necesitaban*** (imp.) *descansar. Se* ***sentaron*** (pret.) *a la sombra de un árbol.*
The soldiers marched one full morning and arrived at the enemy fort at noon when it was very hot. They were tired and needed to rest. They sat down in the shade of a tree.

"Used to" Followed by Infinitive

The English expression **used to** followed by an infinitive is rendered by the imperfect, as this is the tense that designates a habitual action in the past.

Pasábamos *las vacaciones en la costa.*
We **used to spend** the holidays on the shore.

Eran *amigos.*
They **used to be** friends.

Alternatively, the verb *soler* (to be in the habit of) may be used in the imperfect to render the sense of "used to." *Soler* must be accompanied by an infinitive: *solíamos pasar las vacaciones en la costa; solían ser amigos,* etc.

"Was" or "Were" Plus Present Participle

Expressions formed with the past tense of "to be" followed by the present participle of another verb (**was** or **were** doing, singing, studying, etc.) are rendered by the imperfect.

Él ***conducía*** *cuando ocurrió el accidente.*
He **was driving** when the accident occurred.

Pensaban *visitarnos ese verano.*
They **were thinking** of visiting us that summer.

Telling Time in the Past

The imperfect (of *ser*) is used to tell time in the past.

Eran *las tres.*
It was 3 o'clock.

Era *tarde cuando se fueron los invitados.*
It was late when the guests left.

Special Preterites

The preterite of some verbs (such as *conocer, saber, poder, poner, tener,* and *querer*) has a special meaning:

Yo la ***conocí*** *el año pasado.*
I **met** her last year.

Cuando ***supimos*** *la noticia nos pusimos tristes.*
When we **learned/found out** the news we felt sad.

El fugitivo **pudo** *abandonar el país a última hora.*
The fugitive **managed to** abandon the country at the last minute.

Jamás **tuvo** *noticias de su familia.*
She never **received** news of her family.

El ladrón **quiso** *abrir la puerta con una barra.*
The thief **tried to** open the door with a bar.

Juan no **quiso** *pagar la cuenta.*
Juan **refused** to pay the bill.

States of Mind

Normally verbs indicating state of mind (*saber, creer, pensar, comprender, convencerse*, etc.) are expressed using the imperfect unless there is an indication of change in that state. Look for words to indicate this change like *de pronto* (soon), *de repente* (suddenly), *luego que* (as soon as), *cuando* (when), *al* + infinitive (upon + ing).

Juan creía la verdad.
Juan believed the truth.

But:

De pronto *Juan la creyó.*
Suddenly Juan believed it.

"Ago" Statements

"Ago" statements are normally expressed with this formula:

Hace + time + *que* + preterite

Hace dos años que fuimos allí.
We went there two years ago.

"*Hacía*" Statements

To express "had been + ing," use the formula:

hacía + time + *que* + imperfect/past progressive

Hacía dos horas que cantaba/estaba cantando.
He had been singing for two hours.

FUTURE AND CONDITIONAL

Future/Conditional Indicative–Regular: *–ar, –er, –ir*

Since these two tenses use the entire infinitive as their stem, only two examples are given here.

	amar **to love**	***comer*** **to eat**
yo	*amaré/ía*	*comeré/ía*
tú	*amarás/ías*	*comerás/ías*
él/ella/Ud.	*amará/ía*	*comerá/ía*
nosotros, –as	*amaremos/íamos*	*comeremos/íamos*
vosotros, –as	*amaréis/íais*	*comeréis/íais*
ellos/ellas/Uds.	*amarán/ían*	*comerán/ían*

Future/Conditional Indicative–Irregulars

Verbs that drop the *–e* of the infinitive.

caber **to fit**	***haber*** **to have–auxiliary**	***poder*** **to be able**
cabré/ía	*habré/ía*	*podré/ía*
cabrás/ías	*habrás/ías*	*podrás/ías*
cabrá/ía	*habrá/ía*	*podrá/ía*
cabremos/íamos	*habremos/íamos*	*podremos/íamos*
cabréis/íais	*habréis/íais*	*podréis/íais*
cabrán/ían	*habrán/ían*	*podrán/ían*

querer **to want**	***saber*** **to know**
querré/ía	*sabré/ía*
querrás/ías	*sabrás/ías*
querrá/ía	*sabrá/ía*
querremos/íamos	*sabremos/íamos*
querréis/íais	*sabréis/íais*
querrán/ían	*sabrán/ían*

Verbs that change the vowel (*e* or *i*) to a *d*.

poner **to put**	***salir*** **to leave**	***tener*** **to have**
pondré/ía	*saldré/ía*	*tendré/ía*
pondrás/ías	*saldrás/ías*	*tendrás/ías*
pondrá/ía	*saldrá/ía*	*tendrá/ía*
pondremos/íamos	*saldremos/íamos*	*tendremos/íamos*
pondréis/íais	*saldréis/íais*	*tendréis/íais*
pondrán/ían	*saldrán/ían*	*tendrán/ían*

valer **to be worth**	***venir*** **to come**
valdré/ía	*vendré/ía*
valdrás/ías	*vendrás/ías*
valdrá/ía	*vendrá/ía*
valdremos/íamos	*vendremos/íamos*
valdréis/íais	*vendréis/íais*
valdrán/ían	*vendrán/ían*

Verbs that drop the *e* and *c* of the infinitive.

decir **to tell/say**	***hacer*** **to make/do**
diré/ía	*haré/ía*
dirás/ías	*harás/ías*
dirá/ía	*hará/ía*
diremos/íamos	*haremos/íamos*
diréis/íais	*haréis/íais*
dirán/ían	*harán/ían*

Note: Compounds of the above words are conjugated in the same manner (*proponer, detener, contener*). However, ***maldecir*** and ***bendecir*** are conjugated as regular verbs in these two tenses and do not follow the pattern for ***decir***.

Uses of Future/Conditional

Common translations include **will/shall** for the future and **would** for the conditional.

Saldré en seguida.	I shall leave immediately.
Me gustaría saberlo.	I would like to know it.
Juan vivirá conmigo.	Juan will live with me.

Probability Statements or Conjecture

The future tense is used to express **present** probability statements while the conditional expresses **past** probability. These statements in English may be expressed a number of ways.

Present Probability	Past Probability
He **is** probably ill. *Estará enfermo.* *[Debe de estar enfermo.]**	He **was** probably ill. *Estaría enfermo.* *[Debía de estar enfermo.]*
It **must** be 1:00. *Será la una.* *[Debe de ser la una.]*	It **must have been** 1:00. *Sería la una.* *[Debía de ser la una.]*
Where **can** he be? *¿Dónde estará?*	Where **could** he be? *¿Dónde estaría?*
I wonder who he **is**? *¿Quién será?*	I wonder who he **was**? *¿Quién sería?*

* ***Deber de*** + **infinitive** is another way to express probability statements.

Expressing Would, Wouldn't with the Past Tense

When **would** means **used to**, the imperfect tense is used.

When **wouldn't** means **refused**, the negative preterite of *querer* is used.

Cuando era joven, iba al cine a menudo.
When he was young, he would go to the movies often.

No quiso verme.
He wouldn't (refused to) see me.

☞ Drill 2

1. Ninguna de las ventanas está sucia porque la criada las . . . ayer.

(A) limpio (C) limpió

(B) limpiaba (D) limpian

2. Ayer, al levantarme por la mañana, vi que . . . un día estupendo.

(A) hacía (C) hizo

(B) hará (D) había hecho

3. Durante mi niñez siempre . . . a la casa de mis tíos.

(A) iría (C) fui

(B) iba (D) iré

4. Cuando tropezaron conmigo, . . . de salir del cine.

(A) acabaron (C) acabé

(B) acababa (D) acaban

5. Los jugadores no . . . jugar más.

(A) tuvieron (C) quisieron

(B) trataron (D) iban

6. Esta tarde mientras . . . el periódico, sonó el teléfono.

(A) miraré (C) leía

(B) busqué (D) estudio

7. Aunque ella vino temprano, no la . . .

(A) vi. (C) vea.

(B) viera. (D) veré.

8. Al despertarse Ramón se dio cuenta de que . . .

(A) llovió. (C) llovido.

(B) llovía. (D) había llover.

9. El ladrón entró por la ventana que . . . abierta.

(A) estuvo
(B) estaba
(C) estará
(D) estaría

10. La guerra de Vietnam . . . varios años.

(A) duraba
(B) durará
(C) duró
(D) hubo durado

11. . . . tres horas que regresó de su viaje.

(A) Hacen
(B) Ha
(C) Hace
(D) Desde

12. Yo . . . el colegio a los 10 años.

(A) dejé
(B) dejaba
(C) dejara
(D) dejase

13. Yo . . . dormido cuando me llamaste.

(A) estaba
(B) estuve
(C) estoy
(D) estaré

14. Lo . . . la semana que viene.

(A) hicimos
(B) hacíamos
(C) haremos
(D) habíamos hecho

15. Si yo fuera al centro, te . . . algo.

(A) compraría
(B) compré
(C) compre
(D) compraré

16. Cuando era niño, me . . . viendo pasar a la gente por las calles.

(A) divertí
(B) divertía
(C) divertiría
(D) divirtiera

17. ¿Cuánto tiempo . . . que hablabas cuando entraron?

(A) hacía
(B) hizo
(C) hacían
(D) había sido

18. Hacía dos horas que ellos . . . cuando sonó el teléfono.

(A) charlaron
(B) charlan
(C) habían charlado
(D) estaban charlando

19. Ayer al oír al testigo, el juez lo . . .

(A) crea.
(B) creía.
(C) creyó.
(D) creerá.

20. . . . las tres cuando el tren partió.

(A) Eran
(B) Era
(C) Fue
(D) Fueron

21. . . . dos años que terminó la guerra.

(A) Hizo
(B) Hacía
(C) Hace
(D) Hacen

22. Ayer yo . . . a Juan por primera vez.

(A) conocía
(B) conocí
(C) supe
(D) sabía

23. Hace dos semanas que no he visto a Ana. ¿ . . . enferma?

(A) Estará
(B) Esté
(C) Va a estar
(D) Estás

24. Cuando Juan era joven, . . . al cine a menudo.

(A) va
(B) iría
(C) iba
(D) irá

25. Si tengo el tiempo, . . . el museo.

(A) visitaría
(B) visite
(C) visitaré
(D) visitaba

26. ¿Cuánto tiempo . . . que andas sin coche?

(A) hacía
(B) haces
(C) hizo
(D) hace

Drill 2—Detailed Explanations of Answers

1. **(C)** We know that a past tense is needed in this sentence because of the word "ayer" (yesterday). We must then choose between the two past tenses given among the choices: preterite and imperfect. The imperfect tense is often used to imply that a past action was incomplete, i.e., that it had not come to an end, that it was not concluded. In this sentence, however, we know that the maid finished her task of cleaning the windows because we are told that for that very reason the windows are now clean. The preterite tense is used to show that a past action, as viewed by the speaker, is considered completed, over and done with.

2. **(A)** The use of the preterite of the verb "ver" tells us that we are talking about the past. In our sentence, we are describing what the weather was like yesterday morning. The imperfect tense, rather than the preterite, is most frequently used in sentences which describe in the past, particularly if we do not wish to place undue emphasis on the idea that the situation described came to an end. This use of the imperfect tense is especially evident in contexts in which one is setting up the scene or describing the background against which other major events will take place, for example: "Era una tarde triste y lluviosa. No había nadie en la calle." (It was a sad and rainy afternoon. There was no one in the street.)

3. **(B)** In the sentence where you are to fill in the blank, the adverb "siempre" (always) is important. When we are talking about the past and we are referring to a customary or habitual action, as is the case in our sentence, we use the imperfect tense to place emphasis on the idea that the action was performed repeatedly (for an unspecified number of times). In (A), however, the verb "ir" is used in the conditional tense, not the imperfect. English speakers sometimes erroneously use the conditional tense in Spanish to express the idea of "would" in the sense of "used to" simply because English uses the word "would" both as a conditional and also to convey the concept of repeated and habitual past action. This cannot be done in Spanish. Compare the following two English sentences: If he were here, I would know it; Every Saturday when we were at the beach I would swim. Notice that only the second example has to do with a customary and habitual past action. It is in such a case that Spanish would use the imperfect tense instead of the conditional. Choice (C) is wrong because although the sentence refers to the past, it is in the preterite tense. Choice (D) is incorrect also because it is in the wrong tense, the future.

4. **(B)** The verb "tropezar" means "to stumble." The expression "tropezar **con**" means "to meet or encounter." Notice how the preposition "con," when followed by the prepositional pronoun "mí," results in the special form "conmigo." The same thing happens in the second person singular (the familiar form) to produce the word "contigo." The expression "acabar de" + infinitive signifies "to have just" done something. This expression is normally only used in two tenses, the simple present and the imperfect. In the present it means "have or has just." In the imperfect it means "had just." Since our sentence contains a verb in the preterite tense, "tropezaron," we know that we are talking about the past. Therefore, we must logically use the only form of the imperfect that appears among the choices, "acababa."

5. **(C)** (A) is incorrect because "to have to" do something is "tener que" + infinitive, but we have omitted the "que." (B), "trataron," is wrong because we have not included the "de" from the expression "tratar de" + infinitive (to try to do something). In (D), "iban," the preposition "a" is lacking. Remember, "ir a" + infinitive means "to be going to" do something. (C), "quisieron," is the only answer which fits grammatically in our sentence. Try to recall the special meanings which the verb "querer" may have in the preterite tense. If the sentence is affirmative, it may be a synonym for "tratar de" (to try to). "Quisieron venir" would mean "They tried to come." If we simply mean "They wanted to come," we would use the imperfect tense: "Querían venir." If the sentence is negative, then "querer" in the preterite can mean "refused to," as is the case in our sentence. If we simply mean "They didn't want to come," then we would use the imperfect tense again: "No querían venir."

6. **(C)** In our sentence, "mientras" means "while," and "sonó" is the third person singular of the verb "sonar" (to ring—what a telephone does). Do not confuse "sonar" with "soñar" (to dream). Because "sonó" is a past tense, we know that neither (A), "miraré," the first person singular of the future of "mirar" (to look at), nor (D), "estudio" (I study), the first person singular or the present, can be used. Then we are faced with a choice between the first person singular of the preterite of "buscar" (to look for), in (B) "busqué," and "leía," the first person singular of the imperfect of "leer" (to read), in (C), which are both past tenses. When we are talking about the past and we wish to show that an action which was in progress was interrupted by another action, the action in progress is given the imperfect tense and the interrupting action appears in the preterite. In our sentence, the action which was in progress when something else cut across it or interrupted is "I was reading" ("leía"). The action which caused the interruption is "rang" ("sonó").

7. **(A)** After **aunque,** if the present tense is used, the independent clause is generally in the future. In this case, since it is in the past, the preterite indicative is correct. This sentence does not express any uncertainty, but fact. She did arrive, and early. Another statement of fact is that "I did not see her." Therefore, the subjunctive is not needed.

8. **(B)** The correct choice is "llovía" since the imperfect translates a sense of an ongoing event in the past (sometimes, as in this phrase, "intersected" by another discrete event, namely, "se dio cuenta"). The preterite, on the other hand, marks the start, end, or completed duration of an event. In this context such an event is the realizing and not the raining which had already started outside the enunciation, so to speak. This is why choice (A) is incorrect. (As a rule of thumb, if a Spanish verb in the past can be translated into English by means of was + ing, then the Spanish verb can be rendered in the imperfect.) Choices (C) and (D) are wrong for other reasons: "llovido" is a past participle that requires an auxiliary verb ("haber") to function in the present context; and "había llover" is ungrammatical since compound tenses cannot be formed with the infinitive of the main verb.

9. **(B)** The window was already open. The real action of the phrase is the entering. By comparison, the reference to the window is in the mode of a **state** of things or in the mode of a **description**. This is why the correct answer involves an imperfect tense and not a preterite. Choices (C) and (D) do not correlate temporally with "entró."

10. **(C)** Again, the right answer is the preterite because the temporal function of the verb is to designate a duration. Choice (D) is a rarely used formation mostly reserved for literary style. It means the same as the preterite.

11. **(C)** The formula for this kind of expression is **hace** (never in the plural) + **time** + **que** + **preterite** (or **preterite** + **hace** + **time**). In English, this formula translates the particle "ago."

12. **(A)** Choices (C) and (D), both in the subjunctive, are ungrammatical, and (B) is not a good choice in view of the fact that the sentence is about temporal circumscription: the action of quitting school is "bound" by the point in time designated by "ten years." Remember that "imperfect" means incomplete and that an imperfect action is one that the sentence does not mark as ending (or beginning) in the past. The action described in this question, however, is complete; it is a point in time and not an open-ended line.

13. **(A)** Both (C) and (D) make no sense in terms of the temporal frame of the question. Now, the action of calling is in the preterite, which means it did not go on in time and that it is limited and complete in itself. But this is not true of sleeping, which becomes the temporal background for the instance of calling. And here we run into another criterion for learning the difference between preterite and imperfect: when there is a description in the past (as opposed to a main action), the verb used is in the imperfect.

14. **(C)** This item simply tests your understanding that the future tense must be used in the sentence and your recognition of the future tense form of the verb "hacer" (to make or do), "haremos." We know that we must use the future because of the expression "la semana que viene" (next week) in our sentence. (A) "hicimos," is the first person plural of the preterite of "hacer." (B) and (D) give us, respectively, the first person plural of the imperfect, "hacíamos," and of the pluperfect, "habíamos hecho," of the same verb.

15. **(A)** In an "if" clause in the past, using the subjunctive, the conditional is the appropriate form to follow.

16. **(B)** You should first recognize the different forms of "divertirse" given as options and realize, for example, that "divirtiera" is a subjunctive form with no place in the sentence (because there is no "que" followed by a dependent verb). You can also eliminate (C) in order to avoid the contradiction in tense that would result if you put together an imperfect ("era") and a conditional. So the final choice boils down to a choice between the preterite form (A) and the imperfect one (B). The latter is correct because the action of having fun is not circumscribed temporally by any semantic element of the sentence. In other words, you may translate the second part of the sentence with "used to," and being able to do this automatically signals the use of the imperfect.

17. **(A)** In time phrases that use the imperfect tense (hablabas), the third singular of the imperfect of "hacer" is needed. This would eliminate (C) because it is plural and (B) because it is preterite. Answer (D) is a form of the verb **ser**.

18. **(D)** In time phrases beginning with "hacía" either the imperfect tense or, in this case, the past progressive is correct. This would eliminate (A) the preterite and (B) the present tense of charlar. Choice (C) could be used if it were negative.

19. **(C)** Because the action occurred yesterday and "upon hearing" the witness, the preterite of the verb is necessary. If the sentence does not have any indications of past completion, the imperfect answer (B) would be preferred. This would eliminate (A) the subjunctive and (D) the future.

20. **(A)** To express time in the past, the imperfect tense is used. Because it is "three" o'clock and, therefore, plural in Spanish, the plural form of the verb is required. Therefore, choice (B), which is singular, is incorrect. Because both (C) and (D) are in the preterite tense, they are incorrect.

21. **(C)** In order to express "**ago**" in Spanish, an "hace" statement of time will be followed by the preterite tense (in this case "terminó"). "Hace" will be written in the third person singular of the present tense in these statements. Therefore, choice (A) in the preterite, (B) in the imperfect, and (D) in the plural are all incorrect.

22. **(B)** Certain verbs change meaning in the preterite. "Conocer" means "met" in this tense. Because this happened yesterday (ayer) for the first time (por primera vez), we know that the preterite is necessary. This would make choice (A) in the imperfect incorrect. Also, to "meet or know" people requires the use of the verb **conocer**. Therefore, choice (C) "I found out" and (D) "I knew" for the verb **saber** are incorrect in this context.

23. **(A)** This question intimates probability in that it has been two weeks since Ana was seen last. To express present probability, the future tense is used. This may be translated a number of ways: I wonder if she is ill?; Can she be ill?; Is she probably ill? Choice (B), the present subjunctive, and (C), the immediate future, make no sense in this context. Choice (D) is the second singular to refer to Ana, but the third singular is required here.

24. **(C)** In English we often use "would" to refer to something we "used to" do in the past. In Spanish, however, this must be expressed with the imperfect tense, not the conditional. Choice (A), the present tense, (B), the conditional tense, and (D), the future tense are incorrect in this context.

25. **(C)** In this question an understanding of **if** clauses is needed. Commonly when the **if** clause is in the present tense, the other clause will be written in the future tense. Choice (A) is conditional and would call for a past subjunctive to be used in the **if** clause. Choice (B), the present subjunctive, and (D), the imperfect, make no sense when translated in this context.

26. **(D)** Time expressions with **hace** have a certain formula. When asking "how long something **has been** going on," **hace** is paired up with the present tense (or present progressive tense). The other possible time expression would have **hacía** coupled with the imperfect (or past progressive tense). Since "andas" follows **que** and is in the present tense, "hace" must be used in the time expression. Choice (A), the imperfect, and (C), the preterite, are incorrect here. Choice (B) is in the wrong person to be used in an **hace** sentence.

FORMATION OF COMPOUND TENSES

Compound tenses are formed by adding an invariable past participle to the different forms of the auxiliary verb *haber.*

The Past Participle

The past participle in Spanish is formed by appending ***–ado*** to the stem of an *–ar* verb or ***–ido*** to the stem of an *–er* or *–ir* verb,

jugar – jugado (played)
comer – comido (eaten)
recibir – recibido (received)

The Irregular Past Participle

There are 12 irregular past participles.

abrir — abierto (opened)
cubrir — cubierto (covered)
decir — dicho (said)
escribir — escrito (written)
hacer — hecho (done)
imprimir — impreso (printed)
morir — muerto (died)
poner — puesto (put)
resolver— resuelto (solved)
romper — roto (broken)
ver — visto (seen)
volver — vuelto (returned)

Past Participles Ending in *–ido*

Most double voweled infinitives will require an accent mark over the participle ending to separate the diphthong created when the weak vowel ***i*** follows the strong vowel of the stem.

oír – oído (heard) *caer – caído* (fallen) *leer – leído* (read)

Note: Verbs ending in ***–uir*** do not require accents in this form.

huir – huido (fled)
construir – construido (built)

Conjugation of *Haber*: Indicative Mood*

	Present	Preterite*	Imperfect	Future	Conditional
yo	*he*	*hube*	*había*	*habré*	*habría*
tú	*has*	*hubiste*	*habías*	*habrás*	*habrías*
él/ella/Ud.	*ha*	*hubo*	*había*	*habrá*	*habría*
nosotros, –as	*hemos*	*hubimos*	*habíamos*	*habremos*	*habríamos*
vosotros, –as	*habéis*	*hubisteis*	*habíais*	*habréis*	*habríais*
ellos/ellas/Uds.	*han*	*hubieron*	*habían*	*habrán*	*habrían*

* The preterite perfect is a literary tense not commonly used in everyday speech. It is always preceded by a conjunction of time:

luego que	as soon as	*apenas*	hardly, scarcely
en cuanto	as soon as	*cuando*	when
así que	as soon as	*después que*	after
tan pronto como	as soon as	*no bien*	no sooner

Conjugation of *Haber*: Subjunctive and Imperative Moods

	Present	Imperfect
yo	*haya*	*hubiera/hubiese*
tú	*hayas*	*hubieras/hubieses*
él/ella/Ud.	*haya*	*hubiera/hubiese*
nosotros, –as	*hayamos*	*hubiéramos/hubiésemos*
vosotros, –as	*hayáis*	*hubierais/hubieseis*
ellos/ellas/Uds.	*hayan*	*hubieran/hubiesen*

Names of Compound Tenses

Compound tenses are formed by combining different tenses of verbs to create a new one.

Perfect

The present indicative of *haber* with a past participle forms the **present perfect** tense:

He *amado.*
I **have** loved.

Habéis *comido.*
You **have** eaten.

Han *partido.*
They **have** left.

Note: Only *haber* is conjugated. *Amado, comido,* and *partido* do not have to agree in gender and number with their respective subjects.

Pluperfect

The imperfect indicative of *haber* with a past participle forms the **pluperfect** or **past perfect** tense. This tense is used for a past action that precedes another past action:

Había *amado.*
I **had** loved.

Habíais *comido.*
You **had** eaten.

Habían *partido.*
They **had** left.

Future Perfect

The future of *haber* with a past participle forms the **future perfect:**

Habré *amado.*
I **will have** loved.

Habrán *partido.*
They **will have** left.

Note: This tense expresses an action that will take place **before** another. But very commonly the future perfect denotes probability in the past. Compare the following examples:

a) ***¿Habrán partido*** *antes de que comience a llover?*
Will they **have left** before it starts to rain?

b) *Ya* ***habrán partido.***
They **probably left** already.

Conditional Perfect

The conditional of *haber* with a past participle forms the **conditional perfect:**

Habría *amado.*
I **would have** loved.

Habrían *partido.*
They **would have** left.

Perfect Subjunctive

The present subjunctive of *haber* with a past participle forms the **present perfect subjunctive:**

Es increíble que no ***haya amado*** *a nadie en su vida.*
It's incredible that he **has** not **loved** anyone in his life.

Los extrañaremos cuando ***hayan partido.***
We'll miss them when they **have left.**

Pluperfect Subjunctive

The imperfect subjunctive of *haber* with a past participle forms the **pluperfect** or **past perfect subjunctive:**

Yo no habría conocido la felicidad si no ***hubiera amado.***
I would not have known happiness if I **had** not **loved.**

Él siempre había dudado de que sus amigos ***hubieran partido*** *sin despedirse.*
He had always doubted that his friends **had left** without saying goodbye.

Past Participle as Adjective

When the past participle is used with ***haber*** to form the perfect tenses it is invariable. When not accompanied by some form of ***haber***, it functions as an adjective and has four possible forms.

He roto la taza.	I have broken the cup.	[perfect]
La taza está rota.	The cup is broken	[adjective]
una ventana abierta	an open window	[adjective]

THE PRESENT PARTICIPLE

The present participle is formed by appending *-**ando*** to the stem of *–ar* verbs and *-**iendo*** to the stem of *–er* and *–ir* verbs.

andar-andando (walking)　　*escribir-escribiendo* (writing)
vivir-viviendo (living)

Present Participles with a *y*

Double voweled infinitives ending in ***–er*** and ***–ir*** (*creer, leer, oír, caer*, etc.) have a ***y*** in the present participle. It replaces the ***i*** of the participle ending.

caer–cayendo　　*leer–leyendo*　　*oír–oyendo*　　*traer–trayendo*

Exception: *reír–riendo* (laughing)

Present Participles with Stem-changes

Verbs ending in ***–ir*** that have preterite tense stem-changes use the same Stem-Change in the present participle.

*dormir–d**u**rmiendo*	*pedir–p**i**diendo*	*servir–s**i**rviendo*
(ue, **u**)	(i, **i**)	(i, **i**)

Irregular Present Participles

There are four irregular present participles.

ir–yendo *poder–pudiendo* *venir–viniendo* *decir–diciendo*

The Present Participle with *Estar*

The present participle denotes an action in progress and commonly follows the verb *estar*. It corresponds to the "-ing" form of the verb in English. In Spanish it is always invariable. These are called progressive tenses.

Estoy comiendo.	I am eating.
Estaban leyendo.	They were reading.
Estaremos jugando al tenis.	We will be playing tennis.

The Present Participle with Motion Verbs

The present participle may also follow verbs of motion: *ir* (to go), *venir* (to come), *andar* (to walk), *entrar* (to enter), *salir* (to go out), etc.

Ella va corriendo por la calle.
She goes running down the street.

Juan entró riendo pero salió llorando.
Juan entered laughing but left crying.

The Present Participle with *Seguir/Continuar*

Present participles also follow forms of ***seguir*** (*i, i*) (to keep on) and ***continuar*** (*ú*) (to continue). In English "to continue" is often followed by an infinitive. This will **not** occur in Spanish.

Siga leyendo.	Keep on reading.
Ellos continúan hablando.	They continue talking.
	They continue to talk.

The Present Participle Used Alone

The present participle does not need a helping verb to exist. It is often used alone.

Andando por la calle, se cayó.
Walking down the street, he fell down.

No conociendo bien la ciudad, se perdieron.
Not knowing the city well, they got lost.

When Not to Use the Present Participle

Never use the present participle as an **adjective**. Use a clause instead.

un niño que llora	a crying child
un asunto que aterroriza	a frightening event

Never use the present participle as a **noun** (gerund). Use the infinitive instead.

Ver es creer.	Seeing is believing.

Never use the present participle after a **preposition**. Use the infinitive instead.

después de comer	after eating

Never use the present participle of *ir* with the verb **estar**. Use *voy a, vas a, iba a,* etc.

Voy a salir.	I am going to leave.
Iban a comer.	They were going to eat.

REFLEXIVE PRONOUNS

Verbs whose action reflects back upon the subject are called reflexive. Infinitives of reflexive verbs in Spanish end in *–se*. Verbs of this type require the use of the reflexive pronoun group (*me*, *te*, *se*, *nos*, *os*, *se*). English uses pronouns such as myself, herself, themselves, etc., to designate reflexive actions. There are a number of reasons why a verb is reflexive.

1. The verb actually has a "reflexive" translation. I bathe "myself." = *Me baño.*

2. The pronoun is an inherent part of the verb and has no English translation: *atreverse a* (to dare to), *quejarse de* (to complain about), etc.

3. The pronoun alters the meaning of the verb in some way, other than reflexively: *irse* = to go **away**, *caerse* = to fall **down**, etc.

4. To render the meaning "get or become": *enfermarse* (to get ill), *casarse* (to get married), *enojarse* (to get angry), etc.

5. The pronoun is used with the verb when the subject is performing an action **on** his/her own body. *Me rompí la pierna.* = I broke my leg.

Placement of the Pronouns with Verbs

After selecting the pronoun that matches the subject of the verb, it will be placed either **before** the verb or **after** and **attached** to the verb. The following samples demonstrate the placement.

Quiero bañarme.	I want to bathe.	[infinitive]
¡Levántese!	Get up!	[+ command/formal]
¡No te sientes!	Don't sit down!	[– command/familiar]
Estás lavándote.	You are washing up.	[present participle]
Me llamo Juana.	My name is Juana.	[conjugated]

Uses of *Se*

The reflexive pronoun ***se*** is used a number of ways.

1. To express the impersonal **one/people/they** statement with the third person singular of the verb.

   ***se** dice* = one says/people say/they say

2. To render "non-blame" statements when used with certain verbs: *perder* (to lose), *olvidar* (to forget), *romper* (to break), *quemar* (to burn). With statements such as these the speaker is indicating that something happened that was unintentional on his/her part. The *se* will precede the indirect object pronoun (which replaces the subject in English), and the verb will match the noun that follows it.

***se me** rompió el vaso.*	**I** broke the glass.
***se nos** perdió el dinero.*	**We** lost the money.
***se le** olvidaron los libros.*	**He** forgot the books.

Reciprocal Actions

The plural reflexive pronouns (*nos, os, se*) are used to express "each other" in Spanish.

Se escriben.	They write to each other (to themselves).
Nos amamos.	We love each other (ourselves).

Note: Because the above statements could have a reflexive meaning (in parenthesis) as well, one may add the following phrase to clarify:

Se escriben	*uno a otro*	or	*el uno al otro*
	una a otra	or	*la una a la otra*
	unos a otros	or	*los unos a los otros*
	unas a otras	or	*las unas a las otras*

This additional clarifying statement is especially useful with verbs that are already reflexive. In those cases the reflexive pronoun cannot have dual meanings—it must act as a reflexive. As is often the case with these types, there is an accompanying preposition to be dealt with. This preposition is placed in the clarifying statement.

casarse con	to get married to
Se casan uno ***con*** *otro.*	They get married to each other.
burlarse de	to make fun of
Se burlan uno ***de*** *otro.*	They make fun of each other.

Reflexive Substitute for the Passive Voice

It is more idiomatic to replace the passive construction with a reflexive construction using the pronoun ***se*** and the verb in the third person singular or plural. This is especially true of passive sentences that have no expressed agent.

Aquí se habla español.	Spanish is spoken here.

☞ Drill 3

1. Después de dos horas el orador siguió . . .
   (A) hablar. (C) habla.
   (B) hablaba. (D) hablando.

2. . . . olvidó lavar la ropa por la manaña.
   (A) Me (C) Se me
   (B) Se (D) Me lo

3. Los alumnos están . . . la composición.
   (A) escrito (C) analizando
   (B) leen (D) escriben

4. Los vampiros no . . . en el espejo.
   (A) lo ven (C) le ven
   (B) se ven (D) les ven

5. Los trabajadores han . . . su labor.
   (A) terminaron (C) terminados
   (B) terminando (D) terminado

6. Hace mucho tiempo que yo no . . . con mi mamá.
   (A) he hablado (C) estaba hablando
   (B) había hablado (D) hablado

7. . . . el trabajo, pudo salir a tiempo.
   (A) Haber terminado (C) Al terminando
   (B) Estar terminando (D) Habiendo terminado

8. Los problemas . . . , cerró el libro y salió.
   (A) resueltos (C) resolvidos
   (B) resueltas (D) resuelven

9. Para este viernes ellos . . . la película.

(A) habían visto
(B) habrían visto
(C) habrán visto
(D) han visto

10. Ellos vinieron . . . por la calle.

(A) andando
(B) andar
(C) andado
(D) andados

11. . . . , salió del cuarto.

(A) Decírmelo
(B) Me lo decir
(C) Diciéndomelo
(D) Deciéndomelo

12. Juan entró . . . después de oír el chiste.

(A) reír
(B) riendo
(C) reyendo
(D) riyendo

13. No continúes . . . en la iglesia por favor.

(A) hablar
(B) a hablar
(C) hablado
(D) hablando

14. Un niño . . . me causa pena.

(A) que llora
(B) llorando
(C) llorar
(D) a llorar

15. Esto es . . .

(A) vivido.
(B) vivir.
(C) viviendo.
(D) viva.

16. Los chicos . . . por la calle cuando vieron al policía.

(A) eran yendo
(B) estaban yendo
(C) yendo
(D) iban

17. Al . . . el ruido, todos corrieron.

    (A) oír (C) oído

    (B) oyeron (D) oyendo

18. ¡Ay de mí! ¡ . . . el vaso!

    (A) se me rompió (C) se me rompieron

    (B) me rompí (D) me rompieron

19. ¿Quieres . . . antes de ir?

    (A) bañarse (C) bañarte

    (B) báñate (D) bañándote

20. Es importante . . . la mano antes de hablar.

    (A) levantarse (C) que te levantes

    (B) que levanta (D) levantar

21. El sacerdote . . . la pareja.

    (A) se casó (C) casó a

    (B) se casó a (D) casó con

22. Aunque vivimos en distintos lugares, . . . uno a otro cada semana.

    (A) nos escribimos (C) escribimos

    (B) se escriben (D) nos escriben

Drill 3—Detailed Explanations of Answers

1. **(D)** The gerund in Spanish may be used after a conjugated verb, as in this case. The only answer which is correct is **hablando**. The **siguió** is translated as "kept on" or "continued," i.e., verbs of motion.

2. **(C)** There are three different forms in which the verb "olvidar" (to forget) may be used. The simplest of these is "olvidar" used non-reflexively and followed by a noun of an infinitive. For example, "Olvidé lavar la ropa" (I forgot to wash the clothes). Another form is "olvidar**se de**" + noun or infinitive: "**Me** olvidé **de** lavar la ropa." The third form is also reflexive but does not use the preposition "de." It is always accompanied by an indirect object pronoun in addition to the reflexive pronoun: "**Se me** olvidó lavar la ropa." Notice that in this sentence the verb and the reflexive pronoun both are used in the third person singular. This is because the subject of the Spanish sentence is **not** "yo" (I), but rather the infinitive "lavar." In other words, the Spanish literally says "Washing forgot itself." In this sentence, "me" is an indirect object pronoun and means "to me." Therefore, "Se me olvidó lavar la ropa" literally means "Washing the clothes forgot itself to me." One would never say that in English. Instead, we would simply say "I forgot to wash the clothes." The indirect object pronoun, when used this way with the reflexive form of "olvidar," simply shows who is affected by the action of the verb. (A) "Me" will not work here. For it to be correct, we would have to change the verb to "olvidé" and then add the preposition "de."

3. **(C)** In order to form the present progressive tense, we use "estar" + –ndo verb form, meaning "to be doing (something)." Hence, we must say "están analizando" (are analyzing). The progressive tenses place very special emphasis on the fact that the action is (was, etc.) in progress or is (was, etc.) happening at a particular moment. If we do not wish to give that decided emphasis, we just use the simple tenses (present, imperfect, etc.) We can use the progressive form in all of the tenses simply by changing the tense of "estar," for example, "estaban analizando" (they were analyzing), etc. Choice (A) "escrito" is wrong because it is the past participle, not the present participle, of "escribir" (to write). (B) "leen" will not function in our sentence because we cannot have two conjugated verbs, one immediately after the other ("están" and "leen"). The same is true for (D) "escriben."

4. **(B)** "Espejo" indicates that the pronoun needed is reflexive, and the only such pronoun among the choices is (B). The rest are direct object pronouns (A) or indirect, (C) and (D).

5. **(D)** What is needed to fill in the blank is a past participle, which eliminates the first two choices. You also must know that a past participle in a compound tense (following "haber") is invariable in person, gender, and number.

6. **(A)** "Time" statements beginning with **hace** are normally written using the present indicative or the present progressive tenses. Only in the case where the main verb is negative can a perfect tense be used. Choice (B) would be correct if the verb were negative and followed "hacía." Choice (C) also would be found in an "hacía" statement. Choice (D) makes no sense since it is the past participle by itself.

7. **(D)** The translation of this sentence indicates that a participle is required ("Having finished the work,") to make sense. In order for (A) to be correct in the infinitive form, it would have to act as a gerund (i.e., be the subject or object of the verb). Choice (C) is incorrect because **al** must be followed by an infinitive. Choice (B) makes no sense when translated and used in this context.

8. **(A)** The past participle may act as an adjective and in that capacity must match the noun it modifies. Because this noun is masculine and this participle is irregular, (A) is the correct answer. Choice (B) is feminine and (C) is an incorrect form of the past participle. Choice (D) is a conjugated verb and makes no sense in this context.

9. **(C)** By translating this sentence (By this Friday they will have seen the movie.) the proper perfect tense surfaces. Choice (A) "they had seen, (B) "they would have seen," and (D) "they have seen" make no sense in this context.

10. **(A)** Verbs of motion ("vinieron") can be followed by present participles, in this case "andando." They cannot, however, be followed by an infinitive (B) or the past participle (C) and (D).

11. **(C)** This sentence begins with the participial phrase meaning "Saying it to me." Because "Saying" is not the subject of the sentence, it will not be written as a gerund (the infinitive form in Spanish). Therefore, choice (A) is incorrect. Choice (B) is incorrect not only because it is in the

infinitive form but also because pronouns must be after and attached to infinitives. Choice (D) is misspelled.

12. **(B)** Again, verbs of motion may be followed by present participles. Choices (C) and (D) appear to be written in the present participle but are misspelled. Choice (A) is an infinitive and is, therefore, incorrect.

13. **(D)** Unlike English the verb **continue** (continuar) in Spanish cannot be followed by either the infinitive or the present participle. In Spanish, only the present participle is correct with this verb. This would eliminate (A), the infinitive, (B), the infinitive preceded by an "a," and (C) the past participle.

14. **(A)** The present participle in Spanish may not act as an adjective. Phrases such as these must be converted to clauses such as the one found in this sample. Therefore, "a crying child" becomes "a child that cries" in the Spanish sentence. Therefore, (B), the present participle, (C), the infinitive, and (D), the infinitive with "a," are all incorrect.

15. **(B)** In Spanish a verb used as a gerund, either as a subject or the object of the verb, must be in the infinitive form. Therefore, (A), the past participle, (C), the present participle and (D), the present subjunctive, are all incorrect.

16. **(D)** "Ir" may not be used in the progressive tense in Spanish. In order to say that one "is or was doing something," a form of **ir a** (either in the present or in the imperfect tense) is used with the infinitive. Choice (B) is in the progressive tense and choice (A) is a form of **ser** with a present participle, which is never correct. Choice (C) is the present participle alone and makes no sense in the context of this sentence.

17. **(A)** The idiom **al + infinitive** means **upon + –ing**. Because choices (B), the preterite, (C), the past participle, and (D), the present participle, are not in the infinitive form, they are all incorrect.

18. **(A)** This sentence is considered a "non-blame" statement. Certain verbs (such as perder, dejar, caer, romper, etc.) are used in this manner so as to indicate that the subject did not commit the action on purpose. These sentences require using the reflexive pronoun **se**, the **indirect object** pronoun for the subject, and the verb in either the third person singular or plural depending on what follows it. In this case "vaso" is singular and requires a singular verb. Choice (C) is, therefore, incorrect because the

verb is plural. Choice (D) is plural and the reflexive pronoun is missing. Choice (B) would be correct if written as "rompí" alone but would then mean that this action occurred on purpose.

19. **(C)** After a conjugated verb the infinitive is necessary. In this case the subject (tú) requires adjusting the reflexive pronoun to match it. For this reason choice (A) is incorrect because the pronoun (se) does not match the subject (tú). Choice (B) is the familiar singular command and (D) is the present participle, neither of which would follow the conjugated verb in this sample.

20. **(D)** In order to answer this question, one must know the difference between "levantar" and "levantarse." The former means "to raise" while the latter means "to get up." This would then eliminate both (A) and (C). While choice (B) appears to be correct in that it is **not** reflexive, the verb form would need to be subjunctive to fit this particular sentence since it begins with an impersonal expression and there is a change in subject. "Levanta" in this sample is the present indicative.

21. **(C)** This sentence requires knowing the difference between "casarse con" (to get married) and "casar" (to marry). Because the priest is performing the ceremony, choice (C) is correct. The personal **a** precedes the direct object "pareja." Choice (A) is incorrect because it is reflexive and the meaning would not fit this sentence and (B), which is also reflexive, is followed by the wrong preposition. Choice (D) is not correct with "con."

22. **(A)** This is a statement calling for an "each other" translation. The phrase "uno a otro" also indicates this. In Spanish the plural reflexive pronouns are used in these statements. The phrase "uno a otro" is an additional piece so that the translation of the verb will not be confused for "we write to ourselves." Choice (B) is incorrect because the subject in this sentence is **we** (intimated in the first part of the sentence with "vivimos"). Choice (C) requires the matching reflexive pronoun "nos." Choice (D) means "they write to us" and doesn't fit the meaning implied by this sentence.

THE INFINITIVE

The Infinitive as the Subject of the Sentence

When the infinitive is used as the subject of the sentence (gerund) in English, it may be written in the infinitive form or end in –ing. In Spanish this is written only in the infinitive form.

Seeing is believing.	*Ver es creer.*
Eating is important.	*Comer es importante.*

The Infinitive after Prepositions

In Spanish the only correct verb form that can follow a preposition is the infinitive.

antes de salir	before leaving
después de comer	after eating
al entrar	upon entering

The Infinitive with Verbs of Perception

The infinitive is used with verbs of perception ***ver*** (to see) and ***oír*** (to hear) when the sentence has a noun object.

Oí llorar al niño.	I heard the child cry.
Ella vio salir a Juan.	She saw Juan leave.

Verbs Requiring a Preposition Before the Infinitive

Certain verbs require an ***a, en, de, por,*** or ***con*** before the infinitive. See page 131 for a detailed listing.

Verbs Requiring NO Preposition Before the Infinitive

aconsejar	advise to	*pensar (ie)*	intend to
deber	ought to	*permitir*	allow to
dejar	let, allow to	*poder (ue)*	be able to
desear	desire to	*prometer*	promise to
esperar	hope to	*querer (ie)*	wish to
impedir (i, i)	prevent from	*recordar (ue)*	remember to
lograr	succeed in	*rehusar*	refuse to
necesitar	need to	*saber*	know how to
oír	hear	*soler (ue)**	be accustomed to
pedir (i, i)	ask to	*temer*	be afraid to

* This verb is defective and commonly used in two tenses only—the present and the imperfect.

☞ Drill 4

1. Lavé la ropa después de . . .

(A) cenar. (C) comida.

(B) comiendo. (D) había almorzado.

2. Al . . . la alarma, todos abandonaron el hotel.

(A) oyen (C) oír

(B) oyendo (D) oído

3. Orlando oyó . . . a la puerta.

(A) tocó (C) tocando

(B) tocar (D) tocándola

4. El respirar no es . . .

(A) vivir. (C) la vida.

(B) viviendo. (D) vive.

5. Al . . . , le dije adiós.

(A) salir (C) salí

(B) saliendo (D) salido

6. . . . es bueno para el cuerpo.

(A) Corriendo (C) Correr

(B) Corrido (D) Fumar

7. . . . es bueno para la salud.

(A) Dormir (C) Dormido

(B) Durmiendo (D) Dormí

8. Sin . . . , no puedo recomendar la película.

   (A) ver (C) verla

   (B) veo (D) verlo

9. Antes de . . . del autobús, Juan pagó el pasaje.

   (A) bajando (C) bajar

   (B) el bajar (D) baje

10. El policía vio . . . al ladrón del banco.

   (A) salida (C) saliendo

   (B) salir (D) salió

Drill 4—Detailed Explanations of Answers

1. **(A)** "Después de" (after) is a preposition. The only form of the verb we use directly following a preposition is the infinitive. Therefore, we cannot use the present participle, as in (B), "comiendo." The present participle in English is the verbal form ending in –ing: for example, "eating." In English, this form may be used as a noun, in which case we call it a gerund. In a phrase such as "after eating," "eating" is a gerund and means "the act of eating." In Spanish, the form which corresponds to the *–ing*, i.e., words ending in **–ando** and **–iendo**, do not follow a preposition. This is a mistake often made in Spanish by English speakers. Choice (C) is incorrect. If we want to say "after the meal" or "after the afternoon meal," we would have to use the definite article: "después de **la** comida." Choice (D) is also wrong. In Spanish, a conjugated form of the verb does not immediately follow a preposition. We could say, however, "después de haber almorzado" (after **having eaten** lunch). Then the verb is not in a conjugated form.

2. **(C)** Syntactically, the verb forms "oyen" (they hear), the third person plural of the present of "oír," "oyendo" (hearing), the present participle, and "oído" (heard), the past participle, will not fit correctly into this sentence. There is, however, an idiomatic construction based on "al" + **infinitive** which means "upon doing something." We find this form in (C).

3. **(B)** After verbs of perception ("oír", "ver"), the infinitive is used. Therefore, (A), the preterite, and (C) and (D), the present participles, are incorrect.

4. **(A)** Verbs used as gerunds in Spanish (either as the subject or object of the verb) must be in the infinitive form. (B) The present participle and (D) the present tense are incorrect. (C) is incorrect because the infinitive is necessary to maintain parallel structure (infinitive/infinitive).

5. **(A)** The only verbal form that can follow "al" is the infinitive. It means upon + –ing in English.

6. **(C)** The key to this question is to remember that the infinitive can function as the subject of a sentence, but not the gerund (A) or the past participle (B). (D) "to smoke" is not good for "the body."

7. **(A)** This is another example of the use of the infinitive as the subject of the sentence. Therefore, (B) the present participle, (C) the past participle, and (D) the preterite are incorrect.

8. **(C)** After prepositions in Spanish the infinitive must be used. In the context of this sentence, the translation "without seeing it" makes most sense. "It" refers to "película" which is feminine. (A) needs the direct object pronoun "la", (D) has the incorrect direct object pronoun, and (B) is the present indicative, a conjugated verb form.

9. **(C)** The correct verb form after a preposition in Spanish is the infinitive. This would eliminate the present participle (A) and the subjunctive in (D). Choice (B) is a gerund and is not used after a preposition.

10. **(B)** After verbs of perception (ver/oír) the infinitive is used in Spanish. Therefore, the present participle (C), the preterite tense (D) and the noun meaning "departure" in (A) are incorrect.

FORMATION OF THE SUBJUNCTIVE

Present Subjunctive–Regular

	amar **to love**	***comer*** **to eat**	***vivir*** **to live**
yo	*ame*	*coma*	*viva*
tú	*ames*	*comas*	*vivas*
él/ella/Ud.	*ame*	*coma*	*viva*
nosotros, –as	*amemos*	*comamos*	*vivamos*
vosotros, –as	*améis*	*comáis*	*viváis*
ellos/ellas/Uds.	*amen*	*coman*	*vivan*

Present Subjunctive–Irregular

caber	*quepa, quepas, quepa, quepamos, quepáis, quepan*
caer	*caiga, caigas, caiga, caigamos, caigáis, caigan*
dar	*dé, des, dé, demos, deis, den*
decir	*diga, digas, diga, digamos, digáis, digan*
estar	*esté, estés, esté, estemos, estéis, estén*
haber	*haya, hayas, haya, hayamos, hayáis, hayan*
hacer	*haga, hagas, haga, hagamos, hagáis, hagan*
ir	*vaya, vayas, vaya, vayamos, vayáis, vayan*
oír	*oiga, oigas, oiga, oigamos, oigáis, oigan*
poner	*ponga, pongas, ponga, pongamos, pongáis, pongan*
saber	*sepa, sepas, sepa, sepamos, sepáis, sepan*
salir	*salga, salgas, salga, salgamos, salgáis, salgan*
ser	*sea, seas, sea, seamos, seáis, sean*
tener	*tenga, tengas, tenga, tengamos, tengáis, tengan*
traer	*traiga, traigas, traiga, traigamos, traigáis, traigan*
valer	*valga, valgas, valga, valgamos, valgáis, valgan*
venir	*venga, vengas, venga, vengamos, vengáis, vengan*
ver	*vea, veas, vea, veamos, veáis, vean*

Present Subjunctive–Spelling Changes

–car	*atacar*	*ataque, ataques, ataque, etc.*
–gar	*entregar*	*entregue, entregues, entregue, etc.*
–zar	*rezar*	*rece, reces, rece, etc.*
–ger	*coger*	*coja, cojas, coja, etc.*
–gir	*dirigir*	*dirija, dirijas, dirija, etc.*
–guir	*distinguir*	*distinga, distingas, distinga, etc.*

–guar	*averiguar*	*averigüe, averigües, averigüe, etc.*
–uir	*huir*	*huya, huyas, huya, etc.*
–quir	*delinquir*	*delinca, delincas, delinca, etc.*
–cer	*conocer*	*conozca, conozcas, conozca, etc.*
	vencer	*venza, venzas, venza, etc.*
–cir	*conducir*	*conduzca, conduzcas, conduza, etc.*

Present Subjunctive–Stem-changes

If a verb has only one Stem-Change, it will appear in all persons except *nosotros* and *vosotros*. If there are two stem-changes given, the second one will appear in the *nosotros/vosotros* forms of the present subjunctive while the first one will appear in all other persons.

(ú) ***actuar*** **to act**	**(í)** ***enviar*** **to send**	**(ue, u)** ***morir*** **to die**	**(i, i)** ***pedir*** **to request**	**(ie, i)** ***sentir*** **to feel or regret**
actúe	*envíe*	*muera*	*pida*	*sienta*
actúes	*envíes*	*mueras*	*pidas*	*sientas*
actúe	*envíe*	*muera*	*pida*	*sienta*
actuemos	*enviemos*	*muramos*	*pidamos*	*sintamos*
actuéis	*enviéis*	*muráis*	*pidáis*	*sintáis*
actúen	*envíen*	*mueran*	*pidan*	*sientan*

Past (Imperfect) Subjunctive–Regular

To form this tense, remove *–ron* from the end of the third plural of the preterite and add the following endings:

–ra	*–ras*	*–ra*	*´–ramos*	*–rais*	*–ran*
–se	*–ses*	*–se*	*´–semos*	*–seis*	*–sen*

Either set of endings is correct, with the first set being the more widely used.

Past Subjunctive–Irregular

andar	*anduviera or anduviese, etc.*
caber	*cupiera or cupiese, etc.*
dar	*diera or diese, etc.*
decir	*dijera or dijese, etc.*
estar	*estuviera or estuviese, etc.*
haber	*hubiera or hubiese, etc.*
hacer	*hiciera or hiciese, etc.*

ir	*fuera or fuese, etc.*
poder	*pudiera or pudiese, etc.*
poner	*pusiera or pusiese, etc.*
querer	*quisiera or quisiese, etc.*
saber	*supiera or supiese, etc.*
ser	*fuera or fuese, etc.*
tener	*tuviera or tuviese, etc.*
traer	*trajera or trajese, etc.*
venir	*viniera or viniese, etc.*
conducir	*condujera or condujese, etc.*
huir	*huyera or huyese, etc.*

Past Subjunctive–Verbs with Stem-changes

Because the stem for the past subjunctive comes from the third plural of the preterite, it will be affected by verbs that have stem-changes in the preterite.

dormir **(ue, u)** **to sleep**	***sentir*** **(ie, i)** **to feel/regret**	***pedir*** **(i, i)** **to ask for**
durmiera	*sintiera*	*pidiera*
durmieras	*sintieras*	*pidieras*
durmiera	*sintiera*	*pidiera*
durmiéramos	*sintiéramos*	*pidiéramos*
durmierais	*sintierais*	*pidierais*
durmieran	*sintieran*	*pidieran*

Past Subjunctive–Verbs Like *Leer*

Because ***–er*** and ***–ir*** verbs with double vowels (*leer, oír, creer, caer*, etc.) have a ***y*** in the third person of the preterite, this ***y*** will be found in all forms of the past subjunctive.

oír *oyera, oyeras, oyera, oyéramos, oyerais, oyeran*

COMMANDS: FORMAL AND FAMILIAR

The Formal Command

Formal commands (*Ud.* and *Uds.*) are always expressed by the present subjunctive. Some samples follow.

comer: (eat)	*(no) coma Ud.*	*(no) coman Uds.*
volver: (return)	*(no) vuelva Ud.*	*(no) vuelvan Uds.*
tener: (have)	*(no) tenga Ud.*	*(no) tengan Uds.*
atacar: (attack)	*(no) ataque Ud.*	*(no) ataquen Uds.*

The Familiar Command

Unlike the formal commands, which are derived from the same form (the present subjunctive), the familiar commands come from several different verb forms to cover the positive, negative, singular and plural forms.

1. The singular (***tú***) form of the affirmative command is the same as the third person singular of the present indicative.

leer = lee (tú)	*lavar = lava (tú)*	*vivir = vive (tú)*
Read!	Wash!	Live!

2. The plural (***vosotros***) form of the affirmative command is formed by changing the ***–r*** ending of the infinitive to a ***–d***.

leer = leed	*lavar = lavad*	*vivir = vivid*
Read!	Wash!	Live!

3. The negative forms come from the ***tú*** and ***vosotros*** forms of the present subjunctive.

leer = no leas (tú)	*lavar = no laves (tú)*
no leáis (vosotros)	*no lavéis (vosotros)*
Don't read!	Don't wash!

Familiar Commands–Irregulars

The only irregular familiar commands occur in the affirmative singular. All other forms follow the rules stated above.

	tú	*vosotros*	*tú*	*vosotros*
decir	***di***	*decid*	*no digas*	*no digáis*
hacer	***haz***	*haced*	*no hagas*	*no hagáis*
ir	***ve***	*id*	*no vayas*	*no vayáis*
poner	***pon***	*poned*	*no pongas*	*no pongáis*
salir	***sal***	*salid*	*no salgas*	*no salgáis*
ser	***sé***	*sed*	*no seas*	*no seáis*
tener	***ten***	*tened*	*no tengas*	*no tengáis*
valer	***val***	*valed*	*no valgas*	*no valgáis*
venir	***ven***	*venid*	*no vengas*	*no vengáis*

Commands of Reflexive Verbs

Reflexive verbs require the use of reflexive pronouns. The formal command, singular and plural, uses *–se*. The familiar command uses ***te*** (singular) and ***os*** (plural). These pronouns **precede** the **negative command** and are **after** and **attached** to the **positive command**. Any time a pronoun is appended to a command form an accent mark is required. Without it, the stress automatically moves to the next syllable thus affecting the pronunciation.

Bañarse:	*báñese Ud.*	*no se bañe Ud.*
	báñense Uds.	*no se bañen Uds.*
	báñate tú	*no te bañes tú*
	*bañaos vosotros**	*no os bañéis vosotros*

* When ***os*** is appended to the affirmative plural command, the final ***–d*** is dropped (**exception**: ***idos***). If using an ***–ir*** verb, an accent is required over the ***i*** (*divertid + os = divertíos*) to split the diphthong and allow for the ***i*** to be pronounced separately.

"Let's" Statements

There are two ways to express this statement:

1. *Vamos a* + infinitive:

Vamos a comer.	Let's eat.
Vamos a sentarnos.	Let's sit down.
Vamos a leérselo.	Let's read it to him.

2. First plural present subjunctive:

comamos	Let's eat.	(*no comamos*)
*leámoselo**	Let's read it to him.	(*no se lo leamos*)
*sentémonos***	Let's sit down.	(*no nos sentemos*)

Exception: *Vámonos* = Let's go. *No nos vayamos.* = Let's not go. The affirmative is not derived from the subjunctive, but from the indicative.

* Because double ***s*** does not exist in Spanish, this verb form will eliminate one (*leámoselo*).

** Before adding ***nos*** to the reflexive verb form, the final ***–s*** is dropped. An accent mark is needed.

Have/Let/May Statements

Que + third person singular/plural present subjunctive

Examples:	Have her go.	***Que*** *vaya ella.*
	Let him read it.	***Que*** *lo lea.*
	May they do it well.	***Que*** *lo hagan bien.*
	Have them give it to me.	***Que*** *me lo den.*

Note: Pronouns precede these verb forms because they are the conjugated verb of the noun clause.

Dejar is also used to express **let**, with direct object pronouns.

Déjame ver.	Let me see.
Déjanos salir.	Let us leave.

☞ Drill 5

1. No te . . . en el cuarto de Felipe.

(A) acueste (C) acuesten

(B) acostéis (D) acuestes

2. ¡No . . . Ud., por favor!

(A) me hable (C) me habla

(B) hábleme (D) me hables

3. ¡Que lo . . . Ud. bien!

(A) pasar (C) pases

(B) pase (D) pasa

4. Hola, mis amigos. ¡ . . . para hablar conmigo!

(A) Siéntense (C) Sentados

(B) Siéntese (D) Sentaos

5. La madre le dijo a su hijo, –¡ . . . al supermercado!

(A) vete (C) no vaya

(B) váyase (D) no va

6. Antes de salir mi madre me dijo, –¡ . . . el abrigo, hijo!

(A) póngase (C) pónete

(B) póngate (D) ponte

7. Hijos, no . . . mientras estoy hablando.

(A) os reís (C) os reíais

(B) os riáis (D) reíos

8. Juanito, cuando salgas, . . . la luz.

(A) apaga
(B) apague
(C) apagues
(D) apagaste

9. . . . aquí para poder ver mejor.

(A) Nos sentamos
(B) Sentémonos
(C) Sentémosnos
(D) Sentámonos

10. No . . . con vuestros amigos esta noche.

(A) os vayáis
(B) se vayan
(C) os vais
(D) idos

Drill 5—Detailed Explanations of Answers

1. **(D)** This item tests your knowledge of the various forms of the imperative. The choices given are all command forms. We know that we are searching for the "tú" command, i.e., the second person singular imperative, because of the second person singular reflexive pronoun, "te," which is given in the sentence. Furthermore, we know that we must choose a negative imperative from the list because of the "No" in the sentence. Negative familiar singular commands in Spanish correspond to the second person singular of the present subjunctive, which, for "acostarse" (ue) (to go to bed), is "No te acuestes." Choice (A), "acueste," will not work because it is the command form for the third person singular (the "Usted" command), but we are given the second person singular of the reflexive pronoun in the sentence, "te." Choice (B), "acostéis," is the negative command for the "vosotros" form of the verb. Being a negative command, it is also like the corresponding form of the subjunctive of "acostarse," i.e., the second person plural. "Vosotros" is used only in Spain. In all of Central and South America, the third person plural (the "Ustedes" form) is used in its place. "Acostéis" is an incorrect answer here because the reflexive pronoun "te" is not the second person plural form. For (B) to be correct, we would have to say "No os acostéis . . . " (C), "acuesten," is wrong also because the reflexive pronoun for it would have to be "se," the third person plural form.

2. **(A)** The negative formal singular command (Ud.) is required in this sentence. Object pronouns precede negative commands. Choice (B) is incorrect because the pronoun is after and attached to the positive command. Choice (C) is not in a command form, and (D) is the negative familiar command form.

3. **(B)** The exclamatory statement "May it go well for you!" requires the use of the present subjunctive which in this sample is the same as the formal command for "Ud." Choice (A), an infinitive, (C), the "tú" form of the verb, and (D), the present indicative form, are all incorrect.

4. **(D)** The familiar plural positive command is required in this statement ("amigos"). This is formed by removing the **–d** from the infinitive before attaching the reflexive pronoun **os** to the end. Choice (C) is incorrect because the **–d** has been retained. Choices (A) and (B) are both formal commands.

5. **(A)** Because the mother is speaking to her son, the familiar positive command is required in this sample. The familiar singular positive command of **irse** is irregular. Choice (B) is the formal command, (C) is the present subjunctive, and (D) is the present indicative.

6. **(D)** The mother is again addressing her son in this sentence which requires the use of the familiar positive singular command of **ponerse** (to put on). This is irregular. Both (A) and (B) are formal command forms but (B) also has the incorrect reflexive pronoun attached. Choice (C) is an incorrect verb form.

7. **(B)** Because the children are being asked **not** to laugh in this sentence, the negative familiar plural command form is required. This form comes from the second person plural of the present subjunctive. Choice (A) is the second plural of the present indicative. Choice (C) is the second plural of the conditional tense, and (D) is the familiar plural positive command form.

8. **(A)** Because Juanito is being addressed in the familiar ("salgas"), the familiar positive singular command is required. For regular verbs this comes from the third person singular of the present tense. Choice (B) is the formal command, (C) is the second person singular of the present subjunctive, and (D) is the preterite tense.

9. **(B)** One way to express **let's** in Spanish is by using the "nosotros" form of the present subjunctive. If the verb is reflexive, the pronoun **nos** is attached to the end of this form, after removing the **–s**. Choice (A) is the present indicative. Choice (C) has retained the **–s** of the verb, and (D) is not in the present subjunctive.

10. **(A)** Because "vuestros" indicates that the command should be familiar plural and because the sentence is negative, the command form here will come from the "vosotros" form of the present subjunctive. Pronouns precede negative commands. Choice (B) is the third plural of the present subjunctive, (C) is the second plural of the present indicative, and (D) is the familiar plural positive command form.

THE SUBJUNCTIVE–USES

Subjunctive vs. Indicative

The indicative mood tenses express certainty or factual knowledge. The subjunctive mode is used to convey ideas in the realm of all areas other than those of objective fact: concepts that are hypothetical, contrary to fact, those which embody the expression of feelings of the speaker toward a state or action. Because the subjunctive is a **subjoined, subordinate, dependent** verb form, it is logical that it will occur in the **dependent clause** of the sentence. There are four types of clauses that could contain the subjunctive: noun, adjective, adverb, and if.

The Noun Clause

The noun clause is a group of words that acts as the subject or object of the main clause. The subjunctive will occur in this clause if two conditions are met:

1. a change of subject between two clauses
2. a specific category of verb is used in the main clause: wishing/wanting, emotion, impersonal expression, doubt/denial, or indirect command

To join the independent clause to the dependent clause, the relative pronoun ***que*** (that) is required in Spanish. In English we often leave this word out. Note the two possible ways to express the following statement in English.

I hope he's here.	I hope **that** he's here.

Category I–Wishing/Wanting

querer (to want)	*Quiero* ***que Juan vaya***. I want Juan to go.

Others: *desear* (to want), *preferir* (to prefer), *me gusta* (I like), etc.

Category II–Emotion

temer (to fear)	*Temo* ***que Juan vaya***. I fear Juan (may, will) go.

Others: *tener miedo de* (to be afraid of), *lamentar* (to regret), *ojalá que* (if only), *sentir* (to regret/feel)

Category III–Impersonal Expression

An impersonal expression is a combination of **to be** with an adjective. The subject is always **it**. In Spanish **to be** will come from ***ser***.

es importante — *Es importante* ***que Juan vaya***.
It's important for Juan to go.

Others: *Ser* + adjective (*necesario, natural, probable, posible, mejor, lástima, triste*, etc.)

Note: Some impersonal expressions will **not** prompt a subjunctive if they imply **no doubt**. See exceptions on the next page. These expressions will require subjunctive only if negative.

Category IV–Doubt/Denial

dudar (to doubt) — *Dudo* ***que Juan vaya***.
I doubt Juan will go/is going.

Others: *negar* (to deny), *suponer* (to suppose), *puede ser*, (it may be), *creer* (to believe)*, *pensar* (to think)*, *tal vez/quizás* (perhaps)

* *Creer/pensar* commonly take a subjunctive if they are negative or in a question. This is dependent upon the speaker's point of view. If he/she actually believes or thinks what he/she is saying, the indicative will be used.

Category V–Indirect Command

pedir (to ask for)* — *Le pido a* ***Juan que vaya***.
I ask Juan to go.

Others: *decir* (to tell), *sugerir* (to suggest), *exigir*, (to demand), *insistir en* (to insist on), *aconsejar* (to advise), *rogar* (to beg)

Note: Several verbs from this category may be used with the infinitive or the subjunctive.

permitir (to permit)	*dejar* (to allow)
hacer (to make)	*aconsejar* (to advise)
impedir (to prevent)	*mandar* (to command)
prohibir (to prohibit)	*recomendar* (to recommend)

(Te) aconsejo que ***vayas***. or *Te aconsejo ir.*
I advise you to go.

No (me) permiten que ***fume***. or *No me permiten fumar.*
They do not permit me to smoke.

* Many verbs in this category require the use of the indirect object pronoun in the independent clause used with the second subject: *rogar, pedir, decir, aconsejar*, etc.

Example:	*Te ruego que (tú) hables con ella.*
	I beg you to speak with her.

Exceptions

The following expressions are used with the **indicative unless** they are **negative**.

ocurre que	it happens that
sucede que	
es evidente que	it's evident that
es cierto que	it's certain that
es verdad que	it's true that
es seguro que	it's sure that
es obvio que	it's obvious that
es que	it's that
se sabe que	it's known that
parece que	it seems that
no es dudoso que	it's not doubtful that

Sequence of Tenses

Whether the present or past subjunctive is used in the dependent clause is based on the tense used in the independent or main clause. Sequence primarily means the present subjunctive will follow present tense forms while past subjunctive will follow past tense forms. Following is a list of tenses with sequence indicated.

Independent Clause (Indicative)		**Dependent Clause (Subjunctive)**
Present	*espero*	
Present Progressive	*estoy esperando*	***que vaya***
Future	*esperaré*	
Present Perfect	*he esperado*	***que haya ido***
Future Perfect	*habré esperado*	
Command	*espere/espera*	
Preterite	*esperé*	
Imperfect	*esperaba*	***que fuera***

Past Progressive	*estaba esperando*	***que hubiera ido***
Conditional	*esperaría*	***que hubiese ido***
Past Perfect	*había esperado*	
Conditional Perfect	*habría esperado*	

The Adjective Clause

An adjective clause is one that modifies or describes a preceding noun. This noun is called the antecedent and it will determine if the subjunctive will exist in the adjective clause itself. This antecedent must be (1) negative or (2) indefinite for the subjunctive to exist in the adjective clause.

To determine this one must focus not solely on the antecedent itself but the surrounding words (the verb and/or any articles used with that noun).

Compare these two adjective clauses:

Indicative:	**Subjunctive:**
Tengo *un coche que es nuevo.* (antecedent=*coche*) [exists because he **has** it]	***Busco*** *un coche que sea nuevo.* [does not yet exist]
Busco ***el*** *libro que tiene la información.* (antecedent=*libro*) [a specific book exists with the information]	*Busco* ***un*** *libro que tenga la información.* [no specific book]
Hay ***varios*** *hombres que van con nosotros.* (antecedent=*hombres*) [these men exist]	*No hay* ***ningún*** *hombre que vaya con nosotros.* [a negative antecedent]

The Adverbial Clause

An adverbial clause answers the questions when? where? how? why? etc. These clauses are introduced by conjunctions. These conjunctions can be broken down into three separate types:

1. conjunctions **always** followed by the subjunctive
2. the *–quiera* group conjunctions (which are **always** followed by the subjunctive)
3. conjunctions **sometimes** followed by the subjunctive

Always Subjunctive

a fin de que/para que	so that
a menos que/salvo que	unless
con tal que	provided that
antes (de) que	before
en caso de que	in case (that)
sin que	without
a condición de que	on condition that

Examples: *Salió sin que yo lo supiera.*
He left without my knowing it.

Lo haré antes de que lleguen.
I'll do it before they arrive.

The *–Quiera* Group

dondequiera que	wherever
cualquier (a) que	whatever
quienquiera que	whoever
quienesquiera que	whoever (plural)
cuando quiera que	whenever
por + adj/adv + *que*	however, no matter how

Examples: *Dondequiera que vayas, serás feliz.*
Wherever you go, you'll be happy.

Por enferma que esté, ella asistirá.
No matter how sick she is, she'll attend.

Sometimes Subjunctive

Adverbial clauses begun with these conjunctions will be subjunctive only if there is speculation or doubt as to whether the action will take place in the future.

aunque	although
cuando	when
después (de) que	after
en cuanto	as soon as
luego que	
tan pronto como	
así que	
hasta que	until
mientras	while

Subjunctive	Indicative
*Aunque **cueste** mucho, lo quiero.* Although it may cost a lot, I want it.	*Aunque **costó** mucho, lo compré.* Although it cost a lot, I bought it.
*Léalo hasta que **llegue**.* Read it until he arrives.	*Lo leí hasta que **llegó**.* I read it until he **arrived**.
*Dijo que lo haría cuando **llegara**.* He said he would do it when he arrived. [hasn't gotten here yet]	*Lo hizo cuando **llegó**.* He did it when he arrived.

Normally, if the verb in the independent clause is in the future or command form, the subjunctive will be needed in the dependent clause. However, this is not always the case. One must always think in terms of "has this happened yet or not?" and use the subjunctive accordingly.

THE "IF" CLAUSE

The imperfect and pluperfect subjunctives are used in contrary-to-fact statements, as follows:

If Clause	Result Clause
Si yo estudiara/estudiase más, . . . If I studied more, . . .	*recibiría (recibiera) buenas notas.* I would get good grades.
Si yo hubiera/hubiese estudiado más, . . . If I had studied more, . . .	*habría (hubiera) recibido buenas notas.* I would have gotten good grades.

Note: The present subjunctive is **never** used in the **if** clause. Instead the proper sequence (present indicative with future) follows:

Si yo estudio más, . . . If I study more, . . .	*recibiré buenas notas.* I will get good grades.

Como Si (as if) Statements

"As if" statements are always followed by the imperfect or the pluperfect subjunctive.

Habla como si la conociera bien.
He speaks as if he knew her well.

Me castigó como si lo hubiera hecho.
He punished me as if I had done it.

The *–ra* Form as Polite Request

The ***–ra*** forms of the imperfect subjunctive of ***querer, poder***, and ***deber*** are often used instead of the conditional of these verbs to express a polite request or statement.

Quisiera hacerlo.	I would like to do it.
¿Pudieras pasarme la sal?	Could you pass me the salt?
Debieran comprarlos.	They should buy them.

☞ Drill 6

1. Mis padres no deseaban que yo . . . eso.
   - (A) hiciera
   - (B) hacía
   - (C) haría
   - (D) haga

2. Si estuviera aquí, . . . hablar con ella.
   - (A) me gustará
   - (B) podemos
   - (C) tratarían de
   - (D) me negué a

3. Te lo dirán cuando te . . .
   - (A) ves.
   - (B) lo venden.
   - (C) visitemos.
   - (D) ven.

4. Dijeron que nos enviarían el paquete tan pronto como . . .
   - (A) lo recibieron.
   - (B) llegara.
   - (C) tengan tiempo.
   - (D) sabrán nuestra dirección.

5. Me aconsejó que . . .
   - (A) no siguiera la ruta de la costa.
   - (B) duerma más.
   - (C) voy al médico.
   - (D) venga inmediatamente.

6. ¡Ojalá que me . . . un recuerdo de París!
   - (A) traen
   - (B) han comprado
   - (C) enviarán
   - (D) den

7. María le dio el periódico a Enrique para que él lo . . .
   - (A) lee.
   - (B) leyeran.
   - (C) lea.
   - (D) leyera.

8. Si yo fuera al centro, te . . . algo.

(A) compraría (C) compre

(B) compré (D) compraré

9. Yo conozco a un señor que . . . español muy bien.

(A) hable (C) hablando

(B) habla (D) hablara

10. Su madre le dijo que . . . todo o no podría tener postre.

(A) come (C) comía

(B) coma (D) comiera

11. Lo harán cuando . . .

(A) llegas. (C) puedan.

(B) entran. (D) tienen tiempo.

12. Si . . . dinero, iría a Bolivia.

(A) tenía (C) tengo

(B) tuviera (D) tuve

13. . . . que tienes razón.

(A) Creo (C) Niego

(B) Dudo (D) Me alegro de

14. Siento que ellos . . . con Uds. ayer.

(A) no estuvieron (C) no estaban

(B) no estuvieran (D) no estarán

15. Si yo tuviera tiempo a Roma, te . . .

(A) visito. (C) visitaré.

(B) voy a visitar. (D) visitaría.

16. No estoy seguro, pero tal vez él . . .

(A) viniera.
(B) vendrá.
(C) viene.
(D) venga.

17. Mi consejero me dijo que no dijera nada hasta que alguien me lo . . .

(A) pide.
(B) pidiera.
(C) ha pedido.
(D) va a pedir.

18. Se lo expliqué en detalle para que lo . . .

(A) comprendiera.
(B) comprenda.
(C) comprende.
(D) comprendió.

19. Mi madre dice que está bien que vaya mi hermano, con tal de que se lo . . .

(A) cuida.
(B) cuidara.
(C) cuidaba.
(D) cuide.

20. Le pedí que . . . temprano para acabar temprano.

(A) venga
(B) viniera
(C) venir
(D) venía

21. No quiere que su hijo . . . malas costumbres.

(A) tenga
(B) tiene
(C) tengan
(D) tienen

22. No creo que mis amigos me . . . abandonado.

(A) han
(B) habían
(C) hayan
(D) hubieran

23. Si él te . . . un beso, ¿cómo reaccionarías?

(A) daba
(B) da
(C) diera
(D) dar

24. No vendrías si . . . lo que te espera.

(A) sabías
(B) supieras
(C) sabes
(D) supiste

25. Mis padres me compraron un automóvil para que . . . a pasear.

(A) salgo
(B) salir
(C) salga
(D) saliera

26. Por bien que . . . Ana, no quiero jugar con ella.

(A) juega
(B) juegue
(C) está jugando
(D) jugara

27. Habla con ella como si la . . . bien.

(A) conoce
(B) conozca
(C) conociera
(D) conoció

28. Es evidente que los chicos no . . . en sus cuartos.

(A) están
(B) estén
(C) son
(D) sean

29. Mi mamá quería que . . . nuestra tarea a tiempo.

(A) hagamos
(B) hacemos
(C) hiciéramos
(D) hicimos

30. Si yo hubiera sabido la respuesta, se la . . .

(A) diría.
(B) habría dicho.
(C) había dicho.
(D) diga.

Drill 6—Detailed Explanations of Answers

1. **(A)** The verb "desear" can express volition, or desire that something happen. With verbs of this type, if there are two different subjects in the two clauses of the sentence, i.e., if someone is bringing his will to bear on someone or something else, then the subjunctive is required. In our sentence the two different subjects are "Mis padres" and "yo." My parents were exerting their will on me. The sentence, however, requires the imperfect subjunctive, "hiciera," rather than the present subjunctive "haga," because the first verb, "deseaban," is in a past tense, the imperfect. Spanish normally observes a logical tense sequence in sentences requiring the subjunctive. If the first verb, the one that **causes** the subjunctive (in this case, "deseaban"), is in a past tense or the conditional tense, a past subjunctive is required (in this case, the imperfect subjunctive). On the other hand, if the verb that causes the subjunctive is in a present tense or the future, a present subjunctive is used. Note that we would not use the subjunctive, but rather the infinitive, if there were not two separate subjects involved: "Yo no deseaba decir eso" (I didn't want to say that).

2. **(C)** Sentences with subordinate clauses beginning with "si" (if), which establish an unreal or hypothetical situation, contain a past tense of the subjunctive (imperfect of pluperfect subjunctive). Our statement begins with such a clause. In these cases, the other clause (the one which shows what would happen if the "si" clause were true) is in the conditional or conditional perfect tense. Since the "si" clause (the hypothesis) is given here in a simple imperfect subjunctive, rather than the pluperfect subjunctive, we also should use the simple conditional tense in the result clause, rather than the conditional perfect. Note that there are times when one might use the future tense in a result clause, but in those cases the verb of the "si" clause is in the simple present or the present perfect. In such instances, the situation is viewed as much less hypothetical and thus, holding a greater possibility of happening. Compare the following examples: "Si estudia, entonces sacará buenas notas" (If he studies . . . and it is possible he will . . . , then he will get good grades); "Si estudiara, entonces sacaría buenas notas" (If he were to study . . . but he doesn't . . . , then he would get good grades). Only choice (C) could be used in this sentence because it is the only one which appears in the conditional tense. Choice (A) is in the future, (B) is in the present, and (D) is in the preterite. Remember that "tratar de" + infinitive is an idiom meaning "to try to." The expression "negarse a" + infinitive signifies "to refuse to."

3. **(C)** The word "cuando" in our sentence is an adverb which pertains to time. When adverbs of time such as "cuando," "hasta que," "tan pronto como," "así que," "luego que," and "mientras" refer to the future, we are obliged to use the subjunctive following them. Of the four possible choices, the only verb form which is subjunctive is found in (C), "visitemos," the first person plural of the present subjunctive of "visitar" (to visit). In (A), "ves," we find the second person singular of the present indicative of "ver" (to see); (B) gives us the third person plural of the present indicative of "vender" (to sell); in choice (D), we find the third person plural of the present indicative of "ver." Remember that we do not always use the subjunctive after these adverbs of time. If the sentence does not refer to some future time, or if it expresses a customary or habitual situation, the indicative is used: "Siempre los veo cuando **vienen** a nuestro pueblo." (I always see them when they come to our town.) There are even situations in the **past** in which we may refer to some action that was **yet to happen** at some future time. In such instances, a subjunctive is also used following the adverb of time: "Iban a hablarles cuando **llegaran**" (They were going to speak to them whenever they arrived). Note that here we have had to use the imperfect subjunctive of "llegar," rather than the present subjunctive, because we are talking about something that was yet to happen in the past. This sentence implies that they had not yet arrived but were to arrive at some future time. Now, compare the following sentences: "Tratarán de hacerlo cuando tengan tiempo" (They will try to do it whenever they have time); "Dijeron que tratarían de hacerlo cuando tuvieran tiempo" (They said that they would try to do it whenever they had time). In the first example, the verb of the main clause, "tratarán," is future. If the verb of the main clause is future or some present form, then we use a form of present subjunctive. In the second example, the principal verb, "tratarían," is conditional. If the main verb is conditional or a past tense, we use a past form of the subjunctive, in this case, the imperfect subjunctive: "tuvieran."

4. **(B)** For a complete explanation of the use of the subjunctive following adverbs of time such as "tan pronto como" (as soon as), see the explanation for question 3. Also, pay particular attention to the example there which illustrates the use of the past subjunctive after these expressions if the main verb is in a past tense, as is the case in our sentence here. Choice (A) does not qualify because it is in the preterite tense of the indicative. Choice (C) is given in the present subjunctive, rather than the imperfect subjunctive. (D) appears in the future tense of the indicative.

5. **(A)** The verb "aconsejar" (to advise) embodies an expression of will or desire that someone else do something. It carries an implicit com-

mand. After such verbs it is necessary to use a subjunctive form in the dependent clause. Because the main clause of our sentence uses a past tense (preterite) of the verb "aconsejar," we must use a past tense of the subjunctive, the imperfect subjunctive. Choice (B) employs the present subjunctive of the verb; (C) offers us the present indicative; in (D), we once again find a present subjunctive.

6. **(D)** The noun "recuerdo" in our sentence means "souvenir." "Ojalá" and "Ojalá que" both mean "Oh, if only . . . " or "I wish or hope that . . . " They are expressions of desire. Unlike many such expressions, they do not require a change of subject to produce a subjunctive in the following verb. In fact, if there is a verb after them, the subjunctive is obligatory. For that reason choices (A), (B), and (C) are not useful to us. (A) is the third person plural of the present indicative of "traer" (to bring). (B) gives us the third person plural of the present perfect tense of "comprar" (to buy). (C) is the third person plural of the future of "enviar" (to send). Following "Ojalá" and "Ojalá que," if the present or present perfect subjunctive is used, the implication is that the situation is feasible and possible of happening. When we say "¡Ojalá que me den un recuerdo de París!," we mean "I hope that they will give me a souvenir from Paris!" (and it is **possible** that they will). On the other hand, we use a past subjunctive (imperfect or pluperfect) after these two expressions to show that the situation is highly hypothetical, unreal, or impossible: "¡Ojalá que **fuera** millonario!" (I wish I were a millionaire! . . . but I'm not, and probably never will be . . .).

7. **(D)** After the expression **para que,** the subjunctive must be used, and this sentence is in the past. The imperfect subjunctive is used after a principle clause containing the preterite, imperfect, or conditional tenses. Choice (D) is the only one in the imperfect subjunctive which is also singular.

8. **(A)** In an "if" clause in the past, using the subjunctive, the conditional is the appropriate form to follow.

9. **(B)** A known individual or thing does not require the subjunctive, but an unknown, i.e., an indefinite person or thing, does. In this case, it is known, present tense, and indicative. Therefore, choice (B) is correct.

10. **(D)** The imperfect subjunctive is necessary since the verb of the main clause is in the past and it requires the subjunctive following the rule of a verb of request (or similar meaning) directing an action of an object or person different from the subject.

11. **(C)** In our sentence, the word "cuando" is what we term an adverb of time. We can tell from the verb "harán" that we are talking about the future. Whenever an adverb of time refers to the future, we are required to use a subjunctive form of the verb in the following clause. Generally, if the main verb appears in the future or present tenses, we use the present tense of the subjunctive. Among the verbs which are your possible choices, only "puedan" is a present subjunctive form. All of the other choices appear in the present indicative. Even sentences whose main verb is in a past tense may occasionally refer to some future time, e.g., "Dijeron que lo harían cuando **pudieran**" (They said that they would do it whenever they could). Observe that here we cannot use the present subjunctive. We must, on the other hand, use the imperfect subjunctive because we are referring to the past. When the verb does not refer to a future time or when it indicates a customary action, we use an indicative tense following adverbs of time: "Siempre me llaman cuando pueden" (They always call me when they can). Other common adverbs of time which have the same effect are: "hasta que," "tan pronto como," "mientras que," "así que," "luego que," and "en cuanto."

12. **(B)** Dependent clauses beginning with "si" (if) require the use of the **imperfect subjunctive** if they set up an impossible, hypothetical, or unreal situation. Then, in the other clause, we use the **conditional** tense to show what would happen (what the result would be) if that hypothesis were true. The only imperfect subjunctive form appearing among the choices is (B) "tuviera." (A) "tenía" is the imperfect indicative; (C) "tengo" is the present indicative; (D) "tuve" is the preterite. When we say "Si tuviera dinero, iría a Bolivia," we mean "If I had money (but I don't), I would go to Bolivia." In other words, we are emphasizing the unreality or impossibility of my having enough money. If, on the other hand, we wanted to imply that it is not totally unfeasible that I will have the money, we would say in English, "If I have the money, I will go to Bolivia." Notice that here, in the "if" clause, we have used the **present indicative**, and in the result clause, the **future** tense. This pattern would be observed also in Spanish: "Si tengo dinero, iré a Bolivia." Suppose we were talking about a situation in the past and we wanted to set up an unfeasible hypothesis or assumption: "If I had had money, I would have gone to Bolivia" ("Si hubiera tenido dinero, habría ido a Bolivia"). Here we have used compound or perfect tenses: in the "si" clause, the **pluperfect subjunctive**; in the result clause, the **conditional perfect**. Remember this caution: we never use a present or a present perfect subjunctive immediately after the word "si."

13. **(A)** How much do you remember about the uses of the subjunctive as opposed to the indicative? A careful scrutiny of the possible choices reveals that (B) "Dudo" (I doubt), (C) "Niego," (I deny), and (D) "Me alegro de" (I am happy) would require a subjunctive following them if we were to use them in the sentence, but the sentence does not give the subjunctive form of "tener," "tengas," but rather the indicative, "tienes." Consequently, we must use (A) Creo (I believe), which does not cause a subjunctive following it if it is used affirmatively. There are only two possible times when we **may** use the subjunctive after "creer": (1) if "creer" is used negatively, e.g., "No creo que tengas razón" (I don't believe you are right) and (2) if "creer" is used in a question, e.g., "Crees que llueva mañana?" (Do you think it will rain tomorrow?). Even when "creer" is used negatively or interrogatively, the speaker has the **option** of using the indicative, rather than the subjunctive, following "creer" if he wishes to show that he himself feels no doubt about the situation. Earlier, we indicated that the verb "dudar" requires the subjunctive. That is because expressions which cast doubt on the second clause of the sentence bring about a subjunctive in the subordinate verb. The verb "negar" (to deny) produces a subjunctive in the following clause whenever it denies the validity or truth of the subordinate clause. Expressions of emotion, such as "alegrarse de" (to be happy), bring about a following subjunctive only if there is a change of subject between the two verbs. Otherwise, simply the infinitive is used.

14. **(B)** "Siento" is the first person singular of the present tense of "sentir" (ie, i) (to be sorry). "Sentir" is a verb of emotion. It requires a subjunctive in the second part of the sentence when we have two different subjects. For this reason, (A) "no estuvieron," the preterite of "estar" (to be), (C) "no estaban," the imperfect of "estar," and (D) "no estarán," the future of "estar," are all wrong. (B), however, "no estuvieran," the imperfect subjunctive of "estar," is correct. Notice that although "Siento" is given in the present tense, we must use a past tense of the subjunctive because the action of the subordinate clause took place in the past. The word "ayer" (yesterday) is our clue.

15. **(D)** In an "in" clause in the present tense, the independent clause is usually in the future and the dependent clause in the present subjunctive. If, however, the "if" clause is in the past, the independent clause is in the conditional. None of the other answers is correct.

16. **(D)** After the expression **tal vez** indicating a future idea, the present subjunctive is used. Choice (A) is past subjunctive. Only choice (D) is correct.

17. **(B)** The use of the subjunctive is required after **hasta que**. In this case, the sentence is in the past, so the imperfect subjunctive is required, even though the idea of the sentence indicates some action in the future.

18. **(A)** After the expression **para que** the subjunctive can be expected. The introductory sentence begins in the preterite, so the imperfect subjunctive should be chosen.

19. **(D)** After the expression **con tal de que** one expects the subjunctive. It should be noticed that this sentence is in the present tense. The only answer in the present subjunctive is (D). The reflexive in this answer is sometimes referred to as the dative of interest, or it could be considered as the indirect object meaning "for her."

20. **(B)** First you have to decide between the subjunctive and the indicative mood (choice (C), an infinitive, is ungrammatical in the context), and once you decide that the correct mood is the subjunctive (because it is governed by a verb—"pedir"—that always requires a subjunctive), then you have to opt between (A) and (B), that is, the present and the past. Since the main verb is in the past, the subjunctive form to follow must be in the same tense.

21. **(A)** You should first eliminate the last two choices as ungrammatical since they are plural and "hijo" is not. Then you must decide between subjunctive (the correct choice because "querer" always requires the subjunctive) and indicative.

22. **(C)** The four choices break down into two indicatives and two subjunctives. You must choose a subjunctive form at this point because when "creer" is preceded by a negative, it requires the subjunctive mood. Finally, this subjunctive verb must be (like "creo") in the present.

23. **(C)** Three of these choices—(A), (B), and (D)—are ungrammatical, the first two because there is no tense correlation between "daba" (an imperfect form) or "da" (a present) and "reaccionarías" (a conditional form), and the third one because the infinitive must be conjugated. You should also realize that the structure of the sentence is of the "if/then" type, which always requires a subjunctive in the "if" clause.

24. **(B)** This is also an "if/then" clause (inverted: "then/if"). Consequently, the "if" clause must contain a subjunctive form, the only one available being (B).

25. **(D)** Your task in this question is easy if you know that "para que" always takes a subjunctive, though you still have to decide between (C) and (D). The key to this part of the answer is the main verb ("compraron"), which is in the past; therefore, the subjunctive verb that depends on it must also be in the past.

26. **(B)** This adverbial phrase requires the use of the present subjunctive to follow sequence. Therefore, (A) the present tense, (C) the present progressive, and (D) the past subjunctive are incorrect.

27. **(C)** "Como si" is always followed by the past subjunctive. Therefore, choice (A) the present indicative, (B) the present subjunctive, and (D) the preterite are incorrect.

28. **(A)** Although this sentence begins with an impersonal expression and there is a change in subject (i.e., a second clause follows), the subjunctive is not required in the noun clause because there is no doubt implied. Other expressions of this type are "es verdad," "es cierto," "no es dudoso," and "es obvio que." This will eliminate choices (B) and (D) which are both in the present subjunctive. Choice (C) is incorrect because this sentence points out location for which the verb **estar** is used.

29. **(C)** This sentence requires the use of the subjunctive because it begins with a verb of volition and there is a change in subject (from "mamá" to "we"). Because the verb in the independent clause (quería) is in the imperfect tense, to maintain proper sequencing, the past subjunctive is required in the dependent clause. Choice (A) is present subjunctive. Choice (B) the present indicative and (D) the preterite are incorrect since this sentence requires the use of the subjunctive.

30. **(B)** An "if" clause containing a compound verb form (the perfect tense) in the past subjunctive requires the use of a compound tense in the other clause, commonly written in the conditional tense. Choice (A), although it is in the conditional tense, is not compound. Choice (D) is in the present subjunctive and is, therefore, incorrect in this context. Choice (C) is a compound tense but in the pluperfect, not in the conditional perfect tense.

CONJUGATION OF *SER*

Indicative

	Present	Imperfect	Preterite	Future	Condit.
yo	*soy*	*era*	*fui*	*seré*	*sería*
tú	*eres*	*eras*	*fuiste*	*serás*	*serías*
él/ella/Ud.	*es*	*era*	*fue*	*será*	*sería*
nosotros, –as	*somos*	*éramos*	*fuimos*	*seremos*	*seríamos*
vosotros, –as	*sois*	*erais*	*fuisteis*	*seréis*	*seríais*
ellos/ellas/ Uds.	*son*	*eran*	*fueron*	*serán*	*serían*

Subjunctive

	Present	Imperfect
yo	*sea*	*fuera/fuese*
tú	*seas*	*fueras/fueses*
él/ella/Ud.	*sea*	*fuera/fuese*
nosotros, –as	*seamos*	*fuéramos/fuésemos*
vosotros, –as	*seáis*	*fuerais/fueseis*
ellos/ellas/Uds.	*sean*	*fueran/fuesen*

Imperative

Singular	Plural
sé (tú)	*sed (vosotros)*
no seas (tú)	*no seáis (vosotros)*
(no) sea (Ud.)	*(no) sean (Uds.)*

Participles

Past Participle: *sido*
Present Participle: *siendo*

CONJUGATION OF *ESTAR*

Indicative

	Present	Imperfect	Preterite	Future	Condit.
yo	*estoy*	*estaba*	*estuve*	*estaré*	*estaría*
tú	*estás*	*estabas*	*estuviste*	*estarás*	*estarías*
él/ella/Ud.	*está*	*estaba*	*estuvo*	*estará*	*estaría*
nosotros, –as	*estamos*	*estábamos*	*estuvimos*	*estaremos*	*estaríamos*
vosotros, –as	*estáis*	*estabais*	*estuvisteis*	*estaréis*	*estaríais*
ellos/ellas/ Uds.	*están*	*estaban*	*estuvieron*	*estarán*	*estarían*

Subjunctive

	Present	Imperfect
yo	*esté*	*estuviera/estuviese*
tú	*estés*	*estuvieras/estuvieses*
él/ella/Ud.	*esté*	*estuviera/estuviese*
nosotros, –as	*estemos*	*estuviéramos/ estuviésemos*
vosotros, –as	*estéis*	*estuvierais/estuvieseis*
ellos/ellas/Uds.	*estén*	*estuvieran/estuviesen*

Imperative

	Present	Imperfect
	está (tú)	*estad (vosotros)*
	no estés (tú)	*no estéis (vosotros)*
	(no) esté (Ud.)	*(no) estén (Uds.)*

Participles

Past Participle: *estado*
Present Participle: *estando*

Uses of *Ser*

"To be" followed by a predicate noun (a noun that is the same person as the subject) is always *ser.*

*Él **es** médico.*
He **is** a doctor.

Somos *hombres con una misión.*
We **are** men on a mission.

To express origin, ownership, or material consistency.

*¿**Es** Ud. de Atlanta?*
Are you from Atlanta?

*Ese libro **es** de la biblioteca.*
That book **is** the library's.

*Esta mesa **es** de madera.*
This table **is** (made) of wood.

Ser is used to mean "to take place."

*La fiesta **fue** ayer.*
The party **was** yesterday.

*La reunión **es** mañana.*
The meeting **is** tomorrow.

The use of *ser* with an adjective denotes that the speaker considers the quality signified by the adjective an essential or permanent component of the noun.

*El agua **es** clara.*
Water **is** clear.

*La madera **es** dura.*
Wood **is** hard.

*Mi hermano **es** alto.*
My brother **is** tall.

To tell time/dates/seasons:

Son *las dos y media.*	It **is** 2:30.
Es *verano.*	It **is** summer.
Es *el primero de enero.*	It **is** January 1.
Será *tarde.*	It **will be** late.

With "impersonal expressions"—these are expressions with adjectives whose subject is "it."

Es *posible.*	**It's** possible.
Será *imposible.*	It **will be** impossible.
Ha sido *necesario.*	It **has been** necessary.

To express religion or occupation:

Soy *católica.*	I **am** Catholic.
Son *doctores.*	They **are** doctors.

With the adjective *feliz:*

Ella ***es*** *feliz.*	She **is** happy.

To express "passive voice"—when the agent (doer) is expressed:

La información ***fue*** *leída por el profesor.*
The information **was** read by the teacher.

With personal pronouns:

Soy *yo.*	It **is** I.
Es *ella.*	It **is** she.

Uses of *Estar*

Estar is used to express location.

El estadio ***está*** *a dos cuadras.*
The stadium **is** two blocks away.

Los pañuelos ***están*** *en el cajón.*
The handkerchiefs **are** in the drawer.

Estar is used with the present participle of other verbs to form the progressive tense.

Está *lloviendo.*
It **is** raining.

Están *comprando los boletos.*
They **are** buying the tickets.

Estar is used with adjectives to indicate a change from the norm, a temporary state of the subject, or a subjective reaction.

Estaba *gordo cuando lo vi.*
He **was** fat when I saw him.

El postre ***está*** *rico.*
The dessert **is** good.

To express the result of a previous action:

La tarea ***está*** *hecha.*
The homework **is** done.

La casa ***está*** *bien construida.*
The house **is** well built.

With certain idiomatic expressions:

Mi primo ***está de*** *médico allí.*
My cousin **"acts as"** a doctor there.

Estamos *por salir ahora.*
We are in favor of leaving now.

Estoy por *llorar.*
I am about to cry.

Adjectives that Change Meaning with *Ser* or *Estar*

Mi tío ***es*** *bueno.*	My uncle is **good**.
Mi tío ***está*** *bueno.*	My uncle is **in good health**.
Tu perro ***es*** *malo.*	Your dog is **bad**.
Tu perro ***está*** *malo.*	Your dog is **sick**.
La función ***es*** *aburrida.*	The show is **boring**.
Mi esposa ***está*** *aburrida.*	My wife is **bored**.
Mi hijo ***es*** *listo.*	My son is **smart**.
Mi hijo ***está*** *listo.*	My son is **ready**.
Este edificio ***es*** *seguro.*	This building is **safe**.
El portero ***está*** *seguro.*	The porter is **sure**.
Ese hombre ***es*** *cerrado.*	That man is **narrow-minded**.
La puerta ***está*** *cerrada.*	The door is **closed**.
Su hija ***es*** *callada.*	His daughter is **taciturn**.
La noche ***está*** *callada.*	The night is **silent**.

Use of *Lo* with *Estar/Ser*

In Spanish, when a question with a form of ***ser*** or ***estar*** is followed by an adjective, the neuter object pronoun ***lo*** replaces that adjective in the reply.

¿Estás enfermo?	Are you ill?
Sí, ***lo*** *estoy.*	Yes, I am.
¿Son ricos los Garcías?	Are the Garcías rich?
Sí, ***lo*** *son.*	Yes, they are.

☞ Drill 7

1. ¿De dónde . . . Uds.?

(A) van
(B) se dirigen
(C) son
(D) están

2. Esos cocos . . . de Cuba, ¿verdad?

(A) están
(B) estarán
(C) son
(D) sean

3. La boda . . . en la iglesia.

(A) estuvo
(B) fueron
(C) fue
(D) estando

4. Yo . . . dos noches en la selva.

(A) esté
(B) era
(C) estuve
(D) fui

5. El padre de Alicia . . . médico.

(A) está
(B) es
(C) estaba
(D) estará

6. Tú . . . equivocado cuando dijiste que yo no iría a la fiesta.

(A) eres
(B) estás
(C) eras
(D) estabas

7. Los niños han . . . tristes desde que sus padres les prohibieron ver televisión.

(A) sido
(B) sidos
(C) estado
(D) estados

8. El accidente . . . en la esquina, cerca de la tienda.

(A) estuvo (C) está

(B) fue (D) estaría

9. Los deportistas . . . débiles porque no han comido en tres días.

(A) son (C) eran

(B) están (D) habían sido

10. . . . posible hacer la tarea.

(A) Serán (C) Está

(B) Ha sido (D) Estaría

Drill 7—Detailed Explanations of Answers

1. **(C)** The question we most likely want to ask is "Where are you from?" The verb "ser" is used when we are talking about origin; for example, "Soy de los Estados Unidos" (I am from the United States). In our question we are not talking about where these people are, i.e., what their location is. Consequently, "están" (D) would be wrong here. "Estar" does not refer to origin but to location. "Van" (A), and "se dirigen" (B) are normally followed by the preposition "a" (to), because people "go" or "direct themselves" **to** a place, not **from** a place, as "de" would mean.

2. **(C)** The origin of people and things is expressed in the verb **ser**. The subjunctive form is not needed here.

3. **(C)** **Ser** is used for an event or time, and in this case it is singular and in the past.

4. **(C)** To answer correctly, you must understand the differences between the two verbs in Spanish which mean "to be": "ser" and "estar." Only the latter is used to refer to position or location. This immediately eliminates choice (B) "era" (the imperfect of "ser") and (D) "fui" (the preterite of "ser"). (A) "esté" is a form of "estar" but not the right one. It is the first person present of the subjunctive, and there is no reason to use a subjunctive form in this sentence. On the other hand, (C) "estuve" (I was), the first person preterite of "estar," works fine. We have used the preterite of "estar" rather than the imperfect because we know that the action came to an end. The expression "dos noches" puts a limit on the duration of my stay in the jungle ("selva"). Therefore, "estaba" (the imperfect) should not be used here. This particular use of the preterite of "estar" means the same as "pasé" (I spent).

5. **(B)** The only correct way to translate the verb "to be" when the complement is a noun is by means of "ser" and not "estar."

6. **(D)** The primary choice is between "ser" and "estar." In the expression "to be wrong," only "estar" can be used. In addition, you have to realize that the blank has to be filled with a verb in the past to correlate with "dijiste." This eliminates (B).

7. **(C)** The first thing you should notice here is that a form of "haber" is to be followed by some form of "to be." If you analyze the problem in

this way, you'll immediately eliminate (B) and (D), provided you remember that a past participle is invariable in gender and number. Now you are left with the choice between "ser" and "estar," which should go in favor of "estar" because the action (or description "to be sad") began at a certain point and is thus a deviation from the norm (not to be sad).

8. **(B)** If you chose any of the forms of "estar" you might be confusing the sense of location with the notion of occurrence or happening that is translated into Spanish with "ser." To take place ("ser") is not the same as "to be located."

9. **(B)** Now an anomalous element (not eating in three days) has been introduced in the picture of normality described in the previous question, which explains why the right choice is "están" and not any of the other forms of "ser."

10. **(B)** Impersonal expressions (the subject of the verb **to be** is **it** followed by an adjective) require the third person singular of the verb **ser** in Spanish. This would eliminate (C) and (D) since they are both derived from **estar** and (A) because it is plural.

PERSONAL PRONOUNS

Personal Pronoun Chart

Subject		Prepositional		Direct		Indirect	
yo	I	*mí*	me	*me*	me	*me*	to me
tú	you	*ti*	you	*te*	you	*te*	to you
él	he	*él*	him, it–m	*lo*	him, it–m	*le–a él*	to him
ella	she	*ella*	her, it–f	*la*	her, it–f	*le–a ella*	to her
ello	it–neutral	*ello*	it–neutral	*le**	him, you		
Ud.	you	*Ud.*	you	*le*	you	*le–a Ud.*	to you
		sí	("self")			*(se)*	

Subject		Prepositional		Direct		Indirect	
nosotros, –as	we	*nosotros, –as*	us	*nos*	us	*nos*	to us
vosotros, –as	you	*vosotros, –as*	you	*os*	you	*os*	to you
ellos	they–m	*ellos*	them–m	*los*	them–m	*les–a ellos*	to them–m
ellas	they–f	*ellas*	them–f	*las*	them–f	*les–a ellas*	to them–f
Uds.	you	*Uds.*	you			*les–a Uds.*	to you
		sí	("self")			*(se)*	

* *Le* is used to translate **him** or **you**. In Spain the direct object pronouns ***lo*** and ***los*** are often replaced by ***le*** and ***les*** when the pronoun relates to a person or to a thing personified. For the SAT Subject Test, one should follow the Latin American usage and avoid this substitution.

Subject Pronouns

These pronouns are usually omitted in Spanish because the verbal form by itself indicates person and number. (For the sake of clarity, *Ud.* and *Uds.* are usually not omitted.) Naturally, subject pronouns are used when confusion would result otherwise and in order to emphasize a statement. Often the particle *mismo (misma, mismos, mismas)* is used to add emphasis.

***Fue** a comprar vino.*
He went to buy wine.

***Ud. fue** a comprar vino.*
You went to buy wine.

***Ud. mismo fue** a comprar vino.*
You yourself went to buy wine.

Second Person Subject Pronouns

Tú (you, singular) differs from *usted* in terms of familiarity. *Tú* is more intimate; *usted* is more formal. As a rule of thumb, *tú* is used with those people with whom the speaker is on a first-name basis.

In certain parts of Latin America (Argentina, Uruguay, Paraguay, Central America), the form *vosotros* is often used instead of *tú.*

Vos comes with its own verbal forms: *Vos venís a la hora que queréis (Tú vienes a la hora que quieres).* You come at whatever time it pleases you.

Vosotros (you, plural) differs from *ustedes* regionally. In Latin America and in southern Spain, *vosotros* has been replaced by *ustedes.*

Ser Followed by a Subject Pronoun

In Spanish, the subject pronoun follows "to be."

Soy ***yo.***
It is **I.**

Fue ***ella*** *quien me envió el regalo.*
It was **she** that sent me the present.

OBJECT PRONOUNS

The direct object pronouns answer the question "whom" or "what"; the indirect object pronouns answer the question "to (for) whom" or "to (for) what."

Ella ***me*** *dio un regalo.*
She gave **me** a present. (**To whom** did she give a present?)

Nosotros ***lo*** *vimos.*
We saw **him.** (**Whom** did we see?)

Prepositional Complement with Indirect Object Pronoun

The indirect object pronoun can be clarified or emphasized by the addition of a prepositional complement (*a* + prepositional pronoun).

Yo ***le*** *hablé ayer.*
Yesterday I spoke to **him/her/you.**

Yo ***le*** *hablé* ***a ella*** *ayer.*
Yesterday I spoke to **her.**

Special Uses of the Indirect Object Pronoun

a) **Redundant Indirect Object Pronoun.** An indirect object pronoun is used in Spanish even when the indirect object noun is present in the sentence. The latter, however, must designate a person.

Les *dije a* ***los empleados*** *que trabajaran más.*
I told the employees to work harder.

Common verbs of this type are: *pedir* (to ask for), *preguntar* (to ask), *dar* (to give), *decir* (to tell), *gustar* (to like), and *regalar* (to give).

¡Pídaselo a Jorge!	Ask George for it!

b) **Dative of Interest.** Indirect object pronouns are also used to represent the interested party involved in the action designated by the verb. (In these cases English uses a possessive adjective or pronoun.)

Also, when the action results in some disadvantage or loss to the person directly concerned with the action, the indirect object is used. These are usually expressed with **from + person** in English.

Me *robaron la billetera.*
They stole my wallet from me.

Ella siempre ***le*** *esconde la torta* ***al chico****.*
She always hides the cake from the boy.

c) **for + person** is often expressed in Spanish by an indirect object rather than by ***para*** + **person**, particularly when a service is rendered.

Le *lavé la ropa a* ***ella****.*
I washed the clothes for her.

Ella ***me*** *cocinó la comida.*
She cooked the meal for me.

Juan ***nos*** *arregló la puerta.*
Juan fixed the door for us.

Exceptions:	With *ser–*	*Este té es para ti.* This tea is for you.

Where the indirect object is receiving a concrete object, either way is acceptable.

Te traje flores. **or**
Traje flores para ti.

d) **Use the definite article** and indirect object pronoun if the subject of the sentence performs an action on a part of someone else's body.

*Ella **le** lavará la cara a María.*
She will wash Mary's face (for her).

*Julio **le** cortó el pelo a su hijo.*
Julio cut his son's hair (for him).

e) **After *ser* used impersonally**, the indirect object pronoun may be employed to denote the person **to** whom the impersonal expression is applicable.

***Le** será fácil hacerlo.*
It will be easy **for him** to do it.

When Not to Use the Indirect Object Pronoun

In the following two instances, the indirect object pronoun should be avoided and the prepositional phrase used in its place.

a) **After verbs of motion** (*ir, venir, correr,* etc.)

*¡Ven **a mí**, Paco!*	Come to me, Paco!
*El niño corrió **a ellos**.*	The boy ran to them.
*¡No se acerque **a él**!*	Don't approach him!

b) **When the direct object is in the first or second person** (that is, when it is *me, te, nos, os*), Spanish uses the prepositional phrase instead of the indirect object pronoun.

*Me presentaron **a él.***
They presented **me** (D.O.) to him (prepositional phrase).

*Nos mandó **a ellos**.*
He sent **us** (D.O.) to them (prepositional phrase).

Special Uses of the Direct Object Pronoun

a) **Neuter Direct Object Pronoun.** In English the verb "to be" does not require a direct object pronoun, but in some cases both *estar* and *ser* need a **neuter** direct object pronoun to make the sentence grammatical. In these cases ***lo*** refers back to the whole idea expressed in the previous sentence.

¿Es Ud. médico? Sí, ***lo*** *soy.*
Are you a doctor? Yes, I am.

¿Estáis enfermos? No, no ***lo*** *estamos.*
Are you sick? No, we are not.

The neuter direct object pronoun may also be used with the verb "to know."

¿Sabes que Catalina se casó ayer? Sí, ***lo*** *sé.*
Do you know that Catalina got married yesterday? Yes, I know.

¿Tienes dinero que prestarme? ¡Ya ***lo*** *creo!*
Do you have money to lend me? You bet!

b) ***Haber*** **with Direct Object Pronoun.** The verb *haber* sometimes requires the use of a direct object pronoun unknown in English. Note that the direct object pronoun in the following example is no longer neuter.

¿Hay chicas en la fiesta? Sí, ***las*** *hay.*
Are there girls at the party? Yes, there are.

c) ***Todo*** **with Direct Object Pronoun.** A direct object pronoun is required before the verb when the object of the verb is *todo.* Note that the object pronoun agrees in number and gender with *todo.*

Lo *he visto todo.*
I have seen everything.

Las *aprendí todas.*
I learned them all.

d) **Verbs that contain prepositions in their meaning** (*esperar*–to wait **for**, *mirar*–to look **at**, *buscar*–to look **for**, *escuchar*–to listen **to**, etc.) will use the direct object pronouns.

La *miré.*
I looked at her.

Los *buscaré para siempre.*
I'll look for them always.

e) **Verbs used with D.O. + infinitive** = *dejar* (to let), *hacer* (to make), *ver* (to see), and *oír* (to hear).

No lo dejen jugar.
Don't let him play.

Lo hizo recitar.
He made him recite.

La vi entrar.
I saw her enter.

f) **Redundant direct object pronouns** are needed as follows:

1. With the noun when the object is a person or proper name.

   *Conociéndo**la** a Eloisa . . .*
   Knowing Eloisa . . .

   *Ojalá que **lo** cojan al ladrón.*
   I hope they catch the thief.

2. When the object precedes rather than follows the verb.

   La salida (D.O.) ***la** encontrará a su derecha.*
   The exit, you'll find it to your right.

Position of Object Pronouns in the Sentence

Unlike English, object pronouns in Spanish precede the conjugated verb (see examples below). However, they are attached at the end of the verb when the verbal form is an affirmative command, an infinitive, or a present participle.

*Ud. **le** escribe.* You write **to him.**	conjugated—present tense
*¡Escríba**le**!* Write **to him!**	positive command
*Uds. **la** perdonaron.* You forgave **her.**	conjugated—preterite tense
*Hubo que perdonar**la**.* It was necessary to forgive **her.**	infinitive
***Los** dejó sobre la mesa.* He left **them** on the table.	conjugated—preterite tense
*Salió dejándo**los** sobre la mesa.* He went out leaving **them** on the table.	present participle

Note: When the infinitive or the present participle is subordinated to an auxiliary verb such as *querer, ir, poder,* or *estar,* the direct object pronoun can go before these verbs or after, attached to the infinitive or present participle:

I'm going to see **him**.	*Voy a ver**lo**.*
I'm going to see **him**.	***Lo** voy a ver.*
I am looking at **her**.	***La** estoy mirando.*
I'm looking at **her**.	*Estoy mirándo**la**.*

Syntactic Order of Object Pronouns

When a verb has two object pronouns, the indirect object pronoun precedes the direct object pronoun.

Envían una carta.	They send a letter.
***Nos** envían una carta.*	They send a letter **to us**.
***Nos la** envían.*	They send **it to us**.
*¡Envíe**nosla**!*	Send **it to us**!
*¡No **nos la** envíen!*	Don't send **it to us**!

But when the two object pronouns in the sentence are third person pronouns, the **indirect** object pronoun (*le* or *les*) is replaced by *se.*

Escribes una carta.	You write a letter.
***Les** escribes una carta.*	You write a letter **to them**.
***Se la** escribes.*	You write **it to them**.
*¡Escríbe**sela**!*	Write **it to them**!

Prepositional Pronouns

Prepositions are words or phrases that relate words to one another. They may be followed by nouns, pronouns, or verbs (in the infinitive form in Spanish).

Here is a basic list of prepositions:

a	to, at	*excepto**	except
bajo	under	*hacia*	toward
*como**	like	*hasta*	until, as far as, to
*con***	with	*menos**	except
contra	against	*para*	for
de	from, of	*por*	for
desde	from, since	*salvo**	except
durante	during	*según**	according to
en	in, at, on	*sin*	without
*entre**	between, among	*sobre*	on, upon, over, above

* These prepositions are used with **subject** pronouns, not the prepositional group.

según él y yo according to him and me

** With this preposition the prepositional pronouns ***mí, ti***, and ***sí*** combine to form ***conmigo, contigo, consigo***. These combinations are invariable; there are no plural or feminine forms.

Here is a basic list of compound prepositions:

además de	besides	*encima de*	on top of
alrededor de	around	*en cuanto a*	in regard to
antes de	before	*enfrente de*	in front of
a pesar de	in spite of	*en lugar de*	instead of
cerca de	near	*en vez de*	instead of
debajo de	under	*frente a*	in front of
delante de	in front of	*fuera de*	outside of
dentro de	within	*lejos de*	far from
después de	after (time)	*para con**	toward
detrás de	behind	*por + inf.*	because of

* To show an attitude towards, as in "*Es muy cariñoso (para) con su mujer.*" He is very affectionate toward his wife.

Use of *Sí, Consigo*

Sí is a special prepositional form of the pronoun ***se***. It is often combined with a form of ***mismo*** *(–a, –os, –as)* to express "self." Note the difference between these two examples.

Ella no se refiere a sí misma.
She is not referring to herself.

vs.

Ella no se refiere a ella.
She is not referring to her (someone else).

Están disgustados consigo mismos.
They are disgusted with themselves.

vs.

Están disgustados con ellos.
They are disgusted with them (others).

Use of *Ello*

Ello means **it** when referring to situations or statements, but not to nouns.

Todo fue horrible; prefiero no hablar de ello.
It was all horrible; I prefer not to talk about it.

Por vs. *Para*

In general, *por* expresses the ideas contained in "for the sake of," "through," "exchange"; whereas *para* expresses destination, purpose, end, intention.

a) *Por* means "through"; *para* refers to destination.

Iba ***por*** *el parque.*	I was walking **through** the park.
Iba ***para*** *el parque.*	I was **on** my **way to** the park.

b) *Por* refers to motive; *para* to purpose or end.

Lo hizo ***por*** *mí.*
He did it **for** me (for my sake, on my behalf).

El artesano hizo una vasija ***para*** *mí.*
The artisan made a vase **for** me.

c) *Por* expresses the idea of exchange.

Lo cambié ***por*** *una camisa.* I exchanged it **for** a shirt.

d) *Por* denotes a span of time; *para* designates an endpoint in time.

Los exiliados caminaron ***por*** *tres días y tres noches.*
The exiles walked **for** (during, for the space of) three days and three nights.

El traje estará listo ***para*** *el lunes.*
The suit will be ready by Monday.

e) *Para* translates "in order to."

Fui a su casa ***para*** *hablar con él.*
I went to his house **in order to** speak to him.

f) *Por* and *para* have set meanings in certain idiomatic constructions.

por *ejemplo*	**for** example
por lo menos	at least
para *siempre*	**for**ever
No es ***para*** *tanto.*	It's not that serious.

g) Other expressions using *por*.

por ahora	for now
por avión	by plane
por consiguiente	consequently
por desgracia	unfortunately
por ejemplo	for example
por escrito	in writing
por eso	therefore
por fin	finally
por lo común	generally
por lo contrario	on the contrary
por lo general	generally
por regla general	as a general rule
por lo tanto	consequently
por lo visto	apparently
por otra parte	on the other hand
por poco	almost
por si acaso	in case
por supuesto	of course
por teléfono	by phone
por todas partes	everywhere

Idioms with *A, En, De, Sin*

a) Idioms with *a*

a caballo	on horseback
a casa/en casa	at home
a causa de	because of
a eso de	at about (with time)
a fines de	at the end of
a fondo	thoroughly
a fuerza de	by dint of
a la derecha	to the right
a la izquierda	to the left
a la vez	at the same time

a lo largo de	along
a lo lejos	in the distance
a lo menos (al menos)	at least
a mano	by hand
a menudo	often
a mi parecer	in my opinion
a pie	on foot
a pierna suelta	without a care
a principios de	at the beginning of
a saltos	by leaps and bounds
a solas	alone
a tiempo	on time
a través de	across
a veces	at times
a la española (francesa, etc.)	in the Spanish/French way
a la larga	in the long run
a la semana	per week
al aire libre	outside
al amanecer	at dawn
al anochecer	at nightfall
al cabo	finally
al contrario	on the contrary
al día	up to date
al fin	finally
al lado de	next to
al parecer	apparently
al por mayor	wholesale
al por menor	retail
al principio	at first

b) Idioms with *de*

de antemano	ahead of time
de arriba	upstairs
de balde	free
de broma	jokingly
de buena gana	willingly
de cuando (vez) en cuando	from time to time
de día (noche)	by day, at night
de día en día	from day to day
de esta (esa) manera	in this (that) way
de este (ese) modo	in this (that) way
de hoy (ahora) en adelante	from today (now) on

de mala gana	unwillingly
de mal humor	in a bad mood
de manera que/de modo que	so that
de memoria	by heart
de moda	in style
de nada	you're welcome
de ninguna manera/de ningún modo	by no means
de nuevo	again
de otro modo	otherwise
(abrir) de par en par	(to open) wide
de pie	standing
de prisa	in a hurry
de pronto/de repente	suddenly
de rodillas	kneeling
de todos modos	anyway
de uno en uno	one by one
de veras	really

c) Idioms with *en*

en bicicleta	by bike
en broma	jokingly
en cambio	on the other hand
en caso de	in case of
en contra de	against
en cuanto	as soon as
en cuanto a	as for, in regard to
en efecto	in effect
en este momento	at this time
en lugar (vez) de	instead of
en marcha	under way, on the way
en medio de	in the middle of
en ninguna parte	nowhere
en punto	sharp (telling time)
en seguida	at once
en suma	in short, in a word
en todas partes	everywhere
en vano	in vain
en voz alta (baja)	in a loud (low) voice

d) Idioms with *sin*

sin aliento	out of breath
sin cuento	endless
sin cuidado	carelessly
sin duda	without a doubt
sin ejemplo	unparalleled
sin embargo	nevertheless
sin falta	without fail
sin fondo	bottomless
sin novedad	same as usual

Verbs with Prepositions

a) Verbs with *con*

amenazar con	to threaten to
casarse con	to get married to
contar (ue) con	to rely on
cumplir con	to keep (one's word)
encontrarse (ue) con	to run into by chance
enojarse con	to get angry with
estar de acuerdo con	to agree with
meterse con	to pick a quarrel with
quedarse con	to keep
soñar (ue) con	to dream about
tropezar (ie) con	to meet by chance with

b) Verbs with *en*

apoyarse en	to lean on
confiar (í) en	to trust in
consentir (ie, i) en	to consent to
consistir en	to consist of
convenir en	to agree to/on
convertirse (ie, i) en	to become, change into
empeñarse en	to insist on
especializarse en	to major in
fijarse en	to notice, stare at
influir en	to influence
insistir en	to insist on
meterse en	to get involved in
pensar (ie) en	to think about
reparar en	to notice

quedar en	to agree to
tardar en	to delay in

c) Verbs with *de*

acabar de + inf	*Acabo de comer.*	I just ate.
	Acababa de comer.	I'd just eaten.
	Acabé de comer.	I finished eating.

acordarse (ue) de	to remember
alegrarse de	to be glad
alejarse de	to go away from
apoderarse de	to take possession of
aprovecharse de	to take advantage of
arrepentirse (ie, i) de	to repent
avergonzarse (ue) de*	to be ashamed
burlarse de	to make fun of
carecer de	to lack
constar de	to consist of
cuidar de	to take care of
darse cuenta de	to realize
dejar de	to stop (doing something)
depender de	to depend on
despedirse (i, i) de	to say goodbye to
disfrutar de	to enjoy
enamorarse de	to fall in love with
encargarse de	to take charge of
enterarse de	to find out about
fiarse (í) de	to trust
gozar de	to enjoy
olvidarse de	to forget about
oír hablar de	to hear about
pensar (ie) de	to think about (have an opinion)
preocuparse de	to be worried about
quejarse de	to complain about
*reírse (í, i)** de*	to laugh at
servir (i, i) de	to serve as
servirse (i, i) de	to make use of
tratar de	to try to + inf.
tratarse de	to be a question of

* This verb will have a dieresis mark over the *ü* in the present indicative and subjunctive, in all forms except *nosotros* and *vosotros*: *me avergüenzo* but *nos avergonzamos.*

** This verb is conjugated as follows: *reírse* to laugh at

Present Indicative	Present Subjunctive	Preterite	Imperfect Subjunctive
me río	*me ría*	*me reí*	*me riera/se*
te ríes	*te rías*	*te reíste*	*te rieras/ses*
se ríe	*se ría*	*se rió*	*se riera/se*
nos reímos	*nos riamos*	*nos reímos*	*nos riéramos/semos*
os reís	*os riáis*	*os reísteis*	*os rierais/seis*
se ríen	*se rían*	*se rieron*	*se rieran/sen*

Present Participle: *riendo*

Past Participle: *reído*

Formal Commands: *ríase, no se ría* *ríanse, no se rían*

Familiar Commands: *ríete, no te rías* *reíos, no os riáis*

d) Verbs with *por*

acabar por	to end up by
dar por	to consider, to regard as
esforzarse (ue) por	to make an effort
interesarse por	to be interested in
preguntar por + person	to ask for (a person)
tomar por	to take (someone) for

e) Verbs with *a*

Verbs of beginning, learning, and motion are followed by an ***a*** in Spanish.

Beginning

comenzar (ie) a
empezar (ie) a
ponerse a
principiar a

Learning

aprender a	to learn
enseñar a	to teach

Motion

acercarse a	to approach
apresurarse a	to hurry to

dirigirse a	to go toward
ir a	to go to
regresar a	to return to
salir a	to leave to
subir a	to go up
venir a	to come to
volver a (ue)	to return to

Other verbs followed by ***a***:

acertar (ie) a	to happen to
acostumbrarse a	to become used to
alcanzar a	to succeed in (doing something)
asistir a	to attend
asomarse a	to appear at
aspirar a	to aspire to
atreverse a	to dare to
ayudar a	to help
condenar a	to condemn to
convidar a	to invite to
cuidar a	to take care of (person)
decidirse a	to decide to
dedicarse a	to devote oneself to
detenerse a	to pause to
disponerse a	to get ready to
exponerse a	to run the risk of
invitar a	to invite to
jugar (ue) a	to play (game)
negarse (ie) a	to refuse to
obligar a	to obligate to
*oler (ue) a**	to smell like
parecerse a	to resemble
querer (ie) a	to love
resignarse a	to resign oneself to
saber a	to taste like
ser aficionado, –a a	to be fond (a fan) of
someter a	to submit to
sonar a	to sound like
volver (ue) a + verb	to (do something) again

* This verb in the present indicative and subjunctive (except for *nosotros* and *vosotros*) will begin with "*h*." *Él huele a ajo.* He smells like garlic.

Conjunctions

Conjunctions are words or phrases that connect clauses to one another. The following is a basic list of conjunctions:

o (u)	or
y (e)	and
pero, mas, sino que	but
ni	nor, neither
que	that
si	if, whether

Uses of the Basic Conjunctions

a) *O* changes to *u* in front of words beginning with *o* or *ho:*

No sé si lo dijo Roberto ***u*** *Horacio.*
I don't know whether Roberto **or** Horacio said it.

b) *Y* changes to *e* in front of words beginning with *i* or *hi:*

Padre ***e*** *hijo viajaban juntos.*
Father **and** son were traveling together.

Note: *Y* does not change in front of *y* or *hie:*

fuego ***y*** *hielo*	fire **and** ice.
Tú ***y*** *yo.*	You **and** I.

c) *Ni* is the counterpart of *y*. It is often repeated in a sentence to mean "neither . . . nor":

ni *chicha* ***ni*** *limonada* — **neither** fish **nor** fowl

Pero vs. *Sino*

Pero, mas, and *sino* mean "but." (*Mas* with an accent mark, however, is an adverb meaning "more.") *Pero* and *mas* are interchangeable, but *pero* and *sino* have different uses. *Sino* (or *sino que*) has the sense of "rather" or "on the contrary." For *sino* or *sino que* to be used, the first part of the sentence must be negative.

No dije roca ***sino*** *foca.*
I didn't say "rock" **but** "seal."

No vino para quedarse ***sino que*** *vino y se fue.**
She didn't come to stay **but** came and left.

*Mi abuelo ya murió **pero** me dejó un buen recuerdo.*
My grandfather already died **but** he left me good memories.

* When the contrast is between clauses with different verb forms, *que* is introduced.

Correlative Conjunctions

Conjunctions such as *ni...ni* above are not uncommon in Spanish. Other pairs are:

o . . . o	either . . . or
ya . . . ya	whether . . . or, sometimes . . . sometimes
no sólo . . . sino también	not only . . . but also

*Decídete. **O** te vas **o** haces lo que te digo.*
Make up your mind. **Either** you leave **or** you do as I say.

Ella no sólo gana el dinero sino que también lo gasta.
She not only earns the money but also spends it.

Conjunctive Phrases

Some conjunctions may require the use of the subjunctive. (See subjunctive–the adverbial clause.) The others follow:

apenas . . . cuando	hardly . . . when
a pesar de que	in spite of
conque	so then, and so, then
desde que	since
empero	however
entretanto que	meanwhile
más bien que	rather than
mientras tanto	meanwhile
no bien . . . cuando	no sooner . . . than
no obstante	notwithstanding

☞ Drill 8

1. Mi viejo amigo Fernando trabaja . . . la Compañía Equis.

(A) por
(B) a
(C) cerca
(D) para

2. Miguelín . . . trajo café de Colombia.

(A) ti
(B) nos
(C) mí
(D) ella

3. . . . a él, no a ella.

(A) Le parecen
(B) Se lo enseñaron
(C) Se negaron
(D) Los vieron

4. Ayer compré unas sillas nuevas; son muy elegantes y juegan bien con los otros muebles. Son nuevecitas y no quiero que la gente se siente en . . .

(A) las.
(B) ellas.
(C) les.
(D) ella.

5. María me dijo un secreto. . . . dijo el otro día.

(A) Me lo
(B) Lo me
(C) Me los
(D) No me lo

6. Cuando entramos en el dormitorio, nos dimos cuenta de que los ladrones sólo habían robado nuestras corbatas nuevas. . . . llevaron toditas.

(A) Las nos
(B) Nos la
(C) Se las
(D) Me la

7. Invité a Carmela a que fuera . . .

(A) conmigo.
(B) con mi.
(C) con yo.
(D) conmiga.

8. Siempre al comer me gusta el pan con mucha mantequilla. A la mesa tengo que decirles a los otros que . . .

(A) me pasen. (C) me la pasen.

(B) pásenmela. (D) se la pasen.

9. —Mamá, prepáreme la comida. Ella me dice, . . .

(A) «Te lo estoy preparando.»

(B) «Estoy preparándotela.»

(C) «La te preparo.»

(D) «Prepárotela.»

10. Como era natural, el perro salió . . . la puerta.

(A) para (C) a

(B) por (D) de

11. Raúl no entendía el subjuntivo; el profesor . . .

(A) se lo explicó. (C) lo explica.

(B) se los explica. (D) los explicó.

12. Nuestros enemigos están trabajando . . .

(A) con nos. (C) contra nosotros.

(B) contra nos. (D) connos.

13. La silla estaba . . . la mesa.

(A) antes de (C) en cuanto a

(B) detrás de (D) después de

14. Mi novia quería casarse conmigo pero nunca . . . dijo.

(A) se le (C) me lo

(B) se lo (D) lo me

15. Al presidente . . . trataron de asesinar hace varios años.

(A) se
(B) lo
(C) ello
(D) les

16. Carmen es muy bella. Ayer . . . vi.

(A) la
(B) lo
(C) les
(D) se

17. Me pidieron que . . . entregara el informe directamente al jefe.

(A) lo
(B) le
(C) se
(D) la

18. El fugitivo ha regresado; yo mismo . . . vi.

(A) lo
(B) te
(C) les
(D) se

19. Él . . . dio un beso al despedirse.

(A) lo
(B) la
(C) le
(D) se

20. Este político sabe mucho . . . la poca educación que tiene.

(A) a causa de
(B) para
(C) por
(D) porque

21. Todos mis amigos van al mercado menos . . .

(A) mí.
(B) mi.
(C) conmigo.
(D) yo.

22. Ella no es alta . . . baja.

(A) pero
(B) sino
(C) también
(D) sino que

23. Yo no conozco al niño . . . me gusta su coche nuevo.

(A) pero (C) pero que

(B) sino (D) sino que

24. Ella siempre . . . esconde su dinero a mi madre y a mí.

(A) nos (C) les

(B) le (D) los

25. No puedo ver a mis amigas; tengo que . . .

(A) buscarles. (C) buscarlas.

(B) las buscar. (D) las busco.

26. Fue horrible; prefiero no pensar en . . .

(A) lo. (C) ella.

(B) él. (D) ello.

27. Esta taza es . . . café. ¡Démela, por favor!

(A) por (C) en

(B) para (D) con

28. La semana pasada me quedé en casa . . . tres días.

(A) por (C) en

(B) para (D) de

29. ¿Cuánto dinero me dará Ud. . . . mi trabajo?

(A) por (C) de

(B) en (D) para

30. . . . el viernes tenemos esta lección.

(A) En (C) Para

(B) Por (D) De

Drill 8—Detailed Explanations of Answers

1. **(D)** To work **for**, in the sense of "to be employed by," requires the use of "para" rather than "por." For this reason, (A) is wrong, but (D) is right. Thinking that you wanted to say "at," you might have mistakenly chosen answer (B), but the word "a" normally means "at" only when it follows verbs of motion: "Tiró la pelota a la pared" (He threw the ball at the wall). When motion is not involved, we use the preposition "en" to mean "at": "Mi madre está en el mercado" (My mother is at the market). Choice (C) is wrong because "near to" is "cerca **de**" and not simply "cerca."

2. **(B)** In the sentence, the verb "trajo" is the third person preterite of "traer" (to bring). We know that Miguelín brought someone coffee, i.e., Miguelín brought coffee **to** someone. The indirect object pronouns, which mean "to" or "for," are "me" (to or for me), "te" (to or for you, familiar singular), "le" (to or for him, her, you, polite singular), "nos" (to or for us), "os" (to or for you, familiar plural), and "les" (to or for them, you, polite plural). In the list of possible answers, we encounter only one pronoun from this list, "nos." In (A), we see the second person singular familiar form of the prepositional pronoun, i.e., a pronoun which is used following a preposition. Since there is no preposition this choice is incorrect.

3. **(B)** Choice (A) is incorrect because "parecerse a" (to resemble) requires a reflexive pronoun, but we are given the third person singular indirect object pronoun. In (C), we find the reflexive form of "negar," which is used in the idiomatic expression "negarse a" + infinitive (to refuse to). The "a" in our sentence, however, is not followed by an infinitive, but rather by a prepositional pronoun, "él." In (D), we have used the third person plural masculine form of the direct object pronoun. Since we are referring to "él" (him), for this to be correct, we would have to use the masculine singular form of that pronoun, "lo." (B) is correct. It says, "Se lo enseñaron" (They showed or taught it to him). Observe the two object pronouns at the beginning of this answer. Remember that if we have two third person object pronouns (the first indirect, the second direct), the first of these automatically changes to "se." In our sentence, then, the "Se" would actually stand for the word "le." English speakers might question why the indirect object pronoun appears here since later in the sentence we find the prepositional phrase "a él," which means "to him." Nevertheless, the redundant use of the indirect object pronoun is typical of Spanish style,

even though there may be a prepositional phrase later in the sentence which explicitly states the same idea.

4. **(B)** After a preposition, the object pronoun is expressed by the subject pronoun with the exception of the first and second persons singular. In this case, **ellas** is plural and would be the only correct answer because it refers to "chairs."

5. **(A)** The indirect object pronoun always precedes the direct. Both precede the verb unless this is in the infinitive. **Me lo** is the only correct answer because **lo** refers to **secreto**. Choice (D), although grammatically correct, does not follow the train of information given in the first sentence.

6. **(C)** The passive voice in Spanish can be translated by the reflexive **se**, and choice (C) is the only possible one because **las** refers to **corbatas**. (A) has the plural **las**, but the indirect object does not precede the direct.

7. **(A)** The first and second persons singular with the preposition **con** are always **conmigo** and **contigo**. Occasionally **consigo** is used, meaning **con él, con ella,** or **con usted**. The verb **invitar** is one of the verbs which when followed by a change in subject requires the subjunctive, and in this case, it is in the past. **Fuera** is the imperfect subjunctive form of **ir**. (D) is incorrect because **conmigo** is invariable and has no feminine form.

8. **(C)** The indirect object pronoun always precedes the direct. In this case, the subjunctive is required because of the verb **decir**, as a request with a change of subject. The **la** refers to **mantequilla**. (A), (B), and (C) have **me**, but only (C) includes both the indirect and the direct objects in their proper position.

9. **(B)** The use of the auxiliary **estar** is correct with the present participle. The indirect and direct objects are joined in that order following the present participle. **Te** is used because the familiar form is appropriate, and the **la** refers to **comida**.

10. **(B)** **Por** is correct. It is the correct word for "through" in this context.

11. **(A)** The indirect object pronoun **le** is changed to **se** when used in conjunction with a direct object pronoun. **Lo**, in this sentence, refers to the subjunctive in the sentence. Choice (C) is a remote possibility, but is not totally correct grammatically.

12. **(C)** After a preposition, the subject pronoun should be used except for the first and second persons singular. Our enemies are supposedly working "against us," so choice (C) is the only correct answer.

13. **(B)** The preposition "antes de," in (A), means "before." It refers to time, not location. The sentence is talking about the position of the "chair" ("silla"). If we meant "before" in the sense of "in front of," we would have to use the preposition "delante de." The contrary of "delante de" is "detrás de" (behind, in back of), which fits well in our sentence. In (D) "después de" (after), we have another preposition which refers to time, not location. In (C) "en cuanto a" means "about" in the sense of "concerning."

14. **(C)** Neither of the first two choices can be the correct answer because in both "se" refers to a third person not to be found in the question. Choice (D) has the right object pronouns but in the wrong order. Choice (C) is the right answer because it contains the appropriate indirect object pronoun ("she said **to me**") and direct object pronoun ("she said **it** to me") in the correct sequence.

15. **(B)** The correct answer is the only direct object pronoun available. This is a peculiar but common use of the pronoun, which wouldn't be necessary if the sentence were in the normal syntactic order, namely, with the subject in front (an implicit "ellos") and the direct object ("presidente") in back. When the usual order is inverted, then a redundant object pronoun must be introduced.

16. **(A)** The question calls for a direct object pronoun. Of the two available, you need to choose the feminine form to go with "Carmen."

17. **(B)** This question calls for the indirect object pronoun, which you have to identify (there is only one) from the choices offered. The reason for this type of pronoun is that Spanish tends to reinforce the indirect object ("jefe") when it refers to a person.

18. **(A)** Here you need a direct object pronoun that refers to "el fugitivo" and the only possibility among the four choices is "lo."

19. **(C)** The direct object in this sentence is "un beso" and since it is present in the phrase there is no need for a direct object pronoun (such as "lo" or "la"). What the sentence does need is an indirect object pronoun referring to the implicit person (or pet, or whatever) in the statement.

20. **(B)** Para is used whenever the idea of "considering" is implied.

21. **(D)** After certain prepositions (menos, excepto, salvo, entre, como, and según), subject pronouns are used in Spanish. Therefore, choice (A), which is prepositional, is incorrect. Choice (B) means "my" and choice (C) means "with me."

22. **(B)** "Sino" has the sense of "rather" or "on the contrary" and is used as the conjunction in a negative sentence where the second part directly contradicts the first. It is important to note that direct contradictions must be between equal parts of speech, in this case, between the adjectives "alta" and "baja." Choice (A) is incorrect because it cannot be used where a direct contradiction is implied. Choice (C) "also" makes no sense in this context. Choice (D) is used when the direct contradiction is between two conjugated verbs, (i.e., Ella no quiere sentarse sino que quiere levantarse.)

23. **(A)** Even though the first part of this sentence is negative, the second part is not a direct contradiction of the first. Therefore, choice (B) and (D) are incorrect. Choice (C) "pero que" (but that) makes no sense.

24. **(A)** When the action results in some disadvantage or loss ("hides") to the person directly concerned with the action, the indirect object pronoun is used. In English these statements are commonly expressed with **from + person**. Choice (A) is correct because the indirect object must correlate with the phrase "a mi madre y a mí," which is equivalent to **us**. Choices (B) "to him," (C) "to them," and (D) "to you" are also indirect object pronouns but do not correlate with the previously mentioned phrase.

25. **(C)** Verbs which include a preposition in their meaning (buscar–to look for, esperar–to wait for, mirar–to look at) are used with direct object pronouns. Choice (A) is incorrect because it has an indirect object pronoun. Choice (C) has the correct direct object pronoun but it is incorrectly placed. Choice (D) is incorrect because the conjugated verb "busco" cannot follow "tengo que," which requires the use of the infinitive.

26. **(D)** The neuter pronoun "ello" (it) is used to refer to entire happenings, events, or occurrences previously alluded to. Choice (A) is a direct object pronoun and cannot be used after a preposition. Choices (B) "he/it (m)" and (C) "she/it (f)" are incorrect since there is no reference to anything specific that is either masculine or feminine in gender.

27. **(B)** To indicate what something is intended for, use **para**. The intended use of the cup is for coffee.

28. **(A)** **Por** is used to express a length of time. In this example, the length of time is three days.

29. **(A)** **Por** is used when "in exchange for" is intended. In this sample it is money in exchange for work.

30. **(C)** **Para** is used to express some point in future time. In this sample the future time indicated is Friday.

GUSTAR

Gustar and verbs like it follow a certain pattern that is unlike English. These verbs are commonly used in the third person singular and plural in conjunction with the indirect object pronoun group.

Pattern of *Gustar*

Because ***gustar*** means "to be pleasing to," its translation into Spanish from the English "to like" will require setting the verb up according to the following pattern:

I like cars. = Cars **are pleasing** to me.
= *Me* ***gustan*** *los coches.*

In the example given, after rearranging the sentence to fit the Spanish pattern, the indirect object surfaces (to me). In addition, one can see that the new subject (cars) will require using the verb in the third person plural. The following chart shows the indirect object pronoun group with **all** six persons "explained" with the prepositional phrase.

me	*– a mí*	*nos*	*– a nosotros*
te	*– a ti*	*os*	*– a vosotros*
le	*– a él*	*les*	*– a ellos*
le	*– a ella*	*les*	*– a ellas*
le	*– a Ud.*	*les*	*– a Uds.*

This additional prepositional phrase that can accompany each of the indirect object pronouns can be used to:

1. further emphasize the indirect pronoun itself.

   A ***mí*** *me gusta la música clásica.*
   I **really** like classical music.

2. further clarify the meaning of le/les.

   A ella le gustaban las películas de horror.
   She liked horror movies.

3. provide a place to put names/nouns/proper nouns.

   A ***Juan*** *le gustará ir al cine conmigo.*
   Juan will like to go to the movies with me.

   A los chicos *les gustan los coches.*
   Boys like cars.

"*Gustar*" Types

Verbs that follow the "*gustar* pattern":

agradar	to be pleasing	*Nos agrada ir.* It pleases us to go.
bastar	to be enough	*Me basta un traje.* One suit is enough for me.
doler (ue)	to be painful	*Me duele la cabeza.* My head aches.
parecer	to seem	*A él le parece imposible.* It seems impossible to him.
placer	to be pleasing	*Nos place verte.* It pleases us to see you.
quedar	to have left	*Me quedó un buen libro.* I had one good book left.
sobrar	to be left over	*Les sobran tres dólares.* They have $3.00 left over.
tocar	to be one's turn	*A María le toca.* It's Mary's turn.

To Need

To need can be expressed three ways: *falter, hacer falta,* and *necesitar.*

I need a car.	*Me falta un coche.* *Me hace falta un coche.* *Necesito un coche.*
I needed a car.	*Me faltó/faltaba un coche.* *Me hizo/hacía falta un coche.* *Necesité/Necesitaba un coche.*

Note: The verb "*faltar/hacer falta*" is commonly used in the present, preterite, and imperfect tenses. If one needs to express "need" in other tenses, use *necesitar*.

☞ Drill 9

1. A Roberto . . . gusta ir a la playa todos los días durante el verano.

   (A) se (C) le

   (B) os (D) te

2. . . . chico le gusta jugar al tenis.

   (A) El (C) A

   (B) Al (D) nothing needed

3. A Rob y a mí . . . el helado.

   (A) les gusta (C) nos gusta

   (B) les gustan (D) nos gustan

4. Me encanta . . . dinero.

   (A) gastar (C) gastaré

   (B) gastando (D) pasar

5. . . . falta dos dólares.

   (A) Me hace (C) Me haces

   (B) Me hacen (D) Me hago

6. ¿A quiénes . . . toca?

   (A) lo (C) les

   (B) le (D) los

7. A mis amigos . . . el chocolate.

   (A) les gustó (C) le gustó

   (B) les gustaron (D) nos gustó

8. . . . nos encantó la cuidad.

(A) A María

(B) A las mujeres

(C) A vosotros

(D) A los niños y a mí

9. A José . . . dos cursos difíciles.

(A) le bastará

(B) le bastarán

(C) se bastarán

(D) bastarán

10. A Juan no le importaba . . .

(A) los coches.

(B) ir al cine.

(C) estudiando.

(D) a trabajar.

Drill 9—Detailed Explanations of Answers

1. **(C)** Normally, with the verb "gustar" and similar verbs, we use indirect object pronouns (me, te, le, nos, os, les). Although we usually translate "gustar" to mean "to like," we should remember that it literally means "to be pleasing **to**." This explains the use of "A" before "Roberto" in the sentence. It is pleasing "**to** Roberto." The indirect object pronoun can mean "to" or "for." It is for this reason that the indirect object pronoun is required here. Because "Roberto" is a singular noun, we must then use the third person singular indirect object pronoun "le."

2. **(B)** "Gustar" type verbs use indirect object pronouns which can be further clarified by using prepositional phrases. These phrases begin with "a" and normally precede the indirect object pronoun that they go with. Choice (A) is incorrect because the preposition "a" is required. Choice (C) is missing the article "el" which is needed before the noun "chico."

3. **(C)** The "a" phrase contains the hint as to which indirect object pronoun to select. By including "me" with "Rob" the corresponding pronoun is "we" (nos). The verb is singular because the noun "helado" is singular. Choices (A) and (B) have the incorrect object pronoun. Choice (D) has the incorrect form of "gustar."

4. **(A)** If a verb follows any verb used like "gustar," it must be in the gerund form (infinitive) since it is acting as the actual subject of the statement. Choices (B) the present participle and (C) the future tense are both in the incorrect form. Choice (D), although it is an infinitive, is incorrect because this verb means to spend "time," not "money."

5. **(B)** The main verb in this expression (hacer), which means "to need," must match the item(s) needed. In this case two dollars are needed, which is plural. Answer (A) is singular and will not match the subject. Answer (C) the "tú" form of the verb and answer (D) the "yo" form of the verb **hacer** are not acceptable forms of this verb when used in this manner. It must either be third singular or third plural.

6. **(C)** This "gustar" type means "to be one's turn." The prepositional phrase ("a quiénes") contains the hint as to which indirect object pronoun to select. Choices (A) and (D) are direct object pronouns and are not used with "gustar" types. Choice (B) is singular and will not match "a quiénes."

7. **(A)** Because the noun "chocolate" is singular, a singular form of **gustar** is required. The prepositional phrase "A mis amigos" corresponds to the indirect object pronoun "les," Choice (B) is incorrect because the verb is plural. Choices (C) and (D) have the incorrect I.O. pronouns.

8. **(D)** Because the indirect object pronoun "nos" has been used in this sentence, the corresponding prepositional phrase must match it. "A María" (A) would require "le," "A las mujeres" (B) would require "les," and "A vosotros" (C) would require using "os."

9. **(B)** The verb must be plural to match "dos cursos difíciles," and the indirect object pronoun must correspond to the prepositional phrase "A José." Choice (A) has the incorrect verb form. Choice (C) has a reflexive pronoun, and (D) is missing the indirect object pronoun entirely.

10. **(B)** After the verb "importaba" either an infinitive or a singular noun may be used. Choice (A) has a plural noun, and (C) is the present participle of "estudiar." Choice (D) has an additional "a" before the infinitive, which is unnecessary.

DEMONSTRATIVES: ADJECTIVES/PRONOUNS

These two groups share identical forms except that the accent mark is used over the pronouns.

Adjective		**Pronoun**	
this	*este, esta*	this one	*éste, ésta*
that	*ese, esa*	that one	*ése, ésa*
that*	*aquel, aquella*	that one*	*aquél, aquélla*
these	*estos, estas*	these	*éstos, éstas*
those	*esos, esas*	those	*ésos, ésas*
those*	*aquellos, aquellas*	those*	aquéllos, aquéllas

* These demonstratives are used to indicate greater distance from the speaker as well as distance in time. *Ése* (etc.) refers to something near the listener but removed from the speaker, whereas *aquél* (etc.) refers to something far from **both** the speaker and listener.

En aquella época . . .	At that time . . .
Aquellas montañas . . .	Those mountains . . .

Note: The definite article (*el, la, los, las*) followed by ***de*** or ***que*** is often translated as a pronoun.

mi corbata y ***la de*** *mi hermano*
my tie and **that of** my brother

Este libro y ***el que*** *tiene Juan son interesantes.*
This book and **the one that** Juan has are interesting.

NEUTER FORMS

The neuter forms (*eso, esto, aquello*) are used when the gender is not determined or when referring to vague or general ideas. These words do not vary in gender or number, and no accent is required.

¿Qué es esto?
What is this?

Estoy enfermo y esto me enoja.
I'm ill and this makes me angry.

Former and Latter

The pronoun *éste* (*–a, –os, –as*) is used to translate **the latter** (the latest or most recently mentioned), while *aquél* (*–la, –los, –las*) expresses **the former** (the most remotely mentioned).

Juana and Pablo are siblings; the former is a doctor, the latter is a dentist.
Juana y Pablo son hermanos; éste es dentista, aquélla es doctora.

Note: In English we say "the former and the latter," but in Spanish this order is reversed.

☞ Drill 10

1. Querida, ¿no crees que . . . anillo es tan lindo como los otros?

   (A) esto (C) este

   (B) aquello (D) esa

2. Mis nietos me regalaron . . . televisor.

   (A) eso (C) aquel

   (B) esto (D) esté

3. Muéstreme otro apartamento, no me gusta . . .

   (A) esto. (C) esté.

   (B) este. (D) éste.

4. . . . problemas son fáciles de resolver.

   (A) Estos (C) Estas

   (B) Estes (D) Esas

5. Llegó tarde y . . . me hace enojada.

   (A) eso (C) esta

   (B) ésta (D) aquel

6. ¿Qué es . . . ?

   (A) éste (C) ésto

   (B) esto (D) ésta

7. Estas camisas y . . . a lo lejos son caras.

   (A) ésos (C) aquellas

   (B) aquéllas (D) ésas

8. Rolando y Antonia son hermanos; ésta es alta y . . . es inteligente.

   (A) este
   (B) aquel
   (C) aquél
   (D) ése

9. Me gustan . . . guantes porque son de cuero.

   (A) estos
   (B) éstos
   (C) estas
   (D) éstas

10. Mi corbata y . . . Juan son de seda.

   (A) ella de
   (B) ésa de
   (C) éste de
   (D) la de

Drill 10—Detailed Explanations of Answers

1. **(C)** The masculine demonstrative adjective "este" means "this" and should be used to modify a masculine singular noun, just as is required by the sentence. "Esto" (this) in (A) and "aquello" (that) in (B) are pronouns, not adjectives, and they are neuter, i.e., they are neither masculine nor feminine. The neuter pronouns "esto," "eso" (that), and "aquello" (that) are used to refer to ideas or concepts (not specific nouns), for example "Llueve mucho aquí. **Eso** no me gusta." Here the word "eso" does not refer to any particular word, nor does it modify anything. Rather, as a pronoun, it stands for or takes the place of the whole idea which was previously expressed. "Llueve mucho aquí." "Esa" in (D) is clearly wrong because we cannot use a feminine form of the adjective to modify a masculine noun.

2. **(C)** The verb "regalar" means "to give a gift." A "televisor" is a "television set." Choice (D) is inappropriate because it is a form of the present tense of the subjunctive "estar." The syntax of the sentence does not require a verb in the blank. All of the remaining choices are demonstratives, but only one, "aquel" (that), may function as an adjective, which is what we need in the blank in order to modify the word "televisor." (A) "eso" (that) and (B) "esto" (this), are not adjectives, but rather **neuter demonstrative** pronouns. Because they are neuter (neither masculine nor feminine), they cannot be used to refer to any specific noun. Instead, they are used to refer to whole concepts or ideas which have previously been mentioned: Hace mucho calor en esta región y **esto** no me gusta" (It's very hot in this region, and I don't like this). The word "esto" in this sentence refers to no specific noun, but rather to the whole idea previously stated, "Hace mucho calor en esta región . . . "

3. **(D)** The demonstrative adjective form for "this" is converted into a pronoun by using the orthographic accent. (A) **Esto** is considered neuter, since it does not refer to a masculine or feminine noun. Choice (B) is the correct form for the masculine, but it needs the accent. Choice (C) is the correct form for the imperative. Only choice (D) is the proper form.

4. **(A)** "Problema" is masculine, which eliminates (C) and (D). The plural form of este (B) is estos.

5. **(A)** When referring to an entire event, happening, or occurrence, the neuter form "eso" is used. Choice (B) is the feminine singular demon-

strative pronoun meaning "this one." Choice (C) is the feminine singular demonstrative adjective meaning "this." Choice (D) is the masculine singular demonstrative adjective meaning "that" (in the distance).

6. **(B)** The neuter demonstrative is used when one doesn't know the gender of the item asked about. Choice (A) is the masculine singular demonstrative meaning "this one." Choice (C) is incorrect because the neuter forms do not require accent marks. Choice (D) is the feminine singular demonstrative pronoun meaning "this one."

7. **(B)** Because this demonstrative is replacing "camisas," it is being used as a pronoun and must, therefore, have the accent mark to differentiate it from the adjective. Also, "a lo lejos" (in the distance) requires some form of "aquél." Although (A) and (D) are pronouns, neither one is used for distance and (A) is the wrong gender. (C) is the demonstrative adjective meaning "that" and must precede a noun, *not* replace it.

8. **(C)** Latter (a form of "éste") and former (a form of "aquél") are expressed using the demonstrative pronouns. Whereas we say "the former . . . the latter," in Spanish this is reversed. In this sentence the former, Rolando, is being referred to by the statement " . . . es inteligente." Therefore, the masculine singular form "aquél" is needed to express "former." Choices (A) and (B) are incorrect because they are demonstrative adjectives. Choice (D) means "that one" and is not used to express "former or latter" in Spanish.

9. **(A)** "Guantes" (gloves) is the masculine noun requiring the demonstrative adjective. Choice (C) is incorrect because it is feminine. Choices (B) and (D) are demonstrative pronouns and cannot be used to modify nouns.

10. **(D)** Before the preposition **de,** the demonstrative is replaced by the definite article which will have the same gender as the noun referred to, in this case "corbata." Choices (B) and (C) are still in the demonstrative forms. Choice (C) also has the incorrect gender. Choice (A) makes no sense when translated ("she of").

RELATIVE PRONOUNS

Relative pronouns come in both a long and short form as follows:

que	who, that, which, whom	*el que/el cual, los que/los cuales* *la que/la cual , las que/las cuales*
quien	who, whom	
quienes	who, whom (plural)	

***El** hombre **que** vi es médico.*
The man that I saw is a doctor.

*La mujer con **quien** hablé es mi hermana.*
The woman with whom I spoke is my sister.

*Las chicas con **quienes** ando son estudiantes.*
The girls with whom I walk are students.

Note: When referring to people, after a preposition only *quien* or *quienes* may be used.

*La madre de Juan, **la que/la cual** está allí, llegó tarde.*
Juan's mom, who is there, arrived late.

*La madre de Juan, **que/quien** es médica, llegó.*
Juan's mom, who is a doctor, arrived.

*Aquí está la mesa, sobre **la que/la cual**, está la caja.*
Here's the table upon which is the box.

Note: The difference between ***el que/el cual*** is one of formality, ***el cual*** being more formal and less idiomatic than ***el que***.

Use of the Long Forms

With reference to the samples above, the long form of the relative pronoun is preferred when:

1. introducing a parenthetical clause whose antecedent is ambiguous; the long form always refers to the antecedent farthest away from that clause.

   Note: When referring to the closest of the double antecedent, use the shorter form.

2. using a long preposition followed by a relative pronoun.

   Note: ***por, sin,*** and ***para*** must be included since putting ***que*** after these words will result in a change in meaning.

por qué = why	*por la que* = through which
sin que = without + subj.	*sin la que* = without which
para que = so that + subj.	*para la que* = for which

The Neuter Pronouns

1. ***lo que*** — that which, what
   ***Lo que** dijo es verdad.* — What you said is true.
2. ***lo que/lo cual***
   "which" when referring to an entire idea, event, etc.

   Todos los estudiantes salieron bien, ***lo que/lo cual*** *le gustó a la maestra.*
   Everyone passed, which the teacher liked.
3. ***Todo lo que*** means "all that."

Note: ***Lo que/lo cual*** are only interchangeable when used as in (2) above. ***Que*** standing alone cannot be used.

Idiomatic Uses of the Pronouns

el que/quien	he who
la que/quien	she who
los que/quienes	those who
las que/quienes	those who (f)

Note: There are **no** accent marks. ***Quien*** is most commonly used in proverbs.

Whose = *Cuyo* vs. *De Quien*

Cuyo (***–a, –os, –as***) acts as an adjective and will agree with the noun following it.

El hombre cuya hija acaba de graduarse . . .
The man whose daughter has just graduated . . .

Note: When referring to parts of the body, use ***a quien*** instead of *cuyo.*

La niña, a quien la madre lavó las manos, es bonita.
The girl, whose hands her mother washed, is pretty.

De quién/de quiénes is an interrogative and is followed by a verb.

¿De quién es este libro?	Whose is this book?
No sé de quién es.	I don't know whose it is.

☞ Drill 11

1. Los señores de . . . te hablo son extranjeros aquí.

   (A) que
   (B) cuales
   (C) cuyos
   (D) quienes

2. Marta, . . . hijo es ingeniero, vive en Buenos Aires.

   (A) quien
   (B) cuya
   (C) de quien
   (D) cuyo

3. . . . que no puedo entender es por qué se fue sin decir adiós.

   (A) Lo
   (B) Ello
   (C) El
   (D) Esto

4. ¿Conoces a los hombres con . . . el jefe acaba de hablar?

   (A) quien
   (B) quienes
   (C) las cuales
   (D) que

5. . . . estudia, aprende.

   (A) Quienes
   (B) Lo que
   (C) El que
   (D) Él que

6. La chica, . . . la madre cortó el pelo, es mi amiga.

   (A) a que
   (B) a quien
   (C) de quién
   (D) cuya

7. El padre de Anita, . . . es profesora, acaba de morir.

   (A) quien
   (B) la cual
   (C) el cual
   (D) a quien

8. La puerta, por . . . entró la reina, es del siglo IX.

   (A) quien (C) qué

   (B) cual (D) la cual

9. Mi hija Anita juega bien al tenis, . . . es bueno.

   (A) que (C) cual

   (B) lo cual (D) quien

10. En este edificio hay una gran ventana, . . . se ve las montañas.

    (A) por la cual (C) por que

    (B) por cual (D) por el que

Drill 11—Detailed Explanations of Answers

1. **(D)** We need a relative pronoun to complete the sentence correctly. A relative pronoun is one that relates back to a specific noun, pronoun, or idea stated earlier in the sentence (in this case, "señores"). The most common relative pronoun for both people and things is "que," but **following a preposition** (in this case, "de"), if we are referring to people, we may **not** use "que." On the contrary, we use "quien" (if we are referring back to a singular noun) or "quienes" (if we are referring back to a plural noun, as is the case in our sentence). The longer forms of the relative pronoun, "los que" and "los cuales," may also be used in this same situation, but are perhaps less frequent. Note that these must agree in number and gender with the noun to which they refer. Choices (A) and (B) could be correct only if we placed "los" in front of them.

2. **(D)** In our sentence, the word "ingeniero" means "engineer." "Cuyo" is a relative adjective which means "whose." By "relative" we mean a word which relates back to a noun which is previously mentioned in the sentence. In this instance, "cuyo" relates back to "Marta." It is she whose son is an engineer. Since "cuyo" is an adjective, it must agree in number and gender with the noun which follows it. In this case, then, "cuyo" agrees with "hijo," not with "Marta," and must be masculine singular. "Cuyo" and its other forms ("cuya," "cuyos," and "cuyas") are not used as interrogatives, i.e., to ask questions. If we want to ask "Whose is this book?", we would have to inquire "¿De quién es este libro?" Choice (A) "quien" is incorrect, for it is not the masculine form and cannot modify "hijo." (C) "de quien" will not fit because it cannot be followed immediately by a noun. It means "of whom."

3. **(A)** For this answer you need to remember that "que" is preceded by "lo" (a particle that never varies regardless of the context) when the construction can be translated as "that which."

4. **(B)** After a preposition when referring to a person or persons, a form of "quien" or "quienes" is needed. Because the antecedent (hombres) is plural, choice (B) is correct. Choice (C) could have qualified if it were masculine and choice (D) cannot refer to people.

5. **(C)** Although this sentence translates as "he who" studies, learns, the relative pronoun without the accent is the correct answer. Choice (A)

does not qualify because it is plural. Choice (B) means "that which" and choice (D) has an accent and is, therefore, incorrect.

6. **(B)** When referring to parts of the body, use **a quien** instead of a form of **cuyo**, which eliminates choice (D). Choice (C) is incorrect because it means "whose" as an interrogative and would be followed by a verb. Choice (A) means "to which" and makes no sense in this sentence. Also, after a preposition, when referring to people use quien or quienes.

7. **(A)** When referring to the last person mentioned in the double antecedent, a form of "quien" is used. Because it is stated that this person is a "profesora," we know the clause refers to Anita. Choice (C) would be correct if referring to the "padre." Choice (B) is the long form and would need to refer to "padre" which is the wrong gender, and choice (D) means "whom" or "to whom," which is not grammatically correct.

8. **(D)** The longer forms of the relative pronouns follow long prepositions or, as in this case, ones that would change meaning if used with the short form. In this case the translation "through which" cannot be stated using choice (C) "por qué" since that would mean "why." Choice (A) refers to people and choice (B) requires a definite article (in this case **la**) to be correct.

9. **(B)** The neuter form **lo cual** is correct since the second part of the sentence ("which is good") refers to the entire event or occurrence (the fact that Anita plays tennis well) stated in the first part of this sentence Choices (A) and (C) would each need "lo" to be correct. Choice (D) would refer to people.

10. **(A)** Choices (A) and (D) each mean "through which"; however, because the antecedent is feminine (ventana), choice (A) is correct. Choice (B) would need the definite article "la" to be correct. Choice (C) is confusing since it could be "why" if it had an accent.

AFFIRMATIVES AND NEGATIVES

The Affirmative and Negative Words

no	no	*sí*	yes
nadie	nobody, no one	*alguien*	someone
nada	nothing	*algo*	something
tampoco	neither	*también*	also
sin	without	*con*	with
ni . . . ni	neither . . . nor	*o . . . o*	either . . . or
jamás	never, not ever	*siempre*	always
nunca	never		
*ninguno**	no, none	*alguno**	some, any

* See explanation that follows.

Negative Expressions

ni (yo, Juan, ella) tampoco	nor (I, Juan, she) either
ni siquiera	not even
ya no	no longer
todavía no	not yet
sin novedad	nothing new
no . . . más que	only
no . . . más de	no more than
ahora no	not now
más que	more than
mejor que	better than
peor que	worse than
antes de	before
de ningún modo	by no means
de ninguna manera	by no means
apenas	hardly
no sólo . . . sino también	not only . . . but also

The Rules for Usage

Unlike English, statements with double (or more) negatives are correct. A negative sentence in Spanish, whether it has only one negative word or many, **must have** one negative **before** the verb. If there is more than **one** negative, the Spanish sentence may be written two ways.

***No** tengo **nada**.*	***Nada** tengo.*
***No** veo a **nadie**.**	***A nadie** veo.*
***No** como **ni** pan **ni** queso.*	***Ni** pan **ni** queso como.*

Sentences with multiple negatives are common.

No *dije* ***nunca nada a nadie.***
I **never** said **anything to anyone**.

*If a personal *a* is required, it must accompany the negative.

Use of *Ninguno*

The plural forms of ***ninguno***, – ***a*** are no longer used. This word may be used with the noun or to replace the noun. *Ninguno, –a* and alguno, *–a, –os, –as* have shortened forms before masculine, singular nouns: *ningún, algún.*

Ningún *libro . . . no tengo* ***ninguno.***
No book . . . I don't have any.

Ninguna *pluma . . . no hay* ***ninguna*** *aquí.*
No pen . . . there isn't any here.

Ninguno *de ellos salió.*
None of them left.

Ninguna *de ellas irá.*
None of them will go.

¿Tiene amigos Juan?
Does Juan have friends?

No tiene ***ninguno.***
He hasn't any.

Use of *Alguno*

When *alguno*, *–a* follows a noun in Spanish, it makes the negative more emphatic (= at all). This happens with singular nouns only.

Juan ***no*** *tiene* ***ninguna*** *amiga.*
Juan doesn't have **any** girlfriend.

Juan ***no*** *tiene amiga* ***alguna.***
Juan doesn't have a girlfriend **at all**.

Uses of *Jamás* and *Nunca*

The English **"never"** is normally expressed by ***nunca*** and **"never again"** by ***nunca más***. In modern Spanish, ***jamás*** is a learned form mainly in literature. In spoken Spanish it is used to give great emphasis to **never**. In that case it means **absolutely never**.

*No volvió **jamás** a ver a su novia.*
He never again saw his fiancée.

***Jamás** lo sabrás.*
You'll absolutely never know it.

¡Nunca jamás!
Never again!

Jamás also means **ever** in a question expecting a negative answer.

*¿Ha visto Ud. **jamás** nada que iguale a esto? ¡**Nunca**!*
Have you **ever** seen anything to equal this? **Never**!

Nada as Intensifier

Nada may be used adverbially with the meaning "not at all."

Manuel no trabaja nada.
Manuel does absolutely no work.

No hemos dormido nada.
We haven't slept a wink.

No ha sido nada cómodo el cuarto.
The room wasn't comfortable at all.

Algo to Mean "Somewhat"

Algo may be placed before an adjective to express the meaning "somewhat."

Este curso es algo fácil.
This course is somewhat easy.

Estamos algo inquietos.
We are somewhat worried.

Note: *¿Sabes una cosa?*
Do you know something?

¿Sabes algo?
Do you know anything?

Pero vs. *Sino/Sino Que*

Pero, sino, and *sino que* all mean **but**. However, *sino* and *sino que* are used:

(a) when the first clause is negative **and**

(b) the second clause contradicts the first—this contrast must be between two equivalent parts of speech (noun–noun, adjective–adjective, infinitive–infinitive). ***Sino que*** connects the same way but must be followed by a **conjugated** verb.

No habla español, ***sino*** *inglés.* He doesn't speak Spanish, but English.	noun–noun
No le gusta blanco, ***sino*** *azul.* He doesn't like white, but blue.	adjective–adjective
No quiere estudiar, ***sino*** *jugar.* He doesn't want to study, but to play.	infinitive–infinitive
No cerró la puerta, ***sino que*** *la dejó abierta.* He didn't leave the door open, but left it closed.	conjugated verb– conjugated verb

But: *No habla bien,* ***pero*** *me gusta su traje.*
He doesn't speak well, but I like his suit.

Note: *Pero* = "but nevertheless"
Sino = "but on the contrary"

☞ Drill 12

1. Viene a vernos . . .

   (A) nunca. (C) nadie.

   (B) alguien. (D) jamás.

2. No me dijo . . . sobre el asunto

   (A) nadie (C) algo

   (B) nada (D) ninguno

3. ¿Tienes algunos amigos íntimos? No, no tengo . . .

   (A) ningunos. (C) ningún.

   (B) nadie. (D) ninguno.

4. . . . día voy a hacerme médico.

   (A) Alguna (C) Ninguno

   (B) Algún (D) Alguno

5. Nunca hace nada por nadie. No tiene . . .

   (A) amigo alguno. (C) algún amigo.

   (B) ningunos amigos. (D) amigos algunos.

6. Él juega mejor que . . .

   (A) algo. (C) alguien.

   (B) ninguno. (D) nadie.

7. Nadie va con ellos, ni con Juan . . .

   (A) ni. (C) nadie.

   (B) tampoco. (D) también.

8. . . . de las camisas me queda bien.

(A) Nada
(B) Ninguna
(C) Ningún
(D) Ningunas

9. . . . veo en el estadio.

(A) Nadie
(B) Ningún
(C) A nada
(D) A nadie

10. Sin decirme . . . , se fue para siempre.

(A) algo
(B) alguna cosa
(C) nada
(D) ninguno

Drill 12—Detailed Explanations of Answers

1. **(B)** Choices (A), (C), and (D) are all negatives. None of them can be used in the blank because, if a negative word such as "nunca" (never), "nadie" (no one), "ninguno" (none, not any, no one), or "jamás" (never) come after the verb, then there must be a "no" in front of the verb. In other words, we must use a double negative. This does not happen in this sentence. Of the four choices, only the indefinite "alguien" (someone) is acceptable.

2. **(B)** In Spanish the double negative is required when "no" is at the beginning of the sentence, which eliminates (C) because "algo" is a positive particle. Choice (A) is not appropriate because "nadie" refers to persons, and (D) is equally inappropriate because there is no specific antecedent in the question to which "ninguno" could refer.

3. **(D)** "Ninguno" is used exclusively in the singular forms either to modify or refer to previously mentioned nouns. Choice (A) is incorrect because it is plural. Choice (B) means "nobody" and cannot be used to replace the noun "amigos." Choice (C) is apocopated which is not necessary since it does not precede a masculine noun.

4. **(B)** Both "alguno" and "ninguno" have apocopated forms (drop the –o) before masculine singular nouns. "Día" is a masculine singular noun which makes (A) incorrect because it is feminine. Choice (C) and (D) would need to be apocopated to be used correctly before "día."

5. **(A)** When a form of "alguno" is used **after** the noun, it makes the statement more negative and is commonly translated with "at all." Because it is being used like "ninguno" in this type of statement, it will only be correct in the singular forms. Because both (B) and (D) are plural, neither is correct. Although (C) is singular, because "algún" precedes the noun it no longer is a negative and would only be correct in this statement written as "ningún."

6. **(D)** Comparative expressions like "mejor que" (better than), "peor que" (worse than), and "más que" (more than), for example, are negative. Therefore, (A) and (C), which are both affirmative cannot follow this expression. Choice (B), although negative, is incorrect since there is no noun to which it refers.

7. **(B)** The expression "ni . . . tampoco" (nor . . . neither) is used in statements such as this one. "Tampoco" is the negative form of "también" (also). Choice (A) cannot be used because "ni" must be followed by something, a noun, pronoun, verb, etc., to be used. It cannot stand alone. Choice (C) which means "no one or nobody" makes no sense in this statement. "También" (also) is affirmative and cannot be used after the negative "ni."

8. **(B)** Forms of "ninguno" are used only in the singular and modify or refer to nouns. In this statement, this word refers to "camisas" which is feminine. "Ninguna" in this sample is also the subject of "queda." Choice (A), "nada," can not be used to modify nouns. Choice (C) is incorrect because it is apocopated and this can only occur before a masculine singular noun. Choice (D) is incorrect because it is plural.

9. **(D)** Because "nadie" is the direct object of the verb "veo" in this example and also refers to a person, the personal "a" is required before it whether it precedes or follows the verb. Choice (A) needs a personal "a." Choice (B) can only be used before masculine singular nouns. Choice (C) means "to nothing" and makes no sense in this context.

10. **(C)** "Sin" is a preposition that is considered negative. Choices (A) and (B) are both affirmative forms. Choice (D) must have a noun either to modify or to refer to.

INTERROGATIVES

Interrogative Words

qué	what, which, what a + noun
quién, quiénes	who, which one(s)
cuál, cuáles	which, what, which one(s)
cuánto, –a, –os, –as	how much, how many
cuándo	when
dónde	where
adónde	(to) where
por qué	why (answer uses porque)
para qué	why (answer uses para)
cómo	how
a quién, a quiénes	whom
de quién, de quiénes	whose

Note: **All** interrogatives have accent marks.

Uses of *Qué*

a) To ask a definition:

¿Qué es el amor?
What is love?

b) To ask about things not yet mentioned (choice involved):

¿Qué prefieres, manzanas o peras?
Which ones do you prefer, apples or pears?

c) To express **what a**!:

¡Qué día (tan/más) hermoso!
What a beautiful day!

d) To precede a noun:

¿Qué clases te gustan?
What/which classes do you like?

Uses of *Cuál/Cuáles*

a) Followed by *de* = which one(s) of several:

*¿**Cuál** de los libros es más necesario?*
Which of the books is most necessary?

b) Refers to a definite object already mentioned (choice involved):

*Hay dos vestidos, ¿**cuál** prefieres?*
There are two dresses, **which** do you prefer?

c) Followed by ***ser–*** when there are a number of possibilities:

*¿**Cuál** es la fecha?*
What is the date?

*¿**Cuál** es la capital?*
What is the capital?

Por Qué, Para Qué, and *Porque*

Por qué and ***para qué*** both mean *why*. The former is used if the expected answer will begin with ***porque*** (because). The latter starts a question where the expected answer will begin with ***para*** (in order to).

*¿**Por qué** vas al cine?*
Why do you go to the movies?

***Porque me** gusta la película.*
Because I like the film.

*¿**Para qué** vas al cine?*
Why do you go to the movies?

***Para** ver a mi actor favorito.*
In order to see my favorite actor.

Dónde/Adónde vs. *Donde*

a) ***Adónde*** is used with verbs of motion.

¿***Adónde*** vas?
Where are you going?

b) ***Donde*** (without the accent) requires a noun to refer to.

*La casa **donde** vivo es vieja.*
The house **where** (in which) I live is old.

c) ***Dónde*** (with accent) is the interrogative.

*¿**Dónde** está la casa?*
Where is the house?

Note: There are other combinations with ***dónde . . . de dónde***, ***por dónde***, etc.

Cuándo vs. *Cuando*

a) ***Cuando*** (without accent) can be replaced by **as** and not change the meaning drastically.

Te lo diré ***cuando*** *venga Julio.*
I'll tell you **when/as** Julio arrives.

b) ***Cuándo*** (with accent) is the interrogative.

*¿**Cuándo** vas a salir?*
When are you going to leave?

Quién/Quiénes

a) With prepositions to refer to people:

*¿**Con quién** hablas?*
With whom do you speak?

b) With ***de*** to express **whose**:

*¿**De quién** es el carro?*
Whose is the car? (Whose car is it?)

Note: The word order must be changed to express the Spanish sentence correctly: **Of whom** is the car?

A Quién/A Quiénes

Whom is often misused in English. It is used as the object of the verb. **Who**, on the other hand, can only be the subject of the verb. Note the differences below.

Who is the subject of "is."

Who is going with me? *¿**Quién** va conmigo?*

Whom is the object of "see"; the subject is **you**.

Whom do you see? *¿**A quién** ves?*

In Spanish the **whom** statements are actually a combination of the **personal *"a"*** and the words ***quién/quiénes***. In some sentences, the ***"a"*** may act as an actual preposition and have a translation.

*¿**A quién** escribiste?*
To **whom** did you write?

*¿**A quiénes** enviaron el paquete?*
To **whom** did they send the package?

☞ Drill 13

1. ¿ . . . es tu número de teléfono?

   (A) Qué
   (B) Cual
   (C) Que
   (D) Cuál

2. ¿ . . . día es hoy?

   (A) Cuál
   (B) Qué
   (C) Cómo
   (D) A cuál

3. ¿ . . . de los libros es mejor?

   (A) Cuáles
   (B) Cuál
   (C) Qué
   (D) Quiénes

4. Mama, ¿ . . . sirven los anteojos?

   (A) porque
   (B) por qué
   (C) para que
   (D) para

5. ¿ . . . vestidos quieres comprar?

   (A) Cuál
   (B) Qué
   (C) Cuáles
   (D) Cómo

6. El pueblo . . . vivo es viejo.

   (A) donde
   (B) dónde
   (C) a donde
   (D) que

7. No sé . . . es ese carro.

   (A) quién
   (B) de quien
   (C) que
   (D) de quién

8. ¡ . . . día más hermoso!

   (A) Qué un
   (B) Cuál
   (C) Qué
   (D) Qué una

9. ¿ . . . es la astronomía?

   (A) Qué
   (B) Cuál
   (C) Quién
   (D) A quién

10. ¿ . . . son los meses del año?

   (A) Cuál
   (B) Cuáles
   (C) Qué
   (D) De quién

Drill 13—Detailed Explanations of Answers

1. **(D)** From the question marks in our sentence we can tell that we need an interrogative pronoun, a pronoun which asks a question, in the blank. There are only two of these given in the list of possible answers: (A) "Qué" and (D) "Cuál." How do we know that these two are interrogative pronouns? Because this type of pronoun always bears an accent mark. The word "Que," in (C), is a relative pronoun, one that relates back to a previous noun in a sentence: "Los turistas **que** hablan francés . . . " Here the "que" refers back to "turistas." In (B), the word "Cual" is part of another relative pronoun, "el cual," "la cual," "lo cual," which is designed to show gender and is used for the sake of clarity when we have previously been talking about two nouns: "La madre de José, la cual tiene dos hermanos, viaja por España." If we did not use this longer, feminine form ("la cual"), i.e., if we were to say instead "que" or "quien," we would be referring to the noun immediately preceding the relative pronoun ("José"). But since we want to show that it is José's mother, and not José, who has two brothers, then we must use this longer pronoun or its alternate form, "la que." In English, we say "What is your telephone number?" In Spanish, the interrogative word "qué" asks for a definition. If we ask "¿Qué es la física?", we are asking for a definition of what physics is. In our sentence, we do not want to ask for a definition of what one's telephone number is, which is what (A) "Qué" would imply. Instead, we must ask, "Which one" ("Cuál"), out of all the possible numbers in the directory, is your phone number. In other words, "cuál" asks for a choice or selection from a number of possibilities.

2. **(B)** Before a noun "qué" means what/which. Choice (A) is not correct because it cannot modify a noun. Choice (C) means "how" and (D) means "to which."

3. **(B)** "Cuál" is used with a form of **ser** to mean "which." It is also the subject of the verb, which is singular. Choice (A) is incorrect because it is plural. Choice (D) means who and choice (C), which can also mean what/which, cannot be used before a "de" phrase where there is an indication of choice.

4. **(C)** "Para qué" is used when the question intimates "for what purpose/use." Choice (A) "because" and (D) "in order to" are not interrogatives and make no sense. Choice (B) means "why" and does not fit within the intended meaning of this question.

5. **(B)** "Qué" is used before a noun to mean what/which. Therefore, choices (A) and (C) are incorrect since neither can precede a noun. Choice (D) means "how."

6. **(A)** "Donde" without an accent requires a noun to refer to, in this case "pueblo." Because an indirect question is not being asked, choice (B) is incorrect since all interrogatives have accent marks. Choice (C) is used in questions with verbs of motion (i.e., Where are you going?). Choice (D) is the relative pronoun meaning "that."

7. **(D)** Because an indirect question is being asked, the accented form of "whose" is required. This would make choice (B) incorrect. Choice (A) means "who" and choice (C) is a relative pronoun meaning "that."

8. **(C)** Because "¡qué!" in this context means "What a!" and the indefinite article (a) is included in its translation, choices (A) and (D) would be incorrect. Choice (B) is never used to mean "What a!" and again a form of "cuál" is not correct before a noun.

9. **(A)** "Qué" is used before a form of **ser** when asking for a definition, as in this example. Choices (C) "who" and (D) "whom" make no sense. "Cual" precedes a form of **ser** when there are a number of possibilities, which makes choice (B) incorrect.

10. **(B)** A form of "cuál" will precede a form of **ser** when a number of possibilities are given to choose from (i.e., months). Because it is the subject of the verb and because the verb is plural, choice (A) is incorrect. Answer (D) means "whose" and makes no sense in this context. Choice (C) can only be used before a form of **ser** when asking a definition.

THE PERSONAL *A*

Normally the preposition ***a*** means **to** or **at** in Spanish. There are instances when this preposition will appear in the sentence with **no** apparent translation into English. In this case this preposition is called the Personal *A*. This *a* will appear in the Spanish sentence if the **direct object** of the verb:

a) refers to a person in some way:

No veo a Juan/a su amigo/al ejército/a nadie.
I don't see Juan/his friend/the army/anyone.

b) refers to a domestic animal:

Juan ama mucho a su perro, Spot.
Juan loves his dog, Spot.

c) refers to a specific geographical location (if **it does not** have an article):

Visito a España/a Barcelona/a México.
I visit Spain/Barcelona/Mexico.

But: *Visito* ***el*** *Perú.* I visit Peru.

Omission of the Personal *A*

a) After the verb *tener*, unless it means "keep/hold":

Tengo dos hermanos. I have two brothers.

But: *Tengo al culpable en la cárcel.* I have the guilty one in jail.

b) Before an indefinite personal direct object (usually modified by a numeral or an indefinite article):

Vi ***tres*** *hombres en el bosque.* (numeral)
I saw three men in the forest.

Oí ***un*** *ladrón dentro del banco.* (indefinite article)
I heard a thief inside the bank.

c) When the Personal *A* would be in close proximity to another *a* (such as one meaning to, at, toward or the *a* preceding an indirect object):

Presenté mi esposo a mis amigos.
I introduced my husband to my friends.

POSSESSIVES: ADJECTIVES/PRONOUNS

The Possessive Adjectives:

my	*mi, mis*	our	*nuestro, –a, –os, –as*
your	*tu, tus*	your	*vuestro, –a, –os, –as*
his/her/your	*su, sus*	their/your	*su, sus*

The possessive adjectives precede the noun they modify and match it as closely as possible in gender and number.

mi casa, mis casas	my house, my houses
nuestra pluma, nuestras plumas	our pen, our pens

Because the third person adjective has several possible translations, the following may be done for clarification:

su casa =	his house	*la casa* ***de él***
	her house	*la casa* ***de ella***
	your house (s)	*la casa* ***de Ud.***
	their house (f)	*la casa* ***de ellas***
	their house (m)	*la casa* ***de ellos***
	your house (pl)	*la casa* ***de Uds.***

The Possessive Pronouns

The pronoun group is used **to replace** the noun already stated and, therefore, takes on the properties of that noun. This includes retention of the definite article. Also note the difference in translation.

mine	el mío, la mía los míos, las mías
yours	el tuyo, la tuya los tuyos, las tuyas
his/hers/yours	el suyo, la suya los suyos, las suyas
ours	el nuestro, la nuestra los nuestros, las nuestras
yours	el vuestro, la vuestra los vuestros, las vuestras
theirs/yours	el suyo, la suya los suyos, las suyas

Again, because the third person pronouns have several possible meanings, clarification with the prepositional phrase is also possible. With the pronouns, however, the definite article must be retained.

mi coche y el suyo	my car and his	*y **el de él***
	my car and hers	*y **el de ella***
	my car and yours	*y **el de Ud.***
	my car and theirs (f)	*y **el de ellas***
	my car and theirs (m)	*y **el de ellos***
	my car and yours	*y **el de Uds.***

Uses of the Pronouns

The possessive pronouns are used primarily in three areas:

a) As the replacement for the noun:

my house and **ours** — *mi casa y **la nuestra***

b) As an "adjective" with nouns as follows:

several friends of **mine** — *unos amigos **míos***

Note: "of" is **not** expressed.

c) As the possessive used after *ser*:

¿Este vestido?	This dress?
*Es **tuyo**.*	It is **yours**.
¿Estos carros?	These cars?
*Son **nuestros**.*	They are **ours**.

Note: The definite article is normally omitted after *ser*.

Possessives with Clothing/Body Parts

Normally with parts of the body and clothing, the possessive adjective is replaced by the definite article. However, in the following instances, the possessive is correct.

a) With body parts:

1. When ambiguity would result without it.
2. When the body part is modified.

   Ella levantó sus grandes ojos azules.

3. When the body part is the subject.

   Tus manos tienen callos.

b) With clothing:

   1. When the article worn is the subject.

      Su camisa está allí.

   2. When the article is **not** being worn by the subject.

      Encontré ***mis*** *calcetines allí.*

☞ Drill 14

1. Ayer vimos . . . señorita Corrales.
   (A) a la
   (B) la
   (C) a
   (D) la a

2. Mi hermana es más alta que . . .
   (A) la suya.
   (B) el suyo.
   (C) su.
   (D) mía.

3. ¿Conoce Ud. . . . padres?
   (A) mi
   (B) mis
   (C) a mis
   (D) míos

4. Su amigo es más inteligente que . . .
   (A) la nuestra.
   (B) el nuestro.
   (C) los míos.
   (D) la mía.

5. Los hombres se pusieron . . . antes de salir.
   (A) el sombrero
   (B) sus sombreros
   (C) su sombrero
   (D) sombreros

6. Se quitaron . . . al entrar en la casa.
   (A) sus abrigos
   (B) su abrigo
   (C) sus guantes
   (D) el abrigo

7. ¿De quién es este lápiz? –Es . . .
   (A) mío.
   (B) el mío.
   (C) de mi.
   (D) de mí.

8. Mis hermanas y . . . Isabel son bellas.

(A) las que
(C) las
(B) las de
(D) aquellas

9. Tu casa es más grande que . . .

(A) el mío.
(C) mío.
(B) mi.
(D) la mía.

10. Sus pirámides y . . . vienen de épocas distintas.

(A) los nuestros
(C) las nuestras
(B) nuestros
(D) nuestras

11. Tengo . . . padre en el hospital.

(A) mi
(C) a mi
(B) a mí
(D) el

Drill 14—Detailed Explanations of Answers

1. **(A)** The personal **a** must be used when speaking about a person, and the article should accompany a title when not in direct address. The answer (A) is the only one fulfilling these requirements.

2. **(A)** The long form of the possessive is used when the noun is replaced. Because the possessive is now being used as a pronoun, it will take on the properties of the noun it has replaced, including the definite article. The noun in this example is "hermana." Choice (B) is incorrect because it is the wrong gender. Choice (C) is a possessive adjective and must be used with a noun. Choice (D) is the possessive pronoun but needs an article.

3. **(C)** The possessive adjective is required to match the noun "padres." Also, because "padres" is the direct object of the verb and refers to a person, the personal **a** is also required. Choice (A) needs to be plural and have a personal **a**. Choice (B) needs the personal **a** and choice (D) is the possessive pronoun which cannot precede the noun.

4. **(B)** All choices are possessive pronouns but only (B) is the correct gender for "amigo."

5. **(A)** With parts of the body and clothing in Spanish, the possessive is replaced by the definite article. The ownership is established by the reflexive pronoun. In addition, in Spanish, each person wears only **one** hat at a time and even if the subject is plural, the article of clothing remains singular. Answer (C) has the possessive and is incorrect. Choice (B) is plural and has the possessive and choice (D) needs to be singular with a definite article to be correct.

6. **(D)** For the same reason given in number 5 above, each person wears only one coat and the possessive must be replaced by the definite article. Choice (A), therefore, is incorrect because it is plural and has retained the possessive. Choice (B) needs to replace the possessive with the article "el." Choice (C) would be correct if "sus" were replaced with "los" since gloves are worn in pairs.

7. **(A)** The long form of the possessive is used to replace a noun previously referred to. In this example, the noun is "lápiz." Normally, the long form has a definite article. However, after **ser** the article is omitted.

Choice (B) is incorrect because it has the article. Choice (C) means "of my" and choice (D) is incorrect because in spoken Spanish "of me" is not used in this manner. Forms of "mío" are used instead.

8. **(B)** To eliminate **'s** in Spanish, an **of** phrase is used. When replacing a possessive such as this one (Isabel's) wherein there is a name to deal with, the definite article is retained followed by **de**. Because the noun here is "hermanas," the feminine plural article is needed. Neither (C) nor (D) makes sense when placed directly before Isabel. Choice (A) can be translated "those that or those who" but neither makes sense in front of Isabel.

9. **(D)** The long form of the possessive with the definite article is needed to replace the noun previously mentioned ("casa"). Choice (A) is the wrong gender. Choice (B) is the possessive adjective which means "my" and must precede a noun, and choice (C) needs to be feminine with an article to be correct.

10. **(C)** Again, the long form of the possessive with the definite article is needed to replace the noun previously mentioned ("pirámides") which is feminine plural. Choice (A) is the wrong gender. Choice (B) is the wrong gender and needs an article, and choice (D) needs a definite article to be correct.

11. **(C)** The personal **a** is used after **tener** when it means "keep or hold" as it does in this sample. Also, the possessive adjective "mi" has no accent. Choice (A) needs a personal **a**. In choice (B) the accented "mí" means me and is prepositional, not possessive. Choice (D) needs a personal **a**.

THE PASSIVE VOICE

The passive voice is the "mirror image" of the active voice. In passive voice statements the subject receives the action of the verb instead of actually doing it.

Active:	I built the house. *Construí la casa.*
Passive:	The house was built by me. *La casa fue construida por mí.*

The combination of ***ser*** with the **past participle** of the transitive verb constitutes the "true passive" in Spanish. The past participle is used as an adjective and must agree with the subject in number and gender. The formula follows:

ser + **past participle** + ***por*** + **agent** (doer)

Whenever the agent is expressed, this formula is used.

Agent Expressed by *De*

By is normally translated by ***por***. If, however, the past participle expresses feelings or emotion, **by** is translated by ***de***.

Juana es amada (respetada, odiada, admirada) ***de*** *todos.*
Juana is loved (respected, hated, admired) by all.

Reflexive Substitute for the Passive Voice

Commonly when the agent is **not** expressed and the subject is a thing, the passive "Spanish" statement will be written using the third person singular or plural of the verb with the pronoun ***se***.

Aquí ***se habla*** *español.*	Spanish is spoken here.
Se vendieron *guantes allí.*	Gloves were sold there.

Note: The subject follows the verb.

Third Person Plural Active Equivalent for Passive Voice

The best way to avoid using a passive construction is to convert the passive statement to an active one by using the subject **they**.

The house was sold.	=	They sold the house.
Se vendió la casa.	=	*Vendieron la casa.*

No Agent Expressed, Person Acted Upon

In sentences where the agent is indefinite (not mentioned or implied) and a person is acted upon, the indefinite ***se*** is coupled with the **third singular** of the verb.

The man was killed. ***Se mató*** *al hombre.*	He was killed. ***Se le mató.***
The girls will be punished. ***Se castigará*** *a las chicas.*	They will be punished. ***Se las castigará.***

Note: The person acted upon is the direct object of the Spanish sentence. Therefore, direct object pronouns are used to replace it, with one exception—***les*** is used instead of ***los*** for the masculine plural.

The men will be killed. ***Se matará a*** *los hombres.*	They will be killed. ***Se les matará.***

Idiomatic Expressions with *Se*

Se plus the third person singular of the verb will render "impersonal" subject statements. In English we say **people, one, they, you** and the like. This type of statement may also be translated as a passive construction.

se dice =	it is said	***se cree =***	it is believed
[dicen]	people say	***[creen]***	people believe
	they say		they believe
	one says		one believes
	you say		you believe

This may also be rendered with the third plural of the verb.

The Apparent Passive: *Estar* Plus the Past Participle

The true passive in Spanish is formed with *ser* and a past participle. Constructions formed with *estar* and a past participle are different. Instead of expressing an action carried out by an explicit or implicit agent, the apparent passive denotes a state or a condition resulting from a previous action. The past participle becomes an adjective. Compare the following examples:

Apparent Passive

La puerta ***está*** *abierta.*
The door **is** open. (The action of opening it happened earlier.)

True Passive

La puerta ***es abierta*** *(por el niño).*
The door **is opened** (by the boy). (We see the action happening now.)

Apparent Passive

La pieza ***estaba*** *reservada.*
The room **was** reserved. (Someone reserved it earlier.)

True Passive

La pieza había ***sido reservada*** *(por el turista).*
The room had **been reserved** (by the tourist).

☞ Drill 15

1. . . . la mujer.

   (A) Asesinaron a
   (B) Se asesinaron a
   (C) Asesinamos
   (D) Fue asesinado

2. La universidad . . . por el presidente Juárez.

   (A) fundó
   (B) estaba fundado
   (C) fue establecida
   (D) se estableció

3. El asesino fue . . . por el policía.

   (A) muerto
   (B) matado
   (C) morido
   (D) muriendo

4. La ventana . . . abierta por el viento.

   (A) sido
   (B) estuvo
   (C) estaba
   (D) fue

5. La señora García es respetada . . . todos los alumnos.

   (A) de
   (B) por
   (C) a
   (D) con

6. . . . que va a mejorar la economía.

   (A) Se dicen
   (B) Es dicho
   (C) Se dice
   (D) Está dicho

7. Aquí . . . español e inglés.

   (A) es hablado
   (B) se habla
   (C) son hablados
   (D) se hablan

8. ¿Los traidores? . . . matará mañana.

   (A) Se les
   (B) Se los
   (C) Se
   (D) Los

9. Al entrar, vi que las ventanas . . . abiertas.

   (A) fueron
   (B) estaban
   (C) han sido
   (D) han estado

10. Esas casas fueron . . . por un arquitecto famoso.

   (A) construida
   (B) construido
   (C) construidos
   (D) construidas

Drill 15—Detailed Explanations of Answers

1. **(A)** When a person is acted upon in a passive voice sentence, the statement may be expressed three ways: by using true passive (ser + past participle) which matches the noun (thus eliminating answer choice (D)), by using an active voice statement requiring the personal **a** (thus eliminating choice (C)), or by using the third singular of the verb preceded by the reflexive **se** followed by the personal **a** (thus eliminating choice (B)). (A) is correct in the active voice with the personal **a**.

2. **(C)** Choice (A) "fundó" means "founded," but it will not function in the sentence because the "university" ("universidad") did not found anything. On the contrary, it was founded "**by** President Juárez." This gets us into what is called the passive voice. In a passive sentence, the subject is acted upon by someone or something. In our sentence, the subject, "universidad," is acted upon by "el presidente Juárez." To form the passive voice in Spanish, we follow this pattern: the proper tense and form of the verb "ser" + past participle. Look at the correct answer: "fue establecida." You will see that we have followed this pattern. One other thing you will notice is that in the passive voice the past participle always agrees in number and gender with the subject. In our sentence, "establecida" is feminine singular to agree with "universidad." Observe also that the verb "fue" is third person singular since the subject, "universidad," is a singular noun. The passive voice must always be used when the subject is acted upon and the doer of the action is expressed by a "por" phrase ("por el presidente Juárez"). (B) "estaba fundado" is incorrect because (1) we have not used the verb "ser," but rather "estar" (therefore, we are not indicating an action; we are merely describing a state), and (2) the past participle does not agree with the subject "universidad." Now look at (D), "se estableció." Sometimes the reflexive form of the verb can be used as a substitute for the true passive voice, but never when we have a "por" phrase which indicates who did the action, as is the case in our sentence.

3. **(A)** The last two choices are ungrammatical. In order to identify the correct answer, you have to know that the past participle of the verb "matar" is "muerto" when the sentence refers to people.

4. **(D)** To get the right answer you must recognize that this construction is in the passive voice, which means that it's always formed with the

appropriate form of "ser"—but not with the past participle (as in choice (A)) because this particular form needs the support of "haber."

5. **(A)** In a passive voice statement **by** is usually translated by **por**. If the past participle expresses feeling or emotion, rather than action, **by** is translated by **de**. Therefore, choice (B) is incorrect. Because **de** is the only choice to complete this passive statement, (C) and (D) are both incorrect.

6. **(C)** The pronoun **se** used with the third singular of the verb expresses an indefinite subject. This can be translated a number of ways: it is said, people say, they say, one says, etc. Choice (A) is incorrect because the verb is plural. Both (B) and (D) appear to have the literal translation needed but this type of statement is done with **se** + third singular of the verb.

7. **(D)** If the agent (doer) is not mentioned and the subject of the statement is a thing, the reflexive construction is used for the passive. The verb will, in these cases, match the noun. In this case the actual subject ("español e inglés") is plural. Choices (A) and (C) are written in the true passive formula (**ser** + past participle) but cannot be used when the subject is a thing. Choice (B) is incorrect because the verb is singular.

8. **(A)** The indefinite **se** is used when the agent (doer) is indefinite (not mentioned or implied) and a person is being acted upon. In this case the verb is always third singular and the person acted upon becomes the direct object. "Los," however, is the only direct object pronoun not used and is replaced by "les." Therefore, choice (B) is incorrect because "los" has been used. Choice (C) needs the pronoun "les" and choice (D) is simply the direct object pronoun by itself.

9. **(B)** When there is a focus on the "resultant state of a previous action" and **not** on the action itself, a form of **estar** will precede the past participle. The past participle will still be used as an adjective. Therefore, choices (A) and (C) are incorrect because **ser** has been used. Choice (D) when translated (Upon entering, I saw that the windows have been opened.) is incorrect usage of the perfect tense.

10. **(D)** The focus is on the past participle and its function as an adjective in the passive voice statement. It must agree in this sample with "casas." All other answers use incorrect gender or number.

MEASURES OF TIME

The word *tiempo* in Spanish designates both "time" and "weather," as in the following examples:

Ha pasado tanto ***tiempo*** *desde que nos vimos.*
So much **time** has passed since we saw each other.

¿Cómo está el ***tiempo*** *hoy?*
How is the **weather** today?

The following are some of the expressions Spanish uses to measure or divide time.

Seasons of the Year

las estaciones – the seasons
el verano – summer
el otoño – fall
el invierno – winter
la primavera – spring

Months of the Year

el mes – the month
enero – January
febrero – February
marzo – March
abril – April
mayo – May
junio – June
julio – July
agosto – August
septiembre – September
octubre – October
noviembre – November
diciembre – December

Note: In Spanish the names of the months are not capitalized.

Days of the Week

el día – the day
la semana – the week
el lunes – Monday
el martes – Tuesday
el miércoles – Wednesday
el jueves – Thursday
el viernes – Friday
el sábado – Saturday
el domingo – Sunday

Note: The days of the week (which are not capitalized in Spanish) are preceded by the definite article except after a form of *ser*:

el lunes – Monday; on Monday
los lunes – Mondays; on Mondays
Es lunes. – It is Monday.

Other Expressions of Time

hoy – today
mañana – tomorrow*
anteanoche – the night before last
pasado mañana – the day after tomorrow
la madrugada – dawn
el mediodía – noon
la noche – night (time)

ayer – yesterday
anoche – last night
anteayer – the day before yesterday
el día siguiente – the following day
la mañana – the morning*
la tarde – afternoon
la medianoche – midnight

* Be sure to distinguish between *mañana* (tomorrow) and *la mañana* (the morning).

TELLING TIME

When telling the time of day, the word "time" is rendered as *hora.*

¿Qué ***hora*** *es?*	What **time** is it?

When telling the hours of the day, Spanish uses the feminine definite article before the time expression.

Es ***la*** *una.*	It's one o'clock.
Son ***las*** *dos*	It's two o'clock.

Note: To specify A.M. Spanish uses *de la mañana* or *de la madrugada.* (The hours after midnight but before dawn). P.M. is expressed with either *de la tarde* or *de la noche.*

Son las tres ***de la mañana.***	It's three A.M.
Son las cinco ***de la tarde.***	It's five P.M.

To render the half-hour, Spanish uses *media.* To render the quarter-hour, *cuarto* or *quince* are used.

Son las diez y ***cuarto.*** *Son las diez y* ***quince****.*
It's a **quarter** past ten. It's ten **fifteen**.

Son las diez y ***media.***
It's **10:30**. It's **half past** ten.

Son las once menos ***cuarto****. Son las once menos* ***quince****.*
It's a **quarter** of eleven.

Falta un* ***cuarto*** *(Faltan* ***quince****) para las once.*
It's a **quarter** of eleven.

**Faltar* means "to be wanting, lacking."

Note: *y* is used through the half-hour and *menos* is used after the half-hour.

Portions of time other than the half- or quarter-hour are expressed thus:

Son las seis y diez.	It's 6:10.
Son las seis y veinte.	It's 6:20.

Son las siete menos veinte. (Faltan veinte para las siete.)
It's 6:40. (It's twenty of seven.)

At plus the hour is expressed with *a + la/las*.

A la una/A las dos salí.	At one/at two I left.

To tell time in the past, use the imperfect tense.

Era la una/Eran las dos.	It was 1:00/2:00.

To express "a little after" the hour, use ***y pico***.

Llegó a las cinco y pico.	He arrived a little after 5:00.

To express "at about," use ***a eso de*** + the hour.

Salió a eso de las seis.	He left about 6:00.

When **no** exact hour is indicated, "in the morning/afternoon/evening" is expressed with ***por la mañana, por la tarde, por la noche***.

If using the 24-hour clock, the following applies:

1:00 p.m.	*trece horas*
2:00 p.m.	*catorce horas*
8:00 p.m.	*veinte horas*
15:30 (3:30 p.m.)	*quince horas treinta*
20:42 (8:42 p.m.)	*veinte horas cuarenta y dos*
9:10 (9:10 a.m.)	*nueve horas diez*

Note: ***Cuarto, media,*** and **y** are not used.

HACER WITH EXPRESSIONS OF TIME

With expressions of time, *hacer* is an impersonal verb. Only the third person singular is used.

Hace (Tiempo) Que + Present Indicative of Main Verb

This formula shows that the action is still going on in the present. Note that Spanish uses the simple present where English uses the present perfect.

Hace una semana que los equipos no juegan.
The teams have not played for a week.

Hace muchos días que llueve.
It has been raining for many days.

Note: By turning the sentence around, the conjunction *que* can be suppressed. (In negative sentences, it is possible to use a compound tense.)

Los equipos no juegan hace una semana.
(Los equipos no han jugado hace una semana.)
The teams have not played for a week.

Llueve hace muchos días.
It has been raining for many days.

Hace (Tiempo) Que + Preterite of Main Verb

This formula designates the sense of time expressed by the English particle "ago."

Hace tres días que la vi. (La vi hace tres días.)
I saw her three days ago.

Hace años que nos dejaron. (Nos dejaron hace años.)
They left us years ago.

Hacía (Tiempo) Que + Imperfect of Main Verb

This formula shows that the action was still going on in the past.

Hacía tres días que llovía. (Llovía hacía tres días.)
It had been raining for three days.

Hacía tiempo que te esperaba. (Te esperaba hacía tiempo.)
I had been waiting for you for a while.

AGE

Cumplir años and *tener años* are the expressions most commonly used to indicate age:

Mi padre tiene cuarenta y dos años.
My father is 42 (years of age).

Hoy es mi cumpleaños. Cumplo ocho.
Today is my birthday. I turn eight.

To express "at the age of 40 (or any number)," one says "*a los cuarenta años.*"

WEATHER EXPRESSIONS

In English these weather expressions are formed with the verb "to be," in Spanish they are formed with the verb *hacer* used impersonally.

Hace *calor.*	It **is** hot.
Hizo *frío.*	It **was** cold.
Hará *buen tiempo.*	The weather **will be** good.
Hace *sol.*	It **is** sunny.
Hacía *viento.*	It **was** windy.
¿Qué tiempo ***hace****?*	What's the weather like?
Hace *mal tiempo.*	The weather **is** bad.

With *Tener*

When the sentence is personal, Spanish uses *tener* where English uses "to be."

Tengo *calor.*	I **am** hot.
Teníamos *frío.*	We **were** cold.

With *Haber* Used Impersonally

Notice that the third person singular of the present indicative changes from *ha* to *hay* when *haber* is impersonal.

Hay *neblina.*	It **is** misty (foggy).
Hubo *humedad.*	It **was** damp.
Habrá *tempestad.*	It **will be** stormy.

With *Nevar* and *Llover*

"To snow" and "to rain" are rendered by the impersonal verbs *nevar* and *llover,* respectively:

Ayer ***nevó****.*	**It snowed** yesterday.
Mañana ***lloverá****.*	Tomorrow **it will rain**.

CARDINAL AND ORDINAL NUMBERS

The cardinal and ordinal forms of numbers in Spanish are as follows:

Cardinal Numbers

1	*uno/a*	11	*once*
2	*dos*	12	*doce*
3	*tres*	13	*trece*
4	*cuatro*	14	*catorce*
5	*cinco*	15	*quince*
6	*seis*	16	*diez y seis*
7	*siete*	17	*diez y siete*
8	*ocho*	18	*diez y ocho*
9	*nueve*	19	*diez y nueve*
10	*diez*	20	*veinte*
21	*veinte y uno, –a*	300	*trescientos, –as*
22	*veinte y dos*	400	*cuatrocientos, –as*
30	*treinta*	500	*quinientos, –as*
40	*cuarenta*	600	*seiscientos, –as*
50	*cincuenta*	700	*setecientos, –as*
60	*sesenta*	800	*ochocientos, –as*
70	*setenta*	900	*novecientos, –as*
80	*ochenta*	1,000	*mil*
90	*noventa*	1,100	*mil ciento*
100	*cien(to)/a*	2,000	*dos mil*
101	*ciento uno, –a*	1,000,000	*un millón (de)*
200	*doscientos, –as*	2,000,000	*dos millones (de)*

Note: The cardinal numbers from 16 to 29 may be written together: *dieciséis, diecisiete, dieciocho, diecinueve, veintiuno, veintinueve.* Beyond 30, cardinal numbers are written: *treinta y uno, treinta y dos,* etc.

Ordinal Numbers

First	*primero*	Sixth	*sexto*
Second	*segundo*	Seventh	*séptimo*
Third	*tercero*	Eighth	*octavo*
Fourth	*cuarto*	Ninth	*noveno (nono)*
Fifth	*quinto*	Tenth	*décimo*

a) Ordinal numbers are variable in gender and number:

Eres la ***cuarta*** *persona que me pregunta lo mismo.*
You are the **fourth** person to ask me the same thing.

*Los **primeros** en irse fueron los últimos en llegar.*
The **first** to leave were the last to arrive.

b) *Primero* and *tercero* drop their final *"o"* in front of masculine singular nouns:

*el **tercer** ojo*	the **third** eye

c) Ordinal numbers precede the noun except when referring to kings, dukes, popes, or some other kind of succession:

*Juan Carlos **Primero** es el rey de España.*
Juan Carlos I is the king of Spain.

*Juan Pablo **Segundo** es el papa.*
John Paul II is the pope.

d) Usage dictates that after *décimo* no more ordinal numbers are used; they are replaced by cardinal numbers situated after the noun:

*La **décima** carrera fue más emocionante que la (carrera) **once.***
The **tenth** race was more exciting than the **eleventh** (race).

*España no tuvo un rey llamado Pedro **Quince.***
Spain did not have a king named Pedro the Fifteenth.

Un, Una or *Uno*

Un and ***una*** (like the indefinite articles they resemble) are used according to the gender of the noun they precede. ***Uno*** is used alone (i.e., not before a noun).

un** libro, **una** mujer, veinte y **uno

Note: ***un*** will precede a noun that begins with a stressed ***a**– or **ha**– for pronunciation.*

***el** águila = **un** águila*	***el** hacha = **un** hacha*
the eagle = an eagle	the hatchet = a hatchet

Ciento vs. *Cien*

a) ***Ciento*** will apocopate to ***cien*** before any noun or a number larger than itself (i.e., mil, millones).

cien casas	*cien soldados*	*cien mil*	*cien millones*
100 houses	100 soldiers	100,000	100 million

But: *ciento once, ciento veinte y tres, ciento sesenta*

Note: After 100 an **y** is not placed between it and the next number.

b) ***Ciento*** and ***mil,*** when used as collective nouns, may be plural

muchos miles de dólares	*cientos (centenares) de leguas*
many thousands of dollars	hundreds of leagues

Note: *Centenar* is preferred to *ciento* as a collective noun.

c) The multiples of 100 (200–900) have both masculine and feminine forms.

doscientas una mujeres	*quinientos un hombres*
201 women	501 men

d) Although ***ciento*** should be used when the number stands alone, in everyday speech it is apocopated as follows:

Hemos comprado cien.	*Yo vivo en el cien.*
We have bought 100.	I live in number 100.

Expressing Millions

Millón is considered a noun and therefore takes the indefinite article and is followed by the preposition *de:*

un millón de dólares	*doscientos millones de aves*
one million dollars	200 million birds

DATES

Contrary to English usage, **cardinal** numbers are used to indicate dates **except in the case of the first of the month:**

el ***primero*** *de mayo*	the first of May
el ***dos*** *de mayo*	the second of May
el ***tres*** *de mayo*	the third of May
el ***diez*** *de mayo*	the tenth of May
el ***treinta*** *de mayo*	the thirtieth of May

The year may be added to these dates by inserting the preposition *de:*

el tres de octubre ***de*** *1951*	October 3, 1951
el veinte de abril ***de*** *este año*	April 20 of this year

In dating letters the definite article is omitted.

It's common to replace *de este año* by *del corriente* (of the current year):

el veintiocho de febrero del corriente
February 28 of this year

What day is today? may be rendered literally as *¿Qué día es hoy?* or idiomatically as *¿A cómo estamos (hoy)?* The latter expression implies a date as an answer, not just the day of the week:

¿A cómo estamos? Estamos a trece de junio.
What's the date? It is June 13.

¿Qué día es hoy? Hoy es lunes.
What day is today? Today is Monday.

Arithmetical Signs

+	*más*
–	*menos*
×	*por*
÷	*dividido por*

2 + 2 is dos ***más*** *dos*
10 ÷ 5 is *diez* ***dividido por*** *cinco*
3 × 3 is *tres* ***por*** *tres*

Collective Numerals

un par	a pair
una decena	ten
una docena	a dozen
una quincena	fifteen, two weeks
una veintena	twenty
una centena (un centenar)	hundred
un millar	thousand

Pagan cada ***quincena.***
They pay every two weeks.

El libro tiene una ***centena*** *de poemas.*
The book has **one hundred** poems.

Un ***millar*** *de personas*
A **thousand** people

Note: *Quincenal* is an adjective made from *quincena.* Other similar numerical adjectives are *semanal* (weekly), *mensual* (monthly), *semestral* (half-yearly), and *anual* (yearly).

*Una publicación **quincenal***
A **bi-weekly** publication

*Una revista **semestral***
A **half-yearly** magazine

Fractions

1/2	*un medio*	1/3	*un tercio*
1/4	*un cuarto*	1/5	*un quinto*
1/6	*un sexto*	1/7	*un séptimo*
1/8	*un octavo*	1/9	*un noveno*
1/10	*un décimo*		

Two-thirds is either *dos tercios* or *las dos terceras partes*; three-fourths is either *tres cuartos* or *las tres cuartas partes.*

Un medio is only used in arithmetical calculations; the adjective meaning "half" is *medio/a;* the noun meaning "half" is *la mitad:*

*Trabajamos sólo **medio** día hoy.*
Today we only worked **half** a day.

***La mitad** del electorado no votó.*
Half of the electorate did not vote.

☞ Drill 16

1. ¿Cuánto tiempo . . . que esperaban el tren?

    (A) hace
    (B) hizo
    (C) hacían
    (D) hacía

2. . . . tres horas que regresó de su viaje.

    (A) Hacen
    (B) Ha
    (C) Hace
    (D) Desde

3. Mis botas están sucias porque . . . lodo afuera.

    (A) hay
    (B) hace
    (C) es
    (D) está

4. No puedo conducir bien porque . . . neblina.

    (A) está
    (B) es
    (C) hace
    (D) hay

5. Había (231) . . . mujeres en el estadio.

    (A) doscientos treinta y uno
    (B) doscientas treinta y uno
    (C) doscientas treinta y una
    (D) doscientas treinta y unas

6. Ganó (100 million) . . . dólares en la lotería.

    (A) cien millón de
    (B) ciento millón de
    (C) ciento millones de
    (D) cien millones de

7. (The first) . . . de mayo es mi cumpleaños.
   (A) El primero
   (B) El primer
   (C) El uno
   (D) Primero

8. Había (hundreds) . . . de pájaros en San Juan Capistrano.
   (A) cien
   (B) cientos
   (C) centenares
   (D) un cien

9. Juan llegó un poco después de las cinco, o sea, . . .
   (A) a las cinco en punto.
   (B) a eso de las cinco.
   (C) a las cinco y pico.
   (D) hace las cinco.

10. Durante el invierno mi mamá siempre . . .
   (A) está fría.
   (B) tiene frío.
   (C) hace frío.
   (D) es fría.

Drill 16—Detailed Explanations of Answers

1. **(D)** In time expressions involving the verb "hacer," the form of this verb will be third singular. To balance with "esperaban" in the other part of the sentence, "hacer" will be expressed in the imperfect tense also. This renders the translation "had been + ing." Therefore, (A) the present tense and (B) the preterite are incorrect. (C) is incorrect because it is plural.

2. **(C)** The formula for this kind of expression is **hace** (never in the plural) + **time + que** + **preterite** (or **preterite** + **hace** + **time**). In English, this formula translates the particle "ago."

3. **(A)** Weather conditions used with **haber** are "lodo" (muddy), "neblina" (foggy), "polvo" (dusty), "luna" (moonlight), and "nieve" (snow). A good way to remember is that these conditions are visible whereas hot and cold are not. Forms of "estar/ser" (to be) are never used to express weather.

4. **(D)** See the explanation given in number 3 above.

5. **(C)** Because "doscientos" and "uno" have gender and can be feminine, and because they precede a feminine plural noun in this sample, each must also be feminine. It should be noted that "uno" cannot be plural and still mean "one."

6. **(D)** "Ciento" apocopates to "cien" before nouns or numbers larger than itself. "Millón" also has a plural form. It will remain "millón" when accompanied by "un." Whenever a noun follows this number **de** is needed.

7. **(A)** The first of the month is expressed with the ordinal number "primero." All other days of the month use cardinal numbers. "Primero" apocopates to "primer" before a masculine singular noun. In this case it precedes **de** (a preposition) and apocopation is not needed.

8. **(C)** Forms of "centenar" are preferred to forms of "ciento" when used as collective nouns.

9. **(C)** To express "a little after the hour," use **y pico**. "En punto" means "exactly," "A eso de" means "at about," with the hour.

10. **(B)** To express warm or cold personally, **tener** is used. Because "frío" and "calor" are nouns, they do not change in gender to match the subject. "Hace frío" expresses the weather condition itself. Forms of **estar** with "frío/caliente" refer to the warmth or coolness of things (such as soup, tea, coffee, etc.).

VOCABULARY/IDIOMS

Idioms with *Dar*

dar a	to face, to look out upon
dar con	to come upon, to find
dar cuerda (a)	to wind
dar de beber (comer) a	to give a drink to, to feed
dar en	to strike against, to hit
dar gritos (voces)	to shout
dar la bienvenida	to welcome
dar la hora	to strike the hour
darse la mano	to shake hands
dar las gracias (a)	to thank
dar por + past part.	to consider
darse por + past part.	to consider oneself
dar recuerdos (a)	to give regards to
darse cuenta de	to realize
dar prisa	to hurry
dar un abrazo	to embrace
dar un paseo	to take a walk
dar un paseo en coche	to take a ride
dar una vuelta	to take a stroll
dar unas palmadas	to clap one's hands

Idioms with *Haber*

hay	there is, are
había	there was, were
hubo	there was, were (took place)
habrá	there will be
habría	there would be
ha habido	there has been
había habido	there had been
haya	there may be
hubiera	there might be
va a haber	there is going to be
iba a haber	there was going to be
tiene que haber	there has to be
puede haber	there can be
debe haber	there should be
haber de + infinitive	to be (supposed) to
haber sol	to be sunny

haber (mucho) polvo	to be (very) dusty
haber (mucho) lodo	to be (very) muddy
haber (mucha) neblina	to be (very) cloudy, foggy
hay luna	there is moonlight
hay que + infinitive	one must, it is necessary
hay + noun + *que* + inf.	there is/are + noun + inf.

Idioms with *Hacer*

hace poco	a little while ago
hacer buen (mal) tiempo	to be good (bad) weather
hacer (mucho) frío (calor)	to be (very) cold (hot)
hacer (mucho) viento	to be (very) windy
hacer caso de (a)	to pay attention to, to heed
hacer de	to act as, to work as
hacer falta	to be lacking
hacerle falta	to need
hacer el favor de	please + infinitive
hacer el papel de	to play the role of
hacer pedazos	to tear (to shreds)
hacer una broma	to play a joke
hacer una maleta	to pack a suitcase
hacer una pregunta	to ask a question
hacer una visita	to pay a visit
hacer un viaje	to take (make) a trip
hacerse	to become (through effort)
hacerse tarde	to become (grow) late
hacer daño (a)	to harm, to damage
hacerse daño	to hurt oneself

Idioms with *Tener*

tener (mucho) calor (frío)	to be (very) warm (cold)
tener cuidado	to be careful
tener dolor de cabeza (*de estómago,* etc.)	to have a headache (stomach ache, etc.)
tener éxito	to be successful
tener ganas de	to feel like doing something
tener gusto en	to be glad to
tener (mucha) hambre (sed)	to be (very) hungry (thirsty)
tener la bondad de	please + infinitive
tener la culpa (de)	to be to blame (for)
tener lugar	to take place

tener miedo de	to be afraid of
tener por + adj.	to consider
tener prisa	to be in a hurry
tener que	to have to, must
tener que ver con	to have to do with
tener razón (no tener razón)	to be right (wrong)
tener (mucho) sueño	to be (very) sleepy
tener (mucha) suerte	to be (very) lucky
tener vergüenza (de)	to be ashamed (of)

Miscellaneous Verbal Idioms

dejar caer	to drop
echar al correo	to mail
echar de menos	to miss (people)
echar la culpa (a)	to blame
encogerse de hombros	to shrug one's shoulders
estar a las anchas	to be comfortable
estar a punto de + inf.	to be about to
estar conforme (con)	to be in agreement (with)
estar de acuerdo (con)	to agree (with)
estar de pie	to be standing
estar de vuelta	to be back
estar para + inf.	to be about to
guardar cama	to stay in bed
llegar a ser	to become (through effort)
llevar a cabo	to carry out (plans, etc.)
pensar + inf.	to intend
perder cuidado	not to worry
perder de vista	to lose sight of
ponerse + adj.	to become (involuntarily)
ponerse de acuerdo	to come to an agreement
querer decir	to mean
(saber) de memoria	(to know) by heart
tocarle a uno	to be one's turn (uses I.O.)
valer la pena	to be worthwhile
volver en sí	to regain consciousness

Words with the Same English Translation

The following pairs of words cause problems because they share the same translation in English but are not interchangeable in Spanish.

To Know

a) *Conocer* is to know the sense of "being acquainted with" a person, place, or thing.

¿Conoce Ud. a María?	Do you know Mary?
¿Conoces bien a España?	Do you know Spain well?
¿Conoce Ud. esta novela?	Do you know this novel?

Note: In the preterite, *conocer* means **met** for the first time.

La conocí ayer.	I met her yesterday.

b) *Saber* means to know a fact, know something thoroughly, or to know how (with infinitive).

¿Sabe Ud. la dirección?	Do you know the address?
¿Sabes la lección?	Do you know the lesson?
¿Sabes nadar?	Do you know how to swim?

Note: In the preterite, *saber* means **found out**.

Supiste la verdad.	You found out the truth.

To Leave

a) *Dejar* is used when you leave someone or something behind.

Dejé a María en el cine.	I left Mary at the movies.
Dejó sus libros en casa.	He left his books at home.

b) *Salir* is used in the sense of physically departing.

Salió del cuarto.	He left the room.

To Spend

Gastar refers to spending money. *Pasar* refers to spending time.

Me gusta gastar dinero.	I like to spend money.
Pasé mucho tiempo allí.	I spent a lot of time there.

To Play

Jugar refers to playing a game; *tocar* to playing an instrument.

Juego bien al tenis.	I play tennis well.
Juana toca el piano.	Juana plays the piano.

Note: ***Tocar*** has other uses as well:

Le toca a Juan.	It's Juan's turn.
Toqué la flor.	I touched the flower.
Alguien tocó a la puerta.	Someone knocked.

To Take

a) *Llevar* means to take in the sense of carry or transport from place to place or to take someone somewhere. It also means to wear.

José llevó la mesa a la sala.	Joe took the table to the living room.
Llevé a María al cine.	I took Mary to the movies.
¿Por qué no llevas camisa?	Why aren't you wearing a shirt?

b) *Tomar* means to grab, catch, take transportation or take medication.

Ella tomó el libro y comenzó a leerlo.
She took the book and began to read it.

Tomé el tren hoy.
I took the train today.

¡Tome esta aspirina!
Take this aspirin!

To Ask

a) *Pedir* means to request or to ask for something. (If there is a change in subject, it will require the use of the subjunctive.)

Pedí el menú al entrar.	Upon entering I asked for the menu.
Le pido a Juan que vaya.	I ask Juan to go.

b) *Preguntar* means to inquire or ask a question.

Ella le preguntó a dónde fue.	She asked him where he went.

To Return

Volver (*ue*) means to come back; *devolver* (*ue*) to give back.

Volví (Regresé) tarde.	I came back late.
Devuelve el libro.	He returns the book.

To Realize

Realizar means to "make real" one's dreams, ambitions, or desires. *Darse cuenta de* means to "take note."

Juan realizó su sueño de ser doctor.
Juan realized his dream to be a doctor.

Me di cuenta de que no tenía mis apuntes.
I realized that I didn't have my notes.

To Become

a) *Llegar a ser* + noun/adj. means to become something through natural developments of time/circumstance.

Llegó a ser capitán/poderoso.
He became a captain/powerful.

b) *Hacerse* + noun/adj. means to become something through personal will or effort.

Se hizo abogado/indispensable.
He became a lawyer/indispensable.

c) *Ponerse* + adj. indicates a sudden change of emotional state or change in physical appearance.

Ella se puso triste/gorda.
She became sad/fat.

d) *Convertirse* (*ie*, *i*) + noun often indicates a somewhat unexpected change (not a profession).

Hitler se convirtió en un verdadero tirano.
Hitler became a real tyrant.

e) *Volverse* (*ue*) + adj. indicates a sudden or gradual change of personality. [Only adjectives that can be used with **both** *ser* and *estar* may follow *volverse*.]

Ella se volvió loca/alegre/sarcástica.
She became mad/happy/sarcastic.

To Enjoy

a) *Gustar, gozar de, disfrutar de* = to get pleasure from.

Me gusta viajar.
Gozo de viajar/Gozo viajando. I like (enjoy) traveling.
Disfruto de viajar/Disfruto viajando.

b) *Divetirse* (*ie*, *i*) = have a good time, enjoy oneself.

Nos divertimos mucho aquí. We enjoy ourselves a lot here.

To Save

a) *Salvar* means to rescue from destruction.

Ellos le salvaron la vida a ella.
They saved her life.

b) *Guardar* means to keep or put aside.

Voy a guardar mis cuentas.
I am going to keep my bills.

c) *Ahorrar* means **not** to spend or waste.

Vamos a ahorrar agua/dinero.
We are going to save water/money.

d) *Conservar* means to preserve, maintain.

Los indios conservan sus tradiciones.
The Indians preserve their traditions.

To Miss

a) *Extrañar* or *echar de menos* are used when miss = feel the absence of.

¡Cuánto lo extraño/echo de menos!
How much I miss you!

b) *Perder (ie)* means to miss an opportunity, deadline, or transportation.

Perdí el autobús/la última parte de la película.
I missed the bus/the last part of the movie.

c) *Faltar a* means to miss an appointment or fail to attend (as in a class, etc.).

Yo perdí/falté a la clase ayer.
I missed class yesterday.

To Move

a) *Mudarse* or *trasladarse* means to move from place to place (city to city, office to office, etc.)

Cuando era joven, me mudaba mucho.
When I was young, I moved a lot.

La compañía le trasladó a Nueva York.
The company transferred him to New York.

b) *Mover* (*ue*) means to physically move something.

Voy a mover el sofá cerca de la ventana.
I'm going to move the sofa near the window.

To Work

a) *Trabajar* means to work, labor, or toil.

Juan trabaja cada día en la oficina.
Juan works everyday in the office.

b) *Funcionar* means to work, operate, or function.

El coche/tocadiscos no funciona.
The car/record player doesn't work.

To Keep

a) *Quedarse con* means to keep something in one's possession.

Me quedo con la tarea hasta mañana.
I'll keep the homework until tomorrow.

b) *Guardar* means to hold or put away for safekeeping.

Voy a guardar mi dinero en la caja fuerte.
I'm going to keep my money in the safe.

False Cognates

Cognates are words found in different languages, which share the same linguistic origins, and therefore share similar spellings, pronunciations, and meanings. The false cognates, however, cause the most problems, particularly in the reading comprehension passages.

actual	of the present time
antiguo, –a	former, old, ancient
la apología	eulogy, defense
la arena	sand
asistir a	to attend
atender	to take care of
el auditorio	audience
bizarro, –a	brave, generous
el campo	field, country(side)
el cargo	duty, burden, responsibility
la carta	letter
el colegio	(high) school
el collar	necklace
la complexión	temperament
la conferencia	lecture
la confidencia	secret, trust
constipado, –a	sick with a cold
la consulta	conference
la chanza	joke, fun
la decepción	disappointment
el delito	crime
la desgracia	misfortune
el desmayo	fainting
embarazada	pregnant
el éxito	success
la fábrica	factory
la firma	signature
el idioma	language
ignorar	to be unaware
intoxicar	to poison
largo, –a	long
la lectura	reading
la librería	book store
la maleta	suitcase
el mantel	tablecloth
mayor	older, greater

molestar	to bother
el oficio	trade, occupation
la pala	shovel
el partido	game (sports)
pinchar	to puncture
pretender	to attempt
recordar (ue)	to remember
ropa	clothing
sano, –a	healthy
sensible	sensitive
soportar	to tolerate
el suceso	event, happening

☞ Drill 17

1. El tiempo ya había pasado, pero él no . . .

   (A) los realizaba
   (B) lo realizó
   (C) daba cuenta
   (D) se daba cuenta

2. Me gusta juntar dinero para las necesidades del futuro, por eso tengo una cuenta de . . .

   (A) ahorros
   (B) salvos
   (C) guarda
   (D) salvar

3. Ramón no . . . a los padres de su novia.

   (A) muerde
   (B) toca
   (C) conoce
   (D) sabe

4. Ramón no . . . que los padres de su novia son inmigrantes.

   (A) conoce
   (B) sabe
   (C) responde
   (D) pregunta

5. Quiso abrir la puerta del auto pero en ese momento . . . de que había perdido la llave.

   (A) realizó
   (B) se repuso
   (C) se encerró
   (D) se dio cuenta

6. En el estadio . . . muchos espectadores ayer.

   (A) tenían
   (B) habían
   (C) hay
   (D) había

7. La mujer . . . su bolsa en su coche.

   (A) dejó
   (B) partió
   (C) salió
   (D) se quitó

8. Elena . . . los apuntes al profesor.

(A) preguntó
(B) preguntó para
(C) pidió
(D) pidió por

9. Juan . . . la silla de la sala a la cocina.

(A) llevó
(B) levantó
(C) tomó
(D) arrancó

10. Cuando vi el huracán, . . . pálida.

(A) llegué a ser
(B) volví
(C) me hice
(D) me puse

11. Yo sé jugar al golf y mi mejor amigo sabe . . . piano.

(A) jugar el
(B) jugar al
(C) tocar el
(D) tocar al

12. Este alumno no . . . estudiar bien.

(A) conoce
(B) sabe a
(C) sabe de
(D) sabe

13. Basta que los turistas . . . la ciudad antes de salir.

(A) conozcan
(B) sepan
(C) saben
(D) conocen

14. Los estudiantes . . . a la profesora cómo estaba.

(A) pidieron
(B) pusieron
(C) preguntaron
(D) pudieron

15. La señora Gómez . . . el cheque y se fue al banco.

(A) vendió
(B) compró
(C) llevó
(D) tomó

16. Mi hermano quiere . . . doctor.

(A) llegar a ser
(B) volverse
(C) ponerse
(D) convertirse en

17. No me encanta . . . mucho tiempo en la cárcel.

(A) gastar
(B) gastando
(C) pasar
(D) pasando

18. Mis amigas han . . . traer los refrescos.

(A) de
(B) a
(C) por
(D) nothing needed

19. Nuestro cuarto da . . . patio.

(A) por el
(B) para el
(C) al
(D) en el

20. Juan y María hablan de ganar el premio gordo y esperan tener . . .

(A) lugar
(B) el tiempo
(C) hambre
(D) éxito

21. Ese actor sabe bien . . . de Sancho Panza.

(A) hacer caso
(B) hacer falta
(C) hacer el papel
(D) hacer un viaje

22. Tengo que . . . los libros a la biblioteca hoy.

(A) regresar
(B) dejar
(C) devolver
(D) volver

23. Yo quiero que los chicos . . . en la playa.

(A) se diviertan
(B) gocen
(C) gozan
(D) se divierten

24. Cuando me levanto tarde, siempre . . . el autobús.

(A) falto a
(B) pierdo
(C) echo de menos
(D) extraño

25. . . . de Los Ángeles hace cinco años.

(A) Moví
(B) Movía
(C) Me mudé
(D) Me mudaría

26. Por ser tan viejo mi coche rehusa . . .

(A) trabajar
(B) tejer
(C) empezar
(D) funcionar

27. La profesora me dijo, –¡ . . . la tarea para mañana!

(A) quédese con
(B) guarde
(C) salve
(D) gaste

28. Murió sin . . . su sueño de ser doctor famoso.

(A) darse cuenta de
(B) realizar
(C) saber
(D) ponerse

29. . . . mucha tarea . . . hacer esta noche.

(A) Hay . . . para
(B) Hay . . . nothing needed
(C) Hay . . . que
(D) Hay . . . por

30. Tiene que . . . una razón por sus acciones.

(A) haber
(B) estar
(C) ser
(D) pensar

Drill 17—Detailed Explanations of Answers

1. **(D)** **Darse cuenta** must be used here for "to realize." **Realizar** means "to realize" in the sense of gaining or resulting in. (C) would be correct if it were reflexive.

2. **(A)** A "savings account" (**ahorros**) is the only correct answer. None of the other answers indicates this. **Salvar** is "to save," but in the sense of rescuing, not in the banking sense, and **guardar** might mean "to save," but only in the sense "to keep from harm" or "to keep back."

3. **(C)** The correct answer comes down to a choice between "conoce" and "sabe," both modalities of "to know." (The first two choices don't make much sense.)

4. **(B)** Again, an exercise to distinguish between "saber" and "conocer" (and again, the last two choices don't fit semantically or grammatically). When it's a matter of knowing information (as in this case), the correct choice is "saber."

5. **(D)** Choices (B) and (C) simply make no sense in the context. You may think that (A) is the obvious choice since it sounds like it means "realized." It does, but not in the sense demanded by the question, which can only be rendered by (D). ("Realizar" means "to realize" a project or a plan, to make something real.)

6. **(D)** Choice (B) is incorrect because the verb "haber" is impersonal when it translates "there is," "there are," etc. (i.e., when not used in an auxiliary capacity). Choice (C) contradicts the adverb of time in the question ("ayer"), and choice (A) could only be the product of confusion between the meaning and use of "haber" and "tener."

7. **(A)** "Dejar" means to leave something behind. "Salir" means to physically leave a place. "Partir" means to depart, and "quitarse" means to remove (as in clothing).

8. **(C)** "Pedir" means to ask for something or to request, while "preguntar" means to inquire or ask a question. Neither needs "por" nor "para" in this sample.

9. **(A)** "Llevar" means to carry or transport from one place to another or to take someone somewhere. "Tomar" means to take, in the sense of grab or catch. "Levantar" means to lift and "arrancar" means to start, as in an engine.

10. **(D)** "Ponerse" is used with adjectives to indicate a sudden change of emotional state or physical appearance. "Llegar a ser" is used with adjectives/nouns and means to become something through natural developments of time/circumstance. "Harcerse" also used with adjectives/nouns means to become something through effort. "Volverse" is used with adjectives to indicate a sudden or gradual change of personality.

11. **(C)** "Jugar a" is used in connection with sports. "Tocar" is used in connection with instruments.

12. **(D)** "Conocer" means to know or be acquainted with people, places, or things. "Saber" is to know facts or know "how" to do something (when followed by an infinitive).

13. **(A)** The difference betweeen "saber" and "conocer" is given in number 12. One also needs to recognize that the subjunctive is required in this sample. The sentence begins with an impersonal expression ("it is enough") and there is a change in subject.

14. **(C)** "Preguntar" is used to inquire or ask a question. "Pusieron" from "poner" means "they put" and "pudieron" from "poder" means "they were able/managed."

15. **(D)** "Tomar" means to take in the sense of grab or catch. In this sample Mrs. Gomez is "grabbing" the check to take it to the bank. "Vendió" from "vender" means "she sold," and "compró" from "comprar" means "she bought."

16. **(A)** To become something through the natural development of time/circumstance is "llegar a ser." "Ponerse" and "volverse" must be followed by adjectives. "Convertirse en" is used with nouns but indicates a somewhat unexpected change (not a profession).

17. **(C)** To spend **time** is "pasar." "Gastar" means to spend money. Because this verb is the subject of "me encanta," it is a gerund and must be in the infinitive form in Spanish. In Spanish a present participle may not be treated as a noun.

18. **(A)** The idiom "haber de" means to be (supposed) to. Neither "a" nor "por" is used with this verb. "Han" cannot be used alone.

19. **(C)** "Dar a" means to face. "Dar en" means to hit or strike against, which makes no sense in this sentence.

20. **(D)** "Tener éxito" means to be successful. "Tener lugar" means to take place. "Tener el tiempo" means to have the time, and "tener hambre" means to be hungry.

21. **(C)** "Hacer el papel de" means to play a part or role. "Hacer caso de" means to notice. "Hacer falta" means to need and is used like gustar. "Hacer un viaje" means to take a trip.

22. **(C)** To return objects/things one uses the verb "devolver." Both "regresar" and "volver" are intransitive verbs (cannot take direct objects) and are used to indicate a physical return. "Dejar" means to allow/let.

23. **(A)** "Divertirse" means to enjoy oneself. "Gozar" followed by a present participle or "gozar de" followed by a noun means to get pleasure from. Also, one needs the subjunctive here since there is a verb of volition and a change in subject.

24. **(B)** "Perder" means to miss a deadline or transportation. "Echar de menos" and "extrañar" mean to feel the absence of (as in people). "Faltar a" means to miss an appointment or a class, for example.

25. **(C)** To move from place to place is "mudarse." "Mover" is to move objects. The preterite is needed here since this is an "hace" statement meaning **ago**.

26. **(D)** "Funcionar" means to work/operate/function (as in things). "Trabajar" is for people. "Tejer" means to weave, and "empezar" means to begin or start. To start a car, however, is "arrancar."

27. **(A)** "Quédese con" means to keep in one's possession. "Guardar" means to put away for safe keeping (as in money or jewelry). "Salvar" means to save lives and "gastar" means to spend money.

28. **(B)** "Realizar" means to realize one's dreams, hopes, or ambitions. "Darse cuenta de" means to take note. "Saber" is to know facts or how to do something and "ponerse" means to become something unexpectedly (as in pale, sick, angry, etc.).

29. **(C)** These are the missing parts of the idiom "hay + noun + que + infinitive" which is translated: There is a lot of homework to do tonight.

30. **(A)** Through translation "haber" is the logical choice: There has to be a reason for his actions.

THE SAT SUBJECT TEST IN

Spanish

PRACTICE TEST 1

SAT Spanish Practice Test 1

PART A

Time: 1 Hour
85 Questions

DIRECTIONS: In this part you are given incomplete statements or questions, each of which has four possible completions. Choose the most accurate completion and fill in the corresponding oval on the answer sheet.

1. El taxi se encuentra en ------- de aquellas dos calles.

(A) la esquina
(B) el techo
(C) la alfombra
(D) el rincón

2. El hombre que nos atiende en una tienda es el -------.

(A) mercancía
(B) dependiente
(C) cliente
(D) parroquiano

3. ¿Cuándo vas a ------- este libro a la biblioteca?

(A) regresar
(B) devolver
(C) retornar
(D) volver

4. Voy a acostarme porque tengo -------.

(A) sed
(B) hambre
(C) calor
(D) sueño

5. Cuando el autobús llegó al fin de la trayectoria, ------- delante del Museo Arqueológico.

(A) dejó de
(B) cesó
(C) paró
(D) terminó

6. Julio dijo que ------- ayudarnos con la tarea.

(A) ensayaría
(B) trataría de
(C) probaría
(D) se quedaría

7. Mañana voy a pagar ------- de la casa.

(A) los cuentos
(B) los boletos
(C) las cuentas
(D) los billetes

8. ¿Qué piensas ------- estas pinturas?

(A) de
(B) en
(C) a
(D) con

9. Hoy he estudiado demasiado y ------- la cabeza.

(A) me hace daño
(B) me hiere
(C) me daña
(D) me duele

10. Mucha gente lleva abrigo cuando -------.

(A) hace calor
(B) llueve
(C) corre
(D) hace frío

11. Antes de hacer el viaje voy a comprar -------.

(A) una maleta
(B) una máquina de coser
(C) una multa
(D) una muñeca

12. ------- es un lugar, muchas veces en el campo, donde hay muchos árboles.

D

(A) Una verdulería
(B) Una madera
(C) Una leña
(D) Un bosque

13. Felipe se cortó con el cuchillo y tiene ------- en el dedo.

(A) un anillo
(B) una uña
(C) una herida
(D) una oreja

14. Las ovejas producen -------.

(A) lana
(B) seda
(C) jamón
(D) papas

15. Es ------- comer para vivir.

A

(A) preciso
(B) precioso
(C) precario
(D) precoz

16. Tú ------- antes de salir a la calle.

(A) te viste
(B) te vestiste
(C) te pusiste
(D) te pones

17. Todos vamos a ------- en el coche.

(A) caber
(B) empujar
(C) empacar
(D) dejar

18. Al fin de su discurso el general ------- que estaba dispuesto a morir por la patria.

(A) sometió
(B) sumó
(C) agregó
(D) encargó

19. Quisiera ------- al profesor Álvarez.

(A) introduce
(B) presentarte
(C) conozco
(D) saber

20. Hay un ------- en una cámara del piso cuarto.

(A) incendio
(B) huracán
(C) nevada
(D) fogata

21. La comida ha sido buenísima; vamos a dejarle una propina al -------.

(A) cenicero
(B) acero

(C) camarero
(D) bombero

22. No puedo caminar por qué tengo la pierna -------.

(A) puesta
(B) abierta
(C) devuelta
(D) rota

23. Se han apagado todas las luces. Estamos -------.

(A) a la vez
(B) a oscuras
(C) a la luz
(D) a tiempo

24. Anoche ------- a las doce pero no pude dormir.

(A) soñé
(B) me acosté
(C) me desperté
(D) me levanté

25. Enrique y Angela se casaron el sábado. Esta semana fueron --
-----.

(A) a las estrellas
(B) de luna de miel
(C) de miel de abeja
(D) de luna llena

26. Me cuesta trabajo captar la letra de esta -------.

(A) sinfonía
(B) telegrama
(C) baile
(D) canción

27. No me siento bien; tengo un -------.

(A) reloj
(B) enfermedad
(C) resfriado
(D) uña

28. El ruido de esa sirena -------.

(A) me tranquiliza
(B) me molesta
(C) me invita
(D) me da celos

PART B

DIRECTIONS: In each of the following paragraphs, there are numbered blanks indicating that words or phrases are missing. Four completions are provided for each numbered blank. Read the entire passage. For each numbered blank, choose the completion that is the most appropriate given the context of the entire paragraph. Fill in the corresponding oval on the answer sheet.

Una tarde de lluvias primaverales, cuando viajaba sola hacia Barcelona (29) un automóvil alquilado, María de la Luz Cervantes sufrió (30) en el desierto de los Monegros. María de la Luz (31) una mexicana de veintisiete años, bonita y seria, que años antes había tenido nombre como actriz de variedades. Estaba casada con un director de teatro, con (32) iba a reunirse aquel día luego de (33) a unos parientes en Zaragoza. Después de una hora de hacer señas (34) a los automóviles y camiones que pasaban, el conductor de un autobús destartalado paró y (35) ofreció ayuda.

29. (A) conducir
(B) condujo
(C) conduzca
(D) conduciendo

30. (A) una avería
(B) un colapso
(C) una ruptura
(D) una interrupción

31. (A) era
(B) estaba
(C) fue
(D) estuvo

32. (A) que
(B) quien
(C) la que
(D) quién

33. (A) visitando
(B) visitara
(C) visita
(D) visitar

34. (A) desesperado
(B) desesperadas
(C) desesperada
(D) desesperando

35. (A) lo
(B) se
(C) le
(D) la

Marcelo se sorprendió de que Alfredo Zambrano (36) acompañado aquella mañana a Cristina, su esposa. (37) en la mirada del hombre un (38) de odio o (39), algo que le avisara de que Afredo estaba enterado de sus (40) con ella. Pero fue en vano. La (41) del empresario español, lejana, pasiva, no reflejaba nada que (42) ser de cuidado.

36. (A) hubiera
(B) había
(C) haya
(D) habría

37. (A) Busqué
(B) Buscó
(C) Observó
(D) Veo

38. (A) artículo
(B) sentido
(C) indicio
(D) sensorial

39. (A) amistad
(B) deseo
(C) curiosidad
(D) enemistad

40. (A) hijos
(B) relaciones
(C) negocios
(D) obligaciones

41. (A) estatura
(B) emoción
(C) mirada
(D) vista

42. (A) pueda
(B) podía
(C) podría
(D) pudiera

Alrededor de 8.500 personas visitan la Biblioteca Nacional de Buenos Aires todos los meses. (43), no todos quedan (44) con (45) encuentran en el enorme edificio ubicado en Agüero y Libertador, y (46) decepcionados. Aunque los archivos (47) algo más de (48) ejemplares, casi todos son libros editados (49) más de una década. Por eso, (50) buscan información actualizada se ven totalmente frustrados. Por ejemplo, si alguien quiere consultar (51) sobre el conflicto por las Islas Malvinas, no hay nada.

43. (A) Sin embargo
(B) Sin novedad
(C) Sin par
(D) Sin recurso

44. (A) satisfecho
(B) satisfaces
(C) satisfechos
(D) satisfacer

45. (A) lo que
(B) lo cual
(C) el cual
(D) los que

46. (A) se irán
(B) se vayan
(C) se fueron
(D) se van

47. (A) cuentan con
(B) cuenten con
(C) contar con
(D) contaran con

48. (A) uno millón de
(B) millón de
(C) un millión de
(D) un millón de

49. (A) hacía
(B) hace
(C) hacen
(D) hizo

50. (A) los que
(B) quiénes
(C) ellos que
(D) esos que

51. (A) obreros
(B) obras
(C) obradas
(D) obradoras

Hoy en día la ciencia médica aconseja que el hombre siga un (52) alimenticio de legumbres, frutas frescas y cereales. En cambio, la comida típica del norteamericano medio se basa en el consumo (53) de alimentos grasientos, carne roja y carbohidratos, lo cual puede conducir, si no al cáncer o a problemas cardíacos, a (54) casos de obesidad.

A causa de la manía del adelgazamiento y el horror a la obesidad de la gente, ciertos médicos han (55) lo peligroso que puede ser perder mucho peso en poco tiempo; lo cual es posible si seguimos ciertas dietas que (56) se han puesto muy de moda. Tales regímenes, a lo mejor, ayudan a uno a enflaquecer en seguida pero van en contra de las leyes naturales del cuerpo humano.

52. (A) horario
(B) régimen
(C) dietas
(D) esquema

53. (A) reducido
(B) menor
(C) exceso
(D) excesivo

54. (A) severas
(B) difíciles
(C) severos
(D) pesados

55. (A) advertido
(B) advertidos
(C) dicho
(D) dichos

56. (A) actualmente
(B) realmente
(C) definitivamente
(D) jamás

Ya son las diez y media. El tren rápido para Fulango salió hace hora y cuarto y (57) a su destino dentro de hora y media. El tren correo salió para la misma ciudad media hora antes que el rápido y (58) tardará dos horas más en llegar a Fulango.

57. (A) llegaba
(B) llegará
(C) llegó
(D) llegaría

58. (A) ya
(B) nunca
(C) siempre
(D) todavía

PART C

DIRECTIONS: Read the following passages for comprehension. Following each passage are a number of questions or incomplete sentences. Choose the most appropriate response or completion and fill in the corresponding oval on the answer sheet.

A Rafael López, vecino del barrio de Santa Cruz, le ha tocado el gordo de la lotería de Navidad. Antes, el joven sevillano soñaba con ser cantante de música folklórica y hacerse rico y famoso. Mientras tanto, según nos ha contado el propio López, para ganarse la vida, pertenecía a un conjunto musical en el cual tocaba el tambor, pero sólo cuando faltaba alguien. Ahora ya no está apurado y por encima de todo no hay nadie que le desconozca en toda España.

59. ¿Cuál de las oraciones a continuación es cierta?

(A) El joven se hizo cantante popular.
(B) El sevillano fingía ser cantante popular.
(C) Ahora, al joven le hace falta dinero para vivir.
(D) El joven sevillano quería ser cantante.

60. Rafael…

(A) ganó un premio musical
(B) servía de sustituto en una banda
(C) tocaba la guitarra
(D) tenía su propio conjunto

61. Rafael ganó…

(A) un viaje
(B) un conjunto musical
(C) mucho dinero
(D) un tambor

62. El joven sevillano…

(A) es célebre ahora
(B) tiene por qué llorar
(C) sigue careciendo de dinero
(D) tiene prisa

DEPORTES

Jugar al golf en el desierto

Si el golf ya es un deporte que requiere enormes dosis de precisión y habilidad cuando se juega en inmaculados céspedes, hacerlo en un desierto parecía imposible. Sin embargo, ya se puede hacer en el club de golf más insólito del mundo, el Woomera Gold, situado en pleno desierto australiano. En sus áridas instalaciones, los *green* ya no son verdes y los jugadores deben llevar, además de palos y bolas, un pequeño trozo de césped para que el golpe resulte más cómodo. Este campo, de 5.316 metros cuadrados, tiene, evidentemente, los *bunkers* –zonas de arena– más grandes del mundo. Además, los jugadores tienen que contar con dos invitados insólitos: las tormentas de arena y las hormigas. En cualquier caso, ya se ha celebrado el primer trofeo en pleno desierto. Su vencedor, el australiano Paul Nieckel, comentó tras su último recorrido que jugar en el desierto puede ser un buen aprendizaje para ganar en precisión ante los torneos tradicionales.

Cien golfistas participaron en el primer torneo jugado en pleno desierto australiano.

63. ¿Por qué se distingue este club de golf?

(A) Fue diseñado por Paul Nieckel.
(B) Es el primer club de golf construido en Australia.
(C) Es bastante pequeño y es fácil jugar en el.
(D) Está completamente cubierto de arena.

64. Según Paul Nieckel, ¿por qué es bueno jugar aquí?

(A) Es bastante barato y no es necesario ser socio.
(B) Siempre hay competencias con muchos premios.
(C) Es un desafío que ofrece buena práctica.
(D) Tiene los céspedes más inmaculados de Australia.

65. ¿Para qué deben llevar un trozo de césped los golfistas?

(A) Para ponerlo bajo la bola antes de golpearla.
(B) Para tener buen contacto en los bunkers.
(C) Para reparar el daño del golpe del palo.
(D) Para protegerse de las tormentas de arena.

Ayer por la tarde hubo un atraco en un sucursal del Banco Nacional situado en las afueras de la capital. Los reos enmascarados huyeron del lugar del crimen llevándose una cantidad de dinero todavía por determinar y sin ser identificados. Los agentes de la policía armada rodearon el barrio, hicieron una redada y, a las cinco de la tarde, tuvieron éxito en su búsqueda. Se enteraron de que se trataba de una pareja campesina temporalmente radicada en la capital.

66. ¿Cuál de las contestaciones está bien?

(A) Los policías salieron del barrio a las cinco de la tarde.
(B) Los criminales todavía quedan libres.
(C) Se sabe cuánto dinero fue robado.
(D) La policía ha encontrado a los ladrones.

67. El asalto del banco fue llevado a cabo…

(A) a las cinco de la tarde
(B) en el centro de la ciudad
(C) alrededor del barrio
(D) por dos campesinos

68. El Banco Nacional…

(A) cierra a las cinco de la tarde
(B) está situado en el centro de la capital

(C) fue robado ayer por la tarde
(D) es el banco más grande de la ciudad

69. Los guardias

(A) trataron de impedir una rebelión
(B) tuvieron que perseguir a los criminales al campo
(C) supieron quiénes eran los reos
(D) llegaron sin fusiles

70. Los criminales eran

(A) dos chicos del pueblo vecino
(B) dos personas del extranjero
(C) estar disfrazados
(D) los policías armados

En algunas partes de la América Latina la situación económica va de mal en peor a causa de las deudas internacionales que no pueden pagar muchos gobiernos. A esto hay que agregar el aumento del costo de la vida y el paro forzoso.

Teniendo en cuenta la situación inestable de las bolsas internacionales, la bajada del valor del dólar y el desequilibrio de la balanza de pagos, se han reunido los representantes de los poderes más influyentes del mundo económico a fin de llegar a un acuerdo que evite un posible derrumbamiento financiero, para cuyo efecto habrá que obrar con cautela.

71. ¿Cuál de las frases describe mejor la situación?

(A) Suben los precios, hay bastante trabajo y a los gobiernos les falta dinero.
(B) Bajan los precios, hay demasiado trabajo y a los gobiernos les sobra dinero.
(C) Suben los precios, hay mucho desempleo y a los gobiernos les falta suficiente dinero.
(D) Suben los precios, hay mucho paro y los gobiemos consiguen pagar sus deudas.

72. Los delegados de las varias naciones...

(A) quieren estabilizar la economia internacional
(B) apenas se dan cuenta de la seriedad del problema
(C) niegan la gravedad de la situación
(D) van a bajar el valor de la moneda

73. Se entiende que...

(A) el resultado será eficaz
(B) será necesario proceder con cuidado
(C) se efectuará el fin deseado
(D) se logrará el propósito de la conferencia

La gente que tiene animales domésticos en su casa generalmente prefiere gatos y perros y no otros animales como conejos y canarios que también se prestan para la ocasión. Se cree en general que es más fácil hacer migas con perros y gatos que con animales un poco más exóticos. No olvidemos, sin embargo, las diferencias entre perros y gatos: mientras los primeros parecen responder más sistemática y fielmente a los caprichos de sus dueños, los gatos exhiben un individualismo y un oportunismo altamente desarrollados. Es fácil concluir cuando se vive con uno o dos gatos que son éstos quienes controlan a sus dueños y no al revés. Un perro, en cambio, no manda en la casa. Sólo trabaja allí. Pero los gatos nunca tienen una tarea específica como cuidar la casa. Su única misión consiste en ser ellos y hacer sus típicas tonterías que los hacen tan simpáticos, como tenderse de barriga en la alfombra, jugar con un ovillo de lana, treparse por la ropa del dueño y perseguir insectos. Curiosamente sus pequeñas tiranías los hacen más entrañables, lo cual se refleja en el altísimo número de gatos que pululan por las callas de cualquier ciudad y sobre todo por los barrios suburbanos, donde viven muchas veces en casas cómodas y calefaccionadas donde no les falta nada. Pero también hay gente rara que prefiere tener animales más grandes en su casa o jardín, animales como llamas o cabras. Este tipo de animal podría tener su utilidad cortando el pasto o fertilizándolo. Desgraciadamente hay leyes que le impiden a mucha gente guardar animales grandes en el traspatio. Hasta que no cambien estas leyes tendremos que sequir yendo al zoológico para ver cebras y jirafas.

74. ¿Qué cree Ud. que significa "hacer migas"?

(A) pelearse con alguien
(B) amistar
(C) ser indiferentes
(D) comer pan

75. ¿Para qué ocasión se prestan conejos y canarios?

(A) para ser animales domésticos
(B) para hacer migas con gatos y perros
(C) para llevarlos a exposiciones exóticas
(D) para combatir a los vecinos

76. ¿Qué releja el alto número de gatos que existen en las ciudades y áreas suburbanas?

(A) la calidad de la ciencia veterinaria
(B) la existencia de un número igualmente alto de ratones
(C) cll cariño que la gente tiene por los gatos
(D) la amistad de los gatos y los perros

77. Esa mujer quiere

(A) que la gente beba más leche
(B) que su hija se haga estrella
(C) que su hila mantenga su buena salud
(D) que la leche contenga todo lo esencial para la vida

Desde su independencia en el primer cuarto del siglo XIX los países hispanoamericanos han soñado con ser democráticos. Pero la democracia no es fácil de consequir en países con un pasado colonial de tres siglos de duración, siglos en que la América española fue gobernada por españoles nacidos en otro suelo y en que las riquezas del continente fueron manejadas y aprovechadas sólo por la corona española. O sea que los países hispanoamericanos llegaron a la vida independiente sin ninguna tradición propia de gobierno, y sin estructuras políticas desarrolladas. Y tampoco existían estructuras económicas que pudieran servir de base a las nuevas repúblicas. A estos problemas hay que sumar otros cuyo resultado fue muchas veces la dictadura y no la democracia. El período colonial fue un perído de notoria estratificación social. Aunque la sociedad colonial estaba organizada y unificada por la religión católica, sólo un reducido grupo de personas recibían los beneficios económicos y sociales que la sociedad producía. La gran mayoría de la gente eran indios que seguían viviendo de modo ancestral o que hacían el trabajo pesado que sustentaba la economía. Esta división social se agravó en el momento de las guerras de la Independencia y aún sigue siendo un factor que milita contra la democracia. La pobreza y la falta de educación crean situaciones propicias a la dictadura y no a la democracia.

Sin embargo, hoy en día la vasta mayoría de los países hispanoamericanos son democráticos, aunque en los años 70 las dictaduras proliferaron desde Nicaragua hasta la Argentina. Uno de los factores más importantes que deciden el tipo de gobierno en la América Latina es la política exterior de los Estados Unidos, que no siempre está clara. El gobierno norteamericano no puede apoyar la dictadura de Somoza en Nicaragua y a la misma vez pretender que el régimen cubano de Fidel Castro no es legítimo porque es dictatorial.

78. ¿Cuál de las siguientes afirmaciones es falsa?

(A) El período colonial en Hispanoamérica significó una economía controlada por la corona española.
(B) La sociedad colonial era estratificada.

(C) Durante la colonia no se crearon estructuras políticas propias.
(D) El período colonial duró cien años.

79. ¿Quiénes constituían la mayoría de la población en el período colonial?

(A) los indios que hacían el trabajo pesado.
(B) los hijos de los conquistadores.
(C) los negros traídos del Africa para trabajar en las plantaciones de azúcar.
(D) la gente de raza blanca.

80. ¿Cual de las siguientes afirmaciones no se refiere a un factor que pueda explicar la proliferación de dictaduras en la América Latina?

(A) La pobreza y la falta de educación causan la dictadura.
(B) La estratificación social heredada de la colonia causa la dictadura.
(C) La riqueza de los países hispanoamericanos es causa de la dictadura.
(D) La ausencia de estructuras polícticas adecuadas causa la dictadura.

81. ¿Qué tipo de gobierno tenía la Argentina en los años 70?

(A) Democracia.
(B) Parlamentarismo.
(C) Colonial.
(D) Dictadura.

82. ¿Cuál ha sido el gran sueño de los países hispanoamericanos?

(A) de ser democráticos
(B) de ser parte de una dictadura
(C) de unirse con la corona española
(D) de tener una división social

Verdadero rompecabezas para el ser humano es la insoluble cuestión del medio ambiente y cómo conservarlo intacto frente a los avances cada vez más amenazantes de la contaminación tanto del agua como del aire. Fábricas a diario arrojan toneladas de humos nocivos, dejándolos subir a la atmósfera para que caigan después en forma de lluvia perniciosa que perjudica edificios y coches e impide el crecimiento de las plantas.

A veces, la ciencia misma, que debe ser el arma protectora de lo que estudia, es decir, la naturaleza, ha sido la responsable al facilitar nuevos campos de invención industrial como los centrales de energía nuclear. Éstos, muchas veces sin tener en cuenta el bien público, han dejado escapar radiación en cantidades tales que ningún ser podría soportarlas.

Los vertederos de las grandes ciudades van amontonándose de los restos de una civilización que parece tomar como un deber suyo el echarlo todo. Llegará el día cuando habrá que lanzarlos en cohetes rumbo a otro mundo ya que no quedará sitio para ellos o no querrá nadie que se entierren en el huerto detrás de su casa.

83. El autor del artículo parece creer…

(A) que la contaminación del agua es más grave que la del aire
(B) que la naturaleza queda libre de los efectos de la sociedad
(C) que faltan remedios aptos para el problema de la contaminación
(D) que la contaminación del aire es menos seria que la del agua

84. Según el autor, ¿quién tiene la culpa?

(A) la civilización moderna
(B) el medio ambiente
(C) la atmósfera
(D) los vertederos

85. La radiación…

(A) es inaguantable para la vida
(B) es soportable para la vida
(C) es precisa para el bienestar ambiental
(D) es beneficiosa para la vida

SAT Subject Test in Spanish
Practice Test 1

ANSWER KEY

1. (A)	23. (B)	45. (A)	67. (D)
2. (B)	24. (B)	46. (D)	68. (C)
3. (B)	25. (B)	47. (A)	69. (C)
4. (D)	26. (D)	48. (D)	70. (C)
5. (C)	27. (C)	49. (B)	71. (C)
6. (B)	28. (B)	50. (A)	72. (A)
7. (C)	29. (D)	51. (B)	73. (B)
8. (A)	30. (A)	52. (B)	74. (B)
9. (D)	31. (A)	53. (D)	75. (A)
10. (D)	32. (B)	54. (C)	76. (C)
11. (A)	33. (D)	55. (A)	77. (C)
12. (D)	34. (B)	56. (A)	78. (D)
13. (C)	35. (C)	57. (B)	79. (A)
14. (A)	36. (A)	58. (D)	80. (C)
15. (A)	37. (B)	59. (D)	81. (D)
16. (B)	38. (C)	60. (B)	82. (A)
17. (A)	39. (D)	61. (C)	83. (C)
18. (C)	40. (B)	62. (A)	84. (A)
19. (B)	41. (C)	63. (D)	85. (A)
20. (A)	42. (D)	64. (C)	
21. (C)	43. (A)	65. (A)	
22. (D)	44. (C)	66. (D)	

DETAILED EXPLANATIONS OF ANSWERS

PRACTICE TEST I

1. (A)

Esquina means the corner or outer side of an angle formed, for example, by two streets which meet or intersect each other. In the list of choices there appears the word *rincón,* which is not appropriate in this case, although it does mean "corner," but in another sense: the inner side of an angle such as that formed by two walls which meet to form a corner of a room, for example. Obviously, the other two possible answers given (*techo* = "roof" and *alfombra* = "carpet") would not logically be used when talking about streets.

2. (B)

Dependiente means "clerk." This word also has a feminine form which is *dependienta. Atender* (ie) means "to wait on." *Mercancía* means "merchandise." *Cliente* and *parroquiano* both signify "customer."

3. (B)

Devolver means "to return" in the sense of "to give back." The other three possible choices also mean "to return," but only in the sense of "to come or go back." Of these three, *retornar* is the least frequently used.

4. (D)

Tengo sueño signifies "I am sleepy." The verb *acostarse* means "to go to bed." Hence, the other three answers would not apply. Notice how the verb *tener* is frequently used in Spanish to form idiomatic expressions: *tener sed* ("to be thirsty"), *tener hambre* ("to be hungry"), *tener calor* ("to be hot"). To this list we might add other expressions such as: *tener frío* ("to be cold"), *tener razón* ("to be right"), *no tener razón* ("to be wrong"), *tener vergüenza* ("to be ashamed"), *tener ganas de* + infinitive ["to feel like (doing (something)"], *tener celos* ("to be jealous"), etc.

5. (C)
All four of the answers mean "stopped," but the verb *parar* refers to a moving object which comes to a physical halt and movement ceases. *Dejar de* means "to stop doing something" (*Dejé de estudiar a las once* = "I stopped studying at eleven"). Observe that this expression is always followed by an infinitive. *Cesar* and *terminar* also have this meaning. (*Cesó la lluvia a las nueve* = "The rain stopped at nine"). *La fiesta terminó a la medianoche* = "The party ended/stopped at midnight.") The word *trayectoria,* in this case, means "route."

6. (B)
The first three verbs all have to do with the idea of "try," but each is used under very particular circumstances. *Tratar de* + an infinitive is used when we want to say "to try to do something." *Ensayar* and *probar* mean "to try on" or "to try out" but they are generally not followed by infinitives, but rather by nouns. For example, *Voy a probar el agua* ("I'm going to try out the water"). *Ensayar* can also be used to mean "to rehearse," as for a play. In addition, it can occasionally mean "to try on," as with clothing, but the most common verb we use in this instance is the reflexive form of *probar,* i.e., *probarse: Voy a probarme esta blusa* ("I'm going to try on this blouse"). Remember that *probar* can also mean "to prove": *Me probaron que no tenía razón* ("They proved to me that I was wrong").*Quedarse* ("to remain") would be entirely illogical syntactically in this case because it would have to be followed by the preposition *para* ("in order to"), which would be obligatory in front of the infinitive.

7. (C)
Both *boletos* and *billetes* are tickets, for the theater or the train, for example, and would not fit in here with the word *casa* ("house"). *Cuentos* and *cuentas* look rather alike except for the difference in

gender. The first means "story," or in a literary sense, "short story"; the second means "bills," and would, therefore, make sense within the context of the sentence.

8. (A)

Normally, the only two prepositions which appear directly after *pensar* are *de* and *en*. *Pensar de* is most often used in questions to ask for an opinion: *¿Qué piensas de este examen?* ("What do you think about this test?"). *Pensar en* means "to think about" in the sense of concentrating or meditating upon something or someone: *Pienso mucho en mi familia* ("I think about my family a lot," i.e., my family is often on my mind). Remember that when *pensar* is followed directly by an infinitive (with no intervening preposition), the meaning is "to intend" or "to plan on" doing something: *Pienso ir al cine mañana* ("I intend to go to the movies tomorrow").

9. (D)

When a part of the body is causing pain, we use the verb *doler* (ue) preceded by the proper form of the indirect object pronoun (*me, te, le, nos, os, les*) which refers to the person feeling the pain. The subject of the verb *doler* is the part(s) of the body mentioned. Consequently, *doler*, in any tense, will normally be used only in the third person singular and the third person plural. Compare the following sentences: *Le duelen los ojos* ("His eyes hurt him"), *Te dolía una muela* ("Your tooth was hurting you, i.e., you had a toothache"). *Dañar* and *hacer daño* mean "to hurt" in the sense of "to damage" or "harm": *El gato hizo daño a las cortinas* ("The cat damaged the curtains"). *Herir* (ie, i) is related to the noun *herida* (wound), and obviously means "to wound."

10. (D)

To answer properly here it is important to know the meaning of *abrigo* ("overcoat"). This helps us associate the sentence with cold weather and the word *frío* ("cold") in the correct answer. Notice that with many weather expressions we use the third person singular of the verb *hacer*. Other common expressions of this type are *hacer calor* ("to be hot"), *hacer mal tiempo* ("to be bad weather"), *hacer buen tiempo* ("to be good weather"), *hacer viento* ("to be windy"), and *hacer fresco* ("to be cool"). Two common verbs pertaining to weather which do not use *hacer* are *llover* (ue), which means "to rain," and *nevar* (ie), "to snow." Notice the vowel change in *llover* as it appears in answer (B). When it rains you wear a "raincoat," *un impermeable* or *una gabardina*. The verb *correr* ("to run") does not make much sense as a response for this item.

11. (A)
Choosing the right answer here depends first on understanding the expression *hacer un (el) viaje*, which means "to take a (the) trip." Of the four possibilities suggested, only *una maleta* ("a suitcase") has a direct bearing on travel. *Una máquina de coser* is "a sewing machine." *Una multa* means "a fine." *Una muñeca* signifies either "a wrist" or "a doll."

12. (D)
Answering correctly in this case depends on you recognizing the words *lugar* ("place"), *árboles* ("trees"), and *campo* ("countryside"). A place in the countryside where there are many trees is logically woods. A stand of trees is a *bosque*. The word *madera* means "wood" as a building material, for example. *Leña* has a very specific meaning: "firewood" or "kindling." *Verdulería*, although it suggests the idea of *verde* (green), actually means "green grocery," a place where one can buy green vegetables.

13. (C)
Key words in the statement are *se cortó* ("cut himself"), *cuchillo* ("knife"), and *dedo* ("finger"). *Anillo* ("ring") and *uña* ("fingernail") can be related to "finger," but they seem to have no relationship to the idea of Felipe's cutting himself. *Oreja* ("ear") would also be out of place here. *Herida* ("wound"), on the other hand, can be related to the idea of cutting oneself. Notice how, in this case, the verb *cortar* is used in its reflexive form *cortarse*. Reflexive verbs can often be used to show an action which the subject performs on itself: *Se sentó* ("He sat down," i.e., "he sat himself down"); *Me miré en el espejo* ("I looked at myself in the mirror"). In our sentence we did not use the possessive adjective *su* in front of the word *dedo* because in most cases we simply use the definite articles (*el, la, los, las*) with the parts of the body and clothing. The *su* is also unnecessary here because of the verb *tiene*. If

he has *una herida*, he logically has it on his own finger, not on someone else's.

14. (A)
Ovejas are "sheep." They do not produce *seda* ("silk"), *jamón* ("ham"), or *papas* ("potatoes"), but rather *lana* ("wool"). The word *papas* is used in South and Central America. In Spain, the word for "potatoes" is *patatas*.

15. (A)
Preciso ("necessary") is a synonym of *necesario*, which could also be used in this sentence. The three other possible choices, although they look or sound somewhat like *preciso*, are inapplicable here: *precioso* ("precious," "pretty"), *precario* ("precarious," "dangerous'), *precoz* ("precocious"). Clauses beginning with *Es preciso...* or *Es necesario...* are followed by the infinitive if they express a generalization, as is the case in our sentence. If, however, the idea referred to a specific person, we would then be required to use a subjunctive clause, rather than simply the infinitive, for example, *Es preciso que tú comas para vivir* ("It is necessary that you eat in order to live").

16. (B)
To make the right choice for this item you need to know the difference between *vestirse* ("to get dressed") and *ponerse* ("to put on an article of clothing"). Since no item of wearing apparel is mentioned, the two forms of *ponerse* cannot be used; we must say *Tú te vestiste* ("You got dressed"). It could be easy to choose item (A) by mistake because it looks somewhat like several forms of *vestirse*, but remember that *viste* is the second person singular of the preterite tense of *ver* ("to see") and would make little sense here.

17. (A)
The verb *caber* means "to fit." When we follow it by *en*, as in our sentence, we mean "to fit into." *Empujar* (to push) and *empacar* ("to pack") could be relevant to cars but they would not be followed by *en*. Rather, they would require that *coche* be a direct object instead of the object of a preposition. In these two cases, we would have to say *Todos vamos a empujar el coche* ("We are all going to push the car"); *Todos*

vamos a empacar el coche ("We are all going to pack the car"). *Dejar* means "to leave," not in the sense of "to depart," but "to leave behind." It also would not be followed immediately by *en* and would require that *coche* be a direct object, for example: *Vamos a dejar el coche aquí* ("We are going to leave the car here").

18. (C)

The verb *agregar* means "to add," often in the sense of making an additional statement, which, of course, is what we mean in our sentence. Although *sumó* means "he added," it would not apply here because it is used only in a mathematical sense, as in *Sumó la lista de números* ("He added the list of numbers"). Neither *someter* ("to subject or force to surrender") nor *encargar* ("to entrust or to order goods") would be logical in our sentence.

19. (B)

In our sentence, *Quisiera* is the imperfect subjunctive of the verb *querer*. This form is frequently used instead of *quiero*, for example, to express a courteous statement or request, for it is considered more polite. It is appropriate here because we are dealing with a formal situation in which someone is introducing one person to another. For introductions we use the verb *presentar*, not *introducir. Introducir* would not work here anyway because we need an infinitive following *Quisiera*. The *te*, which is attached to *presentar* in (B), is the second person singular direct object pronoun and means "you" (familiar). *Conozco* is also wrong because it is not an infinitive. For us to use *conocer* in the sentence we would have to say *Quisiera conocer al profesor Álvarez* ("I would like to know Professor Álvarez"). This, however, would not refer to an introduction, but would instead simply state my desire to meet Professor Álvarez. In item (D), it is true that we have an infinitive, *saber*, but we cannot use it here, for this verb means to know facts or information, not to know or meet a person.

20. (A)

In our sentence, *cámara* means "room," and *del piso cuarto* signifies "on the fourth floor." It is unlikely that there would be either a hurricane (*huracán*) or a snow storm (*nevada*) at that location. *Fogata* means "bonfire," the kind we have outdoors at picnics. *Incendio* is a more general term for fire and is used to refer to buildings which are on fire. *Fuego*, a synonym for *incendio*, could also have been used in this case.

21. (C)

Propina means "tip," the kind we leave for a waiter or waitress. The verb *dejar* signifies "to leave behind." One of the most common words for waiter is *camarero*, (C). Possible synonyms are *mozo* and *mesero*, which are used in parts of South and Central America. Answer (A) is incorrect; *cenicero* means "ashtray." The word *acero*, in (B), means "steel." In (D), *bombero* is a "fireman." We don't normally give him a tip. Notice the word *buenísima* in our sentence. The *-ísimo* ending may be attached to most adjectives. It signifies "very." Therefore, ***buenísima*** means **muy** *buena*.

22. (D)

Each of the possible answers is a feminine form of the past participle. When past participles are not preceded by some form of the verb *haber*, they function as adjectives and, therefore, agree in number and gender with the word they modify. In other words, we are looking for an adjective which can logically describe the word *pierna* ("leg"). The only logical response here would be *rota* ("broken"). This is the irregular form of the past participle of the verb *romper*. The other possible answers would make little sense here: *puesta* ("placed, put on"), *abierta* ("open"), *devuelta* ("returned," "given back"). In Spanish, if we want to say "Why is your leg broken?", we do not use the possessive adjective *tu*. Instead, by employing the verb *tener* in the second person singular, we know that we are referring to the subject *tú*. That person has his leg broken. Because of the verb *tener*, we can then use *la* instead of *tu* in front of *pierna*. In Spanish, when the meaning is clear, we use the definite article, rather than possessive adjectives,with parts of the body and articles of clothing.

23. (B)

The verb *apagar* means "to turn off," as with lights, etc. It is used in our sentence in the present perfect tense and in the reflexive form. Here it literally means "All the lights have turned themselves off," i.e., "All the lights have been turned off." Notice how Spanish can avoid the use of the true passive voice by substituting the reflexive form of the verb as long as the performer of the action is not mentioned. In the true passive voice our sentence would read as follows: *Todas las luces han sido apagadas*. If all of the lights have been turned off, the implication is that we are "in the dark" (*a oscuras*). Answer (A) is not right because it would mean "at once." Answer (C) is wrong because *a la luz* (in the light) would be contrary to what we expect when the lights are extinguished. *A tiempo* ("on time"), in item (D), has no relation to the fact that the lights have been turned off.

24. (B)
To answer this question correctly, it is necessary to pay particular attention to the second clause of our sentence. The word *pero* ("but") is very important here. If you used answer (A), *soñé* ("I dreamed"), the sentence would be illogical because first you fall asleep, and then you dream, but the second clause says that you "failed to sleep." The preterite tense of *poder* in the affirmative form can mean "to succeed" or "manage to do something." If *poder* is used negatively in the preterite, as in our sentence, it means "to fail" to do something. We hope you didn't confuse *soñar* ("to dream") with *tener sueño* ("to be sleepy"). Answer (C), *me desperté* ("I awakened"), will not work, also because of the word *pero*. Item (D) is illogical. *Me levanté* means "I got up," and should not be confused with *me acosté* ("I went to bed"), the correct answer. Notice that in (B), (C), and (D) the verbs are reflexive because they all show actions which the subject performs on itself.

25. (B)
De luna de miel means "on their honeymoon," which is the only correct answer of the four choices because the first sentence tells us that "Enrique and Angela got married on Saturday." We place the preposition *de* in front of *luna de miel* when it is used with the verbs *ir* ("to go") or *estar* ("to be"). This happens also with other expressions such as *ir de vacaciones* ("to go on vacation") and *estar de vacaciones* ("to be on vacation"). Answer (A) means "to the stars," which is highly improbable. In (C), *miel de abeja* means "bee honey." In (D), *luna llena* signifies "full moon." Observe that in our sentence the verb *casarse* (to get married) is reflexive. The only time this would not be true is when, for example, a father says "I married off my daughter" (*Casé a mi hija*). Here, not only is the verb not reflexive, but also we must use the personal "a" which precedes direct objects referring to specific people.

Remember that "to get married to" is *casarse con*: *Enrique se casó con Angela* ('Enrique got married to Angela").

26. (D)

Cuesta trabajo is a synonym for *es difícil* ("it is difficult"). In any of the tenses, this expression is used only in the third person singular or third person plural, depending on the subject, which in this case is the infinitive *captar*. In this type of expression, it is never plural because the subject is an infinitive. The pronoun *me* is an indirect object meaning "to me" or "for me." In other words, *Me cuesta trabajo...* means "It is difficult for me..." *Costar trabajo* follows the pattern of the verb *gustar*, which also is used only in the third person singular or plural and is also preceded by an indirect object pronoun. The verb *captar* means "to get" or "to catch," in the sense of "to hear clearly." Here, the word *letra* here means "the words of a song." Consequently, *canción* ("song") is the right response. Since a symphony (*sinfonía)*, (A), and a dance (*baile*), (C), do not usually have words, these two answers are wrong. *Telegrama* will not fit in the sentence because it, like many words ending in *-ma, -pa,* and *-ta,* is masculine *(el telegrama, el mapa, el artista*). Also, telegrams are usually read, not heard.

27. (C)

In this sentence, *me siento* comes from the verb *sentirse* (ie, i), which means "to feel." You should not confuse it with *sentarse* (ie) which means "to sit down." Remember that the first person singular of the present of these two verbs looks the same: *me siento*. It is only from the context that we can tell which of the two verbs we are dealing with. If the speaker says *No me siento bien*, followed by *tengo un...*, we must look for an ailment to place in the blank. Consequently, (A), *reloj* ("clock"), and (D), *uña* ("fingernail"), are incorrect. Granted, *enfermedad* means "illness," but it will not fit in the sentence because it is feminine, and the sentence gives us the masculine indefinite article *un*. Normally, words ending in *-a, -dad, -tad, -tud, -ión,* and *-ie* are feminine. The word *resfriado* means a "cold," and fits logically and grammatically in the sentence.

28. (B)

Ruido means "noise." Most people would agree that the sound of a siren tends to bother us. Therefore, we might expect to find some form of *molestar* ("to bother" or "upset") in the answer. The pronoun *me* is an indirect object of the verb *molesta* in this case. Answer (A) is wrong because it says the opposite of what we would normally anticipate: *me tranquiliza* ("calms me"). Answer (C) is wrong because the noise is not an inviting entity. *Me da celos* signifies "makes me jealous." Some form of the verb *dar* is often used in idiomatic expressions to convey the idea of "to make" in the sense of "to cause": *Los perros me dan miedo* ("Dogs make me afraid," i.e., "frighten me," etc.).

29. (D)
In translation, one would need the present participle for this verb form. Also, in Spanish, the verb form that commonly follows verbs of motion (*viajaba*) is the present participle. This eliminates (A) the infinitive, (B) the imperfect tense, and (C) the present subjunctive.

30. (A)
An *avería* refers to the breakdown of a motor. (B) *Un colapso* refers to a breakdown of one's health. (C) refers to a breakdown in negotiations, and (D) refers to an interruption of service.

31. (A)
A form of *ser* is required since *mexicana* indicates nationality. This eliminates choices (B) and (D), which are forms of the root *estar*. The imperfect is preferred because it indicates a characteristic that was ongoing, eliminating (C), the preteritee of *ser*.

32. (B)
In Spanish, expressing "whom" after a preposition requires the use of *quien*, eliminating (A), which cannot be used to refer to persons after a preposition. (C) is the relative pronoun that would be used to refer to a feminine antecedent. (D) is accented and would be used as an interrogative.

33. (D)
The only correct verb form after a preposition (*después de*) is the infinitive. Therefore, (A) the present participle, (B) the past subjunctive, and (C) the present indicative are incorrect.

34. (B)
The past participle is being used here as an adjective and must agree with the noun *señas.* Therefore, choices (A) and (C) are incorrect because they are of the wrong gender. (D) is the present participle.

35. (C)
The indirect object pronoun *le,* meaning "to her," is used with verbs such as this one. One offers help "to" another. Therefore, choices (A) and (D), which are direct object pronouns, and (B), the reflexive pronoun, are incorrect.

36. (A)
Hubiera is correct. The subjunctive is required in the noun clause when the main clause demonstrates wishing/wanting, emotion, an indirect command, doubt/denial, or is an impersonal expression. The verb in the main clause, *se sorprendió* ("was surprised at"), indicates emotion. The past subjunctive is required to follow the sequence established in the main clause (the preterite). Therefore, (B) the imperfect, (C) the present subjunctive, and (D) the conditional tenses are incorrect.

37. (B)
Because the subject is Marcelo and the action is complete, the third person singular of the preterite is needed. Although (C) would also fit this explanation, it doesn't fit contextually. Therefore, (A) preterite ("I looked for") and (D) present ("I see") are incorrect.

38. (C)
The translation, "He looked for a sign of hatred in the man's glance..." indicates that *indicio* is the correct choice. (A) *artículo* ("item"), (B) *sentido* ("sense"), and (D) *sensorial* ("sensory") do not fit in this context.

39. (D)
The noun preceding this choice (*odio*—"hatred") indicates a negative quality. (A) *amistad* ("friendship"), (B) *deseo* ("desire"), and (C) *curiosidad* are incorrect.

40. (B)
Within the context of this sentence, the word "relationship" is most logical: "Marcelo looked for a sign of enmity, hatred, in the man's glance something that would warn him about Alfredo's awareness of his relationship with her." Therefore, (A) *hijos* ("children"), (C) *negocios* ("business"), and (D) *obligaciones* ("obligations") are incorrect.

41. (C)
"Mirada" is correct. Because it is the man's "glance" and not his (A) "height," (B) "emotion," or (D) "sight" that is described as *lejana, pasiva* ("distant, passive"), answer (C) is the correct choice.

42. (D)
The subjunctive is required in an adjective clause with a negative antecedent (*nada*). To maintain proper tense sequence, the past subjunctive is needed (*reflejaba* is in the imperfect tense). Therefore, (A) the present subjunctive, (B) the imperfect tense, and (C) the conditional tense are incorrect.

43. (A)
Sin embargo ("nevertheless") makes sense in this context. (B) means "as usual," (C) means "without equal," and (D) means "without remedy."

44. (C)
The masculine plural adjective form of *satisfacer* ("to satisfy") is needed to match the noun *todos*. (A) is incorrect because it should be plural, (B) is conjugated in the present tense ("he satisfies"), and (D) is the infinitive ("to satisfy").

45. (A)
In context, the translation needed here is "that which" or "what" (*Lo que*). *Lo cual* does not share this same translation, which makes (B) incorrect. Response (C) is incorrect because it is the masculine relative pronoun that could mean who, which, or he who. Choice (D) is the plural relative pronoun meaning "those who."

46. (D)

The present tense predominates throughout this paragraph. Therefore, (A) the future tense ("they will go"), (B) the present subjunctive ("they may go"), and (C) the preterite ("they went") are incorrect.

47. (A)

Again, the present tense is called for in keeping with the meaning of this paragraph. (B) is incorrect because there is no reason for a subjunctive in this statement. (C) is the infinitive: incorrect. (D) is incorrect because it is the past subjunctive.

48. (D)

Un millón de is correct. (A) is incorrect because *uno* must be apocopated before a masculine singular noun, in this case *millón.* (B) is missing the *un.* (C) is misspelled.

49. (B)

Hace followed by a period of time means "ago." No other tense will render this meaning, which makes (A) the imperfect and (D) the preterite incorrect. (C) is incorrect because it is plural.

50. (A)

Los que, "those who," is required in this context. (B) would also mean "those who" if it weren't accented. (C) and (D) are written incorrectly.

51. (B)

Obras are written works. (A) means "male workers," (C) refers to physical work (in farming), and (D) means "female workers."

52. (B)

The masculine singular noun *régimen* means "diet" in Spanish. (A) *Horario* means schedule and refers to time. (C) *Dietas* is a feminine plural noun; thus, it doesn't match the masculine singular adjective *alimenticio.* (D) *Esquema* means scheme and doesn't apply in the context of diets.

53. (D)
The adjective *excesivo* means excessive, and it's the word that fits best contextually. *Excesivo* is frequently found accompanying the noun *consumo* in texts about food and diets. (A) *Reducido* means "reduced" which is contrary to the idea expressed here. (D) "Excess" is a noun, so it's incorrect. (B) "Minor" contradicts the idea that fat foods cause health problems.

54. (C)
Severos ("severe") is frequently found accompanying the noun *casos* ("cases") in medical texts. (A) *Severas* is a feminine noun and doesn't match the masculine *casos.* (B) "Difficult" isn't the best option in this passage. (D) *Pesados* ("heavy") is definitely not applicable in a medical context.

55. (A)
The past participle *advertido* ("warned") accompanies the auxiliary *han* to form a present perfect form. (B) *Advertidos* doesn't apply since past participles do not take plural forms. (C) *Dicho* isn't the best option because it is less descriptive and specific than *advertido.* (D) *Dichos* is an incorrect form of the past participle.

56. (A)
The adverb *actualmente* means "at present," and reinforces the central idea of the passage: nowadays there is a tendency to go on extreme diets that might cause health problems. (B) *Realmente* ("really") and (C) *definitivamente* ("definitively") do not apply in this context. (D) *Jamás* ("never") contradicts the idea of the passage.

57. (B)
is correct. Since the writer of the passage starts in the present tense (*Ya son las diez y media*), we know that the situation is happening right now. Thus, the fast train will arrive (*llegará*) in the near future. Answers (A) "was arriving"—imperfect past, (C) "arrived"—preterite, and (D) "would arrive"—conditional—do not apply here.

58. (D)
Since the story is happening right now, the slow train that carries mail (*el tren correo*) hasn't arrived yet and will take two more hours to arrive in Fulango. In this context, *todavía* means "still." (A) "Already," (B) "never," and (C) "always" do not fit the specific future action here.

59. (D)
The expression *soñar con* means "to dream about" and, in the context of the paragraph, implies a desire on Rafael's part. Consequently, the answer containing the verb *querer* is the most appropriate. Answer (A) would be wrong because *se hizo* means "became," but Rafael did not become a singer. In answer (B), *fingía* means "pretended," but the youth did not pretend he was a singer of popular music. Answer (C) is incorrect because *hacer falta* signifies "to need" ("to be necessary"), but López doesn't need money now that he has won the first prize in the Christmas lottery. In fact, he no longer has any financial problems, we are told. Note the use of the verb *tocar* in the first sentence of the paragraph. When it is preceded by an indirect object, as here, it may be translated as "to win something."

60. (B)
The idiom *servir de* signifies "to serve as." We know that Rafael served as a substitute in a band because we are told that he worked with the bank *sólo cuando faltaba alguien* (only when someone was missing). Here the verb *faltar* has the special meaning of "to be absent." Rafael did not win a musical prize, as (A) says, but rather the Christmas lottery. Answer (C) Rafael played the drum (tambor) not the guitar. Answer (D) tells us that Rafael had his own group (*su propio conjunto*), but the expression *pertenecer a* again indicates that he merely belonged to the group, not that it was his own.

61. (C)
To choose the correct answer, one must know that *ganó* is the past tense of *ganar* and that it means "[he, she] won." As we are told in the first sentence, ...*le ha tocado el gordo de la lotería de Navidad*, he has won the Christmas Lottery. Therefore, he has won a lot of money, which corresponds to answer (C), *mucho dinero*. Note that *el gordo* is the name given to the grand prize in the yearly lottery drawn during Christmas time in Spain. Answer (A) would not be appropriate since

there is no mention of a trip (*un viaje*) in the passage. Answer (B), *un conjunto musical*, refers to the band he plays in, and has nothing to do with Rafael winning the lottery. Answer (D), *un tambor*, is just referring to the drum and it is totally irrelevant to the question.

62. (A)

Getting the right answer here is dependent on knowing that *célebre* means "famous." The last sentence of the reading says that *no hay nadie que le desconozca*. The verb *desconocer* means "not to know or recognize." If there is no one who does not know Rafael, then he is famous. Notice that we have used the present subjunctive of the verb *desconocer*. This is necessary because the *que* refers back to a person whose identity is unknown (*nadie*). Whenever the relative pronoun *que* refers back to someone or something unknown or nonexistent, the verb following the *que* appears in the subjunctive. Compare these two sentences: *No hay nadie que sepa más que tú* ("There is no one who knows more than you"); *Hay muchos que saben más que yo* ("There are many who know more than I"). In the first sentence, we use the subjunctive of *saber* because the relative pronoun refers back to the word *nadie*, a non-existent entity. In the second sentence we use not the subjunctive, but the indicative of *saber* because the relative pronoun refers back to actual existing people, *muchos* ("many"). Answer (B) would be incorrect because of the verb *llorar* ("to cry"). Notice the particular use of *por qué* in answer (B). Here it means "motive" or "reason," but Rafael has little to cry about! To know that (C) is wrong, you must recognize the idiom *carecer de* + noun, which means "to be lacking [something)]." It is used here in the present progressive tense with the auxiliary verb *seguir* ("to continue"), and means "continues to lack" money. We know that this is untrue because Rafael has gotten rich from the lottery. Answer (D) uses the idiomatic expression *tener prisa* (to be in a hurry), which does not pertain to the situation.

63. (D)

In several parts of the article, either sand (*arena*) or the desert (*el desierto*) is mentioned. Paul Nieckel is mentioned as having won the first tournament at this club (*Su vencedor, Paul Nieckel, ...*), making (A) incorrect. Nowhere in the article is there a reference to this being the first golf club in Australia, making (B) incorrect. The club is neither small (*de 5.316 metros cuadrados*) nor easy to play, given its location in the desert, making (C) incorrect.

64. (C)

According to Paul Nieckel, "playing in the desert can be a good learning experience for gaining the precision needed in traditional tournaments" (*puede ser un buen aprendizaje para ganar en precisión ante los torneos tradicionales*). Since there is no mention of fees or membership in the article, (A) is incorrect. (B) is incorrect because Nieckel won the first tournament (*el primer trofeo*) on this course. The most immaculate fairways were mentioned in reference to other golf courses, not this one. Because this course is nothing but sand, (D) is incorrect.

65. (A)

It is stated in the text that the "players should carry a small chunk of sod to cushion the ball strike" (*deben llevar ... un pequeño trozo de césped para que el golpe resulte más cómodo*). Since grass is not used in bunkers, (B) is incorrect. Because the fairways are completely sand, any club strike will not damage them, making (C) incorrect. A chunk of sod will not provide protection from sand storms, making (D) incorrect.

66. (D)

Reo is a synonym for *ladrón* ("thief"). We know that after the holdup at the branch office (*sucursal*) of the National Bank, the criminals escaped (*huyeron*) with an undetermined amount of money, *una cantidad de dinero todavía por determinar. Todavía por determinar* means "yet to be determined." The policemen surrounded (*rodearon*) the district, made a sweep of the area (*hicieron una redada*) and were successful in their search (*búsqueda*). In other words, they found the thieves. Crucial in choosing the right answer is the idiomatic expression *tener éxito* (*en*), which has nothing to do with exits or leaving, but rather means "to succeed [in]" doing something.

67. (D)

The word *asalto* is a synonym of *atraco* ("holdup"), which appears in the first sentence of the reading. The expression *llevar a cabo* means "to realize" or "accomplish." It is used here in the passive voice to mean "was carried out." One finds the clue to the right answer in the phrase *por una pareja campesina temporalmente radicada en la ciudad. Una pareja* means "a pair," "two," "a couple." We know that these individuals were not from the city, but rather the countryside because of the adjective *campesina*. The verb *radicar*, whose past participle, *radicada*, is used as an adjective here means "to be located." We know, consequently, that the pair was temporarily (*temporalmente*) living in the city. Therefore, they were strangers there. Notice that we have used the word *campesinos* in (D)—not *extranjeros*—because the latter would erroneously imply that they were from a foreign country and not just from a different part of the same country. Answer (A) would be wrong because the reading does not say when the holdup took place. (B) is not right since the crime occurred in the outskirts of the city (*las afueras*) and not downtown (*en el centro de la ciudad*). (C) is incorrect because *alrededor de* means "around" in the sense of "surrounding."

68. (C)
Fue robado means "was robbed," another way of conveying the idea of *hubo un atraco*. It is used here in the passive voice. *Ayer por la tarde* means "yesterday afternoon," and appears in the first sentence of the reading. Therefore, the bank was robbed yesterday afternoon. (C) is the correct response according to this first sentence. Answer (A), *cierra a las cinco de la tarde*, is incorrect, since there is no mention of the closing time of the bank in the reading. Answer (B) says the bank is located in the downtown area of the capital, which is incorrect, since the opposite is mentioned in the first sentence of the reading: ...*situado en las afueras de la capital*. The expression *en las afueras* means "in the outskirts." Answer (D) is also incorrect since the actual size of the bank is never discussed in the passage. *Sucursal del Banco Nacional* means "a branch of the National Bank," which may or may not be the largest bank in the city.

69. (C)
The word *guardias* can mean "guards," but here it is used in a more general sense to signify "policemen." In answer (C), we have used the preterite tense of *saber* which can often mean "found out," rather than simply "knew." We see at the end of the story that the police captured the *reos* ("criminals") and identified them as a couple from the country. The policemen did not try to prevent a rebellion, as (A) indicates. The word *radicada* does not refer to "radical." (See explanation 67.) We know that the two criminals were from the countryside, but the police did not have to follow them into the countryside, as (B) says. *Perseguir* means "to pursue" or sometimes "to persecute." We know that the

police force was armed (*armada*). Therefore, answer (D) is wrong because it says that they arrived without *fusiles* ("guns").

70. (C)

We are told in the story that the criminals were *enmascarados* ("masked"). Another way of saying this would be *disfrazados* ("disguised"), as in choice (C). Answer (A) does mention that the criminals are out of towners, but nowhere in the reading does it say that they are kids. Choice (B) is incorrect because *del extranjero* means "from abroad," in other words, "foreigners." Answer (D) is also an inappropriate response because we know it is not the policemen (*la policía*) who robbed the bank.

71. (C)

We learn from the reading that the economic situation in Latin America is going from bad to worse (*va de mal en peor*) because of international debts (*deudas internacionales*) which many governments are unable to pay, the increase in the cost of living (*el aumento del costo de la vida*) and layoffs (*el paro forzoso*). Consequently, governments are lacking sufficient money (*a los gobiernos les falta suficiente dinero*), prices are rising (*Suben los precios*) and there is much unemployment (*desempleo*). Choosing the correct answer here can be aided by a clear understanding of certain other vocabulary and grammatical constructions: the difference between *subir* ("to go up or rise") and *bajar* ("to go down or fall"), *bastante* ("enough") and *demasiado* ("too much"). Notice also the use of the verbs *faltar* ("to be lacking to") and *sobrar* ("to be more than enough"). Both of these verbs follow the pattern of *gustar*, i.e., they are normally used in only the third person singular or plural and are preceded by an indirect object pronoun. If the thing lacking is singular, then the verb will be singular; if it is plural, then the verb will be plural: *Nos falta tiempo* ("We are lacking time"); *Nos faltan amigos* ("We are lacking friends"). The same holds true for the verb *sobrar*: *Nos sobra tiempo* ("We have more than enough time"); *Nos sobran amigos* ("We have more than enough friends").

72. (A)

The delegates (*delegados*) to the international economic conference are concerned by the unstable situation on international stock markets (*la situación inestable de las bolsas internacionales*), the drop in the value of the dollar (*la bajada del valor del dólar*) and the lack of balance in international trade (*el desequilibrio de la balanza de pagos*). They seek to arrive at an agreement (*llegar a un acuerdo*) which will avoid a possible financial collapse (*que evite un posible derrumbamiento*). Consequently, they are trying to stabilize (*estabilizar*) the international economy. The verb *evitar* means "to avoid." We have used it in the present tense of the subjunctive because the relative pronoun *que* refers back to an agreement (*acuerdo*) which is still in doubt, one which will perhaps be arrived at sometime later during the conference. (B) is wrong because *apenas*, meaning "scarcely," would imply that the delegates barely realize (*se dan cuenta de*) the seriousness (*la seriedad*) of the problem. Because of the verb *negar* (ie), "to deny," in answer (C), the statement would be contradictory to what we know. The delegates are not meeting to deny the seriousness (*la gravedad*) of the problem, but rather to remedy it. Item (D) is also wrong; the conferees are not necessarily going to devalue or lower the value (*bajar*) of currency (*la moneda*). In fact, they have not yet decided what they must do.

73. (B)
Se entiende is the reflexive form of the third person singular of the present tense of *entender* (ie), "to understand." Remember that this form of the reflexive can mean "one" does something. It is often used as a substitute for the true passive voice. Here it means "It is understood." Answer (A) tells us that the result (*el resultado*) will be effective *eficaz*, but there is no certainty of that. Item (C) says that the desired goal (*el fin deseado*) will be carried out (*se efectuará*); we have no assurance of that either. In (D), *propósito* means "purpose," and the future tense of *lograrse* signifies "will be accomplished," which is also a shaky assumption. In (B), the correct answer, *será necesario proceder con cuidado* means "it will be necessary to proceed with care." *Haber que* + infinitive, which appears in the third person singular of the future tense in the last sentence of the reading, means "to be necessary to...," and is synonymous to *ser necesario*. The verb *obrar*, which appears in the same sentence, means "to work," and *con cautela* signifies "with caution," and represents the same ideas as *con cuidado* ("with care or carefully").

74. (B)
If you know the word *miga* and choose (D), you have been misled by your knowledge of Spanish. You are better off to think of the connection between *miga* and *amigo* (or *amiga*) and further connect this word with *amistar*. The other choices, at any rate, do not make a great deal of sense.

75. (A)
The last choice is irrelevant; the passage says nothing about neighbors. If you chose (B) or (C) you did not read attentively enough.

76. (C)
Neither vets nor mice are mentioned in the reading, so you can eliminate choices (A) and (B). The key is to read *entrañables* in the passage as related to *cariño* in choice (C).

77. (C)
Although this ad is about drinking milk, question 77 refers to what this particular mother wants specifically for her child. The text, *Hacer que mi hija crezca sana y fuerte es todo para mí*, means she wants her daughter to grow up healthy and strong. This eliminates (A), referring to people's need to drink milk. *Para que brille*, in the ad, refers to her daughter's health, not to her becoming a star, eliminating (B). (D) is generally correct about milk, but is not the point of this particular question.

78. (D)
The false statement contradicts the information supplied in the reading in the sense that the colonial period is stated to have lasted "*tres siglos*."

79. (A)
The word *mayoría* should give you the answer. Notice that (C) is disqualified because there are no references to *negros* in the passage.

80. (C)
Choices (A), (B), and (D) refer directly (and in the same language) to factors identified in the paragraph as contributing to dictatorship. The

correct choice, moreover, contradicts the idea of poverty linked in the passage to Latin America.

81. (D)
The key is to re-read carefully the beginning of the final paragraph.

82. (A)
The first lines of the passage state that *los países hispanoamericanos han soñado con ser democráticos* (they have dreamed of being democratic. Choices (B), (C), and (D) refer to problems they have had for three centuries—forms of government they have been trying to eliminate.

83. (C)
The author of the article apparently believes that there is no handy remedy for the pollution problem. In the first sentence, he refers to it as a *rompecabezas* ("riddle," "puzzle") and an *insoluble cuestión* ("an unsolvable question"). Answer (C) is correct because it tells us that there are no appropriate remedies ("remedios aptos") for the pollution problem. The verb *faltar* in this answer means "to be lacking." Both answers (A) and (D) are wrong because they suggest that either water pollution is more serious than pollution of the atmosphere or the reverse. The article, however, does not say this. It speaks of the *contaminación tanto del agua como del aire*. The construction *tanto... como....* in this particular case means "both... and..." Answer (B) is clearly erroneous, for it says that "nature is free from the effects of society," which is contrary to the whole point of the article. Observe how the verb "quedar," which normally means "to remain," is used in (B) as a substitute for the verb *estar*.

84. (A)
The expression *tener la culpa* is used in the question. It means "to be to blame." The general thrust of the article is that society and the progress of civilization are responsible for polluting the environment. Answer (B) is wrong because *el medio ambiente* is "the environment" itself. Item (C), *la atmósfera* ("the atmosphere"), is not the cause, but the victim of man's effect on the environment. In (D), *los vertederos* ("trash dumps") are not to blame, but rather, man, who creates them.

85. (A)

The adjective *aguantable* is derived from the verb *aguantar* ("to bear") and means "bearable." The prefix *in-* is negative. Consequently, *inaguantable* would be "unbearable," which is exactly what radiation is for life. In (B), the adjective *soportable* is derived from the verb *soportar*, which is a synonym for *aguantable* and, of course, means "bearable." For (B) to be right, we would have to say *insoportable*, rather than *soportable*. In (C), the word *precisa* is a synonym for *necesaria* and, naturally, means "necessary." The word *bienestar*, as you can see, is composed of two words, *bien* ("well") and *estar* ("to be"). It means "well-being." *Ambiental* is an adjective derived from *ambiente* ("environment") and means "pertaining to the environment." Answer (C) claims that radiation is necessary for environmental well-being; quite the opposite is true. In (D), we are told that radiation is *beneficiosa* ("beneficial") to life, an idea which runs contrary to what is said in the article.

THE SAT SUBJECT TEST IN

Spanish

PRACTICE TEST 2

SAT Spanish Practice Test 2

PART A

Time: 1 Hour
85 Questions

DIRECTIONS: In this part you are given incomplete statements or questions, each of which has four possible completions. Choose the most accurate of the completions and fill in the corresponding oval on the answer sheet.

1. Para ser un buen cazador, hay que saber -------.

(A) comer
(B) tirar
(C) dormir
(D) nadar

2. Los Rodríguez van a hacer un viaje por Europa. Sería bueno si tuvieran -------.

(A) mucho sueño
(B) veinte hijos
(C) zapatos apretados
(D) un mapa

3. Ella es mi mejor amiga, por eso -------.

(A) me gusta estar con ella
(B) nunca le escribo a ella
(C) siempre se aleja de mí
(D) canta en voz alta

4. No puedo salir contigo porque no estoy -------.

(A) cansado
(B) vestido
(C) enfermo
(D) sonriendo

5. Él sí es más grande que yo. Con razón, -------.

(A) nunca hace nada
(B) siempre está a tiempo
(C) va a todas partes
(D) pesa más que yo

6. Los trenes corren por -------.

(A) las vías
(B) los canales
(C) las fronteras
(D) las carreteras

7. No me gusta tomar el sol porque siempre -------.

(A) llueve
(B) me quemo
(C) me escribe la familia
(D) me mojo

8. No puedo mover el brazo. Parece que está -------.

(A) de mal humor
(B) lejos de mí
(C) paralizado
(D) fuera de moda

9. Yo no sé cuál ------- escoger para llegar a Madrid.

(A) carta
(B) fruta
(C) oportunidad
(D) camino

10. Mi madre está orgullosa de mí, pues me dice que soy muy -------.

(A) sobrino
(B) listo
(C) nieto
(D) malo

11. Me gusta estar en la panadería por -------.

(A) el olor
(B) la gente
(C) la presión alta
(D) lo mojado que está

12. Yo te ayudaré a ------- las maletas.

(A) estudiar
(B) hacer
(C) comer
(D) beber

13. Aquí tiene usted una gardenia y una azalea. Todas son -------.

(A) árboles
(B) frutas
(C) bebidas
(D) flores

14. Antes de que te cases, mira bien lo que -------.

(A) paces
(B) ases
(C) traes
(D) haces

15. Alguien viene a visitarme. Lo sé porque alguien está -------.

(A) construyendo la puerta
(B) jugando con la puerta
(C) tocando a la puerta
(D) escondiéndose detrás de la puerta

16. Fui a visitar a un amigo en el hospital. No es grave el caso de él; sólo tiene -------.

(A) pie de atleta
(B) polio
(C) pulmonía
(D) dos días de vida

17. Me gusta ir a México porque todo el mundo me -------.

(A) desprecia
(B) critica
(C) repugna
(D) comprende

18. Sin -------, no puedo recomendar la película.

(A) ver
(B) veo
(C) verla
(D) verlo

19. Ella siempre come mucho, y además es buena cocinera. Con razón pesa doscientas libras. Está -------.

(A) larga
(B) delgadísima
(C) con hambre
(D) gorda

20. El avión pasó por unos aires violentos. Algunos de los pasajeros se enfermaron y tenían ganas de -------.

(A) brincar
(B) vomitar
(C) comer
(D) correr

21. En el rancho había mucho ganado, a lo menos tres mil. Ya estaban grandes todos y el ranchero pronto los iba a llevar al -------.

(A) matadero
(B) centro
(C) rodeo
(D) orfanatorio

22. Me encanta esquiar, pero siempre hay riesgos. El año pasado me caí y se me rompió la pierna. En el hospital me la -------.

(A) besaron
(B) pintaron
(C) enyesaron
(D) cortaron

23. Al comenzar el estudio del español, apenas sabía yo los verbos más importantes, pero sí podía -------.

(A) conjugarlos
(B) jugarlos
(C) enjuagarlos
(D) enjaularlos

24. Los deportes me gustan mucho, sobretodo los deportes individuales. Cuando estoy en el rancho, me esfuerzo por montar -------.

(A) el cabello
(B) la caverna
(C) la cebolla
(D) al caballo

25. Un amigo mío tiene unos modales muy diferentes a los míos; él se baña cada sábado, sea necesario o no, y yo me baño todos los días. Por consiguiente, uso más ------- que él.

(A) ropa
(B) jabón
(C) comida
(D) desodorante

26. Federico es joven y fuerte. Todos los días va al gimnasio y levanta pesas. Lo ha hecho por meses y ahora está bien -------.

(A) fornido
(B) cansado
(C) flaco
(D) mal

27. María es amiga de todos. Siempre cuando puede, ayuda a todo el mundo. Ella es muy -------.

(A) desagradable
(B) antipática
(C) detestable
(D) simpática

28. Luisa es una mujer muy bella. Todos los hombres la admiran y hasta las mujeres también. Es una hermosura natural la que tiene; no es necesario -------.

(A) el maquillaje
(B) la máquina
(C) la mantequilla
(D) la maquinista

PART B

DIRECTIONS: In each of the following paragraphs, there are numbered blanks indicating that words or phrases are missing. Four completions are provided for each numbered blank. Read the entire passage. For each numbered blank, choose the completion that is the most appropriate given the context of the entire paragraph. Fill in the corresponding oval on the answer sheet.

Era julio y hacía un calor __(29)__ y no encontraba cómo refrescarme. Aquella noche salí con unos amigos que __(30)__ de los planes de ir a esquiar. Los escuché atentamente por unos minutos y no tenía la menor idea de adónde pensaban ir en agosto. Les __(31)__ adónde __(32)__ a esquiar en agosto. Al oír esto, __(33)__ y me contestaron "Bariloche." Sorprendida y __(34)__ me sentí verdaderamente estúpida. Uno de ellos me explicó que está en la Argentina, como si __(35)__ tonta. Al sur de Sudamérica en las __(36)__ de los Andes hay magníficas __(37)__ de esquiar.

29. (A) intoxicante
    (B) sofocante
    (C) fresco
    (D) encantador

30. (A) hablaban
    (B) hablaron
    (C) hablaran
    (D) hablen

31. (A) he preguntado
    (B) preguntaré
    (C) preguntaron
    (D) pregunté

32. (A) irían
    (B) iría
    (C) iban
    (D) iba

33. (A) se ríen
(B) se rieron
(C) se reían
(D) se reirán

34. (A) confundida
(B) confusa
(C) en desorden
(D) obscura

35. (A) fuera
(B) sea
(C) fui
(D) era

36. (A) laderas
(B) cimas
(C) colinas
(D) alturas

37. (A) pistas
(B) ciudades
(C) vistas
(D) cortes

Pensé un momento y decidí ir con ellos. Por días sólo hablé del viaje; en mi mente sólo tenía mi __(38)__, pero al __(39)__ el día de salir en el largo viaje, me entró tal __(40)__ y ataque de nervios que no __(41)__ podía controlar. Días antes de __(42)__ decidí ser __(43)__ conmigo misma y admitir que el miedo me tenía __(44)__ un saco de nervios. Bueno, con todo fui de viaje y lo __(45)__ muy bien. Descansé y esquié un poco pero __(46)__ más importante fue que enfrenté mi miedo.

38. (A) llegada
(B) emoción
(C) encuentro
(D) aventura

39. (A) acercándose
(B) se acerca
(C) acercarse
(D) se acercaba

40. (A) ansiedad
(B) sonrisa
(C) depresión
(D) alegría

41. (A) la
(B) lo
(C) las
(D) los

42. (A) salgo
(B) salí
(C) salir
(D) saliera

43. (A) controlada
(B) honesta
(C) amistosa
(D) seria

44. (A) hecha
(B) hecho
(C) hacer
(D) haciendo

45. (A) pasé
(B) pasó
(C) pasaba
(D) pasaría

46. (A) el
(B) la
(C) los
(D) lo

Ayer por la tarde hubo un __(47)__ en una __(48)__ del Banco Nacional situado en las afueras de la capital. Los __(49)__ enmascarados huyeron del lugar del crimen llevándose una cantidad de dinero todavía por determinar y sin ser identificados. Los agentes de la policía armada __(50)__ el barrio, hicieron una redada y, a las cinco de la tarde, tuvieron __(51)__ en su búsqueda. __(52)__ de que se trataba de una pareja campesina temporalmente __(53)__ en la capital.

47. (A) agresión
    (B) asalto
    (C) desembarco
    (D) estafa

48. (A) instituto
    (B) rama
    (C) sucursal
    (D) institución

49. (A) criminales
    (B) presos
    (C) culpables
    (D) víctimas

50. (A) cortaron
    (B) pasearon por
    (C) pasaron por
    (D) rodearon

51. (A) éxito
    (B) fin
    (C) fracaso
    (D) gloria

52. (A) buscaron
    (B) se enteraron
    (C) pensaron
    (D) lograron

53. (A) vivida
(B) parada
(C) radicada
(D) situada

Desde hace dos días la familia Rodríguez gozaba de la anticipación del viaje que iba a hacer a Tijuana. Los dos niños expresaban su __(54)__ no sólo con sus preguntas, sino también con la nerviosidad que __(55)__ incesantemente. La abuelita, aunque __(56)__ la misma emoción, por ser mayor hacía todo lo posible por esconderla. Siempre le gustaba ir a Tijuana. Todos deseaban comprar tortillas, pan, jícama, vainilla, hierbas medicinales y, lo más importante, estar en México donde se hablaba español.

54. (A) obsesión
(B) pesar
(C) entusiasmo
(D) delirio

55. (A) demostraban
(B) inhibían
(C) presentaban
(D) escondían

56. (A) sentía
(B) sintió
(C) sentir
(D) ha sentido

PART C

DIRECTIONS: Read the following passages for comprehension. Following each passage are a number of questions or incomplete sentences. Choose the most appropriate response or completion and fill in the corresponding oval on the answer sheet.

Los Estados Unidos no es un país como México o España que dependa económicamente del turismo, pero atrae a cientos de miles de turistas cada año. Resulta interesante ver este país desde la perspectiva de un turista, digamos, sudamericano. Vamos a llamar Claudio a este hipotético turista, y vamos a asumir que vino a los Estados Unidos para conocer lo más posible. O sea que en vez de concentrar el turismo en una sola ciudad como Los Ángeles o Nueva York, Claudio decidió juntarse con un amigo y recorrer ciertas áreas de este país en auto. Lo primero que impresionó a Claudio fue la cultura automovilística de los EE. UU. Esto quiere decir que en este país prácticamente todo el mundo es dueño de un auto, que hay carreteras magníficas y enormes, y que uno no puede andar más de unas cuadras o millas sin toparse con las estaciones de gasolina. Claudio también quedó impresionado porque pudo arrendar un auto en una ciudad y devolverlo en otra. Estas facilidades no existen en su país natal. Pero después de los primeros días la novedad de pasear en auto por todas partes dejó de impactar a Claudio, y éste empezó a aburrirse con la monotonía de las carreteras interestatales, siempre iguales, largas, y sin paisjes pintorescos que admirar. Dejó de tomar fotos, incluso. Pero siguió pensando que una de las grandes diferencias culturales entre los norte y los sudamericanos se centra en el uso y abuso del automóvil. A un sudamericano no se le ocuríría soñar con un Cadillac del 50, por ejemplo, ni asociar su capacidad de conquistar mujeres con la posesión del automóvil adecuado (es decir, no un Yugo sino un Camaro). Claudio piensa que en su país tener un auto cualquiera ya es una gran cosa, y que uno no puede darse el gusto de andar eligiendo marcas. Pero como Claudio vive en una gran ciudad sudamericana, al volver a casa no extrae el auto que no tiene.

Se subió a su ómnibus de siempre y fue a trabajar contento de haber pasado unos días en las carreteras norteamericanas.

57. ¿Cómo se aseguró Claudio de conocer lo más posible de los Estados Unidos?

(A) Comprando un buen mapa
(B) Juntándose con un amigo y alquilando un coche
(C) Casándose con una amiga norteamericana
(D) Entrando desde México

58. ¿Qué piensa Claudio de las carreteras interestatales?

(A) que son magníficas pero aburridas.
(B) que son un buen sitio para tomar fotos pintorescas.
(C) que son iguales a las de su país sudamericano.
(D) no sabe qué pensar porque él anduvo en tren todo el tiempo.

59. ¿Por qué no existe una cultura automovilística en los países sudamericanos?

(A) porque los sudamericanos prefieren tomar el autobús
(B) porque hay muchos analfabetos en Sudamérica
(C) porque el subdesarrollo de los países hace que haya pocos autos entre los cuales elegir y que éstos sean caros
(D) porque hay muy pocos caminos pavimentados

60. ¿Piensa Claudio que hay que tener un buen auto para conquistar a una chica?

(A) Sí, porque a todas las chicas les gusta pasear en auto.
(B) No, con una motocicleta basta.
(C) si, sobre todo un Yugo
(D) no, porque Claudio es sudamericano y no existe una cultura automovilística en su país

No sé cómo me enfermé. La comida será diferente, pero ha sido sabrosa y yo tenía un hambre feroz. Puede ser que haya comido demasiado. De todos modos esta mañana me atacó un retortijón de tripas intolerables que duró casi una hora. Apenas podía yo respirar por el dolor. Hablé con el gerente del hotel cuando pude para que me pusiera en contacto con un médico. Grande fue la sorpresa mía cuando me anunció sin emoción ninguna que aquí en este pueblo no hay médico. Sólo hay un homeópata, pero es bueno y sabe curar. ¿Qué iba yo a hacer? Tenía que ir con él. Después de indicarle las síntomas, me dio ciertas hierbas indicándome cómo hacer el té que debiera tomar. Milagro de milagros. Después de tomar el té, comencé a sentirme mejor y en dos días estaba como nuevo.

61. ¿Dónde se encontraba la persona del cuento?

(A) en ciudad grande
(B) en un hospital
(C) en un pueblo chico
(D) en su casa

62. La persona sufrió de

(A) una jaqueca
(B) dolores fuertes de los intestinos
(C) un resfriado
(D) pies planos

63. El homeópata era

(A) bueno para curar
(B) un matasanos
(C) el gerente del hotel
(D) profesor de escuela

64. La persona debiera hacer el té y

(A) aplicarlo al lugar del dolor
(B) respirar el vapor
(C) tomarlo
(D) mirarlo

10 CONSEJOS PARA HACER LAS PACES

1 Hacer las paces tras una discusión, un conflicto o un malentendido con alguna persona afectivamente cercana no es fácil, pero si dejas pasar demasiado tiempo será aún peor. Corre.

• • •

2 Alguien tiene que dar el primer paso. ¿Por qué no puedes ser tú? Si te pones a investigar quién tuvo más culpa, complicarás las cosas y no encontrarás nunca la reconciliación.

3 No dramatices, que no se hunde el mundo por una rebeldía. Si hubo algo más, ¿no sería mejor analizarlo juntos?

• • •

4 Escucha: dale una oportunidad a la otra parte, tal vez interpretaste mal, o él/ella interpretó mal.

5 A veces la ira es tal que correr a reconciliarse empeora la situación. Espera a calmarte. Da tiempo al tiempo, sin prisa alguna.

• • •

6 No te hagas la ofendida ni la víctima, que no es para tanto, y esas «dignas» actitudes están pasadas de moda. Relaja el gesto y relativiza un poco.

• • •

7 Sostener y no enmendar la falta es nefasto para la felicidad. Si ya sabes que te pasaste, ¿quieres volver a equivocarte al no dar tu brazo a torcer?

• • •

8 Es cierto que en ocasiones nos hieren, o nos hacen algo que no nos gusta, pero dedicarse a mimar tales recuerdos no es nada positivo: se pudren. Olvida. Pelillos a la mar.

• • •

9 Si la otra persona hace el esfuerzo de dar el primer paso, no cometas la imperdonable grosería de hacerte de rogar. Facilítale las cosas. Y agradécele su generosidad.

• • •

10 ¿Qué significa una gotita de enfado en la inmensidad oceánica de una amistad o una pasión, de la que sin duda tienes recuerdos más positivos y vitales?

65. El número 8, según el contexto, ¿qué significa "pelillos a la mar"?

(A) que uno debe enfocar en las heridas para resolverlas
(B) que uno debe pensar en los recuerdos malos
(C) que uno debe ponerlo todo en perspectiva para olvidarlo
(D) que uno debe mimar al herido

66. ¿Por qué sugieren que uno espere antes de reconciliarse?

(A) Cada cual necesita tiempo para pensar con razón.

(B) Cada cual necesita decidir quién tiene la culpa verdadera.
(C) Cada cual necesita consejos de otros primero.
(D) Cada cual necesita ayuda profesional.

67. En cuanto a la "falta,"

(A) Hay que establecer quién la tiene para poder continuar
(B) Hay que examinarla detalladamente
(C) Hay que sostenerla
(D) Hay que hacer caso omiso de ella

Llovía a cántaros y era la medianoche. El tren seguía su trayectoria como de costumbre aunque el ingeniero no podía ver nada, ni las vías. Era fuerte el ojo ciclópico del monstruo de hierro, pero no servía de nada. Era tanta la lluvia que hasta goteaba por el techo de los coches. Unos pasajeros se mojaban, especialmente los que estaban dormidos. Otros, de menos fe en el ingeniero, miraban por las ventanas tratando de penetrar la oscuridad o se daban miradas de sospecha. El tren iba rápidamente, pero ahora comenzaba a caminar más despacio. Eso daba más razón de dudar a los preocupados que demostraban más inquietud como si anticiparan un desastre o algo semejante. Después de un rato no era tanta la velocidad del tren. De pronto el tren se paró. Los pasajeros que dormían se despertaron y por todos los coches se oía el bullicio de comentarios y preguntas. Todos querían saber lo que pasaba.

El ingeniero va delante del tren con su linterna, dijo uno que se asomaba por una ventana.

Esto causó más exitación. Después de unos minutos corrían por todo el tren estas noticias: ¡El ingeniero ha descubierto que la mucha agua ha llevado gran parte de las vías. ¡El tren volverá atrás a la última estación!

68. Llovía y

(A) era de noche
(B) soplaba mucho el viento
(C) brillaba el sol
(D) hacía un frío terrible

69. Confiaban en el ingeniero del tren

(A) unos niños
(B) todos los pasajeros
(C) unos pasajeros
(D) sus hijos

70. Después de examinar las vías, el ingeniero

(A) decidió seguir adelante
(B) mandó repararlas
(C) decidió no mover el tren
(D) decidió regresar a la última parada

71. La mucha agua había

(A) mojado a todos los pasajeros
(B) llevado el tren de la vía
(C) impedido el progreso del tren
(D) apagado la luz

72. Unos de los pasajeros

(A) estaban nerviosos
(B) no pagaron el pasaje
(C) tenían hambre y comenzaron a comer
(D) bajaron del tren

Qué es Metrotour

Si usted ha venido a conocer y disfrutar de nuestra ciudad, hágalo ahora, Metro a Metro, con Metrotour, la tarjeta turística del Metro de Madrid.

La tarjeta Metrotour le permite viajar en Metro durante 3 ó 5 días consecutivos, por sólo 575 ptas. y 850 ptas. respectivamente. Y realizar en ese período todos los trayectos que quiera o necesite en sus desplazamientos.

La tarjeta Metrotour lleva la firma del usuario titular, estando autorizados los empleados del Metro a solicitar su identificación mediante pasaporte o D.N.I. si es necesario. Y se puede adquirir en cualquiera de las taquillas existentes en las estaciones del Metro de Madrid.

Con Metrotour usted sólo obtiene ventajas. Ahorra dinero en sus desplazamientos. Y aprovecha mejor su tiempo conociendo todo lo que Madrid puede ofrecerle.

Pida la tarjeta Metrotour y... ¡feliz estancia en Madrid, Metro a Metro!

¡Bienvenido a Madrid con Metrotour!

¡Descubra Madrid...!

Descubrir Madrid cada día es algo nuevo y diferente. Desde el Madrid de los Austrias, recio y elegante, hasta el Madrid moderno lleno de bullicio y ambiente, Madrid es una ciudad viva y atrayente que gusta a todos los que la visitan.

Para conocer y disfrutar mejor de todos los rincones de esta gran ciudad, utilice la tarjeta Metrotour y siga las rutas que este Madrid, Metro a Metro, le ofrece.

Siempre hay un Metro cerca de usted para llevarle. Mire las líneas y sus estaciones y elija lo que más le interese de Madrid..., en Metro.

73. ¿Cuál es el uso de Metrotour?

(A) Deja que el turista viaje gratis.
(B) Deja que el turista evite el ruido de la ciudad.
(C) Deja que el turista conozca a Madrid por metro sin pagar mucho.
(D) Deja que el turista viaje a Asturias a pago reducido.

74. Se describe a Madrid como

(A) una ciudad sin atracciones modernas
(B) una ciudad con un sistema limitado de transporte
(C) una ciudad donde se identifica mediante un pasaporte
(D) una ciudad que ofrece mucho al extranjero

Cuando Clara canta, hasta los pájaros se callan. Tiene una voz sumamente hermosa, una de ésas que encantan. Y ella nunca ha estudiado; es una voz natural. Creo que nunca le han pagado en ninguna parte, pues ella goza de cantar; es su vida.

Clara siempre ha sido pobre y ha tenido que trabajar para ganar la vida. Un día un director de cine la oyó cantar y decidió ofrecerle un contrato. Ahora es muy famosa; su voz le ha traído riquezas sin par. Antes era el canario, ahora es la cotorra. Pero, no hay mal que por bien no venga. Ya que es rica, tiene muchos pretendientes y dicen que pronto se va a casar.

75. Lo más importante en la vida para Clara es

(A) casarse
(B) firmar el contrato
(C) ganar la vida
(D) cantar

76. Muchos quieren

(A) casarse con ella
(B) apoderarse de su dinero
(C) cantar como ella
(D) conseguir su autógrafo

77. Según el cuento, más vale ser cotorra rica que

(A) golondrina bonita
(B) paloma muerta
(C) pájaro cantante
(D) buitre feo

—No, no quiero confesarme. No sé por qué me tienen preso. No quiero que usted ni nadie me moleste. Lo que sí quiero es vivir y no morir. No me nieguen la vida, es mía y no quiero que me la quiten. Si ustedes son cristianos, ¿por qué me la quieren quitar? Yo quiero vivir. Soy joven y tengo una novia que me quiere mucho, igual que mis padres. Yo sé que usted me dirá que la muerte es la puerta para la vida eterna, pero ésta es la que me vale. No quiero dejar esta vida, ¿me entiende usted? La vida para mí es bella. Si fuera cosa de morir en guerra, eso sería diferente. En ese caso uno moriría con respeto, luchando por una causea honrada y por principios. Eso vale la pena, pero morir ante el paredón, ¡no! Eso no lo entiendo. No tiene sentido morir así. Hasta sería una vergüenza para mí, para la familia, para mi novia y para la humanidad. Es inhumano morir de esta forma.

78. ¿Dónde estará el joven?

(A) con su novia
(B) en la iglesia
(C) sentado a la mesa
(D) en la cárcel

79. ¿Quién vino a estar con él?

(A) un sacerdote
(B) un amigo
(C) su familia
(D) el verdugo

80. ¿Dónde prefereria morir?

(A) cerca de la novia
(B) en el campo de batalla
(C) en el hospital
(D) con la familia

Cuando el marinero se despertó, se encontraba solo y tirado en una playa extensa.

— ¿Sería isla? se decía. — ¿Y dónde están los otros?

El era el único sobreviviente del bergantín naufragado. Él se acordaba de la tempestad violenta y la eminente destrucción del barco y luego esa ola inmensa que lo llevó al mar. Con sus últimos esfuerzos pudo agarrar una tabla suelta. Luego se había despertado adolorido y cansado, pero vivo y pudo ponerse de pie para mirar a su alrededor, buscando otro ser viviente - - pero no había nadie. ¿Qué iba a hacer él? ¿Cómo podría vivir? ¿Qué comería? ¿Cómo podría protegerse de la intemperie? ¡De repente se oye un rugido fuerte! El náufrago quedó petrificado.

81. Por el texto se sabe que el barco era

(A) moderno
(B) insumergible
(C) de tiempos pasados
(D) submarino

82. Llegó a la playa

(A) cantando
(B) nadando
(C) flotando
(D) andando

83. Le molestaba

(A) la soledad
(B) el tráfico
(C) la mucha arena
(D) el sol caliente

84. Estaba preocupado por

(A) su familia
(B) la tripulación
(C) la ropa manchada
(D) su situación física

85. El último temor vino como resultado

(A) de tantos árboles
(B) de los cocos que se caían
(C) de sus zapatos mojados
(D) del gran ruido desconocido

SAT Subject Test in Spanish
Practice Test 2

ANSWER KEY

1. (B)
2. (D)
3. (A)
4. (B)
5. (D)
6. (A)
7. (B)
8. (C)
9. (D)
10. (B)
11. (A)
12. (B)
13. (D)
14. (D)
15. (C)
16. (A)
17. (D)
18. (C)
19. (D)
20. (B)
21. (A)
22. (C)
23. (A)
24. (D)
25. (B)
26. (A)
27. (D)
28. (A)
29. (B)
30. (A)
31. (D)
32. (C)
33. (B)
34. (B)
35. (A)
36. (D)
37. (A)
38. (D)
39. (C)
40. (A)
41. (D)
42. (C)
43. (B)
44. (A)
45. (A)
46. (D)
47. (B)
48. (C)
49. (A)
50. (D)
51. (A)
52. (B)
53. (C)
54. (C)
55. (A)
56. (A)
57. (B)
58. (A)
59. (C)
60. (D)
61. (C)
62. (B)
63. (A)
64. (C)
65. (C)
66. (A)
67. (D)
68. (A)
69. (C)
70. (D)
71. (D)
72. (A)
73. (C)
74. (D)
75. (D)
76. (A)
77. (C)
78. (D)
79. (A)
80. (B)
81. (C)
82. (C)
83. (A)
84. (D)
85. (D)

DETAILED EXPLANATIONS OF ANSWERS

PRACTICE TEST 2

1. (B)

One must know the idiom *hay que* and that *saber* also means "to know how" in order to complete the sentence properly. All the answers are in the infinitive, but only *tirar* has anything to do with being a *cazador*, a "hunter."

2. (D)

It is important to recognize the imperfect subjunctive form of *tener*, *tuvieran*. The only answer appropriate for travelers is *un mapa*, "a map." The other answers are not logical, especially (C) tight shoes.

3. (A)

The *por eso* idiom must be understood to choose "I like to be with her," the only suitable answer to complete the sentence because she is my best friend. Answers (B), (C), and (D) are obviously unsuitable. Answer (C) means "to keep her distance."

4. (B)

An understanding of all possible answers is necessary to connect "I can't go out with you" with "I am not dressed."

5. (D)

The comparative "taller" or "bigger" requires *él pesa más que yo*. The *sí* in this sentence can be translated as "really," and *con razón* as "naturally."

6. (A)
None of the other answers fit the word *trenes*, except the word for "rails" (*vías*); (B) and (D) are routes of other types of travel.

7. (B)
The use of *gustar* is to be translated as "to be pleasing," rather than as in English, "to like." When two verbs are used together, the first is conjugated, the second is generally in the infinitive. Sun bathing can produce a burn. Note the use of the reflexive *quemarse*. None of the other answers can be correct.

8. (C)
Again, two verbs used together, the first is conjugated, the second in the infinitive or sometimes the gerund. *Mover* is a cognate of "to move," as is the proper answer, *paralizado*. Students should take advantage of proper cognate recognition, but should remember too that there are also false cognates.

9. (D)
Cuál may be used with a feminine or masculine noun, so the choice of answer must depend on knowing the meaning of *llegar* connected with Madrid. One gets to Madrid by a road. The other choices are unrelated to the subject.

10. (B)
One must understand the word *orgullosa* in order to answer correctly. If my mother is "proud" of me, then she will most likely tell me I am *listo*, "clever" or "smart." None of the other choices make sense.

11. (A)
The *ia* ending on nouns usually indicates "shop," and in this case refers to a "bakery." The only logical connection with any of the possible answers is "the smell." All the other answers are unpleasant.

12. (B)
One must understand that *hacer* is used with *maleta* as an idiomatic expression for "to pack." The other choices are irrelevant to the subject.

13. (D)
These words all resemble names of flowers.

14. (D)
This is actually an old Spanish proverb. All possible answers contain the assonance rhyme of *a-e*, which might seem confusing. The only suitable answer is *haces*. "Grazing," "grabbing," and "bringing" are inappropriate.

15. (C)
The present participle is used in all the possible answers. Both *jugando* and *tocando* are used for playing; *jugar* for playing a game, *tocar* for playing an instrument. However, *tocar* is also used for "to knock," therefore, answer (C) is correct.

16. (A)
One must understand that *no es grave* means "it is not serious." The only case not serious is (A), "athlete's foot." "Polio," "pneumonia," and "two days to live" are unsuitable.

17. (D)
All the answers but (D) have negative meanings, therefore, "I like to go to Mexico because everyone understands me" is the only feasible answer.

18. (C)
In Spanish, if a verb follows a preposition, the infinitive must be used. In this case, the pronoun *la* is added to the infinitive, which is customary, referring to *película*.

19. (D)
The only relationship between the information in the sentences and the proper answer is *gorda*. Weighing 200 pounds is considered heavy for a woman. *Larga* may resemble the English "large," but actually means "long."

20. (B)
Some of the passengers became ill. The only verb related to the illness is *vomitar*. No one would want to "jump," "eat," or "run" while feeling sick in an airplane.

21. (A)
One must understand the word *ganado* to apply to cattle, otherwise none of the answers have any meaning. The cognate *matar* gives logical sense to *matadero*. (C) is a remote possibility, but unacceptable when compared with the correct response, (A). "Downtown" or "to the orphanage" are inappropriate.

22. (C)
The reflexives *me caí*, and *se me rompió* give the key to the answer. Knowing that *yeso* is plaster helps to understand the verb *enyesar*, "to put on a cast." The other choices, although used in the reflexive, make no sense.

23. (A)
None of the answers have anything to do with the subject of the sentence except (A). One of the first grammar exercises learned by language students is conjugation. (B) "to play with them," (C) "to rinse them," and (D) "to cage them," are incorrect.

24. (D)
There could be confusion among (A), (C), and (D) because of spelling similarities. The sentence indicates a love for individual sports, and *caballo*, "horse," is the only possible answer connected with *rancho*. *Cabello* means "hair," and *cebolla* means "onion."

25. (B)
The only relationship between bathing and the possible answers is (B), "soap," and it is supposed that one who bathes more often uses more "soap," not more "clothing," "food," or "deodorant."

26. (A)
The word *pesas* is a cognate of *peso*, but means “weights” rather than “money.” One must also know that *fornido* means “well-built,” “strong."

27. (D)
Simpática is a false cognate of “sympathetic”; it really means “nice.” Since she is friendly and helpful, she is “nice,” not “disagreeable,” “unpleasant,” nor “hateful.”

28. (A)
The only answer relative to beauty is *el maquillaje*, and since she is a natural beauty, she does not need “make-up.”

29. (B)
Sofocante is correct. It means “impeding respiration,” which is what the air was doing to him. (A) “Intoxicating or poisonous,” (C) “cool, fresh,” and (D) “charmer” are all incorrect.

30. (A)
“They were talking,” *hablaban,* fits perfectly. Although this is an adjective clause modifying the antecedent *amigos,* no subjunctive is required because the antecedent is definite. This eliminates (C) and (D), which are both subjunctive. (B) The preterite is incorrect since a continuous past action is being intimated.

31. (D)
Again, the completed past action (*pregunté*) is required. (A) “I have asked,” (B) “I will ask,” and (C) “they asked” are incorrect.

32. (C)
Iban is correct. (B) and (D) must be eliminated because they are singular. The indirect object pronoun *les* (“to them”), which precedes *pregunté,* indicates that the subject of this verb is plural. (A) “They would go” is incorrect since the translation should be “they were going.”

33. (B)
The preterite (*se rieron*) is correct, since the action is locked into a specific point in time in the past with the statement *al oír esto* ("upon hearing this"). Therefore, (A) the present tense ("they laugh"), (C) the imperfect tense ("they were laughing"), and (D) the future tense ("they will laugh") are all incorrect.

34. (B)
The correct translation for this item is "confused." This eliminates (C) and (D) as possible answers. In most cases, the past participle of a verb acts as an adjective. However, there are exceptions, and this is one of them. Choice (A) is the past participle or verbal form, while choice (B) is the adjective form.

35. (A)
The past subjunctive (*fuera*) is required after "*como si*" ("as if"). Therefore, (B) the present subjunctive, (C) the preterite, and (D) the imperfect are all incorrect.

36. (D)
Alturas ("heights") is correct. The other choices, (A) "sides," (B) "summits," and (C) "hills," do not make sense contextually.

37. (A)
Pistas ("trails") is correct. (B) "Cities," (C) "views," and (D) "courts" make no sense in this context.

38. (D)
Aventura ("adventure") is correct. (A) "Arrival," (B) "emotion," and (C) "encounter" do not translate well in this context.

39. (C)
Al followed by an infinitive means "upon." In this case, the translation is "Upon approaching the day of departure..." (A) The present participle, (B) the present tense ("it approaches"), and (D) "it was approaching" are conjugated and cannot follow *al*.

40. (A)
The choices given here have to make sense when translated. In the context of this statement, the person is referring to a nervous attack. (A) "Anxiety" fits well. (B) "smile," (C) "depression," and (D) "happiness" are incorrect.

41. (D)
The masculine direct object pronoun is a redundant reference to the previously mentioned compound direct object already stated (anxiety and nervous attack). It is common in Spanish, when the direct object precedes the verb, to use a direct object pronoun to refer back to it. Choices (A), (B), and (C) are direct object pronouns that are incorrect in gender and number.

42. (C)
Salir is correct. *Antes de* is a preposition and, in Spanish, the only correct verb form that can directly follow a preposition is the infinitive. In English, we use a present participle in this structure. Because (A), (B), and (D) are all conjugated verb forms, they are not acceptable.

43. (B)
A translation of this sentence would indicate that (B) "honest" makes the most sense. (A) "Controlled," (C) "friendly," and (D) "serious" are not logical contextually.

44. (A)
Hecha is correct. This past participle is being used as an adjective to refer back to the subject (*yo—estaba*), a woman, eliminating (B), which is masculine. (C) The infinitive and (D) the present participle are incorrect verb forms in this context.

45. (A)
The subject (*yo*) is given in the first verb. The completed past (preterite) is required also. Therefore, (B) "it passed," (C) "it was passing," and (D) "it would pass" are incorrect.

46. (D)
Lo used with an adjective or adverb is translated as "part" or "thing." In this case, the sentence means "the most important part/thing was..." (A), (B), and (C) are all definite articles.

47. (B)
The noun *asalto* means "robbery" in Spanish. (A) Aggression implies physical or verbal attack, but not necessarily stealing. (C) *Desembarco* means "landing" or "disembarking" and is used in texts about boats and sailing, or planes and flying. (D) *Estafa* means "swindle" or "fraud."

48. (C)
Sucursal, a feminine noun, is employed to name a branch or subsidiary of a main office. (A) *Instituto* refers to an educational, scientific, commercial, religious, cultural, literary, artistic, or military organization. (B) *Rama* (literally, "branch") is not used much to mean "subsidiary"; this noun is frequently used with the meaning of "part" or "group" of a field of study or occupation. (D) *Institución* is an organization with social, political, cultural, or scientific purposes.

49. (A)
Criminal is a person legally accused of a crime. (B) *Preso* is a prisoner, a person who is in jail. In this context, *reos* is a better option than *presos* because we don't know whether the robbers are in prison yet. (C) *Culpable* ("culprit") stands for someone who is guilty of some kind of offense. (D) A victim (víctima) is a person who was attacked or violated in some way.

50. (D)
Rodearon el barrio means "they surrounded the neighborhood." (A) *Cortaron* ("they 'cut' the neighborhood") is incorrect, as is (C) *pasearon por* ("they 'took a walk or ride around' the neighborhood") and (D) *pasaron por* ("they 'passed by' the neighborhood").

51. (A)
Éxito ("success") is the correct answer because the passage states that the police found the criminals. (B) *Fin* ("end") doesn't match the

phrase *tuvieron... en su búsqueda.* (C) *Fracaso* ("failure") contradicts the idea of the passage. (D) *Gloria* means "fame and acknowledgement," or "greatness and splendor," which do not fit in this context.

52. (B)

Se enteraron means "they found out." (A) *Buscaron* ("they looked for") doesn't compliment the phrase that follows (*de que se trataba de*) (C) *Pensaron* ("they thought") implies that the police hadn't found the robbers yet. (D) *Lograron* ("they were able to") doesn't match the phrase *de que se trataba de.*

53. (C)

Radicado/a is the word frequently employed to mean "established" in a place. (A) *Vivida* ("lived") and (B) *parada* ("stopped" or "standing") are incorrect choices. (D) *Situada* ("situated") refers to someone or something placed in a certain space or position.

54. (C)

Entusiasmo ("enthusiasm") is the best choice contextually. (A) "Obsession" and (D) "delirium" are too strong and extreme. (B) *Pesar* means "grief" or "sorrow," the opposite of what everybody felt at the time of the trip.

55. (A)

"The children showed [*demostraban*] their enthusiasm for the trip." (C) "They presented" isn't an appropriate choice. (B) *Inhibían* ("they inhibited") and (D) *escondían* ("they hid") contradict the main idea of the passage.

56. (A)

The imperfect form, *sentía,* is the best choice here since it expresses feelings. (B) The preterite doesn't match the imperfect form (*hacía*) of the sentence. (C) The infinitive form cannot follow the subject of a sentence. (D) The present perfect tense doesn't fit in a story set in the past.

57. (B)
This is what Claudio does as opposed to focusing on any one place. The passage states that Claudio *pudo arrendar un auto*. You should realize that this expression is equivalent to *alquilando un coche*.

58. (A)
This is the only choice that does not contradict the meaning of the passage. Both adjectives are actually used in the paragraph.

59. (C)
The answer requires a fairly global understanding of the passage. Notice that there is nothing in the paragraph to support the statements of (B) and (C).

60. (D)
Again, the first two choices are fairly gratuitous. The passage does not mention motorcycles nor does it state what (A) does. (C) is meant ironically.

61. (C)
The story indicates there is no doctor available. A large city or a city of any size would probably have had a doctor, so answer (C) is the correct choice. Answer (B) has no basis. Answer (D) is incorrect since the protagonist is speaking with the hotel manager.

62. (B)
The text indicates the illness as un *retortijón de tripas*. One needs only know that *tripas* has its cognate in the English word "tripe," and not necessarily that *retortijón* means "cramps" or "griping." The word "tripe" should suggest "intestine." None of the other indications is appropriate.

63. (A)
Answer (B), a "quack" is not suitable, neither are (C) and (D). The quick cure was evidence of the homeopath's ability to cure, or at least his inability to do more harm.

64. (C)
The *tomarlo* of the correct answer is infinitive, just like the verb *hacer* following the verb *debiera*. They are in parallel usage. Naturally, the answer is that after making the tea, one should drink it. The other answers do not correspond in any way—"applying it to the painful area," "breathing the vapor," or "looking at it."

65. (C)
In item 8, one is told to let "bygones be bygones" (*pelillos a la mar*) by not focusing on who hurt whom or dwelling on negative thoughts, making (A) and (B) incorrect answers. In like fashion, one would not *mimar* ("pamper") the wounded party, making (D) incorrect.

66. (A)
In item 5, it is suggested that one "wait to calm oneself" (*espera a calmarte*) before rushing to reconcile. In the text (item 2), it states that establishing blame (*investigar quién tuvo más culpa*) will only complicate things (*complicar las cosas*), making (B) incorrect. While receiving advice from others (C) and getting professional help (D) are sound ideas, neither is mentioned in this text.

67. (D)
Item 7 states that sustaining (*sostener*) and not mending (*enmendar*) blame hinders happiness. Thus, one should ignore it, making (B) and (C) incorrect answers. Placing blame on an individual is counterproductive to moving forward, making (A) incorrect.

68. (A)
Medianoche is certainly at night and there is nothing in the text about "wind" or that "it was cold." Answer (C) is impossible, since the sun does not shine at midnight.

69. (C)
The expression *como si anticiparan un desastre o algo semejante* indicates that some of the passengers were worried; therefore, (B) is incorrect. On the other hand, some of the other passengers were asleep, indicating their confidence in the engineer.

70. (D)
The text itself indicates that the train returned to the last station. The word *parada*, "stop," indicates then that (D) is the correct answer.

71. (C)
The train was unable to proceed, so its progress was impeded. It was not, however, removed from the track, as (B) indicates.

72. (A)
Some of the passengers demonstrated their uneasiness by anticipating some kind of disaster, as stated in the reading.

73. (C)
Since Metrotour is specifically for tourists who wish to travel at a reduced rate but not for free (*3 ó 5 días consecutivos, por sólo 575 ptas. y 850 ptas. respectivamente*), (A) is incorrect. The idea of the pass is to travel throughout all Madrid, from its most elegant sections (*el Madrid de los Asturias*) to its most modern, making (B) incorrect. There is no mention of *Asturias* for a reduced rate, making (D) incorrect.

74. (D)
Madrid is a city that offers a great deal to the tourist, including modern attractions, making answer (A) incorrect. (B) cannot be deemed correct, because other means of transportation are not featured in this ad such that one could deduce that "there is a limited system of transportation." The passport mentioned in (C) is needed as a form of proof that one is a tourist in orer to purchase the Metrotour pass (*solicitar su identificación mediante pasaporte*).

75. (D)
When the text indicates that Clara "enjoys singing; it is her life," the choice of singing as the most important thing in her life is obvious.

76. (A)
Answer (B) might be considered because it is possible there might be men who would marry Clara for her money, and also many people might want to sing like her or even secure her autograph, but the text

indicates that she had many "pretendientes," "suitors," while none of the other possibilities is mentioned.

77. (C)
A *canario* is a well-known singer, whereas the *cotorra*, "parrot," is a well-known talker, but hardly known for a beautiful voice.

78. (D)
The correct answer is *en la carcel.* Even though the word *carcel* never appears, it is mentioned that he is *preso* ("imprisoned"). The other choices are, therefore, incorrect. He is not "with his girlfriend" nor "in the church," and we have no knowledge of his position ("sitting").

79. (A)
The correct answer is *un sacerdote*. We know this because the protagonist insists that he does not want to *confesarme* ("to confess myself"). The priest has obviously come to give him the Last Rites. The other choices are not acceptable, since there is no indication of "his friend," "his family," or "the executioner" visiting him.

80. (B)
The correct answer is en *el campo de batalla* ("the battlefield"). We know this because he mentions that he could take dying en guerra ("at war"). Thus, the other choices are incorrect.

81. (C)
A brig or brigantine is an old-time ship like the ones used by Columbus; it was neither "modern," "unsinkable," nor a "submarine."

82. (C)
The text indicates that the ship-wrecked sailor was able to grab a plank. Therefore, it is supposed that he floated ashore.

83. (A)
Questions regarding how he would live, what he would eat, and how he could protect himself, indicate that he was concerned about his physical needs. But, his first tragic thought was "there wasn't anyone."

84. (D)
Naturally he was concerned about his ability to stay alive. The necessities of life were not evident anywhere and this concerned him.

85. (D)
His last great fear was the unknown "roar" coming from nowhere. This great noise really frightened him.

THE SAT SUBJECT TEST IN

Spanish

PRACTICE TEST 3

SAT Spanish Practice Test 3

PART A

Time: 1 Hour
85 Questions

DIRECTIONS: In this part you are given incomplete statements or questions, each of which has four possible completions. Choose the most accurate of the completions and fill in the corresponding oval on the answer sheet.

1. La sopa necesita más -------.

(A) aliento
(B) cabello
(C) sal
(D) niebla

2. Mi casa es de -------.

(A) pañuelos
(B) mantequilla
(C) árboles
(D) madera

3. Los obreros se niegan a trabajar; están -------.

(A) de vuelta
(B) de huelga
(C) de pie
(D) de rodillas

4. Mi hijo ------- su abuelo.

(A) es mayor que
(B) se casa con
(C) se parece a
(D) sale de

5. Mario quiere mucho a Angela; le muestra mucho -------.

(A) cariño
(B) desdén
(C) odio
(D) rencor

6. Esta composición es excelente; ------- una nota muy buena.

(A) pierde
(B) merece
(C) debe
(D) agrada

7. ¡Buen viaje! ¡Que lo pases bien en Caracas! Te vamos a echar -------.

(A) a correr
(B) una pelota
(C) de menos
(D) una ojeada

8. Voy ------- para leer un libro para mi clase de inglés.

(A) a la botica
(B) al quiosco
(C) a la librería
(D) a la biblioteca

9. Al oír el chiste, todo el mundo -------.

(A) se rió
(B) lloró
(C) se entristeció
(D) sollozó

10. Los ladrones ------- por la puerta trasera.

(A) huyeron
(B) se quejaron
(C) se burlaron
(D) llevaron

11. Vamos al correo a comprar -------.

(A) cartas
(B) muebles
(C) sellos
(D) revistas

12. Este perfume ------- a flores.

(A) huele
(B) se refiere
(C) suena
(D) sabe

13. No digas eso. Si lo dices otra vez, me voy a -------.

(A) alegrar
(B) golpear
(C) enfadar
(D) pegar

14. Al ver el fantasma, todos -------.

(A) engordaron
(B) crecieron
(C) se asustaron
(D) fumaron

15. Tomás ------- el coche a la playa.

(A) manejó
(B) cocinó
(C) escuchó
(D) revolvió

16. ¿Por qué nunca dices la verdad? ¿Por qué siempre -------?

(A) muerdes
(B) mides
(C) muestras
(D) mientes

17. Me arrepentí ------- lo que había hecho.

(A) de
(B) a
(C) en
(D) con

18. Vamos a ------- en la piscina.

(A) esgrimir
(B) coser
(C) pisar
(D) nadar

19. Este refresco no está frío; voy a echarle un poco de -------.

(A) acero
(B) hielo
(C) hierro
(D) hierba

20. Está lloviendo -------.

(A) a cántaros
(B) en cuenta
(C) por si acaso
(D) en cuanto

21. No he traído el coche hoy porque no ------- bien.

(A) dispara
(B) toca
(C) goza
(D) marcha

22. ¿Qué hay ------- nuevo, Julio?

(A) a
(B) de
(C) en
(D) por

23. Vamos a ------- cuándo sale el autobús.

(A) barrer
(B) encontrar
(C) averiguar
(D) hallar

24. Me ------- con este vestido.

(A) quedo
(B) parezco
(C) pongo
(D) quito

25. Ella ------- almorzar al mediodía.

(A) suele
(B) corre
(C) toma
(D) viene

26. Nuestro apartamento está en ------- del edificio.

(A) la primera flor
(B) el suelo
(C) el tercer piso
(D) el techo

27. ¿De qué ------- este artículo?

(A) factura
(B) se refiere
(C) trata
(D) está

28. Limpiaron toda la casa ------- nuestra alcoba.

(A) menos
(B) con
(C) en
(D) entre

PART B

DIRECTIONS: In each of the following paragraphs, there are numbered blanks indicating that words or phrases are missing. Four completions are provided for each numbered blank. Read the entire passage. For each numbered blank, choose the completion that is the most appropriate given the context of the entire paragraph. Fill in the corresponding oval on the answer sheet.

En algunas partes de la América Latina la situación económica va __(29)__ a causa de las __(30)__ internacionales que no pueden pagar muchos gobiernos. A esto hay que agregar el __(31)__ del costo de la vida y el paro forzoso de trabajadores.

Teniendo en cuenta la situación inestable de las __(32)__ internacionales, la bajada del valor del dólar y el __(33)__ de la balanza de pagos, se __(34)__ los representantes de los poderes más influyentes del mundo económico a fin de __(35)__ a un acuerdo que evite un posible derrumbamiento financiero, para cuyo efecto habrá que obrar con cautela.

29. (A) de bien en mal
    (B) de mal en peor
    (C) de mal en mal
    (D) no hay mal que por bien no venga

30. (A) deudas
    (B) problemas
    (C) situaciones
    (D) ventas

31. (A) disminución
    (B) aumento
    (C) peso
    (D) tópico

32. (A) bolsas
(B) agencias
(C) intercambios
(D) bancos

33. (A) diferencia
(B) descomposición
(C) desliz
(D) desequilibrio

34. (A) han conocido
(B) han preguntado
(C) han reunido
(D) han salido

35. (A) llegar
(B) venir
(C) extender
(D) regresar

No sé cómo me dio indigestión. La comida sí era __(36)__, pero estaba sabrosa y yo tenía un hambre atroz. Puede ser que haya comido demasiado. De todos modos, esta mañana me dio un __(37)__ de tripas insoportable que __(38)__ casi una hora. __(39)__ podía yo respirar de dolor. Hablé con el gerente del hotel cuando pude y le pedí que me __(40)__ en contacto con un médico. Grande fue la sorpresa __(41)__ cuando me __(42)__ sin emoción ninguna que aquí en este pueblo no hay médico.

36. (A) opuesta
(B) distinta
(C) original
(D) anormal

37. (A) torcedura
(B) enrulamiento
(C) retortijón
(D) contracción

38. (A) duró
(B) pasó
(C) sostuvo
(D) cesó

39. (A) Casi
(B) Fácilmente
(C) Apenas
(D) Nunca

40. (A) puso
(B) ponga
(C) pone
(D) pusiera

41. (A) mía
(B) mi
(C) mis
(D) mío

42. (A) gritó
(B) anunció
(C) susurró
(D) pidió

Dicen que las playas de la Costa Brava son __(43)__ de las mejores __(44)__ mundo. Turistas de todas partes __(45)__ a ésas durante todo el año, pero especialmente durante el verano. Se oye una babel de lenguas y el español que se habla representa docenas de __(46)__. Naturalmente, __(47)__ clima es muy agradable y los españoles son sumamente __(48)__. __(49)__ España es el blanco de la mayoría de los turistas europeos, especialmente los ingleses, alemanes, franceses y suecos.

43. (A) las
(B) una
(C) unas
(D) ninguna

44. (A) del
(B) en el
(C) sobre
(D) por

45. (A) se paran
(B) salen
(C) dirigen
(D) se dirigen

46. (A) acentos
(B) jergas
(C) pronunciaciones
(D) sonidos

47. (A) la
(B) un
(C) el
(D) una

48. (A) hostiles
(B) hostales
(C) hospitalidad
(D) hospitalarios

49. (A) Con razón
(B) Con pena
(C) Con creces
(D) Con tal de que

Junto a las costas africanas, cerca del desierto de Sahara, __(50)__ las Islas Canarias, un archipiélago que, __(51)__ los kilómetros que lo separan de la Península Ibérica, forma parte de España. Los __(52)__ pobladores canarios, llamados guanches, rompían la imagen prototipo que el mundo tiene de los españoles, bajitos, y de pelo y ojos oscuros. Los guanches eran altos, con la piel bronceada por el sol, rubios y de ojos azules o verdes. Estas características físicas, tan distintas a __(53)__ de cualquier otro pueblo cercano, son difíciles de explicar, pero __(54)__ estudiosos del tema __(55)__ que eso se debe a que los guanches son descendientes de los __(56)__ de la legendaria Atlántida, un continente del que se dice que, hace muchos años, se hundió para siempre bajo el mar. Los que acceptan esta teoría afirman que las Islas Canarias son los restos de las montañas de la Atlántida, que el agua nunca llegó a cubrir.

50. (A) se parecen
    (B) se hallan
    (C) se descubren
    (D) se miran

51. (A) pese a
    (B) por
    (C) debido a
    (D) entonces

52. (A) añejos
    (B) anticuados
    (C) antiguos
    (D) actuales

53. (A) lo
    (B) el
    (C) las
    (D) los

54. (A) algunos
    (B) algunas
    (C) algún
    (D) alguno

55. (A) insisten
    (B) preguntan
    (C) afirman
    (D) dudan

56. (A) inhabitantes
    (B) población
    (C) vecinos
    (D) habitantes

PART C

DIRECTIONS: Read the following passages for comprehension. Following each passage are a number of questions or incomplete sentences. Choose the most appropriate response or completion and fill in the corresponding oval on the answer sheet.

Hoy en día florecen las agencias de publicidad. Vivimos bajo un sistema que fomenta el consumo por parte del público de una gran variedad de productos, sean los naturales o los que se hacen a mano o en serie en las grandes fábricas. A las empresas mercantiles les hace falta enterarnos, por medio de la televisión o en los diarios y revistas, de las virtudes de lo que nos quieren vender.

Para el que quiera seguir la carrera publicitaria, abundan las escuelas de dibujo que ofrecen el entrenamiento preciso para conseguir un puesto como diseñador. Pero, en la capital, ninguna como la nuestra para brindarle entrada libre y fácil a este campo, cuyas posibilidades no parecen tener límite. Requisitos mínimos. Matrícula razonable. Pagos a plazos. Llame al 39–43–82 o venga a nuestras oficinas: 7 Avenida del Inca.

57. Este pasaje …

(A) critica el sistema capitalista
(B) ofrece empleo en una escuela de dibujo
(C) parece muy optimista
(D) promete un sueldo alto

58. Según el pasaje, …

(A) hay más plazas en el campo que en la ciudad
(B) sólo los grandes negocios se preocupan por la publicidad
(C) la escuela es muy exigente
(D) es fácil encontrar puesto como dibujante

59. Este pasaje es …

(A) un cuento
(B) un anuncio
(C) una advertencia
(D) un brindis

En la actualidad, sigue pendiente el dilema del desarme, sobre todo entre los dos grandes poderes que poseen la mayoría de las armas. ¿Quién sabe si en algún tiempo lejano se planteará de firme la posibilidad de abolir este peligro para la vida? De vez en cuando han surgido propuestas para realizar este sueño pero hasta el momento escasos han sido los resultados.

Los partidarios del desarme opinan que el desarrollo de bombas de rendimiento cada vez más grande podría acarrearnos una catástrofe de dimensiones increíbles. Los informes más recientes vienen apoyando tal teoría. Por otra parte, hay los que están en contra del desarme, creyendo que el enemigo no es de fiar, a no ser que se permita la inspección, la cual presentaría tal vez inconvenientes insuperables para los dos lados. Según los proponentes del desarme, la inspección podría llevarse a cabo contando con una organización internacional como las Naciones Unidas.

Lo obvio es que tenemos que hacer algo a favor de la paz y la supervivencia de la humanidad a la cual pertenecemos todos, amigos y adversarios.

60. ¿Cuál de las respuestas es falsa?

(A) Hay mucho desacuerdo en cuanto a la cuestión del desarme.
(B) Es posible que en el porvenir se resuelva la cuestión del desarme.
(C) De veras, ya se ha solucionado el problema de las armas.
(D) Ya se han sugerido soluciones al problema del desarme.

61. Los que se oponen al desarme ...

(A) son de otra parte
(B) desconfían de la buena voluntad del adversario
(C) son aversos a la supervivencia
(D) apoyan la guerra

62. Los que favorecen el desarme ...

(A) rechazan la idea de la inspección internacional
(B) temen abolir las armas
(C) tienen confianza en el enemigo
(D) están por la inspección internacional

63. Siempre va aumentando ...

(A) la escasez de propuestas
(B) la realización de nuestras metas
(C) la potencia de las bombas
(D) el número de nuestros enemigos

El investigador, don José Alambrés, oriundo de Montevideo, tiene planeado un proyecto de estudio sobre la tasa de la emigración uruguaya durante el siglo pasado. Dicho trabajo exigirá que el estudioso, conforme a los procedimientos más aceptados de su disciplina, recoja de los registros del censo uruguayo los datos más variados sobre el oficio, el parentesco y la afiliación política de los que han emigrado de la patria durante esta etapa de la historia nacional.

Para esta magna empresa, se le ha concedido una beca que le dará lo suficiente para efectuar dichas investigaciones y para realizar después la publicación de los resultados. Advierte Alambrés que, al finalizarse su estudio, éste podrá aportar una nueva perspectiva sobre la disminución de la población nacional durante la época que piensa investigar.

64. ¿Cuál es la profesión de José Alambrés?

(A) policía
(B) psiquiatra

(C) ascensorista
(D) sociólogo

65. ¿Qué tendrá que hacer Alambrés?

(A) exigir mucho
(B) estar conforme
(C) inscribirse en los registros
(D) consultar los censos

66. ¿Qué le han dado al investigador?

(A) una oficina
(B) dinero
(C) unos nombres
(D) una compañía

67. ¿Qué valor tendrán los estudios de Alambrés?

(A) Le traerán mucho dinero.
(B) Harán más fácil la emigración a otros países.
(C) Explicarán por qué ha bajado el número de habitantes.
(D) Causarán un aumento de la población uruguaya.

PROFESIONES

Azafata de vuelo

Para unos no son más que niñas monas; para otros, camareras a bordo. Pero en realidad son mucho más que todo eso. Su nombre técnico es auxiliar de vuelo.

Mari Carmen Pérez Giménez es azafata de vuelo de Iberia desde los 18 años, aunque ahora esté gozando de una excedencia por maternidad. Afirma que toda su vida, desde que se planteó su futuro profesional, quiso dedicarse a esta profesión: «Estaba haciendo COU cuando decidí definitivamente que lo mío era volar, con gran disgusto de mi familia que, al ser hija única, hubiera querido que hiciera una carrera universitaria».

Mari Carmen afirma que la gente, en general, tiene una

LUIS ZAZO

Esta profesión exige tener una auténtica vocación.

idea bastante falsa de cuál es su trabajo; «además de ser mona y saber servir con corrección una naranjada, hay que tener bastante psicología para conocer a la gente y saber tratar a cada persona y, ante todo, hay que saber qué hacer y cómo reaccionar ante una emergencia».

Ventajas e inconvenientes

Esta profesión tiene de todo, como todas las demás. Para Mari Carmen, la ventaja es que a ella siempre le gustó mucho el contacto con la gente —y en su trabajo es diario— y el principal inconveniente es que «con tanto ajetreo de ir y venir te desligas del mundo. Llega la boda de una hermana, por ejemplo, y resulta que tú estás en Tombuctú».

Requisitos necesarios

Para entrar en una compañía aérea se necesita:

- Dar unos mínimos y unos máximos de peso y medida. De medida, el mínimo es de 1,58 metros y el máximo de 1,73 metros. El peso será acorde con la talla.
- Hay que saber inglés.
- Saber nadar.
- Pasar favorablemente una entrevista personal.
- Un *test* de cultura general y uno de inglés.
- Un reconocimiento médico (no se puede usar gafas ni lentes de contacto).

El proceso

Se presenta la instancia en la compañía.

- Si es aceptada, se inician todas esas pruebas antes detalladas. Son eliminatorias; es decir, si no se pasa una no se accede a la siguiente.
- Hay que participar en un cursillo de entrenamiento (técnicas de salvamento incluidas).

68. Para ser auxiliar de vuelo hay que

(A) asistir a la universidad
(B) saber varias lenguas
(C) llevarse bien con la gente
(D) estudiar psicología

69. Mari Carmen no trabaja en este momento porque

(A) está de vacaciones
(B) está embarazada
(C) está estudiando inglés
(D) está en la universidad tomando cursos

70. Los padres de Mari Carmen

(A) querían que ella siguiera estudiando
(B) insistieron en que se hiciera azafata
(C) también eran auxiliares de vuelo
(D) querían que ella llegara a ser psicóloga

71. ¿Cuál de estos requisitos no es verdad?

(A) Las azafatas necesitan saber nadar.
(B) Las azafatas participan en cursos específicos.
(C) Las azafatas tienen que ser de cierto tamaño.
(D) Las azafatas tienen que graduarse de la universidad.

Catalina Levine, joven norteamericana que pasa el verano estudiando en la Universidad Autónoma, ha concedido a este corresponsal una entrevista acerca de sus experiencias durante sus primeras semanas aquí en México. Nos dijo que antes de llegar, no se daba cuenta de lo importante que es el mestizaje en la cultura mexicana. Respecto a esto, hay que constatar que Catalina tiene la cabellera más rubia que el oro. No obstante, en vez de sentirse como una curiosidad entre nosotros, se ha adaptado bien en poquísimo tiempo a una sociedad que antes le era totalmente desconocida.

Viene ella dispuesta a sumergirse en la cultura nuestra puesto que piensa hacerse maestra de español en su propio país y en esta temporada sigue clases en esta materia. A lo mejor, algún día sacará el doctorada en idiomas. Ya ha tenido examen en su clase de literatura colonial. "¡Cuánto duró!" dijo ella, soltando una carcajada, "pero valió la pena."

72. ¿Quién ha hablado con Catalina?

(A) un payaso
(B) un profesor
(C) un mestizo
(D) un periodista

73. Catalina …

(A) se parece a los mexicanos
(B) no se siente como extranjera
(C) busca un puesto
(D) cuenta con el apoyo mestizo

74. Catalina cree que su examen …

(A) fue largo
(B) fue fácil
(C) fue difícil
(D) fue mejor

75. … Catalina al hablar de su examen.

(A) Murmuró
(B) Se rió
(C) Gritó
(D) Lloró

Ayer por la tarde en el Paraninfo ha sido premiado el novelista Javier Requetemacho por su obra más reciente, *Alba de la mujer*. Según el acta del jurado del concurso, se le reconoce la elevada calidad literaria de su novela y su comprensión nada despreciable del papel de la mujer en la sociedad actual.

Requetemacho, catedrático que ejerce su tarea educativa en la Facultad de Filosofía y Letras, en su discurso de respuesta, ha acentuado la rapidez con la que ha ido la mujer ocupando los sitios que antes sólo estaban reservados para el varón y ha apuntado que esto ha sido piedra de escándalo en no pocos hogares, incluso el suyo. Ha elogiado el escritor la valentía con la cual se ha hecho valer la hembra a pesar de los muchos obstáculos con los que se ha encontrado sobre la marcha de la realización de su ser.

En una conferencia de prensa posterior al acto solemne, ha manifestado el premiado, con cierta emotividad, que, a pesar de sus convicciones, le choca mucho que hoy en día la mujer salga sola a la calle y que lleve pantalones. En casa suya, según él, sólo los lleva él. A esto añadió el distinguido hombre de letras que la semana pasada se le huyó de casa la mujer.

76. El novelista ha hablado con …

(A) el ejército
(B) unos actores

(C) unos antifemenistas
(D) los periodistas

77. Requetemacho es ...

(A) inventor
(B) profesor
(C) cura
(D) deportista

78. El escritor Requetemacho ...

(A) ha recibido un premio
(B) ha sido sentenciado
(C) ha condenado a la mujer
(D) ha tomado apuntes

79. ¿Cuál de las frases es la más exacta?

(A) El escritor se ha puesto unos pantalones nuevos.
(B) El novelista es filósofo.
(C) En casa de Requetemacho manda la mujer.
(D) La esposa de Requetemacho se ha fugado.

80. Según los jueces, Requetemacho tiene ...

(A) que pagar una multa
(B) un estilo elegante
(C) la mente cerrada
(D) prejuicios sobre la mujer

Lo primero que hay que entender es que la fiesta brava es, sobre todo, un espectáculo. Es decir que no se trata de un mero deporte como quieren creer muchos extranjeros. A partir del primer paso doble y el desfile de las cuadrillas por el redondel hasta la última estocada, se sigue un ritual establecido ya hace siglos. El arte de torear es una serie de movimientos, cada uno con su propio nombre, que se ejecutan con más o menos destreza, según la habilidad del torero. Pero no se puede negar que éste, por inhábil que sea, no se muestra nada cobarde.

Los hay que ven en el toreo una metafísica del hombre que se enfrenta con la muerte. Lo mismo, quizá, se podría decir del animal, si es que éste piensa en la filosofía. Aunque la fiesta brava apela al sentido visual, muchos la condenan por ser un duelo desigual en el que casi siempre sale perdiendo la bestia. De todos modos, en los países hispanos donde se celebra, parece tener menos aficionados ahora que hace un siglo cuando alcanzó su auge.

81. Podríamos comparar la fiesta brava con ...

(A) un partido de fútbol
(B) la lucha humana con el destino fatal
(C) el toreo
(D) la corrida de toros

82. Desde el principio hasta el fin ...

(A) la fiesta brava muestra mucha ceremonia
(B) todos los toreros son expertos
(C) hay que ver el dolor del torero
(D) desfilan las cuadrillas

83. El toreo

(A) ha perdido algo de su popularidad
(B) se celebra en todos los países hispanos
(C) llega a su auge
(D) les duele a los aficionados

84. En la fiesta brava ...

(A) usualmente muere la bestia
(B) se celebra el auge
(C) los aficionados condenan al torero
(D) se llega a la cumbre

85. Este programa no ofrece

(A) que cada participante termine en 16 meses
(B) que cada participante obtenga ayuda financiera
(C) que cada participante tenga asistencia en hallar trabajo
(D) que cada participante reciba el certificado reconocido en EE.UU.

SAT Subject Test in Spanish Practice Test 3

ANSWER KEY

1. (C)	23. (C)	45. (D)	67. (C)
2. (D)	24. (A)	46. (A)	68. (C)
3. (B)	25. (A)	47. (C)	69. (B)
4. (C)	26. (C)	48. (D)	70. (A)
5. (A)	27. (C)	49. (A)	71. (D)
6. (B)	28. (A)	50. (B)	72. (D)
7. (C)	29. (B)	51. (A)	73. (B)
8. (D)	30. (A)	52. (C)	74. (A)
9. (A)	31. (B)	53. (C)	75. (B)
10. (A)	32. (A)	54. (A)	76. (D)
11. (C)	33. (D)	55. (C)	77. (B)
12. (A)	34. (C)	56. (D)	78. (A)
13. (C)	35. (A)	57. (C)	79. (D)
14. (C)	36. (B)	58. (D)	80. (B)
15. (A)	37. (C)	59. (B)	81. (B)
16. (D)	38. (A)	60. (C)	82. (A)
17. (A)	39. (C)	61. (B)	83. (A)
18. (D)	40. (D)	62. (D)	84. (A)
19. (B)	41. (A)	63. (C)	85. (B)
20. (A)	42. (B)	64. (D)	
21. (D)	43. (C)	65. (D)	
22. (B)	44. (A)	66. (B)	

DETAILED EXPLANATIONS OF ANSWERS

PRACTICE TEST 3

1. (C)

The verb *necesita* means "needs," and *sopa* is "soup." We must, therefore, search for a logical ingredient for soup among the possible choices. That would be *sal* ("salt"). We should not find any of the other items in a pot of soup: (A) *aliento* ("breath"), (B) *cabello* ("hair") or (C) *niebla* (fog).

2. (D)

A form of the verb *ser* followed immediately by the preposition *de* is often used to indicate the materials from which an item is made. That is the case with *es de* preceding the blank in our sentence. Consequently, we need to use an answer which pertains to building materials, since we are talking about a structure, *casa* ("house"). This would not be (A) *pañuelos* ("handkerchiefs") or (B) *mantequilla* ("butter"). Likewise, most houses are not normally constructed of *árboles* ("trees") (C), but rather of the materials that we get from trees, i.e., *madera* ("wood").

3. (B)

The subject of our sentence is *obreros* (workmen). The construction *negarse* (ie) *a* + infinitive signifies "to refuse" to do something. If the workers are refusing "to work" (*trabajar*), then they could be "on strike" (*de huelga*). Notice that all of the possible answers begin with the preposition *de*. There are many expressions like this that indicate a temporary state or condition and are therefore used with the verb *estar: estar de vuelta* ("to be back"), as in (A), *estar de pie* ("to be standing"), as in (C), and *estar de rodillas* ("to be kneeling"), as in (D), etc.

4. (C)

Hijo is "son," and *abuelo* is "grandfather." We should not choose (A) because that would say that the youth "is older than" (*es mayor que*) his grandfather. The expression *se casa con* in (B), means "is getting married to." You might have chosen (D) *sale de* ("is leaving"), but that is wrong. We can only use *salir de* when we are referring to places. If we want to say "to leave" a person, we might use the verb *dejar*. The correct answer, *se parece a*, means "to resemble." Notice that in this context the verb *parecer* is reflexive and is followed by the preposition *a*.

5. (A)

In our sentence, the verb *quiere* means "loves." See how we have had to use the personal *a* in front of "Angela." This is necessary if the direct object of the sentence is a person or people. The personal *a* is not translatable into English. In the second part of our sentence, the verb *muestra*, from *mostrar* (ue), means "to show." In the blank, we need to use a noun that refers to an emotion which one demonstrates toward another whom he loves. This is *cariño* ("affection"). The other three answers are attitudes that are contrary to the situation described: (B) *desdén* ("disdain"), (C) *odio* ("hatred") and (D) *rencor* ("rancor").

6. (B)

The word *nota*, as used in our sentence, means "grade." Of course, it can also sometimes means "note." If the student has written an excellent composition, then he "deserves a very high grade" (*merece una nota muy alta*). Remember that the verb *merecer*, as all verbs whose infinitives end in *-cer*, has an irregular form for the first person singular of the present tense: *merezco*." One of the most common verbs of this type is *conocer* ("to know"): *conozco*. Since we use this form to arrive at the present subjunctive, this irregularity will carry over into that form also: *merezca*, *conozca*. Answer (A) *pierde*, from *perder* (ie), which means "to lose," is incorrect because it says the opposite of what we would expect in this situation. (C) *debe* means "should" or "owes." You might have erroneously chosen (D) *agrada*, since it looks a little like the English word "grade," but the verb *agradar* signifies "to please."

7. (C)
Our sentence obviously deals with the departure of a friend or relative for Caracas. *¡Buen viaje!* means "have a good trip." *¡Que lo pases bien en Caracas!* means "I hope you have a good time in Caracas!" Note that we have used the present tense of the subjunctive after the word *Que*. Sentences beginning with *Que* + the subjunctive mean "I hope that ..." The correct answer, *de menos*, is used with the verb *echar* to express the idea of "to miss" a person or thing, i.e., "to feel nostalgic or melancholy about ..." The expression *echar a correr*, item (A), does exist, but it means "to break into a run." *Echar* can also be used to mean "to throw," but it would be nonsensical to use (B) *una pelota* (a ball) in this context. (D) *Echar una ojeada* means "to glance," which also would have little application here.

8. (D)
Books are available to be read on the spot in a library (*biblioteca*). (C) *librería* ("bookstore") looks like the English word "library," but it is what we call a false cognate, i.e., a word that looks like an English word but one whose meaning is different. The word *quiosco*, in (B), means a bookstall, usually located on the street. It is a place where we may buy magazines, newspapers and books, but we do not read them there. *Botica*, in (A), means "drugstore."

9. (A)
In our sentence, the word *chiste* means "joke." *Al* + infinitive means "upon" doing something. The natural reaction, "upon hearing" (*Al oír*) a joke, is to laugh. The verb *reír* ("to laugh") may be used either reflexively or non-reflexively. There is one idiomatic expression, however, that requires us to use just the reflexive form: *reírse de* ("to laugh at"). The other three possible answers indicate grief: (B) *lloró* ("cried"); (C) *se entristeció* ("became sad"); (D) *sollozó* ("sobbed").

10. (A)
The noun *ladrones* means "thieves." The adjective *trasera* comes from the word *tras*, which means "back of," "behind," "after." By logical extension, then, *la puerta trasera* means "the back door." The only answer that makes sense here is *huyeron* ("they fled"), from the verb *huir* ("to flee"). The remaining answers to this question are illogical: (B) *se quejaron* ("they complained"); (C) *se burlaron*, from the

expression *burlarse de* + infinitive ("to make fun of"); (D) *llevaron* ("they took or carried").

11. (C)
El correo means "the post office." From the list of possible answers, the only items that we can buy at the post office are *sellos* ("stamps"). In many countries in Central and South America, *sellos* are often referred to as *estampillas* or *timbres*. At the post office we do not buy (A) "letters" (*cartas*), although it is possible sometimes to buy "envelopes" (*sobres*). *Muebles*, in (B), is "furniture," and *revistas*, in (D), are "magazines."

12. (A)
The expression "*oler a*" means to smell like. The correct answer says "This perfume smells like flowers." *Referirse* (ie,i) *a*, which is used in the third person singular of the present in (B), means "to refer to" and would make no sense here. The verb *sonar* (ue), in (C), also appears in the third person singular of the present. It means "to sound." When it is followed by the preposition *a*, it means "to sound like." Do not confuse *sonar* with *soñar* ("to dream"). The verb *saber*, in (D), normally means "to know" facts or information, but when it is followed by the preposition *a*, it means "to taste like."

13. (C)
No digas is the negative command for the second person singular (*tú* form) of the verb *decir* ("to say or tell"). The "tú" commands, if they are negative, always correspond to the second person singular of the present subjunctive. *Otra vez* means "again." Our sentence means "Don't say that. If you say it again, I am going to ..." In such a situation one might logically say "to get angry" (*enfadarse*). Notice how it is possible to place the reflexive pronoun *me* in front of the expression *ir a* + infinitive. Of course, it is equally correct to attach it to the end of the infinitive: *voy a enfadarme*. A synonym of *enfadarse* is *enojarse*. Many verbs are used reflexively if they mean "to get or become..." *Alegrarse* ("to become happy"), as used in (A), would be contradictory to the situation and tone of the sentence. *Golpearse* ("to strike oneself"), in (B), would be absurd. The speaker certainly is not going to strike himself. The same would be true in (D) with the verb *pegarse* ("to hit or strike oneself").

14. (C)
El fantasma means "the ghost." Observe that this is one of those words ending in *-ma, -pa, -ta,* which are often masculine. *Al* + infinitive means "upon" doing something. "Upon seeing the ghost," it is likely that "everyone" (*todos*) "became frightened" (*se asustaron*). The remaining answers would not fit in the context: (A) *engordaron* ("got fat"); (B) *crecieron* ("grew"); (D) *fumaron* ("smoked").

15. (A)
La playa means "the beach." The only possible verb form given that applies to "cars" (*coches*) is *manejó* ("drove"). (B) *cocinó* means "cooked." (C) *escuchó* is "listened." (D) *revolvió* signifies "to revolve," "to turn over," "to turn around," "to stir."

16. (D)
If someone never tells "the truth" (*la verdad*), then we might ask him or her "Why do you always lie?" (*¿Por qué siempre mientes?*). Notice that the verb *mentir* has a vowel change (e to ie) in the present in all of the persons of the singular and in the third person of the plural. In the preterite, it changes the *e* to an *i*, but *only* in the third person singular and plural. The same is true of the verb *medir* ("to measure"), which appears in (B). These third person preterite changes occur only with -*ir* verbs which also have a vowel change in the present. For verbs such as *morder* (ue) ("to bite"), in (A), and *mostrar* (ue) ("to show"), in (C), there is no vowel change in the preterite, but in the present the change again occurs in all of the singular forms and in the third person plural.

17. (A)
The expression *arrepentirse de* means "to repent" or "to regret." In the context of our sentence, *arrepentirse* cannot be followed by any other preposition. The verb *arrepentirse* is always used reflexively. Furthermore, it partakes of a vowel change both in the present (*e* to *ie*) and in the preterite (*e* to *i*). It follows the pattern of the verb *mentir* ("to lie"). (See explanation 16.)

18. (D)
La piscina means "swimming pool." Our most natural activity in a swimming pool is "to swim" (*nadar*). The other verbs mentioned are

not things normally done at that location: (A) *esgrimir* ("to fence"); (B) *coser* ("to sew"); (C) *pisar* ("to step on").

19. (B)
A *refresco* is a "soft drink" or "refreshment." If we decide that our *refresco* is not cold, we might choose "to throw into it" (*echarle*) "a little ice" (*un poco de hielo*). The other nouns which are supplied would not go very well with our beverage: (A) *acero* ("steel"); (C) *hierro* ("iron"); (D) *hierba* ("grass"). Notice that in our sentence we have used *está*, rather than *es*, along with the adjective *frío*. This is for two reasons: (1) *estar* is used to show temporary states which may change (We may add ice to the drink. Then it *will* be cold.); (2) the verb *estar* is often used to express one's subjective reaction to a stimulus. In this sense, in our sentence, *está*, although it means "is," also has the implication of "strikes me as being."

20. (A)
Está lloviendo is the third person singular of the present perfect tense of *llover* ("to rain"). You will remember that the progressive tenses are used only when one wishes to place particular emphasis on the fact that an action is (was, etc.) taking place at a given time. If we do not want to be that emphatic about the action's being in progress at a given moment, we just use the simple tenses, for example, *Llueve*. The progressive tenses are formed by using the appropriate tense and person of the verb *estar* + the present participle, i.e., the *-ndo* form of the verb. The word *cántaro*, in (A), means "jug." The idiomatic expression *llover a cántaros*, however, signifies "to be raining cats and dogs, literally, "by the jugfuls." *En cuenta*, which appears in (B), is normally used with the verb *tener*, to mean "to bear in mind" (*tener en cuenta*). In (C), the expression *por si acaso* signifies "in case." *En cuanto*, in (D), means "as soon as." If it is followed by *a*, it means "regarding" or "concerning."

21. (D)
In our sentence, *No he traído el coche* means "I haven't brought the car." If that is the case, there could be something wrong with it. Perhaps "it isn't working well" (*no marcha bien*). In Spanish, when we are talking about machinery and we mean "to work," we normally use

either the verb *marchar*, or sometimes *andar*. (A) *dispara* means "to shoot." *Toca*, in (B), means "touches" or, with musical instruments, "plays." Answer (C) *goza* means "enjoys."

22. (B)
¿Qué hay de nuevo? is a common informal greeting, and might be translated as "What's new?" or "What's up?" One should not use this expression in formal introductory situations. There is a shorter version of the same question that one often hears: *¿Qué hay?* It means the same thing as the longer expression. Only the preposition *de* can be used in this sentence. Consequently, the remaining answers are incorrect. Many idiomatic expressions in Spanish require that a very specific preposition be used with them. Often these prepositions seem illogical or sometimes unnecessary to English speakers.

23. (C)
The verb *averiguar* means "to ascertain" or "to find out" as a result of an inquiry or investigation. The implication in our sentence, then, is that we are going to ask someone when the bus is leaving. The verbs *encontrar*, in (B), and *hallar*, in (D), both mean "to find," but not "to find out." The verb *barrer* ("to sweep"), in (A), is totally irrelevant to the situation.

24. (A)
The word *vestido* means dress. Our sentence could perhaps be spoken by someone who is talking to a clerk in a clothing store. The idiomatic expression *quedarse con* means "to keep," "to take," in the sense of "to buy." We hope that you didn't choose (C) or (D) just because they are expressions which we sometimes use when we are talking about clothing. *Ponerse* + an article of clothing means "to put on," and *quitarse* + an article of clothing means "to take off." Neither of these two verbs will work in our sentence because they would make no sense if followed by the preposition *con*. (B) would require us to use the reflexive verb *parecerse*. This form is followed by the preposition *a* to signify "to resemble," and would have no sensible meaning in our sentence.

25. (A)

In our sentence, the infinitive *almorzar* means "to eat lunch." The verb *soler* (ue) means *tener la costumbre de* (to be accustomed to or to be in the habit of). It is followed directly by an infinitive, and only appears in the present and imperfect tenses. It is a vowel-changing verb in the present only (*suelo, sueles, suele, solemos, soléis, suelen*). (B) *corre*, and (D) *viene*, are unusable in our sentence because both are verbs of motion that require the preposition *a* following them if there is an infinitive immediately afterwards. The verb *tomar* can mean "to take," "to grasp," or sometimes "to drink," and makes no sense here.

26. (C)

Since our sentence refers to an apartment (*apartamento*) and a building (*edificio*), and a form of the verb *estar* appears, we are probably talking about where our home is. It is unlikely that we would be living on the "roof" or "ceiling" (*techo*). You might have thought that *suelo* meant "the ground floor," but that is *la planta baja. Suelo* simply means "ground" or "earth." *La primera flor*, although it might sound like "the first floor" to English speakers, really means "the first flower."

27. (C)

The expression *tratar de* can have two meanings in Spanish. If it is followed by an infinitive, it means "to try to." If it is not followed by an infinitive, it means "to deal with," in the sense of "to treat of," which is what we are aiming for in our sentence. Notice that in a question, we must begin with the preposition *de*, i.e., we must ask "With what does it deal?" or "Of what does it treat?" We know that we can only use the verb "tratar" from the list of answers because it is the only one which can legitimately be followed by the preposition "de." If we were to use (B) "se refiere," we would be required to use the preposition *a: ¿A qué se refiere este artículo?* (To what does this article refer?). The verb *facturar*, appearing in (A), although it makes us think of the English word "facts," actually means something quite different: "to check," as when we check our luggage at an airline desk. (D) is incorrect, for a form of *estar* may not be used in our sentence because of the preposition *de*. If we wanted to ask "What is it about?", we would have to use *es* instead of *está*: *¿De qué es?*

28. (A)

To answer this item correctly, you need to know that the verb *limpiar* means "to clean," and *alcoba* is "bedroom." They certainly did not clean "the whole house" "with" our bedroom, (B) *con*, "in" our bedroom, (C) *en*, or "between" our bedroom, (D) *entre*. The word *menos*, which could be used in our sentence, would mean "except." In addition to *alcoba*, Spanish offers a number of other words that mean bedroom: *cuarto de dormir*, *dormitorio* (used in Spain), and *recámara* (Mexican).

29. (B)

De mal en peor ("from bad to worse") means that the economic situation of some Latin American countries is deteriorating. (A) *De bien en mal* ("from good to bad") is not a Spanish idiom. (C) *De mal en mal* ("from evil to evil") is possible, though the idea of the passage is that things are getting worse, and that is why (B) is a better choice. (D) *No hay mal que por bien no venga* is a proverb that means that every event has a good and bad side.

30. (A)

Deudas ("debts") matches *pagar* ("to pay"). Neither (B) *problemas* ("problems") nor (C) *situaciones* ("situations") can be paid; besides, *problemas* is a masculine noun. (D) *Ventas* ("sales") does not apply here, either.

31. (B)

Aumento means "increase"; an increase in living expenses (*costo de la vida*) is one of the reasons Latin American economies are falling. (A) *Disminución* ("decrease") contradicts the idea of the passage. (C) *Peso* ("weight") and (D) *tópico* ("cliché") do not apply.

32. (A)

Bolsas ("stock exchange") is related to the fall in the value of the dollar (*la bajada del valor del dólar*). (B) *Agencias* ("agencies"), (C) *intercambios* ("exchanges"), and (D) *bancos* ("banks") are not necessarily related to the dollar value.

33. (D)
Desequilibrio ("imbalance") directly relates to *la balanza de pagos* ("the balance of payments"). (A) *Diferencia* ("difference") isn't a specific term that can be used in this context. (B) *Descomposición* ("decomposition") means "separation of the component parts of a thing." (C) *Desliz* ("slip") is incorrect.

34. (C)
Se han reunido ("they have met/have called a meeting") is the best option in this context. (A) *Han conocido* means "they have met for the first time/have become acquaintances." (B) *Han preguntado* means "they have asked about" and (D) *Han salido* means "they have gone out/left."

35. (A)
The expression is *llegar a un acuerdo* ("to reach an agreement"). (B) *Venir* ("to come"), (C) *extender* ("to extend"), or (D) *regresar* ("to return") are not used with *a un acuerdo.*

36. (B)
Comida distinta means "different from what the writer of the passage was used to eating." (A) *Opuesta* ("opposite"), (C) *original,* and (D) *anormal* ("abnormal") are not correct.

37. (C)
Retortijón de tripas ("stomach cramp") is a common phrase in Spanish. (A) *Torcedura* ("sprain") refers to problems of the muscles. (B) *Enrulamiento* means "curling of the hair," and (D) *contracción* means "contraction," referring to muscles and nerves.

38. (A)
Duró means "lasted" ("the stomach cramp lasted almost one hour"). (B) *Pasó* means "went away/disappeared," and doesn't match the period of time mentioned: *casi una hora* ("almost an hour"). (C) *Sostuvo,* as a non-reflexive verb, means "supported." (D) *Cesó* means "ended," and is also incorrect.

39. (C)

Apenas is an adverb that means "almost not" (*casi no*); in this case, the writer could barely breathe. (A) *Casi* is an adverb that means "almost," and doesn't complete the idea. (B) *Fácilmente* means "easily," contradicting the sense of the passage. (D) *Nunca* ("never") doesn't fit either.

40. (D)

The imperfect subjunctive *pusiera* (in English, "I asked him 'to put' me") must be used after *le pedí que*, an introductory phrase of request in the preterite. (A) *Puso* ("he put") is the simple preterite of the indicative mood, which doesn't apply in this tense pattern. (B) *Ponga* is the present form of the subjunctive mood, which cannot follow the past tense. (C) *Pone* ("he puts") is the simple present indicative and is also incorrect.

41. (A)

Since the blank follows the noun *sorpresa* ("surprise"), the correct answer is *mía* ("mine"), a common possessive form in Spanish. (B) *Mi* ("my") would only precede the noun. (C) *Mis* is the plural possessive adjective and must accompany a plural noun. (D) *Mío* ("mine") is masculine and cannot accompany *sorpresa,* a feminine noun.

42. (B)

Cuando me...sin emoción ninguna... ("when he...without any emotion...") calls for the preterite *anunció* ("announced/informed" [me]). (A) *Gritó* means "yelled," a descriptive verb that expresses strong emotion. (C) *Susurró* means "whispered," a verb that also has some emotional connotation. (D) *Pidió* means "requested," and doesn't make sense in this context.

43. (C)

is correct. *Unas de las mejores* [*playas*] means that the Costa Brava beaches are some of the best in the world. (A) Using *las* ("the") is grammatically incorrect. (B) *Una* ("one") is singular and doesn't match *las playas,* a plural noun. (D) *Ninguna* ("none") contradicts the idea of the passage.

44. (A)
The contraction *del* must be used here; in English, it means "in the [world]". (B) *En el* is incorrect, as are (C) *sobre* and (D) *por.*

45. (D)
Se dirigen means "they head towards/to go to." (A) *Se paran* means "they stop" and cannot be followed by *a ésas.* (B) *Salen* means "they go out." (C) The non-reflexive transitive verb *dirigen* means "they direct [something]."

46. (A)
The noun *acentos* ("accents") is correct. The passage refers to different varieties of the Spanish language. (B) *Jerga* ("jargon") refers to the special language of a particular social or professional group. (C) *Pronunciaciones* ("pronunciations") only accounts for the way people articulate words or utterances, and (D) *sonidos* means "sounds" [of a language].

47. (C)
is correct. *Clima* ("climate") is a singular masculine noun and is accompanied by the article *el.* Thus, answers (A) *la,* and (D) *una* are incorrect. (B) The indefinite article *un* ("a") doesn't apply here; the passage refers to a specific climate, that of the Costa Brava beaches.

48. (D)
Hospitalarios means "hospitable." (A) *Hostiles* is "hostile" (aggressive/unfriendly). (B) *Hostales* means "inns." (C) *Hospitalidad* is a noun and cannot accompany the noun *españoles.*

49. (A)
Con razón means "logically/rightly." The idea is that the Costa Brava shores are popular because of the various reasons stated above. (B) *Con pena* ("with sorrow"), (C) *con creces* ("fully/amply"), and (D) *con tal de que* ("provided that") do not apply.

50. (B)
Se hallan ("they are located") is the best choice here. (A) *Se parecen* ("they look like/alike") and (D) *se miran* ("they look at each other") have the wrong meanings and do not work contextually. (C) *Se descubren* means "they are discovered."

51. (A)
Pese a ("in spite of") implies a contradiction in the sentence: "In spite of the many kilometers that separate the Canary Islands from Spain, these islands belong to Spain." (B) *Por* and (C) *debido a* both can be translated as "due to" and have the opposite meaning ("Due to the many kilometers that separate the Canary Islands from Spain, the islands belong to Spain."); these two options don't make sense. (D) *Entonces* ("so") is incorrect.

52. (C)
Antiguos is the correct choice because the others do not fit contextually: (A) *añejos* means "aged," (B) *anticuados* means "old fashioned," and (D) *actuales* means "present."

53. (C)
The pronoun *las* refers to the antecedent *características,* a feminine plural noun (*Estas características físicas, tan distintas a las de cualquier otro...*) The pronouns (A) *lo* and (D) *los* do not convey the correct gender or number. (B) *El* is a definite article and cannot occupy the position of a pronoun.

54. (A)
Algunos is the only indefinite adjective that applies here since it accompanies the masculine plural noun *estudiosos.* (B) *Algunas* is feminine; (C) *algún* and (D) *alguno* are singular.

55. (C)
Afirman ("they state") is the best choice; it is more neutral than (A) *insisten* ("they insist"). The verb insistir also requires the preposition "en." (B) *Preguntan* ("they ask") and (D) *dudan* ("they doubt") do not make sense in this context.

56. (D)

Since the article is *los* (masculine plural), the noun must be masculine plural also, so *habitantes* ("inhabitants") is the best choice. (A) *Inhabitantes* isn't a Spanish word. (B) *Población* ("population") is a singular noun. (C) *Vecinos* means "neighbors."

57. (C)

The word *pasaje* means "passage." It "seems very optimistic" (*parece muy optimista*). It is obviously an advertisement for a school which trains people to be artists and designers for advertisements in the media, and offers "free and easy access" (*entrada libre y fácil*) to a "field" (*campo*) "whose possibilities seem limitless" (*cuyas posibilidades no parecen tener límite*). The reader is given the impression that simply by attending this school, he will be guaranteed a job. Notice that the adjective *optimista* ends in *-a*, even though it modifies a masculine noun (*pasaje*). This happens with all adjectives that end in *-ista* (e.g., *pesimista, oportunista*, etc.). Answer (A) *critica el sistema capitalista* ("criticizes the capitalistic system") is wrong; in reality, the school is part of the capitalistic system and is encouraging others to join that system. (B) *ofrece empleo en una escuela de dibujo* ("offers employment in a school of design"), is in error; the advertisement does not offer employment. Rather, it is seeking students to study at the school. (D), *promete un sueldo alto* ("it promises a high salary"), is also incorrect because no mention is made about what the graduates of the school might make.

58. (D)

The advertisement implies that "it is easy to find a position as a designer" (*es fácil encontrar puesto como dibujante*). The first sentence tells us that "Nowadays publicity agencies are flourishing" (*Hoy en día florecen las agencias de publicidad*). Furthermore, the school, we are told, offers "free and easy access" (*entrada libre y fácil*) to the field of advertising. We hope you didn't choose answer (A), *hay más plazas en el campo que en la ciudad* (there are more positions in the country than in the city), just because the word *campo* appears in the reading. Here the word *campo* means "field of endeavor," rather than "country." Not "just large businesses are concerned with publicity" (*sólo los grandes negocios se preocupan por la publicidad*), as answer (B) would have us believe. The ad also speaks about products that even "are made by hand" (*se hacen a mano*) but are also advertised. We know that (C) *la escuela es muy exigente* (the school is very demanding), is wrong because we are told that their "requirements" (*requisitos*) are "minimal" (*mínimos*).

59. (B)

We can tell by the way this passage is written that it is not (A) *un cuento* ("a short story"). Remember that the feminine form of this word, *una cuenta* means "a bill" (such as you pay when leaving a restaurant). The passage is "an advertisement" (*un anuncio*). You should not have chosen (C) *una advertencia* ("a warning or remark"), just because it looks somewhat like the English word "advertisement." The word *brindis*, which appears in (D), means a "toast" (as when one makes a toast to someone's health). It is related to the verb *brindar* which usually means "to make a toast." This verb, as it appears in the passage, has the special meaning of "to offer."

60. (C)

We know that (C) *De veras, ya se ha solucionado el problema de las armas* (In truth, the problem of arms has already been solved) is false. In the first sentence, we read that "the dilemma of disarmament is still pending" (*sigue pendiente el dilema del desarme*). Remember that both *problema* and *dilema* are masculine words in Spanish. Answer (A) *Hay mucho desacuerdo en cuanto a la cuestión del desarme* ("There is much disagreement concerning the question of disarmament") is true because the article speaks of the controversy between "the supporters of disarmament" (*los partidarios del desarme*) and "those who are against disarmament" (*los que están en contra del desarme*). (B) is also true: *Es posible que en el porvenir se resuelva la cuestión del desarme* ("It is possible that in the future the problem of disarmament will be solved"). Notice that in this sentence we have had to use the subjunctive of *resolverse* (ue) because of the expression *Es posible que*, which implies doubt. *El porvenir* is a synonym for *el futuro*. (D) is also true: *Ya se han sugerido soluciones al problema del desarme* ("Solutions have already been suggested for the problem of disarmament"). We know this because we are told that *han surgido propuestas para realizar este sueño* ("proposals have arisen to realize this dream"). The verbs *sugerir* (ie, i) ("to suggest") and *surgir* ("to arise or appear") should not be confused.

61. (B)

In our sentence, the expression *oponerse a* means "to oppose" or "to be opposed to." (B) *desconfían de la buena voluntad del adversario* ("have no confidence in the enemy's good will"), is correct. We know this because we are told that "those who are against disarmament" (*los que están en contra del desarme*) believe that the enemy *no es de fiarse* ("is not to be trusted"). In (A), *son de otra parte* means "are from somewhere else." We hope you didn't choose this answer just because *parte* was used in the expression *por otra parte*, which means "on the other hand." (C) *son aversos a la supervivencia* ("are against survival"), is clearly wrong. They may be against disarmament, but they surely are not against the survival of humanity. (D) *apoyan la guerra* ("support war"), is also wrong. Those who are opposed to disarmament do not support war, but rather believe that arms may be a deterrence for war. The verb *apoyar* means "to support" in the sense of "to stand behind." On the other hand, when we mean "to support" in the sense of "to give money to," we use the verb *mantener*.

62. (D)

Those who favor disarmament, according to the article, also "are in favor of international inspection" (*están por la inspección internacional*). We read that "the proponents" (*los proponentes*) of disarmament say that international inspection "could be carried out" (*podría llevarse a cabo*) "by counting on an international organization such as The United Nations." (*contando con una organización internacional como las Naciones Unidas*). In the preceding explanation, pay particular attention to certain valuable idiomatic expressions such as *estar por* ("to be for" or "in favor of"), *llevarse a cabo* ("to be carried out or realized") and *contar con* ("to count on or rely on"). The verb *rechazan* ("reject"), in (A), makes that answer incorrect because we know that those favoring disarmament also support international inspection. The verb *temen* ("fear"), in (B), makes that answer wrong because the proponents of disarmament believe that we should try to abolish (*abolir*) arms if there is proper inspection. (C) is also incorrect: *tienen confianza en el enemigo* ("have confidence in the enemy"). We know they don't because they propose international inspection. The word *confianza* in Spanish means "confidence" in the sense of "faith." The word *confidencia*, however, signifies "**a** confidence," i.e. a "secret" which one confides in another.

63. (C)
The infinitive *aumentar* means "to increase." In our sentence, the present participle (the *-ndo* form) of this verb is used along with the third person singular of the verb *ir* ("to go"): *va*. This means "continues to increase." This grammatical construction is similar to the progressive tenses which are based on some form of the verb *estar* + the present participle. In addition to *estar*, frequently other verbs, particularly verbs of motion, can be used in front of the present participle to form variations on the progressive tenses, e.g. *ir, venir, seguir*, etc. What is progressively increasing, according to the article, is the "yield" (*rendimiento*) of the bombs, i.e. their "power" (*potencia*). The article does not indicate that "the scarcity of proposals" (*la escasez de propuestas*) is growing, as (A) says. "The realization of our goals) (*la realización de nuestras metas*) is not on the rise, as (B) says. Nowhere in the article do we find that it says that "the number of our enemies" (*el número de nuestros enemigos*) is increasing either, as (D) sets forth.

64. (D)
Because of the type of project which Alambrés is undertaking, a study of the emigration patterns in Uruguay, we can assume that he is probably a "sociologist" (*sociólogo*), not a "policeman" (*policía*), as in (A), or a "psychiatrist" (*psiquiatra*), as in (B), or an "elevator operator" (*ascensorista*), as in (C).

65. (D)
In our question, *tendrá que hacer* means "will have to do." This is based on the very frequently used construction *tener que* + infinitive ("to have to do [something]"). Alambrés will have to "consult the census records" (*consultar los censos*). He will not have to "demand a lot" (*exigir mucho*) (A), "to be in agreement" (*estar conforme*) (B), or "enroll in the registries" (*inscribirse en los registros*) (C).

66. (B)
Our questions asks, "What have they given to the researcher?" or "What has the researcher been given?" The answer is *dinero* ("money"). This is clear because the article tells us that *se le ha concedido una beca* ("he has been granted a scholarship or fellow-

ship"). Alambrés has not received an "office" (*una oficina*) (A), nor has he been given any "names" (*nombres*) of people, presumably to help him, (C). (D) *Una compañía* ("a company"), is incorrect also. You might have accidentally chosen this answer if you thought that *empresa*, as used in the reading, means "company" or "firm," as it frequently can, but here it means "endeavor."

67. (C)
The word *valor*, as used in our questions, means "value." Sometimes it can also signify "valor" or "courage." This investigator's studies "will explain why the number of inhabitants has declined" (*explicarán por qué ha bajado el número de habitantes*). This may be ascertained from the reading on the basis of the phrase *la disminución de la población* ("the decline in the population"). The noun *disminución* is related to the verb *disminuir* ("to diminish" or "decrease"). It is not suggested in the reading that the investigator's studies "will bring him a lot of money," as (A) would have us believe: *Le traerán mucho dinero;* nor will they "make emigration to other countries easier:" (B) *Harán más fácil la emigración a otros países*. Finally, they will not "cause an increase in the Uruguayan population," (D), *Causarán un aumento de la población uruguaya*. Note that the verb *aumentar* is the contrary of *disminuir*.

68. (C)
The text mentions that one must know how to treat each person (*saber tratar a cada persona*). Attending university and knowing psychology are not mentioned in the requirements for being a flight attendant, making (A) and (D) incorrect. One need only know English well, which makes (B) incorrect.

69. (B)
Mari Carmen is on maternity leave (*gozando de una excedencia por maternidad*), making (A) and (D) incorrect. In order to be a flight attendant, one must know English and not currently be studying it, making (C) incorrect.

70. (A)
Because Mari Carmen is their only daughter (*hija única*), her parents had wanted her to go to a university (*hubiera querido que hiciera una carrera universitaria*), making (B) incorrect. There is no mention of what her parents did for a living, making (C) incorrect. Psychology is mentioned in reference to the flight attendant's need to be able to deal well with people, making (D) incorrect.

71. (D)
Since this question is asking what is *not* true, examining the list of requirements helps one eliminate (A), (B), and (C). Flight attendants must know how to swim (*saber nadar*), must take a training course in life saving (*un cursillo de entrenamiento*), and must be of a certain height and weight (*el peso será acorde con la talla*). Again, there is no mention of one's need to graduate from a university.

72. (D)
The first sentence of the reading tells us that Catalina "has granted" (*ha concedido*) "an interview" (*una entrevista*) to a "correspondent" (*corresponsal*). Therefore, we know that *un periodista* ("a journalist") has spoken with her. (A) *un payaso* is "a clown." (B) *un profesor*, of course, means "a teacher" or a "professor." (C) *un mestizo* signifies "a person of mixed blood" (both Indian and Caucasian).

73. (B)
Catalina does not feel like a foreigner. The last sentence of the first paragraph says that "instead of feeling like a curiosity" (*en vez de sentirse como una curiosidad*), "she has adapted herself well" (*se ha adaptado bien*) "in very little time" (*en poquísimo tiempo*) "to a society which before was totally unknown to her" (*a una sociedad que antes le era totalmente desconocida*). Answer (A) *se parece a los mexicanos*, claims that Catalina "resembles the Mexicans." This is untrue because we know that she is blonde (*rubia*). Answer (C) *busca un puesto*, would have us believe that Catalina "is looking for a job," but she is just a student now. We know that sometime later she would like to become a Spanish teacher, (*piensa hacerse maestra de español*), but not now. We hope you didn't choose this answer just because of the word *que*, which actually means "since" or "in as much as." Answer (D) says that

Catalina "is counting on the support of the mestizos" (*cuenta con el apoya mestizo*), which has no bearing whatsoever on the reading. Several important expressions appear in relation to this question. *Sentirse* (ie, i) is often followed by an adjective, e.g., *Me siento cansado* ("I feel tired"). Notice that it is reflexive. *Parecerse a* means "to look like" or "to count on" or "to rely on." Note that in answer (C), the verb *buscar* means "to look for." Do not use *por* or *para* after it. Also, *hacerse* means "to become." It is used with professions and with the words *pobre* and *rico*.

74. (A)

In the last sentence of the reading, Catalina says *¡Cuánto duró!* when speaking of her "test" (*examen*). This means "How long it lasted!" *Duró* is the third person singular preterite of the verb *durar* ("to last"). It should not be confused with the adjective *duro* which means "hard" or "difficult." For that reason, you should not have chosen (C) *fue difícil* ("it was difficult"). Answer (B) *fue fácil* ("it was easy"), and answer (D) *fue mejor* ("it was better"), have no relation to what the reading says.

75. (B)

Soltar una carajada means "to burst out laughing." The verb *soltar* (ue) literally means "to let loose" or "to free." A *carcajada* is a "raucous laugh." The verb *reírse* (i, i) also means "to laugh." It may be used either reflexively or non-reflexively. *Murmuró*, in (A) means "muttered." In (C), *Gritó* signifies "shouted." In (D), *Lloró* is "cried."

76. (D)

In the first sentence of the last paragraph of the reading, we learn that the novelist held "a press conference" (*una conferencia de prensa*) following the ceremony, at which time he made certain statements. This was obviously before a group of "journalists" (*periodistas*). You should not have allowed the similarity between *ejército* ("army") and the verb *ejercer* ("to exercise or carry out"), in the first sentence of the second paragraph, to lead you to choose (A). Likewise, Requetemacho did not speak before a group of "actors" (*actores*), answer (B), just because of the similarity between this word and the word "acta" ("minutes or official record"), which appears in the second sentence of the reading, or the word *acto* ("act" or "event"), which we find in the first sentence of those listening to Requetemacho were "antifeminists" (*antifeministas*).

77. (B)

We know that Requetemacho is a "teacher" (*profesor*) because we are told that (1) he is a *catedrático*, which means that he is a university professor who holds a "chair" (*cátedra*) at the university, (2) the first sentence of the second paragraph says that he works in "the School of Philosophy and Letters" (*la Facultad de Filosofía y Letras*), where he carries out "his teaching task" (*su tarea educativa*). On the basis of the reading, we can in no way conclude that the novelist is an *inventor* ("inventor") (A), or a "priest" (*cura*) (C), or a "sportsman" (*deportista*) (D). Remember that following any form of the verb *ser* ("to be"), we do not use the indefinite article *un, una,* etc. before a noun indicating profession, unless that noun is modified by an adjeative. Examples: *Josefina es enfermera* ("Josephine is a nurse"); *Josefina es una buena enfermera* ("Josephine is a good nurse").

78. (A)

The verb *premiar* means "to give a prize or reward." In the first sentence, it is used in the passive voice: *ha sido premiado* ("has been given a prize or was given a prize"). Furthermore, in the first sentence of the last paragraph, Requetemacho is referred to as *el premiado* ("the recipient of a prize"). The word *jurado* can mean "jury," as in a court of law. In our reading, it means the panel of judges who chose the prize winner. Therefore, Requetemacho was not in a court of law, and was not "sentenced" (*sentenciado*), as (B) would have it. (C) is wrong also because the novelist has not "condemned women" (*condenado a la mujer*). Instead, he "has praised" (*ha elogiado*) "the valor" (*la valentía*) of "the female" (*la hembra*). You should not have chosen (D) simply because *tomar apuntes* ("to take notes") looks like *ha apuntado* ("has noted," "noted").

79. (D)

The verb *fugarse* is a synonym for *huir* ("to flee" or "escape"). The latter of these two verbs may be used both reflexively and non-reflexively. Requetemacho's wife has fled from her home. This is because her husband is evidently a tyrant. "He, and only he, wears the pants in his family, he insists" (*en casa suya, según él, sólo los lleva él*). In this sentence, the direct object pronoun *los* ("them") refers back to the last word of the previous sentence, *pantalones* ("pants"). There is no mention in the reading that "the writer" (*el escritor*) "has put on new pants" (*se ha puesto unos pantalones nuevos*). Although the novelist teaches in the *Facultad de Filosofía y Letras*, this does not mean that he necessarily teaches philosophy, since many subjects of a liberal arts nature are taught in such a university school. Consequently, (B) is incorrect. Answer (C) is totally contradictory to what Requetemacho himself declares. If he wears the pants in his family, then we cannot conclude that "the female is the boss" (*manda la mujer*) in his house.

80. (B)

According to "the judges" (*los jueces*), one of the reasons they have awarded the prize to Requetemacho is because of *la elevada calidad literaria de su novela* ("the sublime literary quality of his novel"). Therefore, we might conclude that it has "an elegant style" (*un estilo elegante*). You should not have chosen answer (A) *tiene que pagar una multa* ("he has to pay a fine"), simply because of the words *jueces* and *jurado* ("jury" or "panel"). Both (C) tiene la mente cerrada ("he has a closed mind"), and (D) *tiene prejuicios sobre la mujer* ("he has prejudices about women"), will not fit. By reading between the lines, we know that these two things are true, but the judges didn't, and certainly would not have awarded Requetemacho the prize if they had known.

81. (B)

La fiesta brava is "the bullfight." The first sentence of the second paragraph states that there are those who see in the bullfight "a metaphysics" (*una metafísica*), i.e., a philosophy, "of man confronting death" (*del hombre que se enfrenta con la muerte*). Consequently, "we might compare" (*Podríamos comparar*) the bullfight to "the human struggle with fatal destiny," i.e., death (*la lucha humana con el destino fatal*). *El toreo*, in (C), means "bullfighting," and *la corrida de toros*, in (D), means "the bullfight." (C) and (D) are incorrect because they would force us to compare the bullfight with itself. Answer (A) is clearly erroneous. The second sentence of the first paragraph points out that many "foreigners" (*extranjeros*) mistakenly think that the bull-fight is a "sport." If this is wrong, then we cannot compare it to "a football game" (*un partido de fútbol*). The word *partido* means "game" in the sense of a sports event. "*Fútbol*" is the Spanish word for what is called "soccer" in English. If we wish to refer to our "football," in Spanish we must specifically say *el fútbol norteamericano*, which is an entirely different sport and is not played in Spanish-speaking countries.

82. (A)

We know that the "bullfight" (*la fiesta brava*) observes "a ritual already established centuries ago" (*un ritual establecido ya hace siglos*). For that reason, it is correct to say that the bullfight "observes" or "shows" (*muestra*) "much ceremony" (*mucha ceremonia*). Notice that the verb *mostrar* is a vowel-changing verb in the present tense (o to ue). Answer (B) is in error because it says that "all bullfighters are experts" (*todos los toreros son expertos*). The reading, however, establishes that some are and some are not. The last sentence of the first paragraph says that the "movements" (*movimientos*) "are executed with more or less skill" (*se ejecutan con más o menos destreza*) "according to the expertise of the bullfighter" (*según la habilidad del torero*). You should not have chosen answer (C) because there is no mention of the bullfighter's suffering pain (*dolor*). The word *duelo* ("duel") could have misled you if you made this selection. In answer (D), the verb *desfilar* means to parade, and *cuadrilla* signifies the "troop" of bullfighters. When the bullfight begins, they do parade around "the bull ring" (*el redondel*). But remember that the answer says *Desde el principio hasta el fin* ("From the beginning to the end"). Obviously, the parade does not take that long, or the bullfight would never occur.

83. (A)

The last sentence of the reading notes that the bullfight "seems to have fewer fans than a century ago" (*parece tener menos aficionados que hace un siglo*). Consequently, you would be right in saying that "it has lost some of its popularity" (*ha perdido algo de su popularidad*). Notice that in the first of these sentences, *hace un siglo* is how we say "a century ago." The pattern is *hace* + expression of time. The *hace* is always in the present tense when we mean "ago." If there happens to be another verb used in conjunction with this expression, it is used in a past tense, generally the preterite: *Vinieron hace una hora* ("They came an hour ago"). If the time expression starts the sentence, then we use the word *que* to join it to the following verb, provided there is one, and thereby form a dependent clause: *hace una hora que vinieron*. We know that (B) *se celebra en todos los países hispanos* ("it is observed or celebrated in all Hispanic countries"), is wrong because the last sentence speaks only of those Hispanic countries where it is celebrated. In (C), the word *auge* signifies "pinnacle," i.e., its period of maximum development. The bullfight is not reaching that stage now, but did so much earlier. Answer (D) *les duele a los aficionados* ("hurts the fans") is not right, and would only be chosen by those who do not recognize the verb *doler* ("to cause harm or hurt to") or by those who are misled by the noun *duelo* ("duel"), which appears in the second paragraph.

84. (A)

In the bullfight, "the animal usually dies" (*usualmente muere la bestia*), as we see in the second paragraph when it says *casi siempre sale perdiendo el animal* ("the animal almost always comes out the loser, almost always loses"). Notice the use of *salir* as an auxiliary verb in front of the present participle *perdiendo* to form a variation on the present progressive tense. The progressive tenses are generally formed with *estar* + the present participle (the *-ndo* verbal form). Nevertheless, it is not unusual to have other verbs take the place of *estar* in this construction, particularly verbs of motion such as *ir, venir, salir, entrar,* etc. Answer (B) *se celebra el auge* ("the pinnacle is celebrated"), makes no sense with regard to the reading. Answer (C) *los aficionados condenan al torero* ("the fans condemn the bullfighter"), is most certainly not correct within the general context of the passage, although the crowds will sometimes whistle to express their contempt for a bad bullfighter. In (D), the word *cumbre* means "summit" or "pinnacle" and, in this sense, is a synonym for *auge*. But to say that "In the bullfight one arrives at the pinnacle," is not justifiable on the basis of the reading passage.

85. (B)

The focus in this question is on what is *not* offered by this ad. What it does offer is: (A), that each participant finish in 16 months (e*n sólo 16 meses*); (C), that each participant have help in finding work (*permanente asistencia en búsqueda de trabajo*); and (D), that each participant receive certification recognized in the U.S. (*certificado CMA reconocido por todos los hospitales en EE.UU.*). However, although financial help is offered, as stated in (B), it is only available if one qualifies (*ayuda financiera disponible si califica*).

THE SAT SUBJECT TEST IN

Spanish

PRACTICE TEST 4

SAT Spanish Practice Test 4

PART A

Time: 1 Hour
85 Questions

DIRECTIONS: In this part you are given incomplete statements or questions, each of which has four possible completions. Choose the most accurate of the completions and fill in the corresponding oval on the answer sheet.

1. Tengo los pies adoloridos porque vengo de -------.

(A) dormir
(B) nadar en el mar
(C) caminar sobre piedras
(D) quitarme los zapatos

2. En el mes de enero, en los estados del norte, hace mucho frío; la gente en ese tiempo usa ropa -------.

(A) de seda
(B) ligera
(C) pesada
(D) de verano

3. Te digo que no lo soporto, no lo aguanto; -------.

(A) me cae muy mal
(B) me gustaría conocerlo
(C) voy a casarme con él
(D) me encanta hablar con él

4. La última vez que comimos en ese restaurante, no me gustó la comida. La comida estaba muy -------.

(A) sabrosa
(B) insípida
(C) sin color
(D) riquísima

5. Nunca hace la tarea, nunca pone atención, nunca sabe contestar al profesor. Es muy -------.

(A) dedicado
(B) listo
(C) trabajador
(D) perezoso

6. La gente va a los cines a ver -------.

(A) películas
(B) conciertos
(C) obras teatrales
(D) óperas

7. Todas las ciudades grandes suelen tener calles muy sucias; siempre las calles están llenas de -------.

(A) coches
(B) jardines
(C) basura
(D) luces

8. Ha llovido tanto en estos días que me urge tener disponible -------.

(A) un traje elegante
(B) un sombrero de paja
(C) dónde esconderme
(D) algo que me proteja

9. El otro día yo iba manejando a más de 70 millas por hora. Un policía me vio, me paró y me dio un(a) -------.

(A) boleto
(B) multa
(C) carta de recomendación
(D) galleta

10. La esposa de mi hermano es mi -------.

(A) cuñada
(B) tía
(C) sobrina
(D) abuela

11. Rosa está comprando azúcar, arroz, aceite y mantequilla. Ella está en la -------.

(A) peluquería
(B) carnicería
(C) tienda de víveres
(D) panadería

12. Ella come apio, zanahorias, lechuga y rábanos. Podemos decir que a ella le gustan las -------.

(A) frutas
(B) verduras
(C) carnes
(D) cereales

13. Antonio tiene una carie; ayer no pudo dormir. Toda la noche -------.

(A) se peinó
(B) se saludó
(C) se burló
(D) se quejó

14. Acaba de morir la esposa de un buen amigo. Éste está muy triste, naturalmente. Siento la necesidad de decirle algo. Le digo, -------

(A) «Mañana es otro día.»
(B) «Más vale tarde que nunca.»
(C) «Te tengo envidia.»
(D) «Te acompaño en tu dolor.»

15. Ha caído tanta lluvia en estos días que no habrá -------.

(A) cómo encontrar a los amigos
(B) escasez de agua
(C) nada de agua
(D) necesidad de bañarme

16. Mi vecino me dijo que no me va a pagar el dinero que me debe. Yo no quiero perder ese dinero; por eso quiero buscar un buen -------.

(A) abogado
(B) vendedor
(C) empleado
(D) secretario

17. Ésta es la tercera vez que llego tarde a mi trabajo. Mi jefe me vio llegar y yo sentí mucha -------.

(A) pereza
(B) salud
(C) sed
(D) vergüenza

18. Si uno siente el frío cuando otros no, puede ser que -------.

(A) esté enfermo
(B) tiene los ojos abiertos
(C) no duerme bien
(D) no tiene amigos

19. Cada vez que quiero parar mi auto, no sé qué pasa, pero no para inmediatamente. Deben ser -------.

(A) los parabrisas
(B) las luces
(C) los frenos
(D) las llantas

20. Estoy muy enfermo de las anginas. Me duele mucho la -------.

(A) cara
(B) ceja
(C) muela
(D) garganta

21. Los invitados quieren ponerle azúcar al café. Ellos necesitan -------.

(A) cuchillos
(B) cucharas
(C) tenedores
(D) vasos

22. En este cuarto no hay corriente de aire. Voy a poner el ------.

(A) tostador
(B) comedor
(C) ventilador
(D) refrigerador

23. Si quieres abrir esa puerta, tienes que pedir las -------.

(A) llaves
(B) rajas
(C) cerraduras
(D) redes

24. Mi vecino se sacó la lotería por segunda vez consecutiva y yo le dije, -------

(A) «¿Cómo te va?»
(B) «¡Felicitaciones!»
(C) «¡Qué te vaya bien!»
(D) «De todos modos.»

25. ¿Te has superado en tus estudios, verdad? Y yo sé por qué. Es que -------.

(A) estudias mucho
(B) no estás muy aplicado
(C) siempre vas al cine
(D) no te gusta el profesor

26. Cuando fui a la peluquería, el peluquero me dijo, -------

(A) «¡Qué sucia tiene la cara !»
(B) «¿Qué clase de tela quiere?»
(C) «¿Cómo le corto el pelo?»
(D) «¿Cuál es su medida?»

27. Yo sabía que era imposible lo que yo quería, sin embargo ellos me animaban, diciéndome que no me cansara de insistir en mi deseo, que no parara. Pero yo les decía, -------

(A) «Voy a llamar al oculista.»
(B) «Es inútil intentarlo más.»
(C) «Espero que todo salga bien.»
(D) «¡Qué primorosa es la vida!»

28. Cuando Felipe mandó las cartas sin estampillas, su jefe comentó a los demás que -------.

(A) tiene muy poco tiempo
(B) tiene mucha paciencia
(C) no le gusta su trabajo
(D) es muy descuidado

PART B

DIRECTIONS: In each of the following paragraphs, there are numbered blanks indicating that words or phrases are missing. Four completions are provided for each numbered blank. Read the entire passage. For each numbered blank, choose the completion that is the most appropriate given the context of the entire paragraph. Fill in the corresponding oval on the answer sheet.

La cultura mexicana ha sido __(29)__ por otros pueblos a lo largo del tiempo. Una de las influencias fue __(30)__ de los españoles, quienes __(31)__ desde Europa y gobernaron a las gentes de México por muchos años. Los Estados Unidos, vecinos de México, han __(32)__ también a la cultura moderna de este país __(33)__ los programas de televisión, las películas, la música y la moda. __(34)__, los millones de turistas de todo el mundo que visitan México cada año __(35)__ allí un poco de su cultura al marcharse.

29. (A) apoyada
    (B) contribuida
    (C) influida
    (D) intervenida

30. (A) las
    (B) los
    (C) lo
    (D) la

31. (A) navegaron
    (B) volaron
    (C) anduvieron
    (D) salieron

32. (A) contribuir
    (B) contribuido
    (C) contribuyeron
    (D) contribuirían

33. (A) detrás de
(B) dentro de
(C) a través de
(D) además de

34. (A) Actualmente
(B) En actualidad
(C) A lo hecho
(D) De hecho

35. (A) dejan
(B) ceden
(C) adoptan
(D) renuncian

Hace más de 7.000 años, unos __(36)__ montados a caballo __(37)__ de más allá del mar Negro __(38)__ a lo largo de varios milenios todo el continente europeo, desde las estepas al océano. Las lenguas que __(39)__ estos pueblos se diversificaron al entrar __(40)__ las poblaciones que encontraron __(41)__, hasta que a finales del siglo XX el paisaje lingüístico de Occidente presentaba una diversidad que nadie podría haber imaginado. La mayoría de estas lenguas __(42)__ a la misma familia, la indoeuropea. Mucho más tarde, la familia indoeuropea de lenguas llegaría a cruzar el Atlántico, al __(43)__ el español, el portugués, el inglés y el francés en las lenguas dominantes de las Américas.

36. (A) reclutas
(B) caballeros
(C) invasores
(D) ladrones

37. (A) procedentes
(B) derivados
(C) pertinentes
(D) causados

38. (A) evitaron
(B) atravesaron

(C) traspasaron
(D) entraron

39. (A) hablan
(B) hablarían
(C) habían hablado
(D) hablaban

40. (A) en contacto con
(B) en guerra con
(C) en broma con
(D) en confianza con

41. (A) a su paso
(B) en su tierra
(C) a su tiempo
(D) al costado de

42. (A) vienen
(B) se parecen
(C) imitan
(D) pertenecen

43. (A) cambiarse
(B) convertirse
(C) convercerse
(D) persuadirse

Todos los años, a caballo entre julio y agosto, Santo Domingo __(44)__ en el centro de atracción del Caribe con su __(45)__ del merengue. Si en __(46)__ momento del año es difícil pasar unas horas seguidas en __(47)__ país sin escuchar música, en esta semana es imposible. El festival se abre con un vistoso __(48)__ por el malecón, y la ciudad baila __(49)__ de decenas de grupos, entre los que tocan las mejores bandas de merengue dominicanas y caribeñas.

44. (A) se manifiesta
(B) se vuelve
(C) vuelve
(D) se presenta

45. (A) festival
(B) conmemoración
(C) diversión
(D) banquete

46. (A) cualquiera
(B) cualquier
(C) cualesquiera
(D) cualesquier

47. (A) esto
(B) estos
(C) esta
(D) este

48. (A) fiesta
(B) debate
(C) marcha
(D) desfile

49. (A) al compás
(B) al ruido
(C) a la marcha
(D) al fin

Millones de __(50)__ de los puntos más __(51)__ y las culturas más diversas del planeta siguen con pasión el __(52)__ deportivo que más atención despierta en el orbe: el fútbol. La historia moderna del deporte empezó en el momento en que la cadena televisiva Eurovisión __(53)__ por primera vez un __(54)__ del mundial de fútbol por la copa del mundo.

50. (A) público
(B) concurrencia
(C) espectadores
(D) personalidades

51. (A) alejados
(B) cercanos
(C) limitados
(D) ilimitados

52. (A) show
(B) espectáculo
(C) panorama
(D) función

53. (A) exhaló
(B) arrojó
(C) expresó
(D) emitió

54. (A) procedimiento
(B) trato
(C) equipo
(D) partido

La Patagonia chilena es un área montañosa, casi siempre (55) por vientos inclementes, en el (56) sur del continente americano, junto a Tierra del Fuego. (57) nieve en todos lados, y llueve una media de 300 días al año. El navegante Magallanes fue el primer europeo en viajar por la zona en 1520.

55. (A) azotada
(B) golpeada
(C) batida
(D) abrazada

56. (A) punta
(B) término
(C) extremo
(D) extremidad

57. (A) Es
(B) Está
(C) Hay
(D) Aparece

PART C

DIRECTIONS: Read the following passages for comprehension. Following each passage are a number of questions or incomplete sentences. Choose the most appropriate response or completion and fill in the corresponding oval on the answer sheet.

Llegaba el día de su cumpleaños. En unos días ella tendría trece años. Iban a comenzar los años de casi una señorita, y ella ya sentía la nerviosidad de anticipación. Quería estar segura de que sus padres no se habían olvidado de lo que ella quería más que cualquier cosa en el mundo - un reloj de pulsera. Uno de esos de oro con manitas bien adornadas. Un reloj bien pequeño y delicado. Ella sabía que con ese reloj en su muñeca nadie dudaría que ella fuera señorita de verdad. Al pensar en el reloj, su corazón palpitaba más aprisa. ¿Podría ella esperar aquel día? Cada día sería un año, pero ella sería capaz de tener la paciencia necesaria.

Al fin llegó el día. Sus padres la despertaron cantando y presentándole un paquete chiquito envuelto en papel festivo y con un moño precioso. Ella, con manos temblorosas, abrió el paquete, quitando primeramente la cinta y luego el papel. Ella bien sabía que sería el reloj. Al abrir la cajita, ¿cuál cree que fue la sorpresa? Sí, era un reloj, pero no él que anticipaba, sino uno de Mickey Mouse.

58. La muchacha iba a

(A) comprar un reloj
(B) comer mucho pastel
(C) dormir tarde
(D) cumplir años

59. La muchacha quería como regalo de su cumpleaños

(A) un moño
(B) una muñeca
(C) un reloj de pulsera
(D) un rifle

60. Sus padres le presentaron

(A) el desayuno en la cama
(B) una cajita artísticamente adornada
(C) diez dólares
(D) dos de sus mejores amigas

61. Al abrir la cajita, sus manos

(A) temblaban
(B) la acariciaban
(C) quedaron paralizadas
(D) se chocaron

62. La muchacha recibió

(A) algo especial de su abuela
(B) el reloj que anticipaba
(C) otro reloj
(D) otro año de vida

El verano pasado me tocó la buena suerte de estar en el estado de Nueva York, no en una ciudad grande, sino en las montañas del norte del estado donde abundan los árboles que cubren el paisaje. Fui con mi perro cazador y mi rifle porque me habían dicho que los animales de caza menor abundaban también. Yo había alquilado una cabaña solitaria y anticipaba dos semanas de completa distracción y descanso de la rutina de mi trabajo. Apenas podía yo dormir pensando en el gusto que me iba a dar estar solo con mi perro en este ambiente. Cuando llegaron las primeras luces del alba, mi perro, ya anticipando las aventuras del día, me despertó. Tan pronto como pude, me alisté y salí. La niebla agregaba algo misterioso a este evento. El perro iba adelante husmeando uno que otro tronco de árbol y algunas plantas. Después de dos horas yo no había encontrado ningún animal, y decidí volver a seguir mis pasos, pero no pude. Yo estaba perdido. Después de caminar más de una hora, nunca pude encontrar la vereda que venía de la cabaña. Por dicha, el perro comprendió la situación, y de instinto me dejó y fue en busca del rastro. Pronto volvió, meneando la cola. Gracias al perro pude volver a la cabaña.

Como es de esperar, el día siguiente salí con menos entusiasmo y con más cuidado.

63. Este individuo quería gozar de

(A) los deportes de cancha
(B) la cocina continental
(C) las vacaciones al aire libre
(D) estar con gente

64. Su fiel compañero fue su

(A) perro
(B) animal de caza menor
(C) rifle
(D) pájaro carpintero

65. Al salir de la cabaña, se dio cuenta

(A) de la lluvia
(B) de que no llevaba zapatos
(C) de la niebla
(D) que cantaban los pájaros

66. Gracias al perro

(A) pudo encontrar de nuevo el camino
(B) se llenó de pulgas
(C) espantó a todos los animales
(D) pasó la noche al fresco

67. Ya que los perros husmean casi todo, se puede decir que tienen

(A) cola larga
(B) buenas patas
(C) buen olfato
(D) hocico grande

AREAS DE REPOSO

Pueden utilizarse para tomar un pequeño descanso durante el viaje. Los ASEOS GRATUITOS los encontrará en todas las Areas de Servicio y, en caso de urgente necesidad, en las estaciones de peaje.

En caso de AVERIA o ENFERMEDAD, puede pararse en el arcén, señalizando el vehículo de acuerdo con las normas del Código de Circulación y levantando la tapa del motor.

CIRCULACION

No se detenga jamás en un carril de circulación.

Respete estrictamente la señalización.

Circule por la derecha.

No invierta, bajo ningún concepto, el sentido de la marcha: es muy peligroso y está terminantemente prohibido por el Código.

Todo el personal de la autopista está a su servicio para prestarle ayuda en cualquier circunstancia. Por favor, atienda siempre sus indicaciones para una mejor y más fluida circulación.

PEAJE

Es obligatorio detenerse en las estaciones de peaje para pagar el peaje, o recoger el billete de tránsito, según el caso.

Le rogamos no doble ni rasgue el billete de tránsito. El extravío del mismo supone el pago del recorrido más largo posible.

Para su comodidad, procure llevar el importe exacto del peaje.

En todas las cabinas de peaje puede solicitar las tarifas de peaje vigentes.

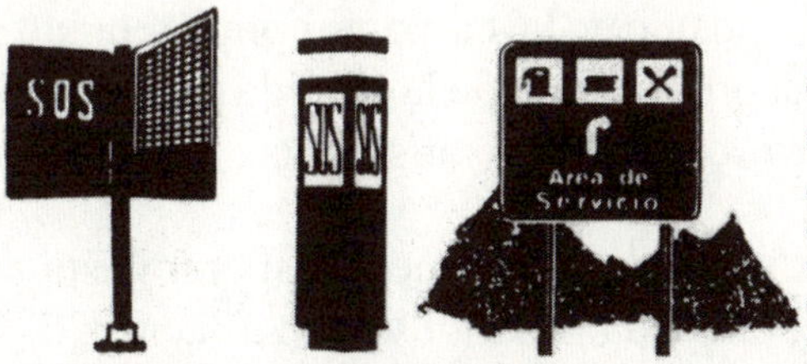

LA AUTOPISTA ES SERVICIO

Vd. no viaja solo.

Su seguridad queda garantizada por un especializado servicio de vigilancia y asistencia que, a través de los Postes de Auxilio (S.O.S.) colocados aproximadamente cada 2 km., está permanentemente alerta para solventar su circunstancia adversa.

La asistencia es total:

- Policía.
- Auxilio mecánico en ruta.
- Remolque del vehículo averiado.
- Ambulancia y servicios sanitarios.

AREAS DE SERVICIO EN AUTOPISTAS

Donde encontrará:

- su cafetería
- su restaurante
- su periódico
- cambio de moneda
- su pequeño "drugstore"
- amplia zona de descanso
- Aseos gratuitos
- Servicio telefónico

Y para su coche:

- carburante (90 n.o., 96 n.o., 98 n.o.)
- accesorios y repuestos
- verificación gratuita de la presión de los neumáticos
- asistencia técnica

En nuestra Area de la Junquera, situada junto a la frontera francesa, le ofrecemos además:

- Oficina de Cambio de Moneda.
- Carta Verde.
- Taller mecánico.

68. Según el artículo, ¿para qué sirven las estaciones de peajes?

    (A) para darle direcciones al conductor
    (B) para proveer comida o descanso
    (C) para ofrecer asistencia médica
    (D) para pagar el derecho

69. En cuanto a la circulación, sabemos que

    (A) se prohibe conducir los fines de semana
    (B) se prohibe circular por la derecha
    (C) se prohibe invertir dirección
    (D) se prohibe pedir asistencia del personal

– Pero Carlos, decía su amigo Rafael, – no puede ser mapa original del tesoro de los piratas, el papel no es viejo.

– Naturalmente, contestó Carlos, – es una copia. Pero sí es verídico, y mañana saldremos para los cayos. ¿Nos acompañas?

– Pues, no debería, pero sí me interesa el proyecto. La mañana siguiente Carlos, Rafael y dos amigos más salieron para *Cayo Hueso*. Llevaban palas, provisiones y una carpa, todo lo necesario para buscar el famoso tesoro del pirata Bracamontes.

Al llegar, primero pusieron la carpa y como tenían hambre, comenzaron con la preparación de la comida también. Todos cooperaron y pronto se quedaron satisfechos.

Uno sugirió que con el calor sería mejor esperar hasta más tarde para empezar la búsqueda. Todos estaban de acuerdo y pronto todos gozaron de los brazos de Morfeo.

Después de la siesta, ya ansiosos por encontrar el lugar indicado en el mapa, alguien preguntó,

– ¿Dónde está el mapa?

Nadie sabía y todos se pusieron a buscarlo. Abrieron todo, hasta revisaron en lugares imposibles, pero no encontraron el mapa. Todos se quedaron estupefactos y se preguntaron,

– ¿Es posible que hayamos dejado el mapa en casa?

Bueno, así era el caso. El viaje fue en vano y todos se sentían estúpidos. Pero, no fue un desastre completo. Todos gozaron de la anticipación de la aventura y ahora podrían fijar otra fecha para el gran descubrimiento.

70. El mapa del pirata que tenían era

(A) original
(B) falso
(C) de seda
(D) copia

71. Se fueron al cayo

(A) en un día de campo
(B) para las olimpiadas
(C) a conocer la playa
(D) a buscar lo indicado en el mapa

72. Cuando llegaron al lugar indicado,

(A) comenzaron a escarbar
(B) pusieron la carpa y comieron
(C) se bañaron en el sol
(D) se bañaron en el mar

73. ¿Dónde estaba el mapa?

(A) Carlos lo había dejado en casa.
(B) Lo perdieron.
(C) Alguien se lo comió.
(D) Lo rompieron.

– Dicen que es casa encantada, pero no lo creo yo.

Javier, que acababa de decir estas palabras, hablaba con los miembros de su fraternidad universitaria.

La casa de que hablaban era una de ésas de ladrillos, construida hace más de cien años, de dos pisos. Nadie había vivido en ella por más de 40 años porque se decía que después del suicidio del dueño, el espíritu de él rondaba por la casa, especialmente por las tempranas horas de la mañana, hora en que el dicho dueño se había ahorcado. La casa había quedado vacía desde esa fecha, pero no completamente, porque todos en el pueblo eran testigos del ruido que emanaba desde adentro. Y en los últimos años, parecía que el ruido aumentaba.

Era de noche, medianoche, y todos los miembros de la fraternidad retaban a Javier a que no se atreviera pasar una noche solo en la casa.

Javier estaba preparado y aceptó el reto. Inmediatamente comenzó con los preparativos. Llevó una cobija, una almohada, una linterna, dos Cocas y su televisor portátil.

Ponga atención, querido lector, que Javier no llevaba nada para protegerse.

Toda la fraternidad se juntó para despedirse del pobre Javier. Ellos no podían entender la valentía, o estupidez, de Javier.

– Adios bobo, así lo despidieron, burlándose de él.

Pero Javier, ignorando los insultos, con calma, entró en la oscuridad de la vieja casa.

Todo se quedó callado.

Los muchachos esperaban oír algo de gritos, pero no había nada. Después de más de dos horas, ya que no oyeron nada de la casa, comenzaron a llamar,

– Javier, ¿dónde estás? ¿Estás bien?

Los muchachos estaban para irse, pero de repente oyeron pasos que venían de la casa. Aparecío Javier en la puerta con dos gatos en los brazos y dijo a los muchachos,

– He aquí sus fantasmas.

74. Javier era el único

(A) miembro de la fraternidad
(B) estudiante
(C) cobarde
(D) valiente

75. Javier llevó con él a la casa

(A) cosas útiles para pasar una buena noche
(B) pistolas para defenderse
(C) mucha ropa extra
(D) una cruz para espantar a los malos espíritus

76. Después de esperar dos horas a la casa, los muchachos

(A) se fueron
(B) comenzaron a comer
(C) se durmieron
(D) vieron a Javier en la puerta

77. Encontró Javier al fantasma.

(A) Era el señor ahorcado.
(B) Eran dos gatos.
(C) Eran unos duendes.
(D) Era la familia del ahorcado.

78. El dicho fantasma, o señor de la casa, murió

(A) ahogado
(B) ahorcado
(C) ahumado
(D) acabado

Es el día de la famosa carrera entre la tortuga y la liebre. Todos los animales están para presenciar el evento. Nunca había tanto ánimo y entusiasmo entre ellos.

El juez es un perro cazador, famoso por su honradez y perspicacia.

La liebre, ya en su lugar, está desesperada, esperando la llegada de la tortuga, que a pasos lentos llegaba. La liebre, confiada en su victoria, se burlaba de las patas cortas de la tortuga.

– ¡Ea, chaparra, levántate, enderézate! No sé por qué me han escogido a mí, que soy tan buen corredor, a que compita contigo, bajita.

– A que gana la tortuga, decía el pato.

– No, dice la ardilla, va a ganar la liebre, no seas tan tonto. Y así arguían todos los animales.

En esos momentos el perro cazador levanta la pistola al aire para dar la señal del comienzo de la carrera.

Reina el silencio por un instante. Todas las apuestas están hechas entre los concurrentes.

¡Pum! El juez dispara la pistola.

La liebre pronto desaparece de la vista. La pobre tortuga no se mueve. Se duerme. Es hora de su siesta. Y así termina la carrera. Gana la liebre, como es de esperarse.

79. Todos los animales se han reunido para presenciar

(A) el casamiento de la liebre y la tortuga
(B) la competencia entre la liebre y la tortuga
(C) la repartición de la herencia entre la liebre y la tortuga
(D) la entrega de trofeos entre la liebre y la tortuga

80. La liebre se burla de la tortuga porque tiene

(A) cola large
(B) patas cortas
(C) cuello arrugado
(D) concha dura

81. Los animales, ¿toman el partido de quién?

(A) Están divididos en su opinión.
(B) Todos favorecen a la tortuga.
(C) Unos creen que saldrán iguales.
(D) Unos son indiferentes.

¿Cómo vencer la timidez?

Es como para pegarse un tiro. Cada vez que me gusta un chico, me quedo bloqueada, con la mente en blanco. Soy terriblemente tímida y no se me ocurre ningún medio para establecer contacto con él. ¿Estrella podrías darme algunos trucos?

Sonia A., 14 años, Burgos.

Por las numerosas cartas que recibo, veo que tu problema afecta a muchísimos jóvenes. En primer lugar, quiero felicitarte por tu capacidad de iniciativa y por distanciarte del arraigado prejuicio de que deben ser los chicos quienes den el primer paso. ¿Trucos que te ayuden a romper el hielo? Nuestras abuelas ya conocían docenas de triquiñuelas para llamar la atención de los caballeros sin salirse de su *rol* de **señoritas recatadas y modosas:** un pañuelo que se deja caer distraídamente, un desvanecimiento oportuno... Hoy día, lógicamente, se aplican estrategias diferentes. Veamos dos de ellas:

Método indirecto

Lo más sencillo es buscar la proximidad física con el chico que te interesa, sentándote junto a él en el autobús, coincidiendo en las actividades deportivas o en la discoteca. Sé amable, pero sin exageraciones, con toda naturalidad. La clave está en que él se perciba de tu presencia y te incorpore en sus pensamientos: ¿Me gusta? ¿Qué puedo hacer para atraerla hacia mí?

Método directo

En esta segunda variante, la relación se entabla de modo activo, recurriendo a un pretexto cualquiera. Pídele algo que sepas de buena tinta que posee: discos, libros, vídeos, etcétera. Solicita consejo o información sobre asuntos que él domine, dile que tienes interés por ver su colección de sellos...

Todas las chicas, incluso las más tímidas, pueden lograr que un chico se fije en ellas. Ya has visto que el primer contacto es relativamente fácil. Ahora le toca a él mostrar interés o reaccionar. Si no se inmuta, acéptalo sin darle más vueltas. ¡Evita el penoso y contraproducente espectáculo de repetir los intentos de aproximación! Pronto se presentará otro chico que te guste. Y, por favor, no te avergüences de tu timidez. Forma parte de ti y, bien llevada, puede ser un encanto más.

82. Sonia se describe a sí misma como una chica

(A) demasiado habladora
(B) bien medrosa
(C) agresiva
(D) cruel

83. ¿Cuál es el problema principal que sufre Sonia?

(A) Su novio se niega a hablar con ella.
(B) Su abuela le ha dado malos consejos a ella.
(C) Su novio tiene celos de ella.
(D) Ella tiene miedo de iniciar conversación con los chicos.

84. ¿Qué habrían hecho las abuelas?

(A) Le habrían ofrecido al chico su pañuelo.
(B) Se habrían aproximado al chico físicamente.
(C) Se habrían desmayado frente al chico.
(D) Le habrían hablado al chico sobre deportes.

85. Si el chico no muestra interés, la chica debe

(A) concentrarse en otro
(B) invitarle al cine
(C) volver a repetirlo todo
(D) pedirle prestados libros o discos

SAT Subject Test in Spanish
Practice Test 4

ANSWER KEY

1. (C)	23. (A)	45. (A)	67. (C)
2. (C)	24. (B)	46. (B)	68. (D)
3. (A)	25. (A)	47. (D)	69. (C)
4. (B)	26. (C)	48. (D)	70. (D)
5. (D)	27. (B)	49. (A)	71. (D)
6. (A)	28. (D)	50. (C)	72. (B)
7. (C)	29. (C)	51. (A)	73. (A)
8. (D)	30. (D)	52. (B)	74. (D)
9. (B)	31. (A)	53. (D)	75. (A)
10. (A)	32. (B)	54. (D)	76. (D)
11. (C)	33. (C)	55. (A)	77. (B)
12. (B)	34. (D)	56. (C)	78. (B)
13. (D)	35. (A)	57. (C)	79. (B)
14. (D)	36. (C)	58. (D)	80. (B)
15. (B)	37. (A)	59. (C)	81. (A)
16. (A)	38. (B)	60. (B)	82. (B)
17. (D)	39. (D)	61. (A)	83. (D)
18. (A)	40. (A)	62. (C)	84. (C)
19. (C)	41. (A)	63. (C)	85. (A)
20. (D)	42. (D)	64. (A)	
21. (B)	43. (B)	65. (C)	
22. (C)	44. (B)	66. (A)	

DETAILED EXPLANATIONS OF ANSWERS

PRACTICE TEST 4

1. (C)

Even though one might not know the word *adoloridos*, the word *dolor* can be seen in it, and this gives the clue. Answer (C) is the only one which would hurt feet. The article (*los*) is used as the possessive adjective when the noun it modifies is a part of the body or an article of clothing. The idiom *venir de* is similar to *acabar de*, and generally means "to have just." Both expressions are followed by an infinitive.

2. (C)

Three clues are given in the statement to permit understanding "heavy clothing" as the correct choice: "the month of January," "northern states" and "it is very cold." Only (C) is appropriate. "Silk," "light," or "summer clothing" would not be suitable.

3. (A)

Soportar is a false cognate and really means "to put up with," so answer (A) is correct. The idiom *caerse mal* has nothing to do with "falling," but means "to impress poorly, negatively." Another clue is the verb *aguantar*, which also means "to put up with." The other answers are positive and pleasant, and therefore could not be confused with the correct answer.

4. (B)

The preterite tense is used for the verb *comer* since it refers to a one-time situation in the past. The imperfect for the verb *estar* is used since the condition of the food remains the same, even though this is in the past. The verb *gustar* is used with the necessary indirect object *me*; the subject is *la comida. Insípida* is a cognate easily recognized and can readily be associated with food that "did not please."

5. (D)
Three very negative descriptions are given about the student: "he never does the homework," "he never pays attention," and "he never knows how to answer the teacher." Naturally, none of the answers given fits the situation except that he is "very lazy."

6. (A)
One must know the difference between *cines* and *teatros*. Answer (A) is the only one that can be seen in a *cine*. The other entertainment is limited to a *teatro*.

7. (C)
Without knowing the verb *soler*, one could guess the answer, but it is easier knowing that it means "usually" + verb. The other answers are easily recognized as positive and natural for a city. "Trash" is the only one that fits *sucias*.

8. (D)
The *llovido* suggests rain and the necessity for protection, but it is necessary to understand the *urge* and the *disponible* in order to choose the correct answer. *Urge* is, of course, suggestive of "urge" or "urgent," but understanding *disponible*, meaning "available," ties the sentence together. Notice that the present subjunctive is used in (D) with the verb *proteger*.

9. (B)
Manejar is the verb "to drive." In combination with the verb *ir*, it generally means "going along driving." At 70 miles per hour one would expect the police to give something unpleasant. One must understand that *multa* is translated "fine" or "ticket." One might be tempted to choose *boleto*, since it means "ticket," but it actually means "an admission ticket." Knowledge of basic vocabulary is important to make wise choices.

10. (A)
Here, one must know family vocabulary and be able to choose the correct word. My brother's wife is my "sister-in-law."

11. (C)
Usually the ending *–ía* on a noun, or some form of the noun, indicates where the product is made. Three of the answers are of this construction: *peluquería*, *carnicería*, and *panadería*. This should make the choice of the correct answer rather simple. *Víveres* is generally translated as "groceries." The information given in the sentence leads one to answer (C).

12. (B)
All of the foods listed in the information sentence are vegetables, so answer (B) is the only correct one.

13. (D)
One must understand the cognate of *carie* in English. An extended vocabulary in English helps the study of Spanish and vice-versa. Not being able to sleep because of his toothache would produce a complaint (*queja*). All of the verbs in the answers are reflexive and in the preterite tense.

14. (D)
The expression *acabar de*, an idiom, means "to have just." It is followed by the infinitive. *Éste* becomes a pronoun. The orthographic accent is not evident because of the capital "E." If a verb follows a preposition, it is always in the infinitive. Answer (B) is a common expression, but does not fit the situation. Answer (D) is the only proper answer.

15. (B)
Escasez suggests its cognate, "scarcity;" this should make the correct choice easy since *tanta lluvia* suggests an abundance of rain. Notice that the past participle of *caer* uses the orthographic accent, *caído*.

16. (A)

Notice the apocopation of *bueno* to *buen* before a masculine, singular noun in the second sentence. The speaker does not want to lose the money; *por eso*, "for that reason," he is looking for a good lawyer, answer (A).

17. (D)

The first word, *ésta*, should have a written accent, but since it is capitalized, it is not shown. Using the two verbs together *ver* and *llegar*, the first is generally translated and the other is left in the infinitive. So, "saw me arriving" gives the clue as to how I felt when I came late – "embarrassed." Notice that all the answers are feminine and singular, a fact clearly appropriate because of the adjective *mucha*.

18. (A)

The correct choice depends upon two conditions: the general knowledge that being ill quite often makes a person feel the cold, and the knowledge of the other answers, which do not fit the situation.

19. (C)

All the answers are plural, as required by the plural use of the verb *deber*. However, the clue is *parar*, "to stop." Stopping a car depends primarily on the "brakes."

20. (D)

The verb *estar* is used with illness or similar bodily condition. *Anginas* may not give a clue as to its meaning. The other answers may be familiar enough to permit choosing the one unknown. *Anginas* are "tonsils."

21. (B)

The use of the indirect object pronoun *le* seems redundant, but it is customary when the noun to which it refers is used or understood and an emphasis wants to be made. To put sugar in their coffee, guests need not "knives," not "forks," not "glasses," but "spoons." So, answer (B) is correct.

22. (C)
The word *corriente* means "current," or even "common" or "ordinary." Here, it means "flow" of air. The answer, then, is going to entail the *ventilador*. *Poner* means "to put" or "to place," but in this case, it means "to turn on." In some Central and South American countries, the verb *prender* is used for this.

23. (A)
The idiom *tener que* is used here meaning "to have to." For opening the door, one must have "keys," so answer (A) is the right choice.

24. (B)
The reflexive *sacarse* indicates "for his benefit." And, since this is the "second time" he won the lottery, "congratulations" are in order. Answer (D) is completely wrong grammatically. Answers (A) and (C) are inappropriate.

25. (A)
The verb *superarse* is a cognate of a familiar Latin word "super," and means "to excel" or "to do exceedingly well." The reason for this is obvious—the student studies a great deal, answer (A). Not liking the teacher, always going to the movies and not being industrious are flimsy excuses and are not reasons for doing well in one's studies.

26. (C)
The word *peluquero* and *peluquería* are related to *pelo*, and this should give a good clue as to the answer, (C). None of the other answers is suitable.

27. (B)
The first sentence and the last clause give the best clues as to the answer. The imperfect subjunctive is used after what they said, asking me "not to become tired" or "not to stop." My answer, however, is answer (B), "It is useless to try any more."

28. (D)
Mandar has several meanings; "to send" and "to command" are two of them. The word *cartas* should indicate which meaning should be used. Other words sometimes used for *estampillas* are *sellos* or *timbres*. The prefix *des-* in Spanish is quite often comparable to the suffix *-less* in English. So, when the boss noticed the letters without stamps, "careless" is the proper description of Felipe.

29. (C)
The past participle *influida* means "influenced." The idea of the passage is that other peoples have influenced Mexican culture throughout history. (A) *Apoyada* means "supported." (B) *Contribuida* ("contributed") is not possible in the past participle form. (D) *Intervenida* means "intervened."

30. (D)
The definite article *la* refers to *una de las influencias* ("one of the influences"), so it must be singular feminine. (A) *Las,* (B) *los,* and (C) *lo* are incorrect answers due to the gender or number they convey.

31. (A)
Because the Spanish came to the Americas by boat, *navegaron* ("they sailed") is the correct answer. (B) *Volaron* ("they flew"), (C) *anduvieron* ("they walked"), and (D) *salieron* ("they went out") do not apply.

32. (B)
The past participle, *contribuido* ("contributed") is necessary, due to the presence of the auxiliary verb *han* (present perfect tense). (A) The infinitive *contribuir* ("to contribute"), (C) the preterite *contribuyeron* ("they contributed"), and (D) the simple conditional *contribuirían* ("they would contribute") are incorrect.

33. (C)
A través de ("by means of") is correct: "The USA has influenced Mexican culture through television, films, music, and fashion." (A) Together, *detrás* and *de* mean "behind." (B) The adverb of place *dentro*

and the preposition *de* mean "inside of" and (D) the adverb of quantity *además* followed by *de* means "besides."

34. (D)
De hecho means "in fact." (A) *Actualmente* is a false cognate that means "at present." (B) *En actualidad* is not a Spanish phrase (however, *en la actualidad* exists and means "at the present time"). (C) *A lo hecho* is part of the phrase *a lo hecho, pecho* (approximately, "offer your chest to what may happen"), which means that we must confront the consequences of our actions, however wrong they were.

35. (A)
Dejan means "they leave behind," meaning that tourists in Mexico leave their customs and culture behind. (B) *Ceden* means "they yield." (C) *Adoptan* ("they adopt") and (D) *renuncian* ("they resign") are incorrect.

36. (C)
Invasores ("invaders") is the best choice. (A) *Reclutas* ("recruits") is used when referring to today's armies. (B) *Caballeros* ("gentlemen") and (D) *ladrones* ("thieves") are incorrect.

37. (A)
Procedentes ("coming from/originating in") is correct: "the invaders came from beyond the Black Sea." (B) *Derivados* ("derived") is used in relation to words/language or chemical substances. (C) *Pertinentes* ("it belongs or refers to") and (D) *causados* ("caused") are incorrect.

38. (B)
Atravesaron... todo el continente europeo means "they crossed the entire the European continent." (A) *Evitaron* means "they avoided." (C) *Traspasaron* means "they went beyond the limits." (D) *Entraron* means "they entered."

39. (D)
The imperfect form *hablaban* is necessary, because it refers to a past ongoing action. (A) *Hablan* applies to the present. (B) *Hablarían* (the

conditional) means "they would speak." (C) *Habían hablado* (the past perfect tense) refers to a time before the past events happened.

40. (A)
The invaders "came into contact with" (*entraron en contacto con*) new peoples. (B) *En guerra con* ("in war with") isn't implied in the passage. (C) *En broma* means "as a joke," and (D) *entraron en confianza con* means "they began to trust [the new peoples.]"

41. (A)
The invaders found peoples "on their way" (*a su paso*). (B) *En su tierra* means "on their land." (C) *A su tiempo* means "at the appropriate time," and (D) *al costado de* means "beside."

42. (D)
The languages belong (*pertenecen*) to the Indoeuropean family of languages. (A) *Vienen* ("they come [from]"), (B) *Se parecen* ("they look like"), and (C) *imitan* ("they imitate/mimic") are incorrect.

43. (B)
Convertirse is the term needed to express "became": "Portuguese, English, French, and Spanish 'became' the most dominant languages in the Americas." (A) *Cambiarse* means "to change/to change oneself." (C) *Convercerse* means "to feel convinced," and (D) *persuadirse* means "to become persuaded."

44. (B)
The reflexive verb *se vuelve* means "turns into" ("Santo Domingo 'turns into' a center of attraction"). (A) *Se manifiesta* means "manifests [itself]/shows/expresses." (C) The non-reflexive *vuelve* means "it returns," and (D) *se presenta* means "presents itself."

45. (A)
Santo Domingo has a "festival" (*festival*—a musical festivity) in July and August. *Conmemoración* ("commemoration") is a ceremony or act in remembrance of an event or a person. (C) *Diversión* is a general word meaning "entertainment," while (D) *banquete* ("banquet") refers to food.

46. (B)
The indefinite adjective *cualquier* ("any") is the apocopated form of *cualquiera,* which must be used before a masculine singular noun (in this case, *momento*). (A) *Cualquiera* is not apocopated. (C) *Cualesquiera* and (D) *cualesquier* are plural forms.

47. (D)
Este ("this") is the form of demonstrative adjective needed to accompany the masculine singular noun *país* ("country"). (A) *Esto* ("this") is a demonstrative pronoun that stands on its own. (B) *Estos* ("these") is the plural form of the demonstrative adjective. (C) *Esta* is the feminine form of *este.*

48. (D)
The passage states that there is an opening parade (*desfile*) at the Malecón when the festival begins. (A) *Fiesta* ("party/celebration") is more general; besides, it is a feminine noun and doesn't match either the indefinite article *un* or the masculine adjective *vistoso.* (B) A "debate" (*debate*) is a discussion in which different points of view are expressed. (C) *Marcha* ("march") is usually employed in relation to the army or a political demonstration.

49. (A)
Al compás is a phrase meaning "to the rhythm/beat of," which makes sense in this context, since the idea is that the whole city of Santo Domingo dances "to the rhythm" of different musical bands. (B) *Al ruido* means "to the noise of." (C) *A la marcha* is "to the march of," and (D) *al fin* means "finally."

50. (C)
The context calls for a plural noun—*espectadores* ("spectators")—that matches *millones de* ("millions of"). (D) *Personalidades* ("personalities") isn't the correct option, since many people, not just celebrities, view soccer. (A) *Público* ("the public") and (B) *concurrencia* are singular nouns.

51. (A)
The idea here is that everybody watches soccer, even people from distant parts of the world; *alejados* ("distant") is the best option. (B) *Cercanos* ("close") contradicts the idea of the passage. (C) *Limitados* ("limited") and (D) *ilimitados* ("unlimited") do not match *puntos* ("points").

52. (B)
Espectáculo ("spectacle") is the best substitute for *fútbol* or sporting event. (A) Although the word "show" is also sometimes used in sports, it isn't the best option. (C) *Panorama* ("panorama") is a wide view of a landscape. (D) *Función* is also used in sports, since it means "show or performance," but doesn't fit in here because it's a feminine noun.

53. (D)
Emitió means "it broadcast." (A) *Exhaló* ("it exhaled") refers to air and breathing. (B) *Arrojó* means "it threw," and (C) *expresó* means "it expressed."

54. (D)
The Spanish word for "match" or "game" is *partido.* (A) *Procedimiento* ("procedure") refers to methods. (B) *Trato* ("deal") and (C) *equipo* ("team") are incorrect.

55. (A)
Azotada is an adjective meaning "violently beaten by the wind or sea." (B) *Golpeada* has the more general meaning of "beat." (C) *Batida* means "beaten as with eggs." (D) *Abrazada* means "hugged" or "embraced."

56. (C)
Extremo ("end") is a masculine singular noun that matches the article *el.* (A) *Punta* ("point") would also be used here if it weren't a feminine noun. (B) *Término* ("conclusion") is incorrect, as is (D) *extremidad* ("extremity"), which refers to the outskirts of a territory.

57. (C)
The present form of the verb *haber* (*hay*) means "there is" ("there exists"). (A) *Es*—verb *ser*—translates as "It is." (B) *Está* means "is temporarily," although this form is incorrect in Spanish. (D) *Aparece* means "appears," which doesn't really make sense contextually.

58. (D)
It should be rather easy to connect *cumplir años* with *cumpleaños*. Add to this the fact that she was going to be thirteen, and the only logical answer is (D).

59. (C)
The word *pulsera* can be remembered because of the traditional location for taking the pulse. This was to be a special kind of wrist watch, a gold one with ornate hands. Alone, *pulsera* means bracelet. *Un moño*, in this context, means "bow," formed by *la cinta*, "ribbon." It can also mean "bun" or "top knot," as in hairstyle. In the passage, *su muñeca* means "her wrist," but *una muñeca* can also mean "a doll."

60. (B)
Notice the indirect object *le*, indicating something to be given to her. Any of the answers fulfill this requirement; however, knowing the subject matter of the story makes the choice simple.

61. (A)
The natural nervousness of the girl opening the hoped-for gift would make her hands tremble. Answer (D) uses the verb *chocar*, which means "to hit together" or "to shake hands."

62. (C)
Understanding the twist in the story makes answer (C) the correct choice.

63. (C)
Notice that the word for "vacation" is always in the plural, *vacaciones*. "In the open air" or "out of doors" is generally translated *al aire libre*.

64. (A)
The answer is his "[faithful] dog." Even though answer (C) could be a possibility, the information given in the story indicates that his dog was his important companion, not his gun.

65. (C)
The idiom *darse cuenta de* is always translated as "to realize" or "to become aware of." When used in front of a verb, *que* must precede the verb, which may never be in the infinitive form. *Niebla* is generally translated as "fog."

66. (A)
Al fresco can also be translated as "out of doors." Occasionally, the expression *de nuevo* is used for "again." In this case, choice (A) is correct since the dog helped him to find the way back.

67. (C)
One must know the verb *husmear*, "to sniff out" or "to smell out." This then gives the clue to answer (C) *buen olfato* because of its cognate "olfactory." The word *hocico* is used for an animal's "mouth" "muzzle," or "snout."

68. (D)
The text states specifically that it is "obligatory to stop to pay the toll" (*es obligatorio detenerse en las estaciones de peaje para pagar el peaje*). Receiving assistance, such as getting directions, is given in the *circulación* areas, making (A) incorrect. Food and rest are provided in the service areas (*áreas de servicio en autopistas*), making (B) incorrect. One can stop along the edge of the road (*arcén*) to get medical assistance, making (C) incorrect.

69. (C)
The text indicates that direction should not be changed under any circumstances. Driving on weekends is not mentioned, making (A) incorrect. A specific direction that is given is to "move to the right" (*circule por la derecha*), so (B) is incorrect. Finally, (D) is incorrect because it is stated that "everyone is at your service to lend help in any

circumstance" (*todo el personal de la autopista está a su servicio para prestarle ayuda en cualquier circunstancia*).

70. (D)
According to the text, the pirate's map was a copy.

71. (D)
Lo indicado is the proper way to give a noun character to *indicado*, and is translated as "that which is indicated." Note that the word *mapa*, even though it ends in –a, is masculine.

72. (B)
Despite the excitement of looking for the treasure, the boys first put up the tent and ate. The verb *escarbar*, in answer (A), means "to dig."

73. (A)
Carlos forgot the map at home. The expression *se lo comió* should be translated as "ate it up." And remember that the verb *romper* not only means "to break," but also "to tear."

74. (D)
This choice is easy. Javier was the only "brave" member of the fraternity.

75. (A)
The exact cognate of *útil* is "utile" or "useful." Javier took only items which would make spending the night more comfortable. The verb *espantar*, in answer (D), means "to frighten."

76. (D)
According to the text, after a couple of hours Javier appeared at the door. Notice that all the answers are in the preterite.

77. (B)
The ghost was two cats. Notice that in Spanish the predicate nominative influences the verb to become plural. In Spanish this sentence is correct: *El fantasma eran dos gatos*.

78. (B)
All answers are possible ways of dying. *Ahumado* has to do with *humo*, "smoke." The story, however, indicates that the man hanged himself.

79. (B)
The word *competencia* should never be *competición*, which might appear to be correct. *Competencia* is always translated as "competition."

80. (B)
Patas are animal feet or furniture legs or anything similar. The word is also used to make fun of human feet.

81. (A)
According to the text, the animals favored either one or the other of the animals. They even placed bets on the outcome.

82. (B)
This question primarily tests one's knowledge of vocabulary. Sonia describes herself as "terribly shy" (*terriblemente tímida*), which is a synonym of *medrosa*. All other answers are adjectives meaning "talkative" (*habladora*), "agresiva" (*aggressive*), and "cruel" (*cruel*), making (A), (C), and (D) incorrect.

83. (D)
Sonia indicates in her letter that she is unable to "establish contact" (*establecer contacto*) because her mind goes blank (*con la mente en blanco*). Therefore, (A) and (C), which both refer to her having a boyfriend, are incorrect. Although grandmothers are mentioned in the text, there is no reference to her having received advice from her grandmother, making (B) incorrect.

84. (C)
Of the two pieces of advice offered in the text, one refers to *un desvanecimiento* ("a fainting fit"), which is synonymous with the verb *desmayarese* ("to faint"). The reference made to the handkerchief (*pañuelo*) has to do with dropping it and not offering it to the boy, so (A) is incorrect. Approaching the boy physically and initiating conver-

sation about sports are two items mentioned under the heading "indirect method" (*método indirecto*), making (B) and (D) incorrect.

85. (A)

At the end of the piece, it is stated that "soon another boy whom you like will present himself" (*Pronto se presentará otro chico que te guste*). Inviting the boy to the movies is not mentioned, making (B) incorrect. The text states that "repeating one's intentions" is to be avoided (*evita el espectáculo de repetir los intentos*), making (C) incorrect. Records and books are mentioned, but in relation to asking about them, not asking to borrow them, making (D) incorrect.

THE SAT SUBJECT TEST IN

Spanish

PRACTICE TEST 5

SAT Spanish Practice Test 5

PART A

Time: 1 Hour
85 Questions

DIRECTIONS: In this part you are given incomplete statements or questions, each of which has four possible completions. Choose the most accurate of the completions and fill in the corresponding oval on the answer sheet.

1. El tiempo fresco de las montañas es bueno para -------.

(A) nadar
(B) darse prisa
(C) caerse
(D) pasear

2. El marido de mi hermana es -------.

(A) soltero
(B) cuñado
(C) mi sobrino
(D) mi padrino

3. Mi casa está hecha de -------.

(A) arcilla
(B) ladrillos
(C) harina
(D) hierro

4. Desde la época de los dinosaurios han pasado -------.

(A) meses
(B) días
(C) semanas
(D) siglos

5. Los árboles crecen en -------.

(A) los pájaros
(B) la pampa
(C) las ramas
(D) el bosque

6. En ------- se nada y se asolea uno hasta cansarse.

(A) el campo
(B) la sierra
(C) la playa
(D) el bosque

7. El bebé lloraba porque ------- leche.

(A) le calentaban
(B) le regulaban
(C) le faltaba
(D) le sobraba

8. Un abogado firma muchos -------.

(A) retratos
(B) recetas
(C) contratos
(D) periódicos

9. El trabajo de los bomberos consiste en -------.

(A) apagar incendios
(B) prender fuegos
(C) conservar el agua
(D) quemar basura

10. En los grandes aeropuertos las autoridades ------- a los pasajeros antes de embarcarse.

(A) asesinan
(B) revisan
(C) besan
(D) dan dinero

11. Se considera ------- como tierras bajas.

(A) al altiplano
(B) a la cordillera
(C) a la llanura
(D) a la sierra

12. Mañana tengo que escribir una ------- a mis padres.

(A) letra
(B) carta
(C) remesa
(D) propina

13. En esa casa encantada el fantasma se ------- todas las tardes a la hora del té.

(A) aparece
(B) parece
(C) representa
(D) permanece

14. Después del accidente el herido fue trasladado a -------.

(A) la enferma
(B) la enfermera
(C) la enfermedad
(D) la enfermería

15. Su esposo ------- de esperarla y se fue.

(A) se casó
(B) se alegró
(C) se cansó
(D) se suicidó

16. No todo lo que brilla es -------.

(A) piedra
(B) oro
(C) barro
(D) ceniza

17. María tiene trece años y ya se pinta -------.

(A) los codos
(B) los ojos
(C) las orejas
(D) la nariz

18. ------- viven en el mar.

(A) Los tiburones
(B) Las serpientes
(C) Las hormigas
(D) Los lagartos

19. Gansos, patos, golondrinas y avestruces son -------.

(A) peces
(B) plantas
(C) minerales
(D) aves

20. Como Lisa tiene veinte años y yo quince, ella es -------.

(A) menor
(B) mayor
(C) mi prima
(D) mi sobrina

21. Llevaremos ------- para comer al picnic de este sábado.

(A) jamón
(B) guantes
(C) zapatos
(D) camisas

22. Ramón no ------- a los padres de su novia.

(A) muerde
(B) toca
(C) conoce
(D) sabe

23. Ramón no ------- que los padres de su novia son inmigrantes.

(A) conoce
(B) sabe
(C) responde
(D) pregunta

24. Caminábamos ------- para llegar más tarde.

(A) fuerte
(B) despacio
(C) rápido
(D) al frente

25. Los árboles y los libros tienen -------.

(A) hojas
(B) ramas
(C) raíces
(D) páginas

26. La segunda ------- mundial terminó en 1945.

(A) garra
(B) guerrilla
(C) guerrillero
(D) guerra

27. Cuando sale el sol, -------.

(A) anochece
(B) atardece
(C) amanece
(D) oscurece

28. Hoy es jueves; ------- fue miércoles.

(A) ayer
(B) mañana
(C) anteayer
(D) pasado mañana

29. Mis tíos tienen ------- donde sus amigos pueden nadar los fines de semana.

(A) un pozo
(B) una piscina
(C) un lavatorio
(D) un charco

30. Cuando la noche está clara, se ven las -------.

(A) nubes
(B) mañanas
(C) estrellas
(D) madrugadas

31. Quiso abrir la puerta del auto pero en ese momento ------- de que había perdido la llave.

(A) realizó
(B) se repuso
(C) se encerró
(D) se dio cuenta

PART B

DIRECTIONS: In each of the following paragraphs, there are numbered blanks indicating that words or phrases are missing. Four completions are provided for each numbered blank. Read the entire passage. For each numbered blank, choose the completion that is the most appropriate given the context of the entire paragraph. Fill in the corresponding oval on the answer sheet.

Al momento de su __(32)__ en 1952 a la edad de 33 años, la __(33)__ primera dama argentina Eva Perón, "Evita" para sus millones de __(34)__, se había convertido en la líder espiritual de la nación, una "santa" cuya dramática vida __(35)__ una devoción casi mítica. __(36)__ en todo el mundo como la musa inspiradora del musical Evita, y tema del filme de Madonna, Eva Perón es uno de los íconos populares del __(37)__ XX.

32. (A) victoria
    (B) elección
    (C) matrimonio
    (D) muerte

33. (A) cruel
    (B) carismática
    (C) entretenida
    (D) caricaturesca

34. (A) seguidores
    (B) opositores
    (C) público
    (D) empleados

35. (A) hubiera inspirado
    (B) inspire
    (C) inspiraría
    (D) inspirará

36. (A) Conocida
(B) Sabida
(C) Hablada
(D) Anónima

37. (A) centuria
(B) siglo
(C) sigla
(D) época

La etapa de _(38)_ musulmán sobre Toledo (años 711–1085) se _(39)_ el mismo año en que las tropas de Tariq cruzaron el estrecho de Gibraltar y _(40)_ al _(41)_ visigodo de don Rodrigo. En poco tiempo, los musulmanes llegaron a la ciudad del río Tajo, que encontraron casi _(42)_ y sin resistencia, ya que la mayoría de sus pobladores crisitianos _(43)_. En cambio, los pobladores judíos _(44)_ en Toledo y colaboraron con los musulmanes, razón por _(45)_ cual recibieron algunos cargos de responsabilidad.

38. (A) dominación
(B) dominio
(C) potencia
(D) absoluto

39. (A) pasó
(B) terminó
(C) inició
(D) perdió

40. (A) golpearon
(B) destrozaron
(C) mataron
(D) derrotaron

41. (A) ejército
(B) armada
(C) militares
(D) marina

42. (A) habitada
(B) despoblada
(C) sola
(D) alejada

43. (A) habían salido
(B) habían ido
(C) habían huido
(D) habían corrido

44. (A) quedaron
(B) pararon
(C) estuvieron
(D) permanecieron

45. (A) las
(B) el
(C) la
(D) una

El mate, testimonio de la cultura americana, de indiscutible __(46)__ indígena y tradición popular, __(47)__ presente en muchos escenarios de la vida moderna—entre ellos la casa, el campo, las __(48)__ de amigos, las playas, y hasta las calles en algunos lugares. "Mate" __(49)__ de la lengua quechua "mati", que quiere __(50)__ "calabaza o calabacita", nombre __(51)__ de la planta Lagenaria Vulgaris, que todos los pueblos han usado y usan como __(52)__.

46. (A) antepasado
(B) patria
(C) origen
(D) pedigree

47. (A) es
(B) está
(C) ser
(D) estar

48. (A) congregaciones
(B) congresos
(C) mitines
(D) reuniones

49. (A) viene
(B) llega
(C) comienza
(D) termina

50. (A) dice
(B) se dice
(C) decimos
(D) decir

51. (A) regular
(B) incorrecto
(C) vulgar
(D) correcto

52. (A) recipiente
(B) tenedor
(C) bañera
(D) receptor

Con la presencia de __(53)__ personalidades de la alta __(54)__, actrices y público invitado, el __(55)__ Di Doménico presentó su nueva colección otoño-invierno. Actrices __(56)__ China Zorrilla, Luisina Brando y Graciela Borges se dieron __(57)__ al pie de la pasarela para apreciar la nueva __(58)__ de uno de los más reconocidos diseñadores argentinos.

53. (A) gran
(B) grande
(C) grandes
(D) granadas

54. (A) arte
(B) ciencia
(C) religión
(D) costura

55. (A) diseñador
(B) estilista
(C) sastre
(D) fabricante

56. (A) así
(B) como
(C) tan
(D) tal

57. (A) reunión
(B) prisa
(C) cita
(D) lugar

58. (A) plan
(B) diseño
(C) llegada
(D) propuesta

Hertz les regala a sus niños un viaje ¡de película! Por cada __(59)__ para adultos que __(60)__ a precio normal, usted recibirá una entrada __(61)__ para niños en los increíbles parques Universal Studios de la Florida y California. Sólo necesita __(62)__ su contrato de alquiler de Hertz en la taquilla. ¡__(63)__ de uno de los mejores parques de atracciones con la compañía que le entrega el mundo en sus manos!

59. (A) pase
(B) cupón
(C) entrada
(D) pasaje

60. (A) venda
(B) adquiera
(C) consiga
(D) pida

61. (A) gratis
(B) libre
(C) cara
(D) barata

62. (A) pasar
(B) demostrar
(C) mostrar
(D) chequear

63. (A) Disfrutan
(B) Disfrutemos
(C) Disfrutó
(D) Disfrute

PART C

DIRECTIONS: Read the following passages for comprehension. Following each passage are a number of questions or incomplete sentences. Choose the most appropriate response or completion and fill in the corresponding oval on the answer sheet.

Los hombres parecen ser más gastadores, aunque las mujeres se llevan toda la fama.

ACTITUDES FEMENINAS Y MASCULINAS ANTE EL CONSUMO

Según se desprende de los últimos estudios, hombres y mujeres gastamos más o menos lo mismo, aunque las actitudes ante el consumo sean diferentes en función de deseos, estado y necesidad.

El progresivo acortamiento de la jornada y de los días laborales de la semana permite cada vez más horas libres que, consecuentemente, inducen a una más elevada tendencia al gasto. El esparcimiento mediante los espectáculos, actos culturales y viajes turísticos se ha incrementado por este motivo.

Teniendo en cuenta la incidencia de todos los factores sociales y culturales antes mencionados, que condicionan en gran medida los comportamientos de los consumidores, entre los que destaca una progresiva emancipación de la mujer, algunos autores deducen que en la actualidad las decisiones importantes respecto al consumo familiar son tomadas en su mayor parte de una forma conjunta, especialmente entre las parejas jóvenes.

La socióloga Asunción Coronado se muestra, sin embargo, algo reticente ante esta teoría, ya que considera que sigue habiendo una clara diferenciación entre los gastos que cubre la mujer y los que realiza el hombre. «Las mujeres siguen ocupándose de los gastos domésticos, aunque éstos no sean ostentosos. No se trata tanto del precio como de las categorías.» La decisión última del coche, la casa o un viaje al extranjero corresponde al hombre.

LA CESTA DE LA COMPRA

El sector alimentación es el que recoge en mayor medida un acercamiento entre los dos sexos a la hora de gastar. El Instituto Nacional de Consumo revela que el 40% de los compradores de los supermercados son hombres y, de ellos, un 70% acude en solitario y un 30% como acompañante. El que un hombre haga la compra se considera algo normal en la actualidad y su comportamiento respecto al de la mujer no varía excesivamente. Algunos estudios demuestran que el hombre compra de forma más planificada y que es más sensible a las marcas que la mujer. Esta, por otra parte, se muestra más receptiva ante los productos en oferta y tiene más capacidad para la improvisación y el ahorro.

INDEPENDIENTES

Los hombres y mujeres independientes económicamente gastan de forma menos compulsiva que aquellos que dependen de otros, ya que, dueños de su situación personal, no necesitan demostrar nada ante los demás.

64. ¿Por qué gastan menos los que viven a solas?

(A) Tiene menos dinero que gustar.
(B) No hay nadie a quien deban empresionar.
(C) Trabajan más dejándoles menos tiempo para ir de compras.
(D) Tienen la ayuda de padres o parientes.

65. Entre las parejas jóvenes

(A) hay tendencia de gastar más
(B) la mujer lo decide todo
(C) quien tiene el sueldo más alto lo decide todo
(D) hay colaboración con respecto al consumo familiar

66. La actitud ante el consumo es más igual en cuanto a

(A) comprar casa o coche
(B) decidir a dónde ir de vacaciones
(C) seleccionar comida
(D) escoger artículos domésticos

Déjenme explicarles cómo es la selva amazónica del Perú, a ustedes que nunca han salido de la capital. Me imagino que algo habrán oído de los mosquitos y víboras y el calor pegajoso que no deja a uno tranquilo. Pero es fácil acostumbrarse a esto, y pronto uno se empieza a fijar en otras cosas, como las increíbles especies do monos que se ven entre las ramas, las orquídeas y las mariposas de colores brillantes. Esto no significa que no sea buena idea llevar un botiquín con medicinas, pero lo que les quiero decir es que no hay que dejarse intimidar por los peligros de la selva. En realidad, creo que lo más peligroso es el vuelo de Lima a Iquitos, la única ciudad importante de la amazonía peruana. El tiempo es turbulento por lo general, y los aviones que hacen el trayecto parecen tener muy poca confianza en sus capacidades mecánicas. De Iquitos uno puede adentrarse en la selva a pie o tomar el río, pero en cualquier caso conviene contratar a un guía. Les pido que si alguna vez vienen a la selva amazónica no cometan el error de algunos turistas americanos que andan preguntando por todos lados dónde quedan las ruinas incaicas más cercanas.

67. ¿A quiénes se dirige el narrador?

(A) a viajeros experimentados en los peligros de la selva
(B) a los turistas americanos
(C) a los habitantes amazónicos
(D) a los habitantes de la capital

68. ¿Cuáles son los atractivos de la selva que el narrador destaca?

(A) los monos y las orquídeas
(B) el calor pegajoso
(C) el viaje en avión
(D) los turistas americanos

69. ¿Qué es Iquitos?

(A) una ciudad selvática importante
(B) la ciudad donde viven los turistas americanos
(C) la línea aérea que vuela desde Lima
(D) unas famosas ruinas incaicas

70. ¿Qué recomienda el narrador a quienes se adentran en la selva?

(A) no pisar las orquídeas
(B) contratar a un guía
(C) contratar a un turista americano
(D) dejar el botiquín médico en casa

¿Por qué lee la gente libros de viajes? Probablemente porque todos queremos viajar pero no podemos, y tenemos que contentarnos con los relatos de otro. Claro que no queremos viajar sólo por viajar, sino que deseamos conocer lugares exóticos. Y justamente la mayoría de los libros de viaje transcurren en lugares alejados y remotos, y muchas veces peligrosos. En realidad, la pregunta que me parece más interesante y difícil de contestar es por qué se escriben los libros de viajes. Y también cuándo se escriben: si durante el viaje mismo o después, en un momento de reflexión. Si el viajero ya ha viajado o mientras viaja, ¿por qué se preocupa de organizar un relato que no podrá ser más emocionante que el viaje en sí? ¿Para recordar los detalles más tarde? ¿Para analizar el significado de la experiencia? ¿O para revivirlo para el lector que no pudo ir de viaje? Esta última razón parece la más probable por qué también explica el por qué se leen los libros de viaje. Cuando los leemos, somos el viajero que en la realidad no pudimos ser. Además hay otra cosa. Los libros de viaje son generalmente más interesantes que los viajes que emprendemos en la realidad. ¿Por qué es esto? ¿Acaso los autores que viajan y luego escriben su viaje son más interesantes que los lectores? Yo creo que no. Lo que pasa es que los autores de estos libros saben antes de viajar que van a escribir un libro de viaje, y hacen lo posible por seguir una ruta llena de aventuras. Viajan por las regiones menos visitadas del país, viajan por tierra y no por aire o mar, y hablan frecuentemente con los lugareños.

71. ¿Por qué se leen tanto los libros de viaje?

(A) porque traen interesantes recetas de cocina
(B) porque traen buenos consejos sobre cómo vivir nuestra vida
(C) porque los lectores son viajeros frustrados
(D) porque cuestan poco dinero

72. ¿Dóndo se ubican los libros de viaje?

(A) sobre todo en las ciudades
(B) en lugares peligrosos y remotos
(C) en los momentos de reflexión
(D) en sitios con muchos animales

73. ¿Por qué se escriben libros de viajes?

(A) para transmitir conocimientos antropológicos
(B) para que el lector envidie al autor que ha viajado
(C) para establecer contacto con los pueblos visitados
(D) para que el lector viva la experiencia del autor

La salud es una preocupación natural de todo ser humano, pero en nuestra sociedad contemporánea se ha convertido casi en una obsesión o en un culto. Los síntomas de este problema se ven en todas partes: la insistencia maniática en tomar sólo alimentos considerados sanos y naturales; la necesidad de ejercitarse hasta el dolor y el agotamiento; el fanatismo de los no fumadores y su agresividad contra quienes gustan de fumar (o lo hacen por vicio), etc. ¿A qué se debe esta situación? Sin duda el puritanismo tradicional de nuestra sociedad—para el cual la higiene es un principio capital—tiene mucho que ver con la obsesión contemporánea con la salud. Pero también parece existir entre mucha gente hoy en día un temor al cuerpo, una inseguridad que traduce un miedo a la muerte. Al cuerpo no hay que mimarlo tanto como se hace hoy. Por supuesto tampoco hay que abusarlo, y si uno vive con moderación no hace falta privarse de todos los alimentos calóricos ni correr hasta la fatiga. Claro que hay una razón más inmediata que explica el culto de la salud en nuestra sociedad, y es la amplia disponibilidad de todos los alimentos y bebidas imaginables. Frente a esta avalancha de cosas deseables hay que saber controlarse. Un último factor que puede ser considerado es la creación de una verdadera industria de la salud, desde los fabricantes de vitaminas y minerales hasta los dueños de gimnasios particulares para correr y jugar tenis en un ambiente de lujo.

74. ¿Qué piensa el autor de los que hacen demasiado ejercicio?

(A) que demuestran síntomas de una preocupación excesiva con la salud
(B) que son buenos amantes
(C) que son muy religiosos
(D) que comen demasiado

75. ¿Cómo se relaciona el puritanismo al culto de la salud?

(A) porque la gente reza para tener buena salud
(B) porque el puritanismo enfatiza la higiene
(C) no se relaciona porque los puritanos desaparecieron hace tiempo
(D) porque la tradición puritana prohibe la carne

76. ¿Significa nuestra actual obsesión con la salud una afirmación del cuerpo?

(A) Sí, el cuerpo es todo lo que verdaderamente poseemos y tenemos que desarrollarlo
(B) Sí, porque el que cree en la salud cree en el cuerpo
(C) No, porque los que se preocupan demasiado de su salud son gente enfermiza que morirá pronto
(D) No, porque preocuparse demasiado de la salud significa desconfiar del cuerpo y temer a la muerte

77. ¿Tiene la abundancia de comida y bebida en nuestra sociedad un efecto negativo sobre la salud?

(A) No, porque la mayoría de la gente no puede darse el lujo de comprar muchas cosas de comer y de beber
(B) Sí, si uno no sabe moderarse
(C) No, porque toda comida y bebida es buena
(D) Sí, porque fumar hace daño

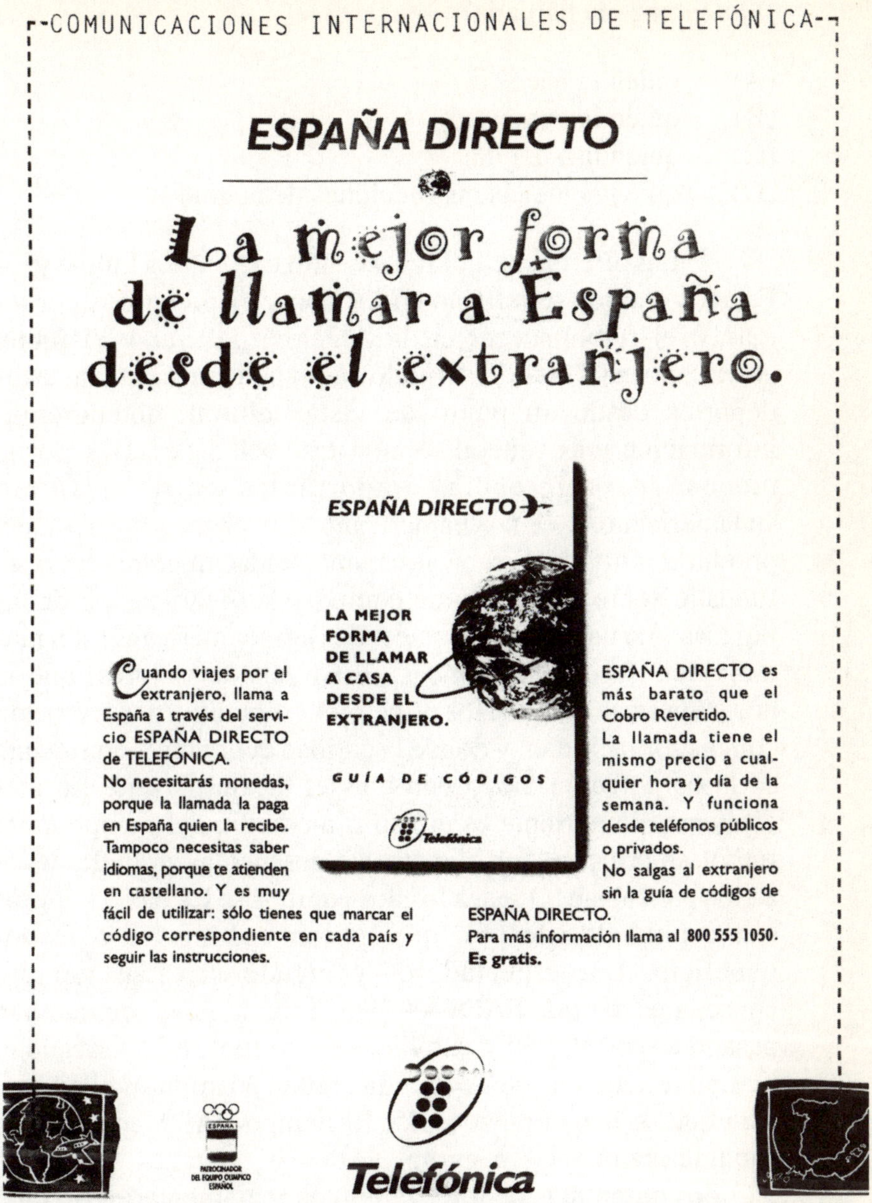

78. ¿Quiénes necesitan esta guía?

(A) los que quieren llamar al extranjero
(B) los que viajan sin mucho dinero
(C) los que hablan muchos idiomas
(D) los que saben los códigos de cada país

79. ¿Quién paga la llamada?

(A) quien la hace
(B) quien la contesta
(C) quien usa la guía
(D) quien sigue las instrucciones de la guía

Las diferencias culturales entre la América Latina y los Estados Unidos se reflejan en los deportes preferidos por las masas: el fútbol-soccer en la América del Sur y el fútbol americano en el Norte. De modo que si podemos analizar estos deportes desde un punto de vista cultural, obtendremos información más general sobre estas sociedades. Hay por lo menos dos diferencias importantes entre el fútbol sudamericano y el norteamericano. En primer lugar, aquél premia el individualismo y la espontaneidad mientras éste está fundado sobre el espíritu de equipo y la planificación de las jugadas. Así también, las sociedades latinoamericanas son más individualistas (más caóticas, dirían sus detractores) que la norteamericana, donde los principios comunitarios se respetan con mayor facilidad, y donde la entidad económica dominante es la corporación, cuyo héroe es el "team-player." La otra diferencia importante es el uso o medición del tiempo en el fútbol americano, que siempre se descuenta, se mide desde arriba para abajo. O sea, a los dos equipos se les da 60 minutos (un capital de tiempo), que gastan con mayor o menor beneficio. Los espectadores y jugadores están siempre conscientes de que FALTAN tantos minutos, no de que han pasado tantos otros. En cambio, en el fútbol sudamericano el tiempo se acumula. No se dice que faltan 20 minutos por jugar, sino que se llevan jugados 25. El tiempo PASA en el fútbol sudamericano, no se agota. (Además, muchas veces los partidos duran más de los 90 minutos reglamentarios, lo cual sería impensable en el fútbol norteamericano. Ahí siempre se juegan 60 minutos, aunque el tiempo real que pasa es a veces 3 horas y media.) ¿Qué puede significar esta diferencia en la concepción del tiempo entre los deportes mencionados?

80. ¿Cuál es el deporte preferido de los latinoamericanos?

(A) remar en bote
(B) el fútbol americano
(C) el análisis cultural
(D) el fútbol-soccer

81. ¿Qué virtudes son importantes para triunfar en el fútbol-soccer?

(A) el espíritu de equipo
(B) la espontaneidad
(C) el ser miembro de una corporación importante
(D) la habilidad de analizar culturalmente al adversario

82. ¿Cómo se mide el tiempo en el fútbol americano?

(A) restándolo
(B) desde adentro para afuera
(C) con relojes nucleares
(D) sumándolo

83. De acuerdo a este análisis de los deportes, ¿Cuál es un rasgo de la sociedad norteamericana?

(A) el caos
(B) la imposibilidad de saber qué hora es
(C) el individualismo
(D) el orden y la planificación

El rasgo más indiscutible de los paises latinoamericanos es la diversidad de sus culturas. Algunos de los países fueron poblados casi exclusivamente por europeos; otros son una mezcla de descendientes de culturas indígenas y españoles; y hay un tercer grupo en que la influencia africana es muy importante. Aparte del aspecto étnico, se deben considerar aspectos geográficos y lingüísticos. El Brasil, por ejemplo, es el país más grande del continente, pero como fue poblado por colonos y aventureros portugueses, no se habla ahí el español. El Caribe forma un submundo en el mundo hispánico, aunque hay naciones en esa región que hablan inglés, francés y hasta holandés. Pero incluso en los países de habla española se encuentran diferencias culturales internas debidas a (o propiciadas por) la geografía. Típicamente los países hispanoamericanos están divididos entre una cultura urbana y una o varias culturas regionales, y la capital muchas veces está sobre el mar mientras que las diversas regiones culturalmente autónomas ocupan las zonas interiores del país. También entre país y país existen importantes diferencias geográficas. Hay algunos situados en la región andina (o sea, en la cordillera de los Andes), otros en la selva amazónica, otros en zonas de climas diversos (como Chile, que se extiende desde el desierto hasta la Antártica), y aún otros en que la planicie domina amplios sectores de la vida cultural y económica del país. A todo esto hay que agregar diferencias históricas y económicas, que explican que ciertos países estén más desarrollados que otros, o que tengan un más alto índice de alfabetización.

84. ¿Cuál de éstas es una importante influencia étnica en las culturas latinoamericanas?

(A) el tabaco y el azúcar
(B) los grupos africanos
(C) los holandeses
(D) los norteamericanos

85. ¿Cómo se divide internamente la cultura de un típico país latinoamericano?

(A) entre la capital y el interior
(B) entre el español y el portugués
(C) entre indígenas y españoles
(D) entre ricos y pobres

SAT Subject Test in Spanish
Practice Test 5

ANSWER KEY

1. (D)
2. (B)
3. (B)
4. (D)
5. (D)
6. (C)
7. (C)
8. (C)
9. (A)
10. (B)
11. (C)
12. (B)
13. (A)
14. (D)
15. (C)
16. (B)
17. (B)
18. (A)
19. (D)
20. (B)
21. (A)
22. (C)
23. (B)
24. (B)
25. (A)
26. (D)
27. (C)
28. (A)
29. (B)
30. (C)
31. (D)
32. (D)
33. (B)
34. (A)
35. (C)
36. (A)
37. (B)
38. (B)
39. (C)
40. (D)
41. (A)
42. (B)
43. (C)
44. (D)
45. (C)
46. (C)
47. (B)
48. (D)
49. (A)
50. (D)
51. (C)
52. (A)
53. (C)
54. (D)
55. (A)
56. (B)
57. (C)
58. (D)
59. (C)
60. (B)
61. (A)
62. (C)
63. (D)
64. (B)
65. (D)
66. (C)
67. (D)
68. (A)
69. (A)
70. (B)
71. (C)
72. (B)
73. (D)
74. (A)
75. (B)
76. (D)
77. (B)
78. (B)
79. (B)
80. (D)
81. (B)
82. (A)
83. (D)
84. (B)
85. (A)

DETAILED EXPLANATIONS OF ANSWERS

PRACTICE TEST 5

1. (D)

The correct choice is *pasear*. None of the other choices makes sense in context. The key to the correct answer is the translation of *tiempo* in the question as "weather" and not "time" (you need to be careful with the meaning of *fresco* as well). If you don't understand *tiempo* properly, you might pick (B) on account of its connection with time. On the other hand, if you pass too lightly over the first half of the phrase and concentrate unduly on *montaña*, you might erroneously choose (C) as the answer. Choice (A) contains an idea related to "pasear" (the correct answer) but contradicts the meaning of the sentence.

2. (B)

You should arrive at the right answer by a process of elimination. Choices (C) and (D) express the incorrect family relation between the husband and the speaker, whereas (A) is obviously contradictory.

3. (B)

The correct answer depends on your ability to differentiate among the different choices. Only one of the materials mentioned fits the bill, the others being more or less irrelevant in the context though plausible for other kinds of construction (except for (C), of course).

4. (D)

The correct choice embraces the widest span of time of any of the four options.

5. (D)

The right answer turns on the ability to relate *árboles* in the question to *bosque*, thus eliminating the other choices, particularly the more ambiguous ones: (A) and (C) are ideas related to "trees" but don't make logical sense in context.

6. (C)

One key to this question is the ability to identify the verbs in the question and then select the one noun among the choices that fits the verbs. (Notice that *asolearse* has *sol* as its main semantic component.)

7. (C)

The correct choice requires an understanding of the verbs *faltar* and especially of the difference between *faltar* and *sobrar*, its opposite pair. Choices (A) and (B) are fairly implausible.

8. (C)

Only one choice refers to documents habitually signed by lawyers. The other options may sound similar but have very different meanings.

9. (A)

All the options contain references to fire or water but only one means "to put out fires," which is what *bomberos* do.

10. (B)

The correct answer consists of identifying the only plausible response to the question, which in turn depends on knowing the correct Spanish verb for "to check," as opposed to the more or less current but anglicized versions *checar* or *chequear*.

11. (C)

To get the right answer you need to know the meaning of *llanura* but also of some of the alternatives, since "plains" is only one of several possible ways to refer to *tierras bajas*. The other three choices in this question all refer to highlands.

12. (B)

Letra sounds like "letter" (the kind one writes and sends off) but the similarity is deceiving. Choices (C) and (D) are ideas linked to one's parents (at least when one is an adolescent) but have nothing to do with writing.

13. (A)

The correct answer depends on the appropriate distinction between *aparecerse* and *parecerse*, which tends to be somewhat blurred in English (both verbs can be translated as "to appear" but are used differently in Spanish).

14. (D)

All the choices are closely related but only one designates the place where the wounded can be taken.

15. (C)

The only choice that completes the question in a logical way is *se cansó*. Choices (A) and (D) are contrary to sense, and (B) is not plausible.

16. (B)

The correct choice requires an understanding of the verb *brillar*. The only choice that refers to the idea of "shining" is *oro*.

17. (B)

The only part of the body (of those mentioned here) that a young girl could "paint" (i.e., with eyeliner) is the eyes. The key to this answer is the verb *pintarse* used in the sense of "to apply make-up."

18. (A)

The key to this answer is the ability to recognize the different animals offered as choices. Only one of these choices refers to a sea-living species.

19. (D)

This question reviews your "fowl vocabulary." In order to choose the correct answer, you must identify the several birds in the question as belonging to the genre *aves*.

20. (B)
The last two choices don't follow logically from the question. The correct answer hinges on your knowing the difference between *mayor* and *menor*.

21. (A)
In order to get the right answer you are expected to distinguish between articles of clothing (choices (B) through (D)) and the only edible item on the list.

22. (C)
The correct answer comes down to a choice between *conoce* and *sabe*, both modalities of "to know." (The first two choices don't make as much sense).

23. (B)
Again, an exercise to distinguish between *saber* and *conocer* (and again, the last two choices don't fit semantically or grammatically). When it's a matter of knowing information (as in this case) the correct choice is *saber*.

24. (B)
The idea is to identify a choice that will complete the sense of the question, i.e., one that will mean "slow" since only this idea will correlate with the last part of the sentence.

25. (A)
This rather playful question asks you to locate the one choice whose meaning applies to both *árboles* and *libros*.

26. (D)
The key to the answer lies in your differentiation of the four closely related choices, only one of which means "war."

27. (C)

Here you have to identify which of the four choices translates the idea of the sun rising. It helps knowing the root words of choices (A) through (C) (*noche, tarde,* and *mañana* respectively). Choice (D) is contradictory in the context of the question.

28. (A)

This question tests your knowledge of the days of the week in Spanish. *Ayer* (yesterday—miércoles), *mañana* (tomorrow—viernes), *anteayer* (day before yesterday—martes), *pasado mañana* (day after tomorrow—sábado).

29. (B)

The correct answer implies knowledge of the verb *nadar* in the question, and the ability to distinguish among several kinds of bodies of water, only one of which can be translated as "swimming pool."

30. (C)

A hasty reading of the question—superficially highlighting *clara*—may result in an incorrect answer (either (B) or (D)). A further obstacle to the correct response is *nubes*, which does make some sense in the context but not as much as *estrellas*. Of course these obstacles can be avoided if you know the meaning of *estrellas* from the outset.

31. (D)

Choices (B) and (C) simply make no sense in the context. You may think that (A) is the obvious choice since it sounds like it means "realized." It does, but not in the sense demanded by the question, which can only be rendered by (D). (*Realizar* means "to realize" a project or a plan, to make something real.)

32. (D)

Muerte ("Death")—due to the possessive adjective *su* ("her")—fits into the passage. (A) *Victoria* (victory) and (B) *elección* (election) both imply a contest of sorts over someone of something and (C) *matrimono* (marriage) do not fit the theme of the reading.

33. (B)
Carismática ("charismatic/with charisma") is the best option here. (A) *Cruel* ("cruel"), (C) *entretenida* ("amusing/entertaining"), and (D) *caricaturesca* ("like a caricature") are incorrect.

34. (A)
Evita had "millions of followers" (*millones de seguidores*). (B) *Opositores* ("opposers") contradicts the idea of the passage, which states that Evita was a popular political figure. (C) *Público* ("public") refers to shows and artistic/sport performances. (D) *Empleados* means "employees."

35. (C)
The passage states that Evita's dramatic life (*dramática vida*) would inspire (*inspiraría*) an almost mythical devotion (*una devoción casi mítica*). (A) *Hubiera inspirado* ("would have inspired"), (B) *inspire* ("that she inspire"), and (D) *inspirará* ("will inspire") do not fit.

36. (A)
Evita is well-known (*conocida*) around the world as the inspiration (*la musa inspiradora*) of the musical *Evita.* (B) *Sabida* ("known") is the past participle of the verb *saber* and refers to knowledge. (C) *Hablada* ("talked about") doesn't fit in the sentence. (D) *Anónima* ("anonymous") conveys the incorrect idea.

37. (B)
The sentence mentions the XX century (*siglo*). (A) *Centuria* also means 100 years, but it is a feminine noun and doesn't agree with the masculine contraction *del.* (C) *Sigla* "abbreviation" and (D) *época* "age/epoch" are incorrect.

38. (B)
Dominio ("dominion/supremacy") is the best choice here. (A) *Dominación* also means "dominion," but it is a feminine noun, which doesn't match the masculine adjective *musulmán* ("muslim"). (C) *Potencia* ("great power/potency") and (D) *absoluto* ("absolute") are incorrect.

39. (C)
The passage states that the muslim dominion started (*se inició*) the same year Tariq crossed the Strait of Gibraltar. (A) *Pasó* ("it passed"), (B) *terminó* ("it finished"), and (D) *perdió* ("it lost") are incorrect.

40. (D)
Tariq's troops (*tropas*) defeated (*derrotaron*) don Rodrigo. (A) *Golpearon* ("they hit"), (B) *destrozaron* ("they smashed"), and (C) *mataron* ("they killed") do not fit.

41. (A)
The contraction *al* is masculine singular and calls for a masculine singular noun: *ejército* ("army"). (B) *Armada* ("navy") is a feminine noun. (C) *Militares* ("military officers") is plural, and (D) *marina* ("marine") is feminine.

42. (B)
The city of the Tajo river (*la ciudad del río Tajo*) was almost deserted (*estaba casi despoblada*) because the Christians had run away. (A) *Habitada* means "inhabited" and denotes the opposite idea. (C) *Sola* ("alone") and (D) *alejada* ("distant") are incorrect.

43. (C)
Most of the Christian inhabitants of Toledo had run away (*habían huido*) from the invaders. (A) *Habían salido* means "they had gone out." (B) *Habían ido* means "they had gone [somewhere]." (D) *Habían corrido* means "they had run."

44. (D)
The Jewish inhabitants (*los pobladores judíos*) stayed (*permanecieron*) in Toledo. (A) *Quedaron* ("were left") requires the reflexive pronoun *se* to mean "they stayed"—*se quedaron.* (B) *Pararon* means "they stopped and stayed there for a while." (C) *Estuvieron* means "they were at."

45. (C)
The feminine singular article *la* refers to *razón* ("reason"). (A) *Las* is

a plural article. (B) *El* is masculine, and (D) *una,* the indefinite article, doesn't fit in the fixed phrase *razón por la cual* ("which was the reason why").

46. (C)
Origen ("origin") is the best choice here. (A) Although *antepasado* ("ancestor") can also be used by extension to mean "origin," that is a secondary meaning. (B) *Patria* ("mother country/homeland") and (D) *pedigree* ("genealogy") are incorrect.

47. (B)
The phrase "is present" calls for *está,* since it conveys the meaning of location. (A) *Es* (the present form of *ser*), (C) *ser* (the infinitive), and (D) *estar* (the infinitive), are incorrect answers.

48. (D)
The correct word here is *reuniones* ("gatherings of friends"). (A) *Congregaciones* ("congregations") refers to large numbers of people, or religious groups. (B) *Congresos* ("conferences") denotes a group of people meeting to discuss a particular issue. (C) *Mitines* ("political meetings") are public meetings at which speakers address the people regarding political or social issues.

49. (A)
The word *mate* comes from the term (*viene de la quechua*) *mati.* (B) *Llega* means "it arrives." (C) *Comienza* means "it starts," and (D) *termina* means "it ends."

50. (D)
The complete phrase is *quiere decir* ("it means"). (A) *Dice* ("it says") is the conjugated form of the verb *decir* and would not follow *quiere.* (B) The impersonal form, *se dice,* means "it is said/they say," and (C) *decimos* means "we say."

51. (C)
The technical term is *nombre vulgar* ("vulgar for"). (A) *Regular* means "so-so" or "usual." (B) *Incorrecto* means "incorrect/wrong," and doesn't apply here. (D) *Correcto* ("right") also doesn't apply.

52. (A)
The gourd is used as a container (*recipiente*) to drink the beverage. (B) *Tenedor* ("fork"), (C) *bañera* ("bath tub"), and (D) *receptor* ("recipient") are incorrect.

53. (C)
The plural *personalidades* requires the plural *grandes* ("important"). (A) The preceding form, *gran,* is singular. (B) *Grande,* too, is singular. (D) *Granadas* means "pomegranates."

54. (D)
La alta costura ("haute couture" or "high sewing") refers to the leading designers and creators of new fashions in clothing for women. (A) *Arte* ("art"), (B) *Ciencia* ("science"), and (C) *religión* ("religion") do not fit the passage, which discusses fashion.

55. (A)
Di Doménico is a designer (*diseñador*) and, according to the passage, he presented his latest fashion line for the fall-winter (*colección otoño-invierno*). (B) *Estilista* (stylist) is used in the context of writing and magazines. (C) *Sastre* ("tailor") is a man who makes and/or fits suits. *Fabricante* "manufacturer" is incorrect.

56. (B)
Como means "like" ("actors like China Zorrilla, Luisina Brando and Graciela Borges"). (A) *Así* means "like this/like that." (C) *Tan* means "so" when followed by an adjective or adverb. (D) *Tal* means "such."

57. (C)
The phrase *se dieron cita* means "they turned up for": in this case, famous actors turned up for Di Doménico's fashion show. (A) *Reunión* ("meeting/gathering"), (B) *se dieron prisa* ("they hurried"), and (D) *lugar* ("place"), do not fit in the passage.

58. (D)
Designer Di Doménico presented his "proposal" (propuesta—feminine noun) for the fall-winter season. (A) *Plan* means "project" and is

a masculine noun that can't accompany the masculine adjective *nuevo.* (B) *Diseño* means "design" and is also masculine. (C) *Llegada* means "arrival."

59. (C)

Entrada means "ticket," in this case, to enter Universal Studios. (A) *Pase* ("pass") refers to a ticket valid for several days or more. (B) *Cupón* is "coupon" and (D) *pasaje* means "fare."

60. (B)

The present subjunctive form *adquiera* means "that you buy." (A) *Venda* ("that you sell"), (C) *consiga* ("that you obtain"), and (D) pida ("that you request") are incorrect.

61. (A)

The passage states that a customer will receive a "free"—*gratis*— ticket each time one regular ticket is purchased. (B) *Libre* means "free from somebody else's dominion, guilt, or obligation." (C) *Cara* means "expensive" and (D) *barata* means "inexpensive," neither of which is correct.

62. (C)

The passage says, "you only need to show your Hertz rental agreement at the ticket office." (*Sólo necesita mostrar su contrato de alquiler de Hertz en la taquilla.*) (A) *Pasar* ("to pass"), (B) *demostrar* ("demonstrate"), and (D) *chequear* ("to check") are incorrect.

63. (D)

The last sentence states, "Enjoy one of the best fairgrounds..." (*Disfrute de uno de los mejores parques de atracciones...*); this requires the imperative form *disfrute.* (A) *Disfrutan* is the third person plural of the simple present indicative. (B) *Disfrutemos* is the plural imperative: "let's enjoy." (C) *Disfrutó* is the past tense: "you/he/she enjoyed."

64. (B)

It states in the box titled *Independientes* that "they don't need to demonstrate anything about others" (*no necesitan demostrar nada ante los demás*). The amount of money earned is not mentioned in the article, making (A) incorrect. The beginning of the article lists a number of reasons for a greater tendency to spend. Among them is "the progressively shortened day and work week" (*el progresivo acortamiento de la jornada y de los días laborales de la semana*), which would not support (C). Parents and relatives are not mentioned in the article, making (D) incorrect.

65. (D)
The article states that "the important decisions with respect to family purchases are done for the most part in collaborative form" (*las decisiones importantes respecto al consumo familiar son tomadas en su mayor parte de una forma conjunta*). None of the information given in (A), (B), or (C) is dealt with in the article.

66. (C)
In *La Cesta de la Compra*, the first sentence states that "in the area of nourishment there is more of an agreement between the sexes" (*el sector alimentación es el que recoge en mayor medida un acercamiento entre los dos sexos*). Buying a house or a car, or deciding on vaction destinations, are primarily men's decisions (*la decisión última del coche, la casa o un viaje extranjero corresponde al hombre*), making (A) and (B) incorrect. Women normally make domestic decisions (*las mujeres siguen ocupándose de los gastos domésticos*), making (D) incorrect.

67. (D)
The answer to this question is made explicit in the first sentence of the narrative, where the *ustedes* makes it clear that the narrator or speaker is addressing city folk who have never left the capital. If you chose (A) you may have missed much of the point of the passage, and its tone, which is playful at the expense of those who know little or nothing about the jungle, especially the American tourists alluded to at the end, who are unaware of the great distances separating the Amazonian region of Peru from its Andean zone (where the Incas lived). It should be clear that these tourists are not being addressed by the speaker, which eliminates (B) as the correct answer. (C) is wrong because there is no mention of aborigines in the passage.

68. (A)
Choices (B) and (C) are clearly not tourist attractions, especially as the plane trip from the capital to the jungle is described as the most dangerous aspect of the experience. You'll choose (D) only if you are not paying attention and draw a facile connection between tourism and the attractions of an exotic place. The question is also plural, requiring a plural response.

69. (A)
By now you should find the references to American tourists disturbing, and should realize that they are made in the same playful spirit as the original reference in the narrative passage. By now you should also have re-read the end of that passage carefully if only to figure out just what is going on with these recurrent tourists. If you've done this, then you probably didn't pick (B) as your answer, since you are likely to know that no particular city is mentioned in connection with the tourists. However, two cities are indeed mentioned, and one is Iquitos, about which it is explicitly stated that it is the only important Amazonian city in Peru. The other two available choices, (C) and (D), are factually incorrect, though a careless reading of the passage could have been responsible for choosing either one or the other as the correct answer.

70. (B)
Conviene contratar a un guía, it says in the passage, and this is the phrase that supports (B) as the correct answer. (D) could not be it since it directly contradicts narrative information. (A) and (C) are fairly ludicrous choices, and you won't find the narrative passage consistent with either one of them.

71. (C)
None of the incorrect choices are actually mentioned explicitly or implicitly in the passage, so if you chose any of them, you probably didn't read carefully. In fact, it's hard to imagine that anything in the passage could be misinterpreted to coincide with any of the wrong answers, though (B) could be more easily arrived at by a process of distortion or overreading. The phrase that you needed to key on for the correct answer is *cuando los leemos, somos el viajero que en la realidad no pudimos ser*.

72. (B)
Here it helps to know the verb *ubicar* in the question, which can anyway be deduced from the several choices (*ciudades, lugares, sitios* all suggest the idea of location or setting). Knowing this, and keying on the last two sentences of the narrative, you should have picked the right answer. The others are all plausible, but (A) contradicts the narrative information (which speaks of the less frequented regions of a country), (C) misunderstands the appropriate passage in the narrative (where it says that travel books might be written in moments of reflection), and (D) is an invention not supported by any textual evidence.

73. (D)
The correct answer is explicitly stated in the narrative passage, which claims that travel books are probably written to revive the travel experience for the reader who couldn't go on a trip. The remaining choices are not totally implausible, except for (B), but are not supported by the passage either.

74. (A)
There are certain references in the passage that might lead a careless reader to choose (C) or (D), such as the references to Puritanism and to the abundance of food in our society, but these allusions appear in a different context and refer to something else in the passage. (B) is a gratuitous answer since there are no references to sex at all. (A), on the other hand, is the right choice because that passage explicitly states the link between over-exercising and a modern obsession with health.

75. (B)
The passage defines Puritanism in terms of the capital principle of hygiene. Choices (A) and (C) are naive answers not supported by any textual evidence, and there is no reference to the Puritan religion forbidding meat anywhere in the passage.

76. (D)
To choose the right answer you have to ask yourself what the passage states concerning the status of the body in a society obsessed by health practices. And what it says is that our society's obsession with clean living represents a fear of the body and of death, an insecurity

concerning our body which motivates over-exercise and food prohibitions. This is essentially what (D) states. The other choices might be internally consistent but do not accord with the line of the argument.

77. (B)

This is the kind of question that requires a yes-or-no type of answer. So first you have to make up your mind what it is to be, and once you've decided that according to the logic of the passage abundance of food and drink is indeed deleterious to one's health, your next step is to choose between the two positive answers. (D) is the wrong choice not because it isn't internally consistent but because there is nothing said in the passage about smoking. (B), on the other hand, restates one of the points explicitly made in the passage (using a different vocabulary: "moderarse" instead of *controlarse*, and *abundancia* instead of *disponibilidad*).

78. (B)

The text states, "you will not need coins" (*no necesitarás monedas*). Since this *guía* is for those who want to call home from outside the country (*llamar a casa desde el extranjero*), (A) is incorrect. The text indicates that one need not know other languages (*tampoco necesitas saber idiomas*) because one is assisted in Castilian (*porque te atienden en castellano*), making (C) incorrect. One need not know the codes (*códigos*) for each country since that is what this guide is for, making (D) incorrect.

79. (B)

The text states that "the one who receives the call in Spain pays for it" (*la llamada la paga en España quien la recibe*), making (A), the one who makes it, (C), the one who uses the guide book, and (D), the one who follows the instructions of the guide book, all incorrect.

80. (D)

This is a very simple question that refers you to the opening sentence of the paragraph. Choice (C) is deliberately mystifying and (A) refers to nothing whatsoever in the passage.

81. (B)

Choices (A) and (C) could only be the product of a misreading, since these qualities apply to American football or to American society but not to soccer or to Latin American societies. (D) will not mystify those who have read the passage carefully and who know that in it soccer and spontaneity are linked together.

82. (A)

This is a more complicated question because it depends on your having followed a potentially ambiguous argument, namely, the whole question of the use of time in the two different sports at issue. The correct answer is (A) ("subtracting it"), which restates what the paragraph says about spending (*gastar*) time in American football. The idea is that you are given a "capital" of time that you have to "invest" carefully and wisely, and that the time used is to be subtracted from the original total as an expenditure is from a sum total. You also have to know that in Spanish *restar* means "to subtract" (just as *sumar* means "to add"). Now you know why (D) is wrong. (B) is a sort of pun on a phrase in the passage (*desde arriba para abajo*). You have to be careful here not to be misled by appearances. (C) is deliberate nonsense.

83. (D)

(A) contradicts the information given in the passage, namely, that it is Latin American societies whose detractors refer to them as chaotic. By the same token, (C) is wrong because the passage makes the point that individualism is a trait of Latin American societies. (B), needless to say, is whimsical.

84. (B)

(A) is incorrect because tobacco and sugar cannot be thought of as "ethnic" influences. (C) is wrong because all that the passage says about the Dutch is that their language is spoken locally in the Caribbean, but not that they are an ethnic influence. Nothing is said about the Americans, who at any rate don't constitute an ethnic group or influence in Latin America.

85. (A)

(D) sounds like a plausible answer if it wasn't so general. A more specific point is made by the passage in question, where it says that *típicamente los países hispanoamericanos están divididos entre una cultura urbana y una o varias culturas regionales.* You simply have to connect the "interior" with the notion of regional cultures and you have the answer.

THE SAT SUBJECT TEST IN

Spanish

ANSWER SHEETS

THE SAT SUBJECT TEST IN
SPANISH
PRACTICE TEST 1
ANSWER SHEET

1. Ⓐ Ⓑ Ⓒ Ⓓ
2. Ⓐ Ⓑ Ⓒ Ⓓ
3. Ⓐ Ⓑ Ⓒ Ⓓ
4. Ⓐ Ⓑ Ⓒ Ⓓ
5. Ⓐ Ⓑ Ⓒ Ⓓ
6. Ⓐ Ⓑ Ⓒ Ⓓ
7. Ⓐ Ⓑ Ⓒ Ⓓ
8. Ⓐ Ⓑ Ⓒ Ⓓ
9. Ⓐ Ⓑ Ⓒ Ⓓ
10. Ⓐ Ⓑ Ⓒ Ⓓ
11. Ⓐ Ⓑ Ⓒ Ⓓ
12. Ⓐ Ⓑ Ⓒ Ⓓ
13. Ⓐ Ⓑ Ⓒ Ⓓ
14. Ⓐ Ⓑ Ⓒ Ⓓ
15. Ⓐ Ⓑ Ⓒ Ⓓ
16. Ⓐ Ⓑ Ⓒ Ⓓ
17. Ⓐ Ⓑ Ⓒ Ⓓ
18. Ⓐ Ⓑ Ⓒ Ⓓ
19. Ⓐ Ⓑ Ⓒ Ⓓ
20. Ⓐ Ⓑ Ⓒ Ⓓ
21. Ⓐ Ⓑ Ⓒ Ⓓ
22. Ⓐ Ⓑ Ⓒ Ⓓ
23. Ⓐ Ⓑ Ⓒ Ⓓ
24. Ⓐ Ⓑ Ⓒ Ⓓ
25. Ⓐ Ⓑ Ⓒ Ⓓ
26. Ⓐ Ⓑ Ⓒ Ⓓ
27. Ⓐ Ⓑ Ⓒ Ⓓ
28. Ⓐ Ⓑ Ⓒ Ⓓ
29. Ⓐ Ⓑ Ⓒ Ⓓ
30. Ⓐ Ⓑ Ⓒ Ⓓ
31. Ⓐ Ⓑ Ⓒ Ⓓ
32. Ⓐ Ⓑ Ⓒ Ⓓ
33. Ⓐ Ⓑ Ⓒ Ⓓ
34. Ⓐ Ⓑ Ⓒ Ⓓ
35. Ⓐ Ⓑ Ⓒ Ⓓ
36. Ⓐ Ⓑ Ⓒ Ⓓ
37. Ⓐ Ⓑ Ⓒ Ⓓ
38. Ⓐ Ⓑ Ⓒ Ⓓ
39. Ⓐ Ⓑ Ⓒ Ⓓ
40. Ⓐ Ⓑ Ⓒ Ⓓ
41. Ⓐ Ⓑ Ⓒ Ⓓ
42. Ⓐ Ⓑ Ⓒ Ⓓ
43. Ⓐ Ⓑ Ⓒ Ⓓ
44. Ⓐ Ⓑ Ⓒ Ⓓ
45. Ⓐ Ⓑ Ⓒ Ⓓ
46. Ⓐ Ⓑ Ⓒ Ⓓ
47. Ⓐ Ⓑ Ⓒ Ⓓ
48. Ⓐ Ⓑ Ⓒ Ⓓ
49. Ⓐ Ⓑ Ⓒ Ⓓ
50. Ⓐ Ⓑ Ⓒ Ⓓ
51. Ⓐ Ⓑ Ⓒ Ⓓ
52. Ⓐ Ⓑ Ⓒ Ⓓ
53. Ⓐ Ⓑ Ⓒ Ⓓ
54. Ⓐ Ⓑ Ⓒ Ⓓ
55. Ⓐ Ⓑ Ⓒ Ⓓ
56. Ⓐ Ⓑ Ⓒ Ⓓ
57. Ⓐ Ⓑ Ⓒ Ⓓ
58. Ⓐ Ⓑ Ⓒ Ⓓ
59. Ⓐ Ⓑ Ⓒ Ⓓ
60. Ⓐ Ⓑ Ⓒ Ⓓ
61. Ⓐ Ⓑ Ⓒ Ⓓ
62. Ⓐ Ⓑ Ⓒ Ⓓ
63. Ⓐ Ⓑ Ⓒ Ⓓ
64. Ⓐ Ⓑ Ⓒ Ⓓ
65. Ⓐ Ⓑ Ⓒ Ⓓ
66. Ⓐ Ⓑ Ⓒ Ⓓ
67. Ⓐ Ⓑ Ⓒ Ⓓ
68. Ⓐ Ⓑ Ⓒ Ⓓ
69. Ⓐ Ⓑ Ⓒ Ⓓ
70. Ⓐ Ⓑ Ⓒ Ⓓ
71. Ⓐ Ⓑ Ⓒ Ⓓ
72. Ⓐ Ⓑ Ⓒ Ⓓ
73. Ⓐ Ⓑ Ⓒ Ⓓ
74. Ⓐ Ⓑ Ⓒ Ⓓ
75. Ⓐ Ⓑ Ⓒ Ⓓ
76. Ⓐ Ⓑ Ⓒ Ⓓ
77. Ⓐ Ⓑ Ⓒ Ⓓ
78. Ⓐ Ⓑ Ⓒ Ⓓ
79. Ⓐ Ⓑ Ⓒ Ⓓ
80. Ⓐ Ⓑ Ⓒ Ⓓ
81. Ⓐ Ⓑ Ⓒ Ⓓ
82. Ⓐ Ⓑ Ⓒ Ⓓ
83. Ⓐ Ⓑ Ⓒ Ⓓ
84. Ⓐ Ⓑ Ⓒ Ⓓ
85. Ⓐ Ⓑ Ⓒ Ⓓ

THE SAT SUBJECT TEST IN
SPANISH
PRACTICE TEST 2
ANSWER SHEET

1. Ⓐ Ⓑ Ⓒ Ⓓ
2. Ⓐ Ⓑ Ⓒ Ⓓ
3. Ⓐ Ⓑ Ⓒ Ⓓ
4. Ⓐ Ⓑ Ⓒ Ⓓ
5. Ⓐ Ⓑ Ⓒ Ⓓ
6. Ⓐ Ⓑ Ⓒ Ⓓ
7. Ⓐ Ⓑ Ⓒ Ⓓ
8. Ⓐ Ⓑ Ⓒ Ⓓ
9. Ⓐ Ⓑ Ⓒ Ⓓ
10. Ⓐ Ⓑ Ⓒ Ⓓ
11. Ⓐ Ⓑ Ⓒ Ⓓ
12. Ⓐ Ⓑ Ⓒ Ⓓ
13. Ⓐ Ⓑ Ⓒ Ⓓ
14. Ⓐ Ⓑ Ⓒ Ⓓ
15. Ⓐ Ⓑ Ⓒ Ⓓ
16. Ⓐ Ⓑ Ⓒ Ⓓ
17. Ⓐ Ⓑ Ⓒ Ⓓ
18. Ⓐ Ⓑ Ⓒ Ⓓ
19. Ⓐ Ⓑ Ⓒ Ⓓ
20. Ⓐ Ⓑ Ⓒ Ⓓ
21. Ⓐ Ⓑ Ⓒ Ⓓ
22. Ⓐ Ⓑ Ⓒ Ⓓ
23. Ⓐ Ⓑ Ⓒ Ⓓ
24. Ⓐ Ⓑ Ⓒ Ⓓ
25. Ⓐ Ⓑ Ⓒ Ⓓ
26. Ⓐ Ⓑ Ⓒ Ⓓ
27. Ⓐ Ⓑ Ⓒ Ⓓ
28. Ⓐ Ⓑ Ⓒ Ⓓ
29. Ⓐ Ⓑ Ⓒ Ⓓ
30. Ⓐ Ⓑ Ⓒ Ⓓ
31. Ⓐ Ⓑ Ⓒ Ⓓ
32. Ⓐ Ⓑ Ⓒ Ⓓ
33. Ⓐ Ⓑ Ⓒ Ⓓ
34. Ⓐ Ⓑ Ⓒ Ⓓ
35. Ⓐ Ⓑ Ⓒ Ⓓ
36. Ⓐ Ⓑ Ⓒ Ⓓ
37. Ⓐ Ⓑ Ⓒ Ⓓ
38. Ⓐ Ⓑ Ⓒ Ⓓ
39. Ⓐ Ⓑ Ⓒ Ⓓ
40. Ⓐ Ⓑ Ⓒ Ⓓ
41. Ⓐ Ⓑ Ⓒ Ⓓ
42. Ⓐ Ⓑ Ⓒ Ⓓ
43. Ⓐ Ⓑ Ⓒ Ⓓ
44. Ⓐ Ⓑ Ⓒ Ⓓ
45. Ⓐ Ⓑ Ⓒ Ⓓ
46. Ⓐ Ⓑ Ⓒ Ⓓ
47. Ⓐ Ⓑ Ⓒ Ⓓ
48. Ⓐ Ⓑ Ⓒ Ⓓ
49. Ⓐ Ⓑ Ⓒ Ⓓ
50. Ⓐ Ⓑ Ⓒ Ⓓ
51. Ⓐ Ⓑ Ⓒ Ⓓ
52. Ⓐ Ⓑ Ⓒ Ⓓ
53. Ⓐ Ⓑ Ⓒ Ⓓ
54. Ⓐ Ⓑ Ⓒ Ⓓ
55. Ⓐ Ⓑ Ⓒ Ⓓ
56. Ⓐ Ⓑ Ⓒ Ⓓ
57. Ⓐ Ⓑ Ⓒ Ⓓ
58. Ⓐ Ⓑ Ⓒ Ⓓ
59. Ⓐ Ⓑ Ⓒ Ⓓ
60. Ⓐ Ⓑ Ⓒ Ⓓ
61. Ⓐ Ⓑ Ⓒ Ⓓ
62. Ⓐ Ⓑ Ⓒ Ⓓ
63. Ⓐ Ⓑ Ⓒ Ⓓ
64. Ⓐ Ⓑ Ⓒ Ⓓ
65. Ⓐ Ⓑ Ⓒ Ⓓ
66. Ⓐ Ⓑ Ⓒ Ⓓ
67. Ⓐ Ⓑ Ⓒ Ⓓ
68. Ⓐ Ⓑ Ⓒ Ⓓ
69. Ⓐ Ⓑ Ⓒ Ⓓ
70. Ⓐ Ⓑ Ⓒ Ⓓ
71. Ⓐ Ⓑ Ⓒ Ⓓ
72. Ⓐ Ⓑ Ⓒ Ⓓ
73. Ⓐ Ⓑ Ⓒ Ⓓ
74. Ⓐ Ⓑ Ⓒ Ⓓ
75. Ⓐ Ⓑ Ⓒ Ⓓ
76. Ⓐ Ⓑ Ⓒ Ⓓ
77. Ⓐ Ⓑ Ⓒ Ⓓ
78. Ⓐ Ⓑ Ⓒ Ⓓ
79. Ⓐ Ⓑ Ⓒ Ⓓ
80. Ⓐ Ⓑ Ⓒ Ⓓ
81. Ⓐ Ⓑ Ⓒ Ⓓ
82. Ⓐ Ⓑ Ⓒ Ⓓ
83. Ⓐ Ⓑ Ⓒ Ⓓ
84. Ⓐ Ⓑ Ⓒ Ⓓ
85. Ⓐ Ⓑ Ⓒ Ⓓ

THE SAT SUBJECT TEST IN
SPANISH
PRACTICE TEST 3
ANSWER SHEET

1. Ⓐ Ⓑ Ⓒ Ⓓ
2. Ⓐ Ⓑ Ⓒ Ⓓ
3. Ⓐ Ⓑ Ⓒ Ⓓ
4. Ⓐ Ⓑ Ⓒ Ⓓ
5. Ⓐ Ⓑ Ⓒ Ⓓ
6. Ⓐ Ⓑ Ⓒ Ⓓ
7. Ⓐ Ⓑ Ⓒ Ⓓ
8. Ⓐ Ⓑ Ⓒ Ⓓ
9. Ⓐ Ⓑ Ⓒ Ⓓ
10. Ⓐ Ⓑ Ⓒ Ⓓ
11. Ⓐ Ⓑ Ⓒ Ⓓ
12. Ⓐ Ⓑ Ⓒ Ⓓ
13. Ⓐ Ⓑ Ⓒ Ⓓ
14. Ⓐ Ⓑ Ⓒ Ⓓ
15. Ⓐ Ⓑ Ⓒ Ⓓ
16. Ⓐ Ⓑ Ⓒ Ⓓ
17. Ⓐ Ⓑ Ⓒ Ⓓ
18. Ⓐ Ⓑ Ⓒ Ⓓ
19. Ⓐ Ⓑ Ⓒ Ⓓ
20. Ⓐ Ⓑ Ⓒ Ⓓ
21. Ⓐ Ⓑ Ⓒ Ⓓ
22. Ⓐ Ⓑ Ⓒ Ⓓ
23. Ⓐ Ⓑ Ⓒ Ⓓ
24. Ⓐ Ⓑ Ⓒ Ⓓ
25. Ⓐ Ⓑ Ⓒ Ⓓ
26. Ⓐ Ⓑ Ⓒ Ⓓ
27. Ⓐ Ⓑ Ⓒ Ⓓ
28. Ⓐ Ⓑ Ⓒ Ⓓ
29. Ⓐ Ⓑ Ⓒ Ⓓ
30. Ⓐ Ⓑ Ⓒ Ⓓ
31. Ⓐ Ⓑ Ⓒ Ⓓ
32. Ⓐ Ⓑ Ⓒ Ⓓ
33. Ⓐ Ⓑ Ⓒ Ⓓ
34. Ⓐ Ⓑ Ⓒ Ⓓ
35. Ⓐ Ⓑ Ⓒ Ⓓ
36. Ⓐ Ⓑ Ⓒ Ⓓ
37. Ⓐ Ⓑ Ⓒ Ⓓ
38. Ⓐ Ⓑ Ⓒ Ⓓ
39. Ⓐ Ⓑ Ⓒ Ⓓ
40. Ⓐ Ⓑ Ⓒ Ⓓ
41. Ⓐ Ⓑ Ⓒ Ⓓ
42. Ⓐ Ⓑ Ⓒ Ⓓ
43. Ⓐ Ⓑ Ⓒ Ⓓ
44. Ⓐ Ⓑ Ⓒ Ⓓ
45. Ⓐ Ⓑ Ⓒ Ⓓ
46. Ⓐ Ⓑ Ⓒ Ⓓ
47. Ⓐ Ⓑ Ⓒ Ⓓ
48. Ⓐ Ⓑ Ⓒ Ⓓ
49. Ⓐ Ⓑ Ⓒ Ⓓ
50. Ⓐ Ⓑ Ⓒ Ⓓ
51. Ⓐ Ⓑ Ⓒ Ⓓ
52. Ⓐ Ⓑ Ⓒ Ⓓ
53. Ⓐ Ⓑ Ⓒ Ⓓ
54. Ⓐ Ⓑ Ⓒ Ⓓ
55. Ⓐ Ⓑ Ⓒ Ⓓ
56. Ⓐ Ⓑ Ⓒ Ⓓ
57. Ⓐ Ⓑ Ⓒ Ⓓ
58. Ⓐ Ⓑ Ⓒ Ⓓ
59. Ⓐ Ⓑ Ⓒ Ⓓ
60. Ⓐ Ⓑ Ⓒ Ⓓ
61. Ⓐ Ⓑ Ⓒ Ⓓ
62. Ⓐ Ⓑ Ⓒ Ⓓ
63. Ⓐ Ⓑ Ⓒ Ⓓ
64. Ⓐ Ⓑ Ⓒ Ⓓ
65. Ⓐ Ⓑ Ⓒ Ⓓ
66. Ⓐ Ⓑ Ⓒ Ⓓ
67. Ⓐ Ⓑ Ⓒ Ⓓ
68. Ⓐ Ⓑ Ⓒ Ⓓ
69. Ⓐ Ⓑ Ⓒ Ⓓ
70. Ⓐ Ⓑ Ⓒ Ⓓ
71. Ⓐ Ⓑ Ⓒ Ⓓ
72. Ⓐ Ⓑ Ⓒ Ⓓ
73. Ⓐ Ⓑ Ⓒ Ⓓ
74. Ⓐ Ⓑ Ⓒ Ⓓ
75. Ⓐ Ⓑ Ⓒ Ⓓ
76. Ⓐ Ⓑ Ⓒ Ⓓ
77. Ⓐ Ⓑ Ⓒ Ⓓ
78. Ⓐ Ⓑ Ⓒ Ⓓ
79. Ⓐ Ⓑ Ⓒ Ⓓ
80. Ⓐ Ⓑ Ⓒ Ⓓ
81. Ⓐ Ⓑ Ⓒ Ⓓ
82. Ⓐ Ⓑ Ⓒ Ⓓ
83. Ⓐ Ⓑ Ⓒ Ⓓ
84. Ⓐ Ⓑ Ⓒ Ⓓ
85. Ⓐ Ⓑ Ⓒ Ⓓ

THE SAT SUBJECT TEST IN
SPANISH
PRACTICE TEST 4
ANSWER SHEET

1. Ⓐ Ⓑ Ⓒ Ⓓ
2. Ⓐ Ⓑ Ⓒ Ⓓ
3. Ⓐ Ⓑ Ⓒ Ⓓ
4. Ⓐ Ⓑ Ⓒ Ⓓ
5. Ⓐ Ⓑ Ⓒ Ⓓ
6. Ⓐ Ⓑ Ⓒ Ⓓ
7. Ⓐ Ⓑ Ⓒ Ⓓ
8. Ⓐ Ⓑ Ⓒ Ⓓ
9. Ⓐ Ⓑ Ⓒ Ⓓ
10. Ⓐ Ⓑ Ⓒ Ⓓ
11. Ⓐ Ⓑ Ⓒ Ⓓ
12. Ⓐ Ⓑ Ⓒ Ⓓ
13. Ⓐ Ⓑ Ⓒ Ⓓ
14. Ⓐ Ⓑ Ⓒ Ⓓ
15. Ⓐ Ⓑ Ⓒ Ⓓ
16. Ⓐ Ⓑ Ⓒ Ⓓ
17. Ⓐ Ⓑ Ⓒ Ⓓ
18. Ⓐ Ⓑ Ⓒ Ⓓ
19. Ⓐ Ⓑ Ⓒ Ⓓ
20. Ⓐ Ⓑ Ⓒ Ⓓ
21. Ⓐ Ⓑ Ⓒ Ⓓ
22. Ⓐ Ⓑ Ⓒ Ⓓ
23. Ⓐ Ⓑ Ⓒ Ⓓ
24. Ⓐ Ⓑ Ⓒ Ⓓ
25. Ⓐ Ⓑ Ⓒ Ⓓ
26. Ⓐ Ⓑ Ⓒ Ⓓ
27. Ⓐ Ⓑ Ⓒ Ⓓ
28. Ⓐ Ⓑ Ⓒ Ⓓ
29. Ⓐ Ⓑ Ⓒ Ⓓ
30. Ⓐ Ⓑ Ⓒ Ⓓ
31. Ⓐ Ⓑ Ⓒ Ⓓ
32. Ⓐ Ⓑ Ⓒ Ⓓ
33. Ⓐ Ⓑ Ⓒ Ⓓ
34. Ⓐ Ⓑ Ⓒ Ⓓ
35. Ⓐ Ⓑ Ⓒ Ⓓ
36. Ⓐ Ⓑ Ⓒ Ⓓ
37. Ⓐ Ⓑ Ⓒ Ⓓ
38. Ⓐ Ⓑ Ⓒ Ⓓ
39. Ⓐ Ⓑ Ⓒ Ⓓ
40. Ⓐ Ⓑ Ⓒ Ⓓ
41. Ⓐ Ⓑ Ⓒ Ⓓ
42. Ⓐ Ⓑ Ⓒ Ⓓ
43. Ⓐ Ⓑ Ⓒ Ⓓ
44. Ⓐ Ⓑ Ⓒ Ⓓ
45. Ⓐ Ⓑ Ⓒ Ⓓ
46. Ⓐ Ⓑ Ⓒ Ⓓ
47. Ⓐ Ⓑ Ⓒ Ⓓ
48. Ⓐ Ⓑ Ⓒ Ⓓ
49. Ⓐ Ⓑ Ⓒ Ⓓ
50. Ⓐ Ⓑ Ⓒ Ⓓ
51. Ⓐ Ⓑ Ⓒ Ⓓ
52. Ⓐ Ⓑ Ⓒ Ⓓ
53. Ⓐ Ⓑ Ⓒ Ⓓ
54. Ⓐ Ⓑ Ⓒ Ⓓ
55. Ⓐ Ⓑ Ⓒ Ⓓ
56. Ⓐ Ⓑ Ⓒ Ⓓ
57. Ⓐ Ⓑ Ⓒ Ⓓ
58. Ⓐ Ⓑ Ⓒ Ⓓ
59. Ⓐ Ⓑ Ⓒ Ⓓ
60. Ⓐ Ⓑ Ⓒ Ⓓ
61. Ⓐ Ⓑ Ⓒ Ⓓ
62. Ⓐ Ⓑ Ⓒ Ⓓ
63. Ⓐ Ⓑ Ⓒ Ⓓ
64. Ⓐ Ⓑ Ⓒ Ⓓ
65. Ⓐ Ⓑ Ⓒ Ⓓ
66. Ⓐ Ⓑ Ⓒ Ⓓ
67. Ⓐ Ⓑ Ⓒ Ⓓ
68. Ⓐ Ⓑ Ⓒ Ⓓ
69. Ⓐ Ⓑ Ⓒ Ⓓ
70. Ⓐ Ⓑ Ⓒ Ⓓ
71. Ⓐ Ⓑ Ⓒ Ⓓ
72. Ⓐ Ⓑ Ⓒ Ⓓ
73. Ⓐ Ⓑ Ⓒ Ⓓ
74. Ⓐ Ⓑ Ⓒ Ⓓ
75. Ⓐ Ⓑ Ⓒ Ⓓ
76. Ⓐ Ⓑ Ⓒ Ⓓ
77. Ⓐ Ⓑ Ⓒ Ⓓ
78. Ⓐ Ⓑ Ⓒ Ⓓ
79. Ⓐ Ⓑ Ⓒ Ⓓ
80. Ⓐ Ⓑ Ⓒ Ⓓ
81. Ⓐ Ⓑ Ⓒ Ⓓ
82. Ⓐ Ⓑ Ⓒ Ⓓ
83. Ⓐ Ⓑ Ⓒ Ⓓ
84. Ⓐ Ⓑ Ⓒ Ⓓ
85. Ⓐ Ⓑ Ⓒ Ⓓ

THE SAT SUBJECT TEST IN

SPANISH

PRACTICE TEST 5
ANSWER SHEET

1. Ⓐ Ⓑ Ⓒ Ⓓ
2. Ⓐ Ⓑ Ⓒ Ⓓ
3. Ⓐ Ⓑ Ⓒ Ⓓ
4. Ⓐ Ⓑ Ⓒ Ⓓ
5. Ⓐ Ⓑ Ⓒ Ⓓ
6. Ⓐ Ⓑ Ⓒ Ⓓ
7. Ⓐ Ⓑ Ⓒ Ⓓ
8. Ⓐ Ⓑ Ⓒ Ⓓ
9. Ⓐ Ⓑ Ⓒ Ⓓ
10. Ⓐ Ⓑ Ⓒ Ⓓ
11. Ⓐ Ⓑ Ⓒ Ⓓ
12. Ⓐ Ⓑ Ⓒ Ⓓ
13. Ⓐ Ⓑ Ⓒ Ⓓ
14. Ⓐ Ⓑ Ⓒ Ⓓ
15. Ⓐ Ⓑ Ⓒ Ⓓ
16. Ⓐ Ⓑ Ⓒ Ⓓ
17. Ⓐ Ⓑ Ⓒ Ⓓ
18. Ⓐ Ⓑ Ⓒ Ⓓ
19. Ⓐ Ⓑ Ⓒ Ⓓ
20. Ⓐ Ⓑ Ⓒ Ⓓ
21. Ⓐ Ⓑ Ⓒ Ⓓ
22. Ⓐ Ⓑ Ⓒ Ⓓ
23. Ⓐ Ⓑ Ⓒ Ⓓ
24. Ⓐ Ⓑ Ⓒ Ⓓ
25. Ⓐ Ⓑ Ⓒ Ⓓ
26. Ⓐ Ⓑ Ⓒ Ⓓ
27. Ⓐ Ⓑ Ⓒ Ⓓ
28. Ⓐ Ⓑ Ⓒ Ⓓ
29. Ⓐ Ⓑ Ⓒ Ⓓ
30. Ⓐ Ⓑ Ⓒ Ⓓ
31. Ⓐ Ⓑ Ⓒ Ⓓ
32. Ⓐ Ⓑ Ⓒ Ⓓ
33. Ⓐ Ⓑ Ⓒ Ⓓ
34. Ⓐ Ⓑ Ⓒ Ⓓ
35. Ⓐ Ⓑ Ⓒ Ⓓ
36. Ⓐ Ⓑ Ⓒ Ⓓ
37. Ⓐ Ⓑ Ⓒ Ⓓ
38. Ⓐ Ⓑ Ⓒ Ⓓ
39. Ⓐ Ⓑ Ⓒ Ⓓ
40. Ⓐ Ⓑ Ⓒ Ⓓ
41. Ⓐ Ⓑ Ⓒ Ⓓ
42. Ⓐ Ⓑ Ⓒ Ⓓ
43. Ⓐ Ⓑ Ⓒ Ⓓ
44. Ⓐ Ⓑ Ⓒ Ⓓ
45. Ⓐ Ⓑ Ⓒ Ⓓ
46. Ⓐ Ⓑ Ⓒ Ⓓ
47. Ⓐ Ⓑ Ⓒ Ⓓ
48. Ⓐ Ⓑ Ⓒ Ⓓ
49. Ⓐ Ⓑ Ⓒ Ⓓ
50. Ⓐ Ⓑ Ⓒ Ⓓ
51. Ⓐ Ⓑ Ⓒ Ⓓ
52. Ⓐ Ⓑ Ⓒ Ⓓ
53. Ⓐ Ⓑ Ⓒ Ⓓ
54. Ⓐ Ⓑ Ⓒ Ⓓ
55. Ⓐ Ⓑ Ⓒ Ⓓ
56. Ⓐ Ⓑ Ⓒ Ⓓ
57. Ⓐ Ⓑ Ⓒ Ⓓ
58. Ⓐ Ⓑ Ⓒ Ⓓ
59. Ⓐ Ⓑ Ⓒ Ⓓ
60. Ⓐ Ⓑ Ⓒ Ⓓ
61. Ⓐ Ⓑ Ⓒ Ⓓ
62. Ⓐ Ⓑ Ⓒ Ⓓ
63. Ⓐ Ⓑ Ⓒ Ⓓ
64. Ⓐ Ⓑ Ⓒ Ⓓ
65. Ⓐ Ⓑ Ⓒ Ⓓ
66. Ⓐ Ⓑ Ⓒ Ⓓ
67. Ⓐ Ⓑ Ⓒ Ⓓ
68. Ⓐ Ⓑ Ⓒ Ⓓ
69. Ⓐ Ⓑ Ⓒ Ⓓ
70. Ⓐ Ⓑ Ⓒ Ⓓ
71. Ⓐ Ⓑ Ⓒ Ⓓ
72. Ⓐ Ⓑ Ⓒ Ⓓ
73. Ⓐ Ⓑ Ⓒ Ⓓ
74. Ⓐ Ⓑ Ⓒ Ⓓ
75. Ⓐ Ⓑ Ⓒ Ⓓ
76. Ⓐ Ⓑ Ⓒ Ⓓ
77. Ⓐ Ⓑ Ⓒ Ⓓ
78. Ⓐ Ⓑ Ⓒ Ⓓ
79. Ⓐ Ⓑ Ⓒ Ⓓ
80. Ⓐ Ⓑ Ⓒ Ⓓ
81. Ⓐ Ⓑ Ⓒ Ⓓ
82. Ⓐ Ⓑ Ⓒ Ⓓ
83. Ⓐ Ⓑ Ⓒ Ⓓ
84. Ⓐ Ⓑ Ⓒ Ⓓ
85. Ⓐ Ⓑ Ⓒ Ⓓ

THE SAT SUBJECT TEST IN

Spanish

INDEX

A

B

C

D

E

Research & Education Association
REA
ESL
BEGINNER
ENGLISH AS A SECOND LANGUAGE
Made Nice and Easy!
MAKES LEARNING THE
BASICS OF ENGLISH GRAMMAR
EASY AND FUN
THROUGH THE USE OF:
• Illustrations
• Reviews
• Reading Passages
• Listening Exercises
• Group Activities
AN INVALUABLE BOOK FOR:
■ ESL students and teachers
■ ACT ESL Placement test-takers
■ Adult education students
■ Anyone looking for a review of English grammar